FOUNDATIONS OF SPORT MANAGEMENT

2nd Edition

Titles in the Sport Management Library

— • —

Case Studies in Sport Marketing

— • —

Developing Successful Sport Marketing Plans, 3rd Edition

— • —

Developing Successful Sport Sponsorship Plans, 3rd Edition

— • —

Economics of Sport, 2nd Edition

— • —

Ethics & Morality in Sport Management

— • —

Financing Sport, 2nd Edition

— • —

Foundations of Sport Management, 2nd Edition

— • —

Fundamentals of Sport Marketing, 3rd Edition

— • —

Media Relations in Sport, 2nd Edition

— • —

Sport Facility Management: Organizing Events and Mitigating Risks

— • —

Sport Governance in the Global Community

— • —

Sport Management Field Experiences

FOUNDATIONS OF SPORT MANAGEMENT

SECOND EDITION

Andy Gillentine, PhD
UNIVERSITY OF MIAMI

R. Brian Crow, EdD
SLIPPERY ROCK UNIVERSITY

EDITORS

Fitness Information Technology
a Division of the International Center
for Performance Excellence
West Virginia University
262 Coliseum, WVU-PASS
PO Box 6116
Morgantown, WV 26506-6116

Library of Congress Card Catalog Number: 2009930513

ISBN: 978-1-885693-94-5

Cover Design: Bellerophon Productions
Cover Photos: Silhouettes from line art © kjpargeter, bigstockphoto.com. Stadium photo by Andy Gillentine.
Interior Photos: Andy Gillentine (unless noted otherwise)
Production Editor: Val Gittings
Copyeditor: Mark Slider
Typesetter: Bellerophon Productions
Cover Design: Bellerophon Productions
Printed by Data Reproductions Corporation

10 9 8 7 6 5 4 3 2 1

Fitness Information Technology
A Division of the International Center for Performance Excellence
West Virginia University
262 Coliseum, WVU-PASS
PO Box 6116
Morgantown, WV 26506-6116
800.477.4348 (toll free)
304.293.6888 (phone)
304.293.6658 (fax)
Email: fitcustomerservice@mail.wvu.edu
Website: www.fitinfotech.com

Dedication

This book is dedicated to my father, Frank Gillentine, who embodied the meaning of hard work, ethical behavior, love of family, and an understanding of all that sport has to offer. I appreciate and miss you every day.

—AG

This book is dedicated to my two children, Sam and Hannah. Reach for the stars!

—RBC

Contents

Acknowledgments ix

Guest Foreword xi
    Steve Moore

Foreword xiii
    Rick Burton

Preface xv
    Andy Gillentine and R. Brian Crow

Chapter 1

Introduction to the Sport Industry 1
    Andy Gillentine, R. Brian Crow, and Josh Harris

Chapter 2

Why Sport Management Matters 15
    Catriona Higgs and Betsy McKinley

Chapter 3

Communication and Media Relations in Sport 29
    Andy Gillentine, R. Brian Crow, and Cheri Bradish

Chapter 4

Management and Leadership in the Sport Industry 43
    Jeremy S. Jordan, Aubrey Kent, and Matthew B. Walker

Chapter 5

An Introduction to Sport Economics 71
    Matthew T. Brown and David Matthew Zuefle

Chapter 6

Sport Finance 91
    Tom H. Regan and Matthew Bernthal

Chapter 7

Sport Marketing 123
    John Clark

Chapter 8

Sponsorship and Sales in the Sport Industry 145
    Nancy L. Lough

Chapter 9

Sport Facility and Event Management 161
    Bernard Goldfine and Tom Sawyer

Chapter 10

Sport Industry and the Law 187
    Paul J. Batista

Chapter 11

Sport Governance 207
    Dennis Phillips

Chapter 12

Ethics in the Sport Industry 225
    Lynn L. Ridinger and T. Christopher Greenwell

Chapter 13

Global Sport Industry 243
    Artemisia Apostolopoulou and Dimitra Papadimitriou

Chapter 14

Sport Management Internships 265
    John J. Miller

Chapter 15

Your Future in the Sport Industry 281
    Benjamin D. Goss, Colby B. Jubenville, and Craig Crow

Glossary 299

Index 313

About the Editors 321

About the Authors 323

Acknowledgments

I wish to acknowledge my wife, Glenna, for her continued patience and support for the duration of this revision. Thanks for always being a great sounding board for good ideas and bad ones and loving me enough to tell which ones were which and when to quit talking and get back to work.

I would like to recognize the chapter authors for their work and contributions to this second edition and the many students without whom this book would not exist. I should also recognize all of the sporting events and venues that allowed me to take countless photographs in order to shoot the select few used in this edition of the text.

Thanks to the publisher and editors at FIT for their continued support of this text.

Finally, I wish to acknowledge my friend and co-editor Brian Crow, Thanks B., it has been fun as always.

—AG

The success of this textbook is due to the contributions of each chapter author—your initial work and subsequent updates have made this project fun and inspiring. Andy Gillentine—it's always a pleasure to be your colleague and writing partner. From our brief time together at USM to now, it's been a great ride. Andy Ostrow—thanks for the encouragement to put this book together.

—RBC

Guest Foreword

My theory is that sport management was invented 50,000 years ago when Neanderthals battled giant mammoths with stones and spears.

Men, women, and children would gather around and watch mammoths get clobbered and hunters get squashed. Sometimes the Neanderthals won and sometimes the mammoths won. It was an exciting spectacle with tons of body contact.

I imagine that one day a slightly more evolved Neanderthal, who was sitting out the season with a torn knee ligament and had lots of time to think, got a brilliant idea:

"Hey, maybe we should charge admission."

Next thing you know, the Neanderthals were organizing teams and hiring coaches and setting up vendors ("Yo, raw meat! Get yer raw meat here!") and selling merchandise and promoting the events in the mass media.

The Mammoth Games probably weren't huge moneymakers, but player salaries back then were a fraction of what they are today, so the overhead was less.

Since those times, there have been brief periods where sport management has tapped into the public's fascination with athletes in a big way—the Olympians in ancient Greece, the gladiators in Rome, those knucklehead jousters in Europe.

But it's only been within the last few decades that sports have crossed the threshold into Big Business.

I first became aware that something big was happening when I was a sports editor back in the 1980s. I was fresh of out journalism school and working for *The Maui News*. (Yeah, I know. Tough gig. I covered Hawaiian canoe races, surfing contests, the NFL Pro Bowl, tennis tournaments. Once, after a match in Lahaina, I asked John McEnroe a really stupid question and his answer was, "That's a really stupid question.")

A perfect storm was brewing in sports. There were brilliant athletes such as Joe Montana, Magic Johnson, Larry Bird, and Wayne Gretzky. ESPN was born. Monday Night Football was in its glory days. Marketing geniuses turned player endorsements into multimillion dollar deals and team brands into a merchandising bonanza.

It all came together and suddenly it wasn't enough to just say, "OK, everyone get out there and kill a mammoth—and have fun!"

Sport management ascended into the Big Leagues.

Everyone got real serious about the business—and forgot about the game.

Players' egos soared along with their salaries. Ticket prices doubled, tripled, quadrupled. Bench-clearing brawls, once an annoying quirk of hockey, spread to baseball, basketball, and football. Even fans lost their playfulness and found ever more blatant ways to disrupt a game.

I started the "In the Bleachers" cartoon in 1985 for two reasons. First, I needed the money. Hawaii's an expensive place to live, and journalists don't get lucrative shoe endorsement deals. And second, I wanted to create a sports feature that would deliver this message to a world gone crazy over sports:

Lighten up. It's just a game.

If, after reading Foundations of Sport Management, 2nd Edition, you decide that this is the career for you, please do yourself a favor. Every now and then, walk out of your office and look out onto the field or the court or the rink or the mammoth arena. Take a deep breath. Look around. Thnk back to when you were a kid and the games were just games.

Then go back into your office and crunch numbers and sign contracts and deal with the media and fire the peanut vendor.

You'll have a lot more fun.

STEVE MOORE
CREATOR OF "IN THE BLEACHERS"

Foreword

Not long ago as I was walking across the campus at the United States Olympic Committee Training Center in Colorado Springs (on a beautiful sunny September day in the mid-seventies), I said a small prayer of thanks for how my career had unfolded to date. I was in the process of asking myself, "How many cool jobs are there in the sports world?" because, as the chief marketing officer of the USOC, I felt I surely had one of them.

This place is sacred in ways that the old Yankee Stadium or Lambeau Field are sacred. Fenway Park. Madison Square Garden. The Big House at Michigan. The Carrier Dome, Mac Court, and Cameron Indoor Stadium. The Rose Bowl. Wembley. Rod Laver Arena. The Melbourne Cricket Ground (the MCG). The Indianapolis Motor Speedway. Daytona. Talladega. All of them and more.

But I digress.

We are surrounded here in Colorado Springs not only by a fantastic setting (Pikes Peak, the Garden of the Gods, the Broadmoor) but also by amazing athletes striving to achieve their Olympic dreams. They come here to swim, to wrestle, box, shoot, spike, and cycle (to name just a few Olympic sports), and they come here in all genders, shapes, sizes, heights, weights, ethnicities, religious beliefs, places of origin, and competitive convictions. These people are, more often than not, doing what they love—not for the money or fame, but for the chance to represent their country at the Olympics.

And those athletes, making that commitment in the afterglow of the great Beijing 2008 Olympic Games, know that Michael Phelps won eight gold medals. That Shawn Johnson won gold at 16 years of age. That Dara Torres won silver at 41. That Henry Cejudo, a child of illegal Mexican immigrants, won gold against all odds. That Lopez Lomong, one of the "Lost Boys of the Sudan" carried our American flag at the Beijing Opening Ceremonies and that his first race in Beijing was his first international race ever. These athletes are not just inspirational, they are beacons of what Olympic sport produces every day.

What does that have to do with you, the reader of this foreword? Well, my guess is that you are considering a career in sports that involves working in this business as opposed to competing. Maybe you are just looking for a course that broadens your appreciation of the world around you. Or maybe you needed a class that started after 10 a.m. and this one fit the bill.

In all cases, this textbook, *Foundations of Sport Management, 2nd Edition*, is designed to give you a very informed look at one of the world's largest businesses. Yes, sports is big business and, on the surface, it looks glamorous. But like any business (or elite sport performance), it requires intense commitment, extraordinary discipline, long hours spent learning the craft, creativity, maturity and "hustle."

You may or may not feel that you really care about those traits or that working hard is your scene. But I can assure you, as one of those people who feels blessed every day by what he gets to do, that the sport management journey is worth it. Here in Colorado Springs we talk about that journey with a slogan that simply says, "Amazing awaits." I could not think of better words as you get ready to read this textbook. There is amazing material in this book.

So choose carefully where you apply your intentions and passion. This book is a roadmap for a specific journey, and it is one that recognizes not only the hard work and discipline needed for success but also the aptitude. This book grasps that the core subject matter is complex, ever-changing and worthy of real knowledge.

Said another way, it means there is really good "stuff" in this book and if you want to get into this industry, you have to pay attention and learn the fundamentals.

Use this roadmap and ask for directions (from your professor or instructor) along the way.

RICK BURTON
FORMER CHIEF MARKETING OFFICER, USOC
PRINCIPAL, BURTON MARKETING GROUP

Preface

The continued dramatic growth of the sport industry over the last 30 years has given many individuals the initiative to pursue careers in this dynamic industry. In order to prepare these future sport administrators, it is important that educators continue to monitor and adjust educational programs and professional preparation needs. The second edition of *Foundations of Sport Management* is designed to provide an initial introduction to the sport industry to those students interested in a career in sport. In order to have an opportunity to succeed in this industry, it is important for the future administrator to move beyond water cooler or ESPN SportsCenter discussions and recognize the multiple and often complex components of the sport industry.

This text is written in a contemporary manner to enhance comprehension and to minimize the shock factor for those examining the sport industry for the first time. The contents of the text were designed to address the core competencies initially identified by the North American Society of Sport Management (NASSM) and the National Association of Sport and Physical Education (NASPE) and now supported by the Commission on Sport Management Accreditation (COSMA). It is the goal of the editors to briefly introduce each of the core competencies and instill a sense of excitement in the student regarding each subject. We hope that the reader will leave each chapter with a feeling of "Wow! That's cool! I'd like to know more about this!"

Each chapter is designed to both inform and entertain the student. Cartoons from the popular comic strip "In the Bleachers" by Steve Moore have been used to make the text more enjoyable for students than the ordinary type-filled pages they might have come to expect from regular college textbooks, and to perhaps match, if only in some small way, some of the passion and excitement they might feel for the subjects of sport and sport management. Additionally, supportive quotes from a variety of sources are used to introduce areas of importance. Key words are highlighted in each chapter to help emphasize main points and important terminology. Review questions are supplied at the conclusion of each chapter to help the student master the material provided.

It is our hope that instructors will appreciate the availability of PowerPoint presentation for each chapter. The slides are designed to allow for simple modification by individual instructors. A comprehensive test bank has also been made available for instructors and consists of a wide variety of objective questions.

Too often textbooks fail to identify their targeted audience and consequently try to be everything for everyone, from the casual reader to the Ph.D. student. The authors of this text have chosen to target undergraduate students, and this book is written to address that specific audience. The intent of this text is not to teach individual subjects in their entirely, but simply to introduce them and generate interest and understanding in continued study of the sport industry. Each of the chapter authors was selected as a recognized expert in his or her area and represents the next generation of sport industry authorities.

You are about to embark on the study of one of the most dynamic, exciting, and visible industries in the world today. Throughout your academic career, you will be exposed to a variety of topics, career options, and issues to research; embrace them, and become passionate about your study of sport management. Oftentimes in sport, there are hundreds of applicants for a single job—what will make your resume stand out? As you read this, think of the classmates in your Introduction to Sport Management class. What makes you different? You can distinguish yourself by understanding and applying the principles found in this text, along with gaining practical experience in a variety of sport settings. Best wishes as you embark on your academic study of the sport industry.

For the Student

Chapter One

INTRODUCTION TO THE SPORT INDUSTRY

ANDY GILLENTINE • R. BRIAN CROW • JOSH HARRIS

"SPORT IS NOT SIMPLY ANOTHER BIG BUSINESS. IT IS ONE OF THE FASTEST GROWING INDUSTRIES IN THE U.S., AND IT IS INTERTWINED WITH VIRTUALLY EVERY ASPECT OF THE ECONOMY—FROM THE MEDIA AND APPAREL TO FOOD AND ADVERTISING . . . SPORTS IS EVERYWHERE, ACCOMPANIED BY THE SOUND OF A CASH REGISTER RINGING INCESSANTLY."

—MICHAEL OZANIAN

Cost of an average college degree in sport management:
$60,000

Number of weeks you will work nights and weekends in this industry:
52

Percentage of friends who will ask for free tickets:
100%

Seeing your stadium full of cheering fans despite a poor record:
Priceless

Welcome to the Sport Industry!

IN THE BLEACHERS — *BY STEVE MOORE*

TAYLOR! GET YOUR HEAD IN THE GAME!!

LEARNING OBJECTIVES

Upon completion of this chapter, the reader should be able to
* Understand the growth of the sport industry;
* Describe the growth of the academic study of sport management;
* Identify the myths surrounding the sport industry;
* Discuss the unique features of the sport industry; and
* Elaborate on the challenges of selecting a career in the sport industry.

Introduction

The sport industry represents one of the largest and fastest growing industries in the United States and the world (Pitts & Stotlar, 2002; *SportsBusiness Journal*, 2003; The Sport Industry, 2007). This accelerated growth has fueled the continued desire of many people to pursue a career in the sport industry. Thousands of students each year, in the U.S. and abroad, enter academic programs specializing in the study of sport management to prepare for a future in sport.

In addition to the rapid growth of the sport industry, the nature of sport business has changed as well. Sport is now a major component of the entertainment industry, competing for the discretionary income of fans worldwide. Gone are the days of collecting gate receipts in "cigar boxes" (Gillentine, 2004). Sport is now a multibillion-dollar industry and growing. This increases the need for sound administrative and business practices and for individuals specifically educated for the unique nature of the sport industry.

Why a Career in Sport?

Before launching into a college degree program and professional career in sport, individuals should fully understand the commitment and dedication required for success in this field. In order to evaluate their current status, it is important to answer the most basic of Socratic questions, "Why?"

Probably the most common answer to this question is "I love sports!" While it is important to have a passion for your work, a love of sports is probably not enough to ensure a happy and productive career in the sport industry. Upon entering the sport profession, this "love of sport" becomes a job and, like all jobs, will have its good moments and bad. If your motivation also includes "getting to watch lots of games," your time and money may be better spent purchasing a 52-inch plasma television. When you choose sport as a career, you will be preparing for the upcoming event while others are tailgating in the parking lot; most likely you will be working during game time, in addition to several hours after the event. Your passion has now become your occupation. Helping others enjoy watching the event while you earn your paycheck is the reality.

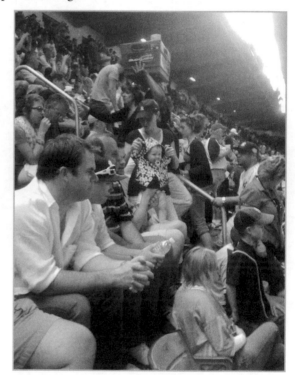

Another common answer is "I hope to rub elbows with the rich and famous." While you may have greater access to well-known athletes and coaches, don't be misled in thinking they will be your new lunch buddies. Frequently entry-level sport managers find themselves disappointed after meeting the "star player" of their new employer. According to David Sampson, President of the Florida Marlins, "Quite often you will find these guys are immature, overpaid, and over indulged, just because they can throw hard" (Sampson, 2004).

Others enter the sport industry with dollar signs in their eyes. The sport media is full of stories chronicling the astronomical salaries and monies generated in the sport industry. While it is true that a lucrative living can be made in the sport business, the reality is few in the administration of sport receive those salaries. The vast fortunes of the owners of today's professional sport franchises were typically made outside of the sport industry. Don't be disappointed, though; a comfortable living can be made in sport management . . . but individuals must be prepared and patient to work toward that level of compensation.

Opportunities in Sport: Myth and Reality

The sport industry is subject to a high level of public scrutiny. Daily fans evaluate every move made not only by the players on the field, but also by the executives directing the organization. This constant evaluation, however, does not ensure the credibility of those making the evaluation. Therefore many "myths" regarding the sport industry flourish (additional myths are also discussed in various chapters). Many of these myths focus on the potential for a career in the sport industry. Most of these myths are based upon antiquated ideas and/or outdated information, while others merit closer analysis because they also infuse accurate information but are presented in a questionable context. Listed below are some of the most frequently cited myths, complied from a variety of sources, regarding seeking a career in the sport industry.

1. **Opportunities are limited and the field is saturated with applicants.**

   It seems almost paradoxical to state that sport is one of the fastest growing industries worldwide and in the next breath state that opportunities are limited. While obviously there are not an unlimited number of jobs available in the sport industry, there are, in fact, jobs available. In order to be successful in the sport industry, individuals must be mobile. Opportunities in sport are found in locations ranging from New York City to Stillwater, Oklahoma, to Portland, Oregon, and all points in between. Individuals wishing to enter the sport industry must be willing to "go where the jobs are." Often people are too myopic in their vision of where they are willing to work and therefore limit their access to jobs. With regard to over-saturation of the job market, most administrators will agree there are never enough qualified applicants for positions, while there are always too many unqualified ones. It is important for individuals to appropriately prepare and position themselves to become attractive to potential employers.

2. **Short-term opportunities are not worthwhile.**

   One of the quickest and most effective ways to enter the sport industry is through internships (see Chapter 14). Quite often these positions are designed to be seasonal or short-term. They do, however, provide the individual with the experience necessary to apply for better full-time opportunities as they arise. Often individuals will fill multiple short-term internships in order to gain valuable experience and to begin networking in the sport industry. During events such as the Sony Ericsson Open, the fifth largest professional tennis tournament in the world, numerous volunteer and intern opportunities exist. Over 2,000 volunteers and staff work together to produce an event that has become one of the most popular tennis tournaments among fans and players alike. Opportunities such as this are not only good résumé builders, but also provide you with an avenue to showcase your skills to today's sport industry executives. Furthermore, do not be discouraged from accepting positions that initially indicated a specific beginning and ending date. View each of these opportunities as a chance to gain new skills and to showcase your abilities.

3. **Opportunities for minorities are limited.**

   While the number of minorities holding high-ranking sport industry positions is verifiably low, these numbers are improving (Lapchick, 2008). As more and more minorities decide to pursue a managerial career in the sport industry and prepare themselves for that career, we will see a continued change in the demographic make-up of sport managers. The process is, and will be, slower than any of us desire, but the sport industry has always been willing to allow individuals the opportunity to pursue this career option and is often more willing than the rest of society to judge a person on their successes rather than on their race, ethnicity, or gender. With the recent formation of organizations such as the National Association of Black Sports Professionals (NABSP), whose mission is increasing opportunities for minorities by enhancing their presence, awareness, and industry exposure (*SportsBusiness Journal*, 2007), the number of minorities in administrative positions should continue to increase. Becoming successful in a management position in the sport industry requires the same skills athletes must have to succeed: dedication, commitment, and a willingness to work harder than your competitors.

4. Opportunities for females are limited.

As you will learn in Chapter 2, there are laws protecting the rights of women in the workplace. But beyond that, the sport industry is witness to an unprecedented growth in the number of females entering and advancing in the workplace. There certainly is, however, much room for improvement. One only needs to look in the "Careers" section and the "People" section in a recent issue of the *SportsBusiness Journal* to see that while women are represented, all things are not equal. In fact, look at the *SBJ* Top Forty Under Forty, or the listing of Top Sport Executives, and notice the number of women.

Despite the continued existence of these myths, the sport industry does offer many exciting, challenging, and rewarding positions for those deciding to pursue this career path. Managerial challenges in the sport industry may be compared to completing a crossword puzzle. You can clearly see the problem that needs to be solved; there is at least one clue to help identify the best possible answer; the answer's position in relationship to the entire situation is evident; and once the answer is found, immediate gratification is mentally and visually present.

The Evolution of Sport Management Education

The growth of the sport industry far exceeded the expectations of scholars and researchers in the late 20th century, who projected that the GNP for the industry would consume more than $121 billion (Rosner, 1989; Meek, 1997; Pitts, 2001). However, actual estimates after the turn of the century show these numbers to be far too conservative, with various researchers putting the number somewhere between $200 billion and $250 billion (SBJ, 2003; Pitts & Stotlar, 2002; The Sport Industry, 2007). These estimates have varied widely due to the unimaginable explosion of opportunities within this industry, which is good news for those who want to pursue a sport-related career.

As employment opportunities in the sports industry have grown, the need for training of sport professionals has received much attention. Universities have quickly tried to develop sport management curricula at the graduate and undergraduate levels to fill the need for professionals trained specifically in sport management/administration (Stier, 1993). In fact, as of June 2008, the North American Society of Sport Management (NASSM) website identified the number of universities offering a sport management curriculum at approximately 230, a substantial increase from the first established program in 1966. In addition, membership in NASSM, including sport management faculty members and students, has reached over 1,000 for the first time in its history.

As the interest and participation in sport have grown to all-time highs, so has the need for professional preparation of sport managers and administrators. Large numbers of undergraduates and sport professionals are rapidly returning to the campus to take discipline-specific courses to improve their current or potential employment opportunities (Parkhouse, 1996). The impetus for the development of a sport administration academic program developed when Walter O'Malley (of the Brooklyn Dodgers) urged University of Miami (FL) educator James Mason to imagine the effectiveness of individuals specifically trained to deal with the business of the growing sport industry (Mason, Higgins, & Owens, 1981).

> "I ask the question, where would one go to find a person who by virtue of education had been trained to administer a marina, race track, ski resort, auditorium, stadium, theatre, convention or exhibit hall, a public camp complex, or a person to fill an executive position at a team or league level in junior athletics such as a Little League baseball, football, scouting, CYO, and youth activities, etc. . . . A course that would enable a graduate to read architectural and engineering plans; or having to do with specifications and contract letting, the functions of a purchasing agent in plant operations. There would be problems of ticket selling and accounting, concessions, sale of advertising in programs, and publications, outdoor and indoor displays and related items." (Mason et al., 1981, p. 44)

From this modest and carefully orchestrated beginning, sport management and sport administration programs have grown rapidly throughout the United States and the world. While the University of Miami may claim to be the "birthplace of sport management education," the curriculum proposed by Mason in 1957 was considered "ahead of its time" and was not implemented by the Coral Gables institution (Sawyer, 1993). Mason started the first graduate program in sport administration at Ohio University in 1966. Ironically, Biscayne College, now known as St. Thomas University, located only 15 miles from the University of Miami campus, became the first university to establish an undergraduate program in sport administration (Masterlexis, Barr, & Hums, 2005). The state of Florida remains a leader in sport management education with no fewer than 18 colleges and universities offering academic programs (*SportsBusiness Journal*, 2004). Many public and private high schools have established special academic programs for high school students wishing to pursue a career in the sport industry (High School of Sports Management, 2008; OneCommunityOneGoal Annual Report, 2004).

The expansion of academic programs was not confined to undergraduate and master's degree programs. Results of a study completed in 1996, and re-confirmed as recently as 2008 from the NASSM website, showed that no fewer than 22 universities offered doctorate programs with at least an emphasis area in sport administration and/or sport management (Gillentine & Crow, 1996). Despite this finding, sport administration/management academic programs struggle to find enough discipline-specific trained professionals to fill their faculty needs (Mahony, Mondello, Hums, & Judd, 2004).

The rapid development of sport management graduate programs occurred through the independent efforts of various universities throughout the country. The lack of coordination between schools caused a fragmentation in the development of programs. Each university or department was free to establish its own priorities and areas of emphasis (NASPE/NASSM, 1993). The sport management/administration programs were established and housed in different departments (general business, physical education, management, etc.) according to university preference (Bridges et al., 1992).

The Sport Management Arts and Science Society (SMARTS), a group organized at the University of Massachusetts, Amherst, first examined this curricular fragmentation (Masteralexis et al., 2005). From the initial explorations of the SMARTS organizations, greater emphasis was placed on the academic credibility of graduate sport management programs. The recognized need for a standardized review of sport management curricula and programs prompted the formation of the North American Society of Sport Management (Parkhouse, 1996).

The National Association for Sport and Physical Education (NASPE) organized a Sport Management Task Force in 1986 to begin the development of standardized core competencies. The NASPE task force formed a partnership with the North American Society for Sport Management (NASSM) to further explore and develop the standardized core requirements for sport management programs (see Table 1.1). The recommended standards established by the joint task force identify minimum competencies that should exist in undergraduate and graduate programs. Standards were also established identifying the minimum number of course offerings and faculty needed to offer a program. The Sport Management Program Review Council (SMPRC) was created through the NASPE/NASSM task force to help universities "attain and maintain excellence in undergraduate and graduate education for sport management" (NASPE/NASSM, 1993). For 15 years the SMPRC reviewed programs, volunteering for the approval process through use of the identified criteria and evaluated the program curriculum by area and as a whole.

The development of minimum program requirements and the move toward standardization were the first steps to establish credible sport administration and sport management curricula. In 2005 representatives from NASSM and NASPE reconvened to discuss organizing a body for the *accreditation* of sport management programs. Two committees were developed to explore the accreditation process and the identification of appropriate standards for accreditation. Nine months from their

Table 1.1. NASSM/NASPE Core Competencies for Undergraduate Programs

1. **Socio-Cultural Dimensions in Sport**—enables the student to recognize that sport is a microcosm of society and is influenced by cultural traditions, social values, and psychosocial experiences.

2. **Management Leadership and Organization in Sport**—to enable the student to define and understand the concepts of management and leadership in sport.

3. **Ethics in Sport Management**—students should be able to recognize and identify moral issues related to sport in its intrinsic and extrinsic dimensions.

4. **Marketing in Sport**—the student will be able to apply fundamental marketing concepts to the sport industry.

5. **Communication in Sport**—students will become familiar with the principles of interpersonal communication, mass communication, and interaction with the public as they relate to the sport industry.

6. **Budget and Finance in Sport**—the student will understand why budget and finance in sport is a critical component of all sport-related industries.

7. **Legal Aspects of Sport**—the student will become familiar with the legal concept in those areas that they are likely to encounter in the sport workplace.

8. **Economics in sport**—the student will obtain an understanding of economic principles and their application in the sport industry.

9. **Governance in sport**—the student will be familiar with various governing agencies in sport and examine their authority, organizational structure, and function.

10. **Field Experiences in Sport Management**—the student will benefit from a culminating in-depth practical experience, bridging the gap between classroom learning and practical application in the sport industry.

(NASPE/NASSM, 1993)

---

inception, the committees provided their preliminary reports to representatives of NASSM and NASPE. The leadership from both organizations solicited and collected feedback from all constituencies regarding the movement toward program accreditation. From the subsequent discussions a proposal for the formation of a Sport Management Accreditation body was developed (Sport Management Accreditation, 2007).

Through the joint efforts of NASSM and NASPE, the Commission on Sport Management Accreditation (COSMA) has been created to provide accreditation and related services for sport management programs (see Table 1.2). As required by accepted academic accreditation policies and procedures, COSMA will exist as an independent accrediting body, with a Board of Commissioners formed from its membership. NASSM and NASPE identified a timeline to officially launch the COSMA organization in July 2008 (COSMA History, 2008). The failure to properly train and prepare managers and administrators is the number one cause of management failure today. Over 98 percent of managers are placed in positions for which they have not been properly trained (Bridges et al., 1992). To help ensure that sports professionals do not follow the same pattern of failure, it is imperative to continue developing quality sport management programs. In order for the sport industry to maintain consistent educational and preparation standards, it is important that universities recognize and implement the recommended standards, ultimately leading to program accreditation.

PURPOSE OF THE COSMA

The purpose of the COSMA is to promote and recognize excellence in sport management education in colleges and universities—at both the undergraduate and graduate levels—through specialized accreditation. Institutions, students, employers, and the general public all benefit from the external verification of quality provided through the COSMA's accreditation process. They also benefit from the process of continuous quality improvement that is encouraged by the COSMA's developmental approach to promoting excellence in sport management education.

Table 1.2. Characteristics of Excellence in Sport Management Education

Excellence in sport management education has many different components that must be considered during the evaluation process.

Excellence in sport management education normally displays the following characteristics:

* The sport management program has a clearly defined and relevant mission and broad-based goals that are consistent with those of the institution.
* The sport management program has a strategic plan that is in touch with the realities of sport management education and the marketplace, and that is consistent with the strategic plan of the institution. This strategic plan is driven by the approved mission and broad-based goals of the sport management program.
* The sport management program has developed and implemented an outcomes assessment process that promotes continuous improvement in the sport management programs and operations, and that is linked to the strategic plan of the sport management program.
* Students in the sport management program develop, both personally and professionally, into well-educated, ethical, competent sport management professionals.
* The sport management program operates in an environment that encourages and promulgates innovation and creativity in sport management education.
* The sport management program has meaningful and effective linkages between the classroom and practitioners in the sport management community, thereby providing assurance of relevancy and currency in the academic programs.
* The sport management program encourages cooperative relationships with other educational units, both external and internal, which are consistent with its mission and broad-based goals.
* Faculty in the sport management program model ethical character and integrate ethical viewpoints and principles in their teaching.
* Faculty in the sport management program are effective teachers who are current in their fields and active in their professional contributions to their institution and discipline. Further, the faculty are positively engaged within their sport management program and contribute to its mission and broad-based goals through appropriate faculty development and faculty evaluation processes.
* The mix of academic and professional credentials of the sport management faculty is worthy of the respect of the academic and sport marketplace communities.
* The mission of the institution and its sport management program is effectively communicated to current and prospective students.
* The institution provides adequate resources to the sport management program to accomplish its mission and broad-based goals.
* The curricula in the sport management programs reflect the mission of the institution and its academic unit, and are consistent with current, acceptable practices and principles of professionals in the academic and sport marketplace communities.
* The curricula in the sport management programs ensure that students understand and are prepared to deal effectively with critical issues in a changing global environment.
* The content of sport management courses is delivered in a manner that is appropriate, effective, and stimulates learning.
* The sport management program recognizes the role of practical and experiential learning as a relevant component of sport management curricula.
* The institutional organizational structure supports excellence in sport management education.

Source: Commission on Sport Management Accreditation.

The rapid development of sport management academic programs also created another point of confusion within the industry . . . the name. Individuals examining sport management academic programs will find them listed under a variety of different titles. The most common names for academic programs are either sport(s) management or sport(s) administration. While most professionals agree that the particular name of the program is much less important than program course content, it is important to understand why there are differences in *sport* and *sports, management* and *administration*. The early academic programs in sport were frequently housed in departments of physical education. Therefore, the programs were referred to as *sports* management or *sports* administration. The term *sports* typically refers to separate sports activities such as football, baseball, etc. The implication, then, is

What's the Deal with the Name?

that *sports* management would therefore encompass only the management of these sports activities. *Sport*, on the other hand, offers a more universal description of the variety of activities and occurrences in the sport industry as a whole. These activities may include planning, organizing, and controlling sport programs (discussed in Chapter 4). Parks and Quarterman (2002) offer a clarifying analogy by surmising that the difference between sport and sports is similar to the difference between religion and religions. While *religions* refers to the different beliefs and denominations (i.e., Catholic, Baptist, Jewish, Muslim, etc.), *religion* is a broader term that encompasses leadership, belief, operation, and function.

The variance between the use of administration or management also traces its origins to its original home department. The term *administration* was typically associated with those programs and individuals working in the public sector, such as high school or university athletic directors. Since many early programs were housed in physical education departments, the use of this term seemed most logical. The term *management* was typically associated with those organizations and individuals working in the private sector. As graduates of those early programs often saw a larger job market available in educational settings, many programs adopted the term *administration* in their name. Regardless of the name, the true test of an academic degree lies in the program content.

Unique Aspects of the Sport Industry

The need for discipline-specific academic preparation for the sport industry is magnified by the uniqueness of several primary features included in the discipline. While at an elementary level these features are similar to skills needed in other business ventures, closer analysis clearly identifies how this industry differs from others. Mullin (1980) first identified three unique features of sport management: marketing, finance, and career paths. Parks et al. (2002) suggested that the social influence of sport was an additional unique feature of this industry. In addition to these unique features, we believe that the customer base (fans) and the venues also separate the sport industry from other business enterprises.

MARKETING

The marketing aspects of sport offer a great many challenges to the sport professional. Not only does the sport marketer have to clearly identify who the customer is, it is also necessary to recognize where the customer will consume the product. Unlike many products, the same sport product may be consumed in multiple ways simultaneously. Additionally, the sport product is commonly produced and consumed at the same time, offering the marketer little room for adjustment. The specifics of the unique features of sport marketing are covered in Chapter 7.

FINANCE

A brief overview of sport finance will quickly indicate the unique components of this industry. Few industries generate the multiple sources of revenue that the sport product does. In many instances, more revenue is generated for these alternate revenue streams than from the core product itself. The sport product also differs from other industries in that multiple forms of business enterprise (corporations, partnerships, sole proprietorships, and non-profit) exist within the same environment. Additional detailed explanation of these varied financial and economic differences will be offered in Chapter 6.

CAREER PATHS

As the sport industry continues to mature and evolve, new positions and job descriptions will emerge. There are few areas of career emphasis that are not currently available through the various branches of the sport industry. In addition to the emergence of new positions in the sport industry, the current trend toward diversification of the sport industry workforce will continue. The move toward diversification will generate additional positions for underrepresented groups throughout the sport industry. Future changes in technology will serve only to launch new positions within the industry.

SOCIAL INFLUENCE OF SPORT

In order to view the social impact of sport, one needs only to attend a sporting event and observe the myriad of emotions and actions of the crowd. Not only will they support their chosen team, they will suffer with them if they are not successful. Fans demonstrate their emotional and psychological attachment through their attendance and consumption of the sporting event itself; they most frequently also now even show their involvement through the purchase of ancillary items related to the sport product. From the playing fields to the water cooler, sport is pervasive throughout our country. In 2004, the U.S. was blanketed with a sea of yellow wristbands, indicating support for Lance Armstrong and others who had battled back from cancer. What started as a small show of support soon became a national phenomenon. In the summer of 2008, it is estimated that just over 2 billion people—almost one third of the world's population—watched the Beijing Summer Olympics Opening Ceremony (Opening Ceremony, 2008). These social implications of sport will be discussed in greater detail in Chapters 2 and 13.

CUSTOMER BASE (Fans)

Fans (customers) are yet another consideration that adds to the unique aspects of the sport industry. Rarely is such an intense sense of loyalty found in other industries. Sport fans also often exhibit intense levels of identification with the sport product through which the fan feels psychologically connected to a team (Wann, Merrill, Russell, & Pease, 2001). This connection is not deterred by poor seasons or regional location, which allows for expansion of the sport product. Fans also add to the uniqueness of the sport product in that they can influence potential revenue streams of the sport organization in a variety of ways outside of consumption of the core product. Team names and logos are present on almost any product imaginable and are purchased by fans. While loyal customers may have strong feelings regarding a particular consumer good, rarely do you find them painted in corporate colors cheering for their favorite detergent!

SPORT VENUES

Lastly, the venues in which sport events take place further separate sport from most industries. Most often an industry operates in a single setting that typically offers a quite controlled environment. The sport industry, however, produces and displays its product in a variety of settings that are subject to a variety of external influences. The sport product may also be consumed in a variety of venues at the same time. This consumption can take place at the stadium or arena, the consumer's home, a sports bar or restaurant, on a radio, or even via the Internet. While sport managers may not be able to control these environments, they must recognize the impact they may have on the sport product. Sport managers must recognize the potential impact that the venue has on customer satisfaction with the sport product.

Summary

The sport industry is a dynamic, exciting, and visible field for career opportunities and academic study. Ultimately, your mastery of the field will provide you with the opportunity to advance beyond entry-level work to a rewarding career. As you look back at the information in this chapter regarding the growth of sport and the study of sport management, think of ways you can improve upon the body of knowledge contained herein. You represent the future of the sport industry, and therefore are responsible for knowing the history and fundamentals of the field, as well as building upon it for the future.

DISCUSSION ACTIVITIES

1. What are some of the myths surrounding employment in the sport industry? Why do they continue to exist?
2. Identify and discuss the unique aspects of the sport industry.
3. What professional opportunities are available in the sport industry?
4. Explain the differences between sport and sports, and management and administration.

SUGGESTED READINGS

Brassie, P. S. (1989, November/December). A student buyer's guide to sport management programs. *Journal of Physical Education, Recreation, & Dance, 60*(9), 25–28.

Danylchuk, K. L., & Judd, M. (1996) *Journal of Sport Management*: Readership survey. *Journal of Sport Management, 10*, 188–196.

Hardy, S. (1987) Graduate curriculums in sport management: The need for a business orientation. *Quest, 39*, 207–216.

Olafson, G. A. (1995) Sport management research: Ordered change. *Journal of Sport Management, 9*, 338–345.

Slack, T. (1996). From the locker room to the boardroom: Changing the domain of sport management. Journal of Sport Management, 10, 97-105.

Stier, W. (1993). Alternate career paths in physical education: Sport management. Washington, DC: Eric Digest—Clearing House on Teaching and Teacher Education.

Weese, W. J. (1995). If we're not serving practitioners, then we've not serving sport management. *Journal of Sport Management, 9,* 237–243

Weese, W. S. (2002). Opportunities and headaches: Dichotomous perspectives on the current and future hiring realities in the sport management academy. *Journal of Sport Management, 16,* 1–17.

Zakrajsek, D. B. (1993). Sport management: Random thoughts of one administrator. *Journal of Sport Management, 7,* 1–6.

References

Brassie, P. S. (1989, November/December). A student buyer's guide to sport management programs. *Journal of Physical Education, Recreation, & Dance, 60*(9), 25–28, 404–498.

Bridges, J. B., & Roquemore L. L. (1992). *Management for Athletic/Sport Administration.* Decatur, GA: EMS.

Boucher, R. L. (1998). Toward achieving a focal point for sport management: A binocular view. *Journal of Sport Management, 12,* 76–85.

COSMA History (2008). Retrieved September 25, 2008, from: http://iweb.aahperd.org/naspe/cosma/template.cfm?template=history.html

Cuneen, J., & Sidwell, J. (1998, Winter). Evaluating and selecting sport management undergraduate programs. *The Journal of College Admissions,* 6–13.

Danylchuk, K. L., & Judd, M. (1996) Journal of sport management: Readership survey. *Journal of Sport Management, 10,* 188–196.

Gillentine, A. (2004). "Moving mountains": Encouraging a paradigm shift in sport administration/management. Paper presented at the Annual Convention of the Florida Alliance of Health, Physical Education, Recreation, & Dance. Oct. 13. Orlando, FL.

Gillentine, A. (2000). The evolution of sport administration/management graduate programs. *MAHPERD Journal, 4*(1), 7–10.

Gillentine, A., & Crow, B. (1997). *Sport management doctoral programs.* Paper presented at the Annual Convention of the Southern District Alliance of Health, Physical Education, Recreation, & Dance. Feb. 13. Biloxi, MS.

Hardy, S. (1987) Graduate curriculums in sport management: The need for a business orientation. *Quest, 39,* 207–216.

High School of Sports Management (2008). Retrieved September 25, 2008, from: http://insideschools.org/index12.php?fso=1444&all=y

Lapchick, R. (2008). *2007 Racial & gender report card.* Orlando, FL: The Institute for Diversity and Ethics in Sport.

Lapchick, R. (2007). Group's growth a positive step for diversity in sports business. *Sports-Business Journal.* Retrieved August 15, 2008, from: http://sportsbusinessjournal.com/article/57402

Mahony, D., Mondello, M., Hums, M., & Judd, M. (2004). Are sport management doctoral programs meeting the needs of the faculty job market? Observations for today and the future (Perspectives). *Journal of Sport Management, 18,* 91–110.

Mason, J. G., Higgins, C., & Owen, J. (1981). Sport administration education 15 years later. *Athletic Purchasing and Facilities,* 44–45.

Masterlexis, L. P., Barr, C. A., & Hums, M. A. (2005). *Principles and practice of sport management* (2nd ed.). Sadbury, MA: Jones & Bartlett.

Meek, A. (1997). An estimate of the size and supported economic activity of the sports industry in the United States. *Sport Marketing Quarterly, 6*(4), 15–21.

Mullin, B. J. (1987) Sport management: The nature and utility of the concept. *Arena Review, 4*(3), 1–11.

NASPE-NASSM Joint Task Force on Sport Management Curriculum and Accreditation. (1993). Standards for curriculum and voluntary accreditation of sport management education programs. *Journal of Sport Management, 7*(2), 159–170.

Olafson, G. A. (1995) Sport management research: Ordered change. *Journal of Sport Management, 9,* 338–345.

Opening Ceremony draws 2 Billion Viewers (2009). Retrieved September 25, 2008, from http://blog.nielsen.com/nielsenwire/media_entertainment/beijing-opening-ceremonys-global-tv-audience-hit-2-billion/

Parkhouse, B. L. (2005). *The management of sport: Its foundation and application* (4th ed.). New York: McGraw-Hill.

Parks, J., & Quarterman, J. (2002). *Contemporary sport management*. Champaign, IL: Human Kinetics.

Pitts, B. (2001). Sport management at the millennium: A defining moment. *Journal of Sport Management, 15*(1), 1–9.

Pitts, B. G., & Stotlar, D. K. (2002). *Fundamentals of sport marketing* (2nd ed.). Morgantown, WV: Fitness Information Technology.

Pitts, B. G., Fielding, L. W., & Miller. L. K. (1994) Industry segmentation theory and the sport industry. *Sport Marketing Quarterly, 3*(1), 15–24.

Rosner, W. (1989). The world plays catch-up: Sport in the 90s. *Sports Inc., 2,* 6–9.

Sampson, D. (2004). Personal correspondence. January 14. Sunrise, FL.

Sawyer, T. H. (1993). Sport management: Where should it be housed? *Journal of Physical Education, Recreations, & Dance, 64*(9), 4–5.

Slack, T. (1996). From the locker room to the boardroom: Changing the domain of sport management. *Journal of Sport Management, 10,* 97 105.

Sport Management Accreditation (2007). Retrieved September 25, 2008, from: http://www.nassm.com/Members/Accreditation

Stier, W. (1993). *Alternate career paths in physical education: Sport management*. Washington, DC: ERIC Clearinghouse on Teaching and Teacher Education.

The Sport Industry (2007). *SportsBusiness Journal*. Retrieved June 20, 2008, from http://www.sportsbusinessjournal.com/index.cfm?fuseaction=page.feature&featureld=43

Wann, D., Merrill, J., Russell, G., & Pease, D. (2001). *Sport fans*. New York: Routledge.

Weese, W. J. (1995). If we're not serving practitioners, then we've not serving sport management. *Journal of Sport Management, 9,* 237–243.

Weese, W. S. (2002). Opportunities and headaches: Dichotomous perspectives on the current and future hiring realities in the sport management academy. *Journal of Sport Management, 16,* 1–17.

Zakrajsek, D. B. (1993). Sport management: Random thoughts of one administrator. *Journal of Sport Management, 7,* 1–6.

Chapter Two

WHY SPORT MANAGEMENT MATTERS

CATRIONA HIGGS · BETSY MCKINLEY

© 1997 Universal Press Syndicate   www.uexpress.com

UNABLE TO COPE WITH PRESSURE OF BEING A ROLE MODEL

LEARNING OBJECTIVES

By the end of this chapter, the student should be able to
- Describe the reasons why sport managers should study sport;
- Identify current myths in sport;
- Know what we can learn from studying sport;
- Understand the relationship between society and sport;
- Describe why diversity is such an important topic for sport managers;
- Outline the major laws that prohibit discrimination in the workplace; and
- Describe the major methods utilized in socio-cultural studies to understand sport behavior.

Introduction

Sport is one of the largest and most influential industries in the United States, eclipsing real estate, retail trade, health care, banking, and transportation (Coakley, 2007). The phenomenal global impact of sport has resulted in the academic study of sport from a variety of different perspectives. Sports are popular, public activities that offer many exciting opportunities for examining their sociological and cultural relationship to society. The financial impact of sport on society increases the need to analyze the political and cultural importance of sport from both a national and international perspective. *Sport sociologists* focus on many of these issues, including the analysis of sport as an industry, the political and cultural implications of sport, sport and globalization, the relationship between gender, class and economics, deviance in sport, and the social organization of sport (Woods, 2007). Careful *sociological analysis* of sport enables us to learn more about human social organization and its relationship to individual and group behavior within the sport environment (Coakley, 2007).

While many students are interested in sport and have a good working knowledge of trivia, statistics, and teams, few students understand the complexities of sport as a *social institution* and phenomenon. In many sport management classes, the primary focus of learning for students is, of course, on management. We might think we know a great deal from buying into the myths perpetuated by many of those involved in the management and organization of sport. It is important to distinguish the truth from falsehoods so we can gain a clear idea of the role of sport in our lives. Students will gain a great deal from an analysis of sport from a socio-cultural perspective that is both applicable to their future roles as sport managers and to their own knowledge base in sport.

Why should we study this subject and why is it important to dispel the myths surrounding this activity? Understanding the answers to those questions will ultimately enable you to become a better consumer of sport, a more knowledgeable fan, and a better sport manager.

Why Should We Study Sport?

Undoubtedly, why we should study sport is an important question for any student and appears to be easily answered by the following examples:

- *Sport is omnipresent.* It is all around us and affects our lives in a myriad of different ways. It is an important part of our lives and thus merits our attention. We all know of people whose lives revolve around their favorite team or athlete. These individuals (fans) often know more about sport trivia than what is happening economically or politically in the U.S. or the world. Why are people so interested in what appears to be a relatively trivial and unimportant part of society? The answer is fairly simple—sport is a fascinating and multidimensional activity, full of daring, drama, and spectacle. In many ways, it is far more interesting than many other things in our lives. Why do we know so much about sport? It's similar to learning the words of a song—the tune appeals to us and we commit it to memory. We love sport and most of us want to know and learn more about it (Davis, 2002).

- *Sport coverage has increased dramatically over the past decade.* It would be impossible to pick up a newspaper or switch on the radio or television and not see some form of sports coverage. Television in particular has been responsible for bringing sport to the masses. Network and cable stations utilize sport to attract viewers and advertise other television programs. The Super Bowl, the Olympic Games and other major sporting events attract hundreds of millions of viewers each year and command billions of dollars in advertising revenues and sponsorship.

- *Many of the role models adopted by our children are athletes.* Athletes such as Michael Phelps, Lebron James, Kobe Bryant, Maria Sharipova, Sydney Crosby, and Tom Brady are instantly recognizable and have an impact on the way our children act, dress, and think. Similar to other media figures, sports stars are entertainers and may provide a distraction from reality. The media coverage afforded to these sport stars is phenomenal. As a public, we appear unable to get enough of watching our favorite sports stars both on and off the court/field.

Myths in American Sport

Myths are stories that often become our realities. Beneath the visible, explicit surface of sport, there lies a whole other world comprised of hidden beliefs and motives. As sport managers, we are assailed by a number of myths or misperceptions that appear to be real. In effect, our feelings and attitudes about sport have been largely shaped by the media and cultural beliefs. An overwhelming number of people get their information from watching television, socializing with others, or accessing the Internet, rather than reading a textbook or conducting their own research. We do not reflect upon sport programs or sport information, we experi-

"Sports do not build character . . . they reveal it."

—John Wooden

ence them. As such we fall victim to the ways in which the media and our upbringing shape our perceptions of sport. In effect, the information often presented to us is highly subjective. An analysis of the socio-cultural aspects of sport reveals the following myths/misconceptions:

- College sports programs generate millions of dollars, making huge profits for their universities.
- *Title IX* has resulted in complete equity for men's and women's education-based athletic programs.
- *Title VII* has resulted in complete employment equity for men and women outside the education setting.
- Gambling in sport poses no risk to the sport or its participants.
- Sport is a wonderful way for all children (regardless of skill level) to help build their self-esteem.
- Politics does not affect sport.
- Most communities benefit economically and psychologically from supporting a professional sport franchise, and therefore the community should pay for expensive renovations or building new stadiums.
- Drug abuse is not a problem in professional sports.
- Sport is one of the few places in society where African Americans receive equitable treatment.

What Can We Learn from Studying Sport?

Sport is an important element of American life that is so pervasive we are all affected by it. Studying sport from a social perspective will help us understand the *culture* of our society and help dispel some of the myths that have been purported (Donnelly, 2004). Imagine that a Martian spaceship landed in America on the day a major sports event was being held. What could those visitors learn about our society from watching that sports event and our reactions to it? If the event was the Super Bowl, perhaps the Martians could conclude that we as Americans loved activities that were fast-paced, competitive, exciting, and aggressive. In addition, the signage around the stadium may help the aliens conclude that there are major connections between sports and the business world. In watching the advertisements shown during the breaks in competition, they may also understand how economics play an important part in defining what sport is in this country. In short, studying sport from a social perspective facilitates learning and understanding more about our culture.

Culture represents the norms and values of individuals and groups within society. Sport in America mirrors what is occurring in the rest of our society. Politics, economics, inequities, social relationships, and deviance in society can all be viewed through an analysis of sport. Sport, in essence, is a microcosm of American culture. Thus, the more we understand about sport, the more we can reflect on what is happening in the rest of society.

Not everyone agrees with what is important in studying sport and society. The method of analyzing sport from a cultural perspective has resulted in the development of a sub-discipline called *sport sociology*. Sports sociologists are interested in how humans relate to each other in the sport context, how values affect these relationships, and how humans organize sport activities (Coakley, 2007). Sport sociology is a science and derives most of its methods and theories from its parent subject: sociology. Sport sociology is often a difficult and complex area to analyze because social phenomena in the sports world are complex, subtle, and elusive. Sport is a *dynamic* activity that is constantly evolving and changing. Sport sociologists conduct research into the development of sport, patterns of culture, social perspectives, values, and sports organizations. Sport sociologists have many questions about what is important and what is not. To that end, cultural practices in sport are studied from a number of different perspectives. Understanding and applying these perspectives to a study of sport in the social context can be a valuable tool for students who wish to further their understanding of this area.

Theories are valuable ways to examine the effect of sport on society. Theories attempt to examine patterns and provide answers for why things happen in sport. The important thing to remember, however, is that no one theory can hope to explain all parts of the sport experience because of the inherent limitations of each one. Hopefully what these theories can offer us are methods by which we can answer questions related to the values of our culture and the relationship of these values to sport.

Frameworks for Understanding the Relationship Between Sport and Society

Sociologists study sport in a variety of different ways (Eitzen, 2002). The focus of analysis is not confined solely to elite athletic experiences (such as professional, Olympic, or intercollegiate participation); rather, we are interested in all facets of involvement in sport and physical activity. Areas of consideration include, but are not limited to, the following:

- Sport and Social Values
- Socialization into Sport
- Youth Sport
- Sport and Education (interscholastic and intercollegiate)
- Sport and the Economy
- Sport and the Political System
- Violence in Sport
- Use of Performance-Enhancing Substances
- Gambling and Sport
- Sport and Religion
- Sport and the Mass Media
- Social Stratification
- Diversity Issues in Sport
- Future of Sport

What Areas Do Sport Sociologists Investigate?

Analyzing these areas permits us to look beyond statistics, teams, and trivia into a more meaningful exploration of the impact that sport has on our everyday lives. The analysis of sport from a longitudinal perspective (e.g., youth sport through inter-scholastic, intercollegiate, and professional participation) gives us an opportunity to review the major influences in our decision to engage in this practice and to explore the reasons for our continuance/non-continuance in this activity. Questions like the following can be answered by reviewing our own experiences:

- Why did we play the sports we played?
- How did we become interested in those particular activities as opposed to others? How were those early experiences related to social class, race, gender, and community?
- What was the role of our parents/guardians in learning to love sports?

An investigation of the close relationship between the economy and sport reveals the multidimensional nature of this activity. To say that sport is "big business" is truly an understatement in the 21st century. Similarly, those who believe that politics have no impact on sport need to understand and appreciate how local and national governments affect sport participation and sport consumption.

A brief review of the political events that have surrounded the last 100 years of Olympic competition is enough to convince anyone that political interventions, particularly boycotts, are a fundamental part of international sport competition. Major problems in society (e.g., drugs, violence, gambling) can also be analyzed in the sports context. Understanding why these social problems exist in sport helps to explain the motivation of athletes to engage in these practices and the pressures that lead to these abuses. Why do athletes commit violent acts on and off the field? Why do athletes take performance-enhancing substances? Why do fans riot? Why do male athletes abuse women? All these questions can be addressed from a sociological perspective.

DEVIANCE IN SPORT

A quick review of any local/national newspaper, sports channel, or specific sports event quickly reveals that some athletes (like some non-athletes) are engaged in deviant activities. Floyd Landis, Kobe Bryant, Marion Jones, Michael Vick, Barry Bonds, Mike Tyson, O. J. Simpson, and Adam "Pacman" Jones are examples of athletes who have recently been accused or convicted of committing deviant acts on and off the field. Are athletes more deviant than others, or are they just more visible in the media and their deviant acts therefore more noticeable? *Deviance* is any act that violates the norms of an activity (Coakley, 2007). What is considered normal in sport (e.g., aggressive plays, violent actions on the court/field), however, would be considered deviant in other areas of society. Sport requires a measure of competitiveness and aggression that would be frowned upon in any other social sphere. However, even in sport there are normative (acceptable) behaviors for athletes. Athletes are expected to pursue victory as zealously as possible, but we do not expect them to apply a "win at all costs" mentality to this quest (at least not if this involves cheating to win). Unfortunately the focus on achievements, winning, and victory often leads athletes to make choices between what is morally right and what may give them a "competitive" edge (Woods, 2007). Taking performance-enhancing substances to improve performance, for example, has become one of the most important areas for discussion and policy among sport organizations and sport sociologists. The use of drugs in sport is a not a new phenomenon (Goode, 1992); however, it has recently garnered a great deal of attention from fans, Congress, and the general public. Although steroid use has been the focus of much of this attention, athletes in a variety of sports use drugs to improve their performance. Wrestlers and jockeys have used diuretics for many years to make weight, cyclists in the Tour de France have been accused of taking stimulants to remain competitive, Olympic archers and biathletes have taken "downers" (such as alcohol and beta blockers) to steady nerves and dampen arousal levels, and world class skiers such as Bode Miller have endorsed the use of erythropoietin (EPO) to increase endurance.

Most sport organizations have responded to the rampant use of drugs in sport and devised drug-testing policies and procedures to try to combat this problem. However, their efforts have been hampered by the increasing sophistication of drug compounds that cannot be detected and the scientific use of masking agents and stacking (cycling on and off drugs) regimens used by athletes. This issue will likely remain at the forefront of modern sports well into this century.

Another concern of many sport sociologists is the incidence of on- and off-field violence in sports. Football is the most popular sport in the U.S. primarily because it appeals to us as Americans on many levels. It is a tough, aggressive, competitive activity that reflects Americans' cultural values. We watch this sport and revel in the aggressive nature of the plays. The media often highlights the most violent of acts (tackles, sacks) and replays these events numerous times. A measure of risk is assumed by all athletes on the field; however, the concern of many is when athletes have problems in turning off this aggression off the field. The number of violent incidences that athletes have been involved with over the past decade suggest that there is some cause for concern, especially when we look at the rise in violence against women by male athletes (Crosset, 1999). Mike Tyson's conviction of rape is one example of the blatant misuse of women by athletes; however there is no definitive research that proves that athletes are more likely to commit offenses against women than non-athletes.

DIVERSITY AND SPORT

Perhaps the most important area for sport managers to appreciate and understand is that of *diversity* (Cunningham, 2007). In the 21st century, a focus on all discriminatory practices related to diversity in the workplace is critical (Robinson & Dechant, 1997). Functioning as an effective and efficient sport manager requires an understanding, true appreciation, and constant application of non-discriminatory practices (Fink & Pastore, 1999). Diversity is more than just an analysis of *racism* and *sexism*. According to the U.S. Equal Employment Opportunity Commission (U.S. EEOC), federal laws including Title VII of the Civil Rights Act of 1964, the Americans with Disabilities Act (ADA) and the Age Discrimination in Employment Act (ADEA) specifically address the illegality of any employment-based *discrimination* with regard to race, color, religion, gender, national origin, disability, or

"PREJUDICE IS A BURDEN WHICH CONFUSES THE PAST, THREATENS THE FUTURE, AND RENDERS THE PRESENT INACCESSIBLE."

—MAYA ANGELOU

age (Carr-Rufino, 2007). Sexual harassment is also addressed but sexual orientation is not protected by federal laws.

Race/Color Discrimination

Although African Americans represent a large percentage of those who participate in collegiate and professional sports, the opportunities for advancement to the administrative, front office, and coaching ranks are sadly limited for this minority group (Feagin, 2001; Lapchick, 2006). Additionally, the contributions of Mexican Americans, Native Americans, and Asian Americans to sport have largely been ignored (Lapchick, 2006). Focusing on these issues is critical to our understanding of sport and to enhancing our role as sport managers in a diverse and complex society.

Title VII of the Civil Rights Act of 1964 covers federal, state, and local governments, employment agencies, labor organizations, and private employers of 15 or more people. It is unlawful to discriminate against any employee or applicant for a position based on his or her race or color (U.S. EEOC, 2006). The law prohibits discrimination in all phases of the hiring, employment, promotion, work compensation, and termination spectrum. Further, it is illegal to discriminate based on personally held or social stereotypes and assumptions about the competence, characteristics, or performance of any racial group. For example, the sport manager would be creating a hostile work environment by telling jokes that portray an individual or group in a negative light (either to the individual or behind his or her back). Such actions are illegal. Examples of stereotyping that may lead to a negative work environment also include the use of disparaging remarks and criticisms or negative statements made in relation to a person's race or color (Landry, 2005). Such actions are termed "verbal harassment." Race/color discrimination violations also include isolating one group from interaction with others in the work place (segregation) and requesting pre-employment information regarding race that may be used in excluding a job candidate from selection for employment.

Sex Discrimination

While sport is largely considered to be a meritocratic organization that does not discriminate according to sex, an analysis of stratification and diversity issues in sport can quickly reveal the realities (National Women's Law Center, 2002). Sport has long been a male preserve, and females have been excluded from participating in sport-related activities (Acosta & Carpenter, 2006). Federal laws prohibit such discrimination. In reference to the school and university setting, *Title IX* was passed in 1972 as part of the Educational Amendments Act and prohibits sex discrimination in education agencies that receive federal funding. Title IX has been effective in many ways by improving participation levels of females in sport associated with educational settings (Carpenter & Acosta, 2005). The law, however, has not completely erased personal prejudice and discrimination against women athletes and administrators.

Title VII of the Civil Rights Act of 1964 prohibits sex discrimination in areas outside the education setting, such as in fitness centers, sport arenas, and other venues. Because sport is still organized and controlled primarily by men, the "glass ceiling" that exists in the business world is certainly restrictive to women who wish to advance to upper management and front office positions in the sports world (U.S. Glass Ceiling Commission, 1995). Though the private sector has seen an increase in women in managerial positions from 29 percent in 1990 to over 38 percent in 2006, at the same time, women comprise 48 percent of the private sector workforce (U.S. EEOC, 2006). It is imperative that sport managers ensure that management positions are equally representative of all facets of the public sector, and do not reflect bias in hiring based on the sex of the applicant.

Sexual Harassment

Title VII also protects men and women against workplace sexual harassment, including requests for sexual favors from those in a position of power (i.e., supervisors) or those serving as co-workers, workplace conditions that create a hostile or unwelcome environment for either gender, or same-sex harassment. EEOC statistics for fiscal year 2006 show 23,247 charges of sex-based discrimination. During the same time, 23,364 sex-discrimination charges were satisfied, resulting in recovery of monetary benefits of more than $99.1 million. Sexual harassment can be found in many forms in the workplace. *The Pregnancy Discrimination Act*, an amendment to Title VII of the Civil Rights Act of 1964, provides protection for pregnancy-based discrimination including pregnancy, childbirth, and pregnancy-related medical conditions. Further, pregnancy cannot be used as a reason to refuse to hire a woman. It is within the bounds of the law for an employer to request a doctor's statement regarding any work-related limitations due to pregnancy; however, an employer must hold open a position that was temporarily vacated due to a pregnancy leave.

Obviously, it is imperative that the sport manager understands and implements workplace practices that are free of all forms of sexual discrimination (Landry, 2005). Programs focusing on the prevention of sexual harassment include sensitivity training for all managers and employees, the establishment of a procedure for filing complaints, and quick resolution/action regarding every sexual harassment issue filed (Marshall, 2005).

Religious Discrimination

It is illegal for employers or employees to discriminate based on religious beliefs in the workplace (U.S. Commission on Civil Rights, 2005). This includes during the hiring process, during the creation of work schedules, during the promotion process, or in establishing workplace rules. In fact, a manager is to make reasonable efforts to provide workplace flexibility regarding various religious convictions of workers, as long as those accommodations do not infringe on the beliefs or work environment of other employees. The manager must also take care to prohibit workplace religious harassment among employees and ensure that one person's religious beliefs do not result in negative workplace business interests for others in the facility. For example, managers must take care to assure that additional business costs are not incurred as a result of their decisions regarding workers' religious convictions, and that one group of employees does not receive special considerations regarding salary, work schedule, or work materials to the detriment of other groups or individuals.

Disability Discrimination

The Americans with Disabilities Act (ADA) of 1990 protects individuals with disabilities from being discriminated against in the workplace. The ADA delineates a person with disabilities as an individual who "has a physical or mental impairment that limits one or more major life activities, has a record of such impairment, or is regarded as having such an impairment" (EEOC). As in previous areas of discrimination, the manager has the responsibility of accommodating schedules, modifying facilities, and adjusting policies and operating procedures for individuals with disabilities. Again, there is an undue hardship consideration wherein the accommodations enacted by the manager must not involve additional expense or hardship for the business owner, and the work or product produced by the facility must be of the same quality as expected from all employees (Sharp, Moorman, and Claussen, 2007).

Age Discrimination

Because many organizations have less than 20 employees, thus generally negating the position of a human resource officer for the company, it is critical for the sport manager to be aware of and implement non-discrimination in all areas of the workplace. This is true when working with individuals who are given less than satisfactory entry opportunities, job placement, work scheduling, and promotion/retention opportunities. *The Age Discrimination in Employment Act (ADEA) of 1967* was initially passed to protect workers age 40 and older from age discrimination in the above-mentioned areas. The ADEA was amended by the *Older Workers Benefit Protection Act of 1990 (OWBPA)* to include a focus on age discrimination and loss of workplace benefits. The OWBPA also provided for older worker protection in the area of protocol establishment that must be followed when employers are asked to waive their rights when filing settlement claims regarding age discrimination. This legislation is particularly critical to workers who have been affected by company mergers, acquisitions, and job displacement due to downsizing.

METHODS USED IN SOCIO-CULTURAL STUDIES TO UNDERSTAND SPORT BEHAVIOR

Sport sociologists largely rely on the methods of the parent discipline (sociology) to research areas in sport. Sport sociology is a science, and, as such, the concentration of research in the area is geared toward the collection of accurate and verifiable evidence. *Surveys* (questionnaires) are valuable methods of learning about group and individual preferences and opinions. Sometimes the facts we need are not recorded by anyone and we have to ask people questions. For example, asking fans what motivated them to attend a particular sports event can provide us with very valuable information regarding consumer (fan) behavior. A questionnaire can be completed by individuals in a fairly short period of time and may produce a large volume of data that can be analyzed quickly and efficiently. *Interviews* with fans, participants, and sport consumers are also widely used to explain various aspects of sports participation and consumption. Interviews can be more revealing than surveys, especially when open-ended responses are used to gather information. A close-ended (yes/no) response tells the researcher very little about the actual reasoning behind a decision. Asking questions such as "why" can be far more revealing, and some of the most interesting studies are ones that use this approach singularly (e.g., ethnographic studies). *Observational studies* also produce data that can help a sport sociologist understand aspects of sports participation. For example, subjects who are unaware that they are being watched and their behavior recorded are acting naturally in their environment and are not being asked to recall past information or misrepresenting their experiences (as in an interview). There are many other methods of collecting data; however, the main responsibility of the researcher in this area is to accurately collect, record, analyze, and interpret the facts. In our search for the truth, we rely on scientific methods of data collection to accurately describe what really exists as precisely and objectively as possible.

Summary

Examining sport from a socio-cultural perspective is critical for those entering the sport management profession. Concepts related to sport and other social institutions are important for the sport manager to understand. The development of modern sport has been influenced by many factors that have affected our perceptions about this topic. In addition, the concepts of diversity discussed in this chapter are also critical from many perspectives. The workplace is changing and evolving, and the kinds of people that we now see and service in sport are from diverse backgrounds. An examination of the demographic shifts likely to occur in this century reaffirms the need to be well versed in multiculturalism and inclusion. A good sport manager is one who affirms diversity in the workplace and accepts all individuals for their contributions to the sport organization. Differences should be embraced and not feared, and individuals should be judged on their merit, not on the color of their skin or what they choose to believe. Confronting prejudice and discrimination in the workplace is a difficult thing to do, but as a manager it is important to realize that part of your responsibility lies in challenging the barriers to employment diversity, thereby providing a safe and secure workplace for all employees. Strategies for managing diversity are important for achieving workplace equity; however, the first step in the process must be a review of one's own prejudices and an examination of why these prejudices exist. Only when we confront our own fears and discriminatory behaviors can we begin to effect change in others.

LEARNING ACTIVITIES

1. Does sport bring people together or tear them apart? What specific instances can you think of to support your view?
2. What impact does legislation have on managing a sport organization? Provide specific examples from this chapter to support your answer.
3. Describe any personal experiences that you have had with discrimination. How did these situations affect you, and what did you learn from these experiences?
4. How can the rampant use of drugs in sport be curbed? Do current drug testing policies work?

PROJECTS TO BE COMPLETED OUTSIDE OF CLASS

1. Go to the website of a professional franchise or college athletic department and access the page that introduces their management team. Record the following:
   a. Number of male vs. female managers
   b. Types of managers by gender (e.g., is the athletic director a man or woman? is the assistant director of marketing a man or a woman?)
   c. If pictures are provided—how many minority managers are there in this organization?

   Once you have collected this data, answer the following questions:

   a. Is there a disparity in gender of those associated with the franchise or sport organization?
   b. Are the administrative positions staffed by only men, only women, or a percentage of both?
   c. Are the administrative positions staffed only by Caucasian personnel, or are underrepresented groups evident in top management?
   d. Is the wording used by the franchise or sport organization inclusive or exclusive according to gender, race, or ability? Provide specific documentation of your findings.
2. Choose two of the myths outlined in this chapter. Using the web or other resources, provide two examples of specific information that helps to refute each myth.
3. Attend a sports event at your college or university. Observe how the sports event is presented to the audience. Report on the relationships and connections you witness between the event and the concepts discussed in this chapter (i.e., signage, ages of spectators, promotions for spectators, reactions of fans to calls by officials, reactions of fans to opposing fans).
4. Analyze the content of a sports section of a local or national newspaper. Record the following information:
   a. The number of articles featuring male athletes
   b. The number of articles featuring female athletes
   c. The number of photographs featuring female athletes
   d. The number of photographs featuring male athletes

e. The number of articles featuring minority athletes

f. The number of photographs featuring minority athletes

g. Answer the following questions: Who does the media choose to focus on with regard to sport? Which gender/races are most included? Which gender/races are most excluded?

5. Review the drug-testing policies of the NFL, NBA, MLB, and NHL. Compare and contrast the efficacy of each.

DISCUSSION ACTIVITIES

1. **Hitting a Triple.** In groups of three, determine three reasons why sports coverage has increased dramatically over the past decade. You have three minutes to complete this activity. Be prepared to share your reasons with the rest of the class!

2. **Once Upon a Time.** Many athletes are viewed as role models by children and youth. With a partner, write a fairy tale ("Once upon a time, there was a child who . . .), in which the child in the story emulates undesirable attributes of professional athletes (i.e., greed, drug abuse, gambling, poor sportsmanship, bullying). The negative attributes should not contribute positively to the growth or social interaction of the child in any way. Share your story with another pair in the class. Then, correct the two stories so that "all lived happily ever after!"

3. **The Three R's.** A female employee is being sexually harassed and is told by her boss that it is not a good time to "make waves." With a partner, analyze this scenario using the following three steps: 1. REFLECTION: "How did the events in the scenario relate to one another?" 2. RESEARCH: "What concepts or principles in the field of sport management will help us to understand what happened?" 3. RESPOND: Ask the students to list specific actions that should have been added, omitted, or applied differently to "fix" the scenario. An extension of this activity is to have students create different scenarios, using chapter material

4. **Shared Feelings.** Create a list of words that describe you and your experiences. Include reference to gender, race, marital status, year in school, favorite food, hobby, religion, political affiliation, club membership, athletic team membership, sports you like to watch, sports you like to play, favorite dessert, pet ownership, favorite vehicle, socioeconomic status, favorite chain restaurant, favorite sports teams. Share this list with two other people, and compare your similarities and differences. What does this exercise tell you about yourself and those in your class, as related to this chapter?

5. **Ready, Set, Go.** Get ready, because this active learning strategy adds the element of *time* in decision making. Each student in class is given a scenario relating to a diversity problem or issue. Seated face to face in two concentric circles, each pair of students has 60 seconds to share their scenarios and to elicit a solution to each. At the end of a minute, the outer circle of students is cued to move one seat to the left. The sixty-second timer is restarted, and the process begins again. Remember to take notes on each collaboration, for discussion at the end of the activity. Stop this activity after 8 or 9 rotations. Students will take turns sharing their solutions to their scenarios. Was thirty seconds enough time to "solve" each scenario? In real world settings, time is always a critical factor during decision making. Therefore, care must always be taken to arrive at solutions in both an appropriate and timely fashion.

SUGGESTED READINGS

Burstyn, V. (1999). *The rites of men: Manhood, politics, and the culture of sport.* Toronto, ON: University of Toronto Press.

Cahn, S. (1995). *Coming on strong: Gender and sexuality in twentieth-century women's sport.* Boston, MA: Harvard University Press.

Waddington, I. (2000). *Sport, health and drugs: A critical sociological perspective.* New York: Routledge.

References

Acosta, V., & Carpenter, L. (2006). *Women in intercollegiate sport: A longitudinal study—29 year update—1977–2006.* Unpublished manuscript, Brooklyn College, NY.

Americans with Disabilities Act (1985) C.F.R. 843 (j) (2) (i).

Carpenter, L., & Acosta, V. (2005). *Title IX.* Champaign, IL: Human Kinetics.

Carr-Ruffino, N. (2007). *Managing diversity.* Boston, MA: Pearson.

Coakley, J. (2007). *Sport in society: Issues and controversies* (9th ed.). Boston, MA: McGraw Hill.

Crosset, T. (1999). What do we know and what can we do about male athletes violence against women? *Quest.* (August).

Cunnigham, G. B. (2007). *Diversity in sport organizations.* Scottsdale, AZ: Holcomb Hathaway.

Davis, R. (2002). *Inclusion through sports.* Champaign, IL: Human Kinetics.

Donnelly, P. (2004). Interpretive approaches to the sociology of sport. In J. Coakley & E. Dunning (Eds.), *Handbook for sport studies* (pp. 77–91). London: Sage.

Dunning, E. (1999). *Sport matters: Sociological studies of sport, violence and civilization.* London: Routledge.

Eitzen, S. (2002). *Sociology of North American sport* (7th ed.). Boston, MA: McGraw Hill.

Equal Employment Opportunity Commission (2006). *Sex based charges.* Retrieved November 30, from http://www.eeoc.gov/stats/sex.html

Feagin, J. (2001). *Racist America: Roots, current realities and future reparations.* London: Routledge.

Fink, J., & Pastore, D. L. (1999). Diversity in sport? Utilizing the business literature to devise a comprehensive framework of diversity initiatives. *Quest, 51,* 310–327.

Goode, E. (1992). *Drugs in American society.* New York: McGraw Hill.

Landry, F. J. (Ed) (2005). *Employment discrimination litigation: Behavioral, quantitative and legal perspectives.* San Francisco, CA: Jossey Bass.

Lapchick, R. (2006). *Race and gender report card.* Retrieved on November 30, 2007, from http://www.bus.ucf/sport

Marshall, A. M. (2005). *Confronting sexual harassment: The law and politics of everyday life.* Burlington, VT: Ashgate.

National Women's Law Center (2002). *The battle for gender equity in athletics: Title IX at 30.* June, Washington, DC.

Robinson, G., & Dechant, K. (1997). Building a business case for diversity. *Academy of Management Executive, 11*(3), 21–31.

Sharp, L. A, Moorman, A. M., & Claussen, C. L. (2007). *Sport law: A managerial approach.* Scottsdale, AZ: Holcomb Hathaway.

U.S. Commission on Civil Rights (2005). Clearinghouse Publication, 70.

U.S. Glass Ceiling Commission (1995). *Good for business.* U.S. Department of Labor.

Woods, R. B. (2007). *Social issues in sport.* Champaign, IL: Human Kinetics.

Chapter Three

COMMUNICATION AND MEDIA RELATIONS IN SPORT

ANDY GILLENTINE • R. BRIAN CROW • CHERI BRADISH

LEARNING OBJECTIVES

Upon completion of this chapter, the reader should be able to
- Understand the important role of communication in the sport industry;
- Identify the various components of effective communication;
- Recognize the barriers to effective communication;
- Discuss the importance on nonverbal communication; and
- Appreciate the role of media relations in the sport organization.

Introduction

Sport organizations, like all other enterprises, strive to send a unique message to their many stakeholders. For example, consider the Florida Marlins of Major League Baseball. The Marlins have been pursuing the construction of a new $515 million dollar stadium that the team maintains will help them to compete financially and on the field with other teams in the league (Rabin, 2008). The owner of the team (as well as other team officials) is in constant communication with fans, sponsors, researchers, broadcasters, fantasy league players, schools, community groups, city officials, employees, volunteers, suppliers, vendors, licensees, and dozens of other individuals and organizations on a daily basis (Table 3.1). This information exchange occurs in a variety of ways: via phone calls, email, personal meetings, text messages, visits to a web page, written correspondence, visits to schools or hospitals, and other various methods of communication. If the Marlins failed to maintain open lines of communications with each of these groups, it is doubtful that they would be able to generate the approval needed for the new stadium. It is clear that sport organizations rely on communication to survive in today's media savvy environment. A clear and consistent message is more likely to be understood by the recipient and responded to in a positive manner.

Effective communication in sport is one of the most important and pervasive qualities and competencies a sport manager can possess. Communication can run the gamut from interpersonal and small group communication to public mass communication networks. The importance of developing communication skills necessary for success in the sport industry is heightened by the tremendous growth of electronic media. The expansion of media coverage of the sport industry will only continue to grow as innovative technologies offer sport managers new avenues through which to communicate. Therefore, it is essential that sport managers have a strong appreciation of the power of contemporary communication media, both as a means of connecting with key constituents and as an advantage that requires increasingly greater management skill and coordination.

Sport mangers must constantly refine their communication skills in order to effectively deliver information to the diverse groups with which they may interact. From casual conversation with colleagues to formal meetings with financial sponsorship partners, the sport manager must be prepared to maximize the effectiveness of communication. The development of effective communication skills requires sport managers to (1) acknowledge the importance of effective communication, (2) commit to an honest and frequent appraisal of their communication strengths and weaknesses, and (3) demonstrate a willingness to invest the time and effort to improve them.

Interpersonal and Small Group Communication

KEYS TO EFFECTIVE COMMUNICATION

In order to become an effective communicator, the sport manager must understand that communication is a multifaceted skill. The sport manager must recognize the multiple techniques for effective communication, evaluate the various methods through which communication can occur, and select the most appropriate action or actions. Effective *planning* is an often overlooked step in the communication process, compromising the usefulness of the information. After determining the most effective method(s) to utilize, the sport manager must effectively plan the content of the message, the timing for release of the information, and estimate the content, speed, and consequences of the recipient's feedback.

Table 3.1. Sport Managers Communication Demands

- Team Owners/Administration
- City Officials
- Coaches
- Vendors
- Competing Sport Organizations
- Sponsors
- Staff members
- Researchers
- The media
- Game Officials
- Boosters
- Players
- Fans
- Parents
- Faculty

Modified from Anshel (1997)

Once the plan is in place, the sport manager must ensure the integrity of the information to be distributed. It is important that the *content* of the message is accurate and free from bias or inflammatory language. It is also important for the sport manager to establish his or her *credibility* with the intended audience. The credibility of the sender directly affects the perception of the receiver regarding the content of the message. Credibility is enhanced through an established reputation, a long history of truthful and accurate communication, and legitimacy. *Personal credibility* goes hand-in-hand with *message credibility*. Honest communication from the organization results in trust from the audience. Failure to be honest—for example, repeatedly denying trade rumors that ultimately prove to be true—will often damage the organization and administrator's credibility. Never distribute information before it has been checked for accuracy. It is better to have a short delay in sending a message than to send one with inaccurate information.

Additionally, the sport manager must consider the *type of information* being transferred. *Complex* information may be potentially confusing and must be carefully presented, to not create additional communication problems. Also, the *emotional content* of the message has to be considered. Often the information transmitted

Table 3.2. Guidelines for Effective Communication

- Plan for communication
- Be honest
- Establish consistent daily communication
- Encourage upward, downward, and lateral communication
- Respect other viewpoints
- Praise (in public) and criticize (in private) behavior, not the person
- Utilize humor
- Do not use sarcasm or embarrass others
- Never use stereotypes or prejudicial statements
- Avoid negative humor and obscene language

Table 3.3. Barriers to Effective Communication

- Linguistic barriers
- Psychological barriers
- Environmental barriers

Table 3.4. Components of Linguistics

Phonetics: different sounds that are employed across all human languages
Phonology: patterns of a language's basic sounds
Morphology: the internal structure of words
Syntax: how words combine to form grammatical sentences
Semantics: the meaning or interpretation of words
Sociolinguistics: the effect of all aspects of society, including cultural norms, expectations, and context, on language

from the sport organization—for example, the trading of a star player or firing of a coach—contains emotionally charged content for recipients (i.e., fans, boosters, players). These messages must be delivered in the most positive manner possible. Also, specific words can be emotion laden. Words related to sex, religion, and politics may themselves evoke a response from recipients that may affect the delivery of the message.

BARRIERS TO EFFECTIVE COMMUNICATION

Sport managers must also recognize that there are inherent *barriers to effective communication*. These barriers may be typically categorized into three distinct categories: (1) linguistic barriers, (2) psychological barriers, and (3) environmental barriers. While it may be impossible for the sport administrator to completely eliminate these barriers, methods to minimize the potential impact of each should be considered during the communication planning process.

The classic Abbot and Costello comedy routine "Who's on First?" depicts a conversation between two friends regarding the players on a baseball team. The ensuing miscommunication is a perfect example of a *linguistic* barrier to effective communication. Visit http://www.youtube.com/watch?v=sShMA85pv8M to see the full video clip.

Linguistics is defined as "the study of the nature, structure, and variation of language, including phonetics, phonology, morphology, syntax, semantics, sociolinguistics, and pragmatics" (*The American Heritage Dictionary of the English Language: Fourth Edition*, 2000).

While each of the above areas identifies an important component in the study of linguistics, perhaps the most important components are *semantics* and *sociolinguistics*. Semantics is defined as the meaning or the interpretation of a word and/or sentence. Individuals often define terms differently, which could impact the content of the message. The sport administrator must be cautious in the selection of terminology to ensure the proper interpretation of the message. This difference can lead to miscommunication or disagreement over a topic that both groups may actually agree on. Closely related to semantics and an area of great importance is sociolinguistics.

Sociolinguistics refers to the impact that differing social and/or cultural groups have on the meaning and interpretation of language. Very often words or phrases have a very different meaning from group to group. Social variables that could impact communication may include ethnicity, religion, economic status, and level of education. Given the diverse audience the sport manager interacts with on a regular basis, it is critical these differences be noted. For example, certain language used by college students during a college athletic event might be interpreted differently by a 51-year-old man and his 18-year-old daughter (Cramer & Schietzer, 2004).

The *environment* may also pose barriers to effective communication. The designated audience may not effectively receive verbal messages delivered in a crowded, noisy, or uncomfortable room. Distractions may impede a person's ability to hear and accurately interpret the message. The temperature and other weather conditions, such as high winds, rain, and snow, can promote levels of discomfort that may impede communication. While it is impossible for sport managers to control all of these environmental barriers, it is important to recognize them and to minimize their impact.

Additional environmental concerns can involve the physical structure of the facility. Aside from noise issues, inadequately furnished facilities may also create a level of discomfort, which might in turn impede effective communication. In an attempt to offset this problem, many administrators have turned to feng shui experts to help them design meeting spaces that incorporate comfortable seating and facilitate an effective communication environment (Broadhead, 2001).

Additional potential barriers to effective communication in the sport industry are *psychological* barriers. Psychological barriers are outside the scope of linguistic and environmental barriers, manifesting instead in the mind of the intended audience. While these barriers are among the most difficult to identify, the sport manager must recognize these potential barriers and take actions to offset or change them. Foremost among the psychological barriers is the *perception* of the information or sender. Perception is defined as the "recognition and interpretation of sensory stimuli based chiefly on memory" (*The American Heritage Dictionary of the English Language, Fourth Edition*, 2000). Individuals often rely on past experiences to positively or negatively interpret newly received information. While positive perceptions will most likely help the sport administrator, negative perceptions regarding the administrator, organization, or situation can damage the effectiveness of the message. Public perception and attitudes toward the organization must be continually monitored. If negative perceptions are ignored and immediate action to correct them is not taken, innuendo, rumors, and other misinformation can be perceived as factual.

THE COMMUNICATION NETWORK

Peterson, Miloch, and Laucella (2007) stated that "the sport organization is created, developed, and maintained through the communicative actions of the stakeholders" (p 124). In order for these actions to be effective, the sport manager must recognize the importance of the *flow of communication* among all stakeholders. The sport organization must develop an information flow that moves downward, upward, and laterally.

Downward communication refers to information that is transmitted from the upper levels of management to the middle and lower levels of the organization. Frequently sport managers maintain communication systems that allow only for downward communication, eliminating the opportunity to receive valuable information and feedback from others in the organization.

The *upward* flow of information allows for upper management to receive information from subordinates, customers, suppliers, etc., that may be useful in correcting current operations and/or determining the future direction of the organization. Failure to develop an effective system to gather *feedback* from within the organization and its customers results in upper level management that is out-of-touch with its constituents.

Lateral communication refers to communication that flows between the various individuals or groups at the same or equivalent levels of management. This exchange of information is important to ensure that duplication of materials and information is not occurring within the organization. This type of communication can also be useful to help foster employee involvement and empowerment within the organization.

The communication network also includes identifying the medium through which the communication will be transmitted. These communication networks include *verbal communication*, *non-verbal communication*, and *mass media communication*. Each of these communication media requires specific levels of understanding by the sport manager in order to maximize its effectiveness.

The most commonly used method of communication is verbal communication. Estimates indicate that 70 percent of a person's day is spent in at least one form of verbal communication (Sarthe, Olson, & Whitney, 1973). Verbal communication consists of speaking, listening, reading, and writing. In order to improve verbal communication, it is important for sport managers to consider multiple components of spoken communication. Aside from the credibility of content addressed earlier, sport managers need to consider articulation, tempo, and volume. These components are referred to as paralanguage, the features which accompany verbal communication but are not considered part of the language system.

Articulation refers to the ability to clearly enunciate words. Speakers may need to overcome national or regional accents that may impact the listener's understanding of the message. Speakers should also be aware of the correct pronunciations of words and terms used in delivery. Mumbling is another aspect of articulation that can impact the message. Speakers should strive to speak as clearly as possible and to carefully enunciate each word during a presentation. Although the speaker may initially feel awkward in this careful manner of speech, the reward is an audience that properly decodes the message.

Tempo refers to the speed at which we speak. Novice speakers often have a tendency to speak too rapidly in an important situation. This can be due to increases in adrenaline or general nervousness. No matter what the reason, effective communication requires speakers to speak slower than normal when addressing a group. Another aspect of tempo that should be avoided is a sing-song manner of speech, in

Table 3.5. Verbal Communication
We hear half of what is said: **50 percent**
We listen to half of that: **25 percent**
We understand half of that: **12.5 percent**
We believe half of that: **6.25 percent**
And we remember half of that: **3.125 percent**
Martens, 1987

which the pitch and timing of words follow a pattern that can be distracting to the listener.

Speakers should also be aware of the volume of their voice. In additional to always speaking slower than normal, speakers should also speak louder. A general rule of thumb is to speak in a manner such that someone in the back of the room can easily hear you. This should be a consideration when a addressing a large group. Often it is better to err on the side of caution and utilize a microphone than not be heard.

Another important aspect of verbal communication is listening. Research indicates that individuals spend nearly half of their daily verbal communication listening. The late Mark McCormack, founder of International Management Group (IMG), stated that the most important skill an administrator could have is effective listening. McCormick advocated active listening, a method through which the listener actively and physically participates with the speaker.

NONVERBAL COMMUNICATION

Powerful nonverbal messages are transmitted through the mannerisms and physical actions of the sport manager. The way the speaker utilizes the space in which he/she is delivering the message, and the presentation of their physical attributes and appearance, sends additional information to the recipient, which may or may not reinforce their verbal message. Sport managers must be aware of the importance of these nonverbal communication cues and take the appropriate actions to manage them effectively.

The study of how individuals communicate through their use of space is referred to as *proxemics*. This form of communication includes not only the amount of space between the receiver and the sender, but also how the speaker utilizes the environment. The appropriate use of space can have a dramatic impact on the effectiveness of communication. Often individuals are able to disengage from the speaker if specific personal space or physical barriers are present. It is important for a sport manager to effectively use the space available to deliver his or her message. Space may also provide the speaker with a "buffer zone" to increase his or her own level of comfort (Table 3.7).

The appearance and physical mannerisms of a speaker are referred to as *kinesics*. This may include the speaker's posture, gestures, facial expressions, and eye movement. It is important for a speaker to demonstrate good posture when speaking to an audience. Good posture—standing erect, shoulders back, head up—gives the image of a confident speaker, which may help with credibility issues mentioned earlier. The sport administrator may increase the effectiveness of the message through the use of effective eye and facial movements. Occasionally, speakers unintentionally send messages to listeners through inappropriate facial or eye movements. Presidential candidate Al Gore was publicly criticized for his facial and eye movements during the 2000 presidential debates. Head Coach John Gruden of the Tampa Bay Buccaneers is often lampooned for his animated fa-

Table 3.6. Steps to Improve Listening

- Be prepared to listen
- Listen openly
- Concentrate on message
- Do not judge speaker
- Observe mannerisms and gestures of speaker
- Identify main concepts and points
- Eliminate distractions
- Be committed

adapted from Martens, 1987

Table 3.7. Hall's Proxemic (Distance) Model

Public Distance: **10' or more**
Social/consultive Distance: **4'–10'**
Personal/casual Distance: **1 1/2'–4'**
Intimate Distance: **0"–18"**

Hall, 1959

cial expressions. Speakers must carefully study their own appearance in order to make appropriate changes or modifications in both of these areas.

The use of physical gestures, including touching, can help the speaker in emphasizing important points of information and also in conveying the sincerity of the message. Simple gestures can send a variety of messages to the audience, and it is important for speakers to review the gestures they commonly use or to identify ways to increase their use. In today's litigious society, sport managers need to exercise caution, though, when touching individuals. It should be recommended that the speaker know the recipient well before initiating any physical contact. Casual touching can increase the level of perceived familiarity with the speaker through appropriate use of space as mentioned earlier.

Mass Media Communication

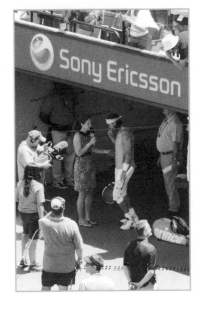

"THE MEDIUM IS THE MESSAGE"

First penned by Marshall McLuhan, it has long been regarded that "the medium is the message." This indicates that, in fact, the means of interaction and communication often serve as the most pivotal means of the message in communication. This is true also of sport. There has been a longstanding relationship, even synergies, between sport and the medium of communication.

Sport Media

Sport media is a broad term encompassing many aspects of how sport consumers receive information. This information can be delivered directly by a team, league, or sport organization (via direct mail or the Internet) or through mass media (newspapers, radio, television, magazines, or the Internet). The growth of sport in the United States, both in participation and spectatorship, can be, in part, attributed to the increasingly complex role media play in our lives. All the issues to be considered when dealing with sport and media are too numerous for one textbook chapter. However, several important topics will lead you to a greater understanding of the role media play in our participation and consumption of sport.

HISTORICAL PERSPECTIVES

Print Media

Organized sport in the United States has evolved tremendously in the past 150 years. Along with that evolution has come an increased thirst for information regarding those sports. Initially, the limited coverage of sport events, and even more limited advertising and promotion of those events, was through *newspapers*. These papers had narrow circulation and quite often not even one writer solely responsible for sport. Compare that to 2008, where most metropolitan newspapers employ several dozen sportswriters. Sports writing improved dramatically after World War I, as the US population became increasingly literate.

Sport, however, continued to grow in popularity, and many professional sport organizations, as well as the precursor to the NCAA, were formed around the turn of the twentieth century. Media coverage of sport continued to evolve as well, with *radio* becoming a major influence beginning in the 1920s. The first radio broadcast of a professional baseball game was in 1921, on KDKA radio in Pittsburgh. This new competition forced sportswriters to change their style of writing; since the game itself was on the radio, they had to provide in-depth, comprehensive information not available on the radio broadcast.

When television became a permanent fixture in the 1950s, sports writers had to change again, becoming investigative reporters and explaining how and why things happened instead of what happened. Today, newspapers devote 20–25 percent of their space to sports news (Nichols, Moynahan, Hall, & Taylor, 2002).

Radio

By the 1930s, nearly 300 million radios were being used in the United States. All 16 Major League Baseball teams broadcasted their games live. Interestingly, play-by-play announcers did not travel with the team in those days; they would recreate the broadcast using Western Union tapes of the game (Nichols, et al., 2002). Radio went from local broadcasts in its early days, to national network broadcasts in the middle of the twentieth century, back to broadcasts aimed at local audiences after World War II (Nichols, et al., 2002). In 2005, national radio broadcasts are again becoming popular, with the advent of satellite radio competitors Sirius Radio and XM Radio.

Television

The first televised sporting event was in 1939—a baseball game between Columbia and Princeton. The growth of professional sport and the growth of television as a viable medium run parallel. In the late 1940s and early 1950s, television in the US was fledgling, with only 190,000 TV sets in use in 1948. Sport—because the events already existed, and there were no sets to build and no actors to hire—became attractive programming (http://www.museum.tv/archives/etv/S/htmlS/sportsandte/sportsandte.htm).

Sport was popular with television executives for several reasons: (1) it attracted a regular weekend audience, (2) it created cross-promotion, (3) it was popular with viewers, and (4) ownership of sports rights adds "credibility" to a network or cable outlet. Today there are more than 500 national and regional cable networks, and over 80 percent of homes subscribe to cable. ESPN, established in 1979, was the first 24-hour, all-sports network. Television rights fees are a significant source of revenue for professional and intercollegiate teams.

Television specifically and media in general impact our sport consumption daily. For example, prior to 2000, it was rare to see a major college football game played on any day but Saturday or Thursday, or a professional game on any day but Sunday or Monday. But in 2004, ESPN proudly announced it would telecast live NCAA and NFL football over 19 straight days. College teams from less visible conferences such as the Sun Belt and Mid-American Conference grudgingly play on Tuesday, Wednesday, or Friday evening for two reasons: exposure and revenue.

Several issues related to televised sport are currently being debated. One involves the limited coverage of women's sports, which is somewhat of a catch-22. Perhaps the popularity of women's sports is narrow because it is rarely televised; and it is rarely televised because of its limited popularity. Another current issue is the rise in the use and popularity of digital video recorders (DVRs). These devices allow viewers to manually edit live broadcasts and skip any portion they may not want to see (i.e., commercials). Since networks and cable broadcasters generate the majority of their income from advertisers, the impact of this new technology remains to be seen. Recent reports regarding the consumption of sport via the use of DVRs indicate that most sport-related programming is played back the same day it was recorded and interestingly a high percentage of the viewers do not skip through the commercials (McDonough, 2007; Vasquez, 2008). For a detailed discussion of sport and television, see http://www.museum.tv/archives/etv/S/htmlS/sportsandte/sportsandte.htm.

Internet

A discussion of various forms of sport media would not be complete without mentioning the World Wide Web. Most sport management undergraduates cannot remember a time when streaming video, real-time information, and instantaneous communication via the Internet were not available. Those of us a few years older, however, remember with a little fondness the pre-Internet days. Today, every sport organization has an official website and hundreds, if not thousands, of unofficial sites created by loyal fans. Official sites specifically are a vast resource of information, as they include schedules, team news, player profiles, historical data, stadium information, and much more.

Every major news organization, media outlet, television and radio station, newspaper, and magazine has its own website, with material to supplement its mainstream offerings. Many web-only sport media organizations have been created as well, with the list too long to even count. The rapid development and availability of blogs and podcasts have also added to the availability of sport-related information to consumers. A blog is a website that displays written entries in which readers are given the opportunity to comment (Blogger.com, 2008). The term *blog* is short for "weblog," a term popularized by Jorn Barger, a weblogger in the late 1990s (Duncan, 2005). A *blogger* is the term used to describe the editor and/or writer of a specific blog. The popularity of blogs has caused ripples throughout the sport industry. Blogs can be developed and launched with little or no monetary investment and can actually generate money for the web editor through the use of banner ads and other advertising options. This has encouraged many individuals to start their own sport-related blogs. Both professional and collegiate sport organizations have been forced to recognize the impact of these bloggers and to take steps to clarify their access to information. In 2006, MLB prohibited bloggers with no affiliation to the recognized mainstream outlets access to stadium press boxes. Television and radio rights holders pay big money in order to broadcast sports. And in turn, they expect something of an exclusive when it comes to the money they pay

(McErlain, 2007). The question of blogger's access was also brought to light when Dallas Mavericks owner Mark Cuban banned full-time bloggers from the team's locker room regardless of their media affiliation (Jacobson, 2008).

For an example of sports blogging, visit www.sportstcurmudgeon.com.

The NCAA has also prohibited live blogging from the press box at its events (Ballard, 2007). A reporter for *The-Courier-Journal* in Louisville was escorted from the press box at an NCAA Super Regional baseball game for live blogging. The NCAA has adopted the position that live blogging infringes upon the assigned broadcast rights of other organizations by providing a live description of the action. "The limitation against play-by-play on the Internet is intended to support our media partners' efforts to provide guaranteed, comprehensive coverage," according to NCAA spokesman Bob Williams. Current NCAA guidelines state that bloggers can only describe the atmosphere, crowd, and other non-play related details. In an effort to meet consumer interest in sport blogging of live events, many sport organizations have employed their own blog editors and allow them the ability to report live from the event.

Podcasting is a result from the popularity of blogs. A podcast is a digital media file that is distributed over the Internet using syndication feeds for playback on portable media players and computers (Starak, 2005). Podcasts serve the sport consumer who prefers to listen to audio commentary rather than to read Internet blog posts and commentaries. The popularity of podcasts also benefited from the availability of high-speed Internet connections which allow for rapid downloading of audio files. Podcasts allow developers the ability to produce their own audio commentaries for a limited cost. While the quality and content of podcasts varies, many podcasts have a very professional presentation. Consumers must be wary, however, because there are very few systems in place to check the veracity and accuracy of information available through podcasts and blogs.

Sport will continue to grow along with new forms of media. In 2004, viewers of the NCAA Division I men's basketball tournament could answer various questions during the broadcast by sending SMS (short message service) text messages from their Cingular Wireless (NCAA sponsor) phones. Current cellular phones, such as the iPhone, allow sport consumers to receive and monitor sports scores and news through their cellular phone provider. Many of the phones also allow for the viewing of live televised events, offering the consumer a "third screen," and yet another way to experience a sport event.

Sports Information

The current relationship between sport and the media has come a long way from the "good old days" when beat writers were on professional sport team payrolls and traveled with their team, in large part to share a public relations "goodwill" account with local and very loyal fans. Today, the relationship between sport and the media has become more tenuous, juxtaposing a more critical, yet accountable forum regarding professional sport organizations and athletes, while at the same time providing a multitude of enhanced outlets to promote and discuss these same sport products.

Table 3.8. Sports Information Outputs

The sports information or media relations director is responsible for delivering many outputs to their media outlets on a very regular and timely basis.

These include the following pieces:

Media Releases

Designed to positively position the sport organization and disseminate information about future developments or happenings within the organization.

Fact Sheets

Delivered in a more timely matter, these are designed to showcase future opportunities for the organization as well as highlight specific facts.

Pre-game Notes

Similar in nature to fact sheets, these are produced prior to sporting events to profile key players and match-ups, as well as interesting and informative team notes.

Hometown Features

Geographically targeted to correspond to key targets, these are developed to highlight key individuals in their hometown region, while also positioning the organization in a positive light.

Media Guides

A very detailed analysis of all facets of the organization, including in-depth profiles of team members, an organization management overview, and information related to each competition (home and away).

Game Programs

For distribution at every home game, these are intended for both consumers and the media to profile the particular match-up and current happenings of the organization.

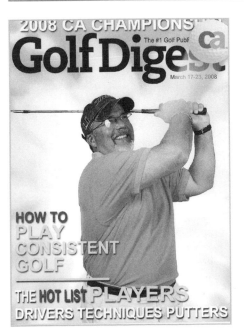

Historically, the formalization of "media relations" departments occurred similarly to the development of the sport industry during the 1950s. In response to the rise in interest of spectator sport, media outlets—specifically, local papers and radio outlets—increased their coverage and requests for information from sport organizations at both the professional and collegiate sport levels. As these requests intensified, the need for full-time sports information directors emerged and the official office of media relations was born. Today, this department works very closely within the greater public relations umbrella of the sport organization, which includes the growing area of community relations. Not only is this unit responsible for the ongoing dissemination of sports information outputs (Table 3.8), but it is also regarded as the first point of contact within the sport organization. It is essential that this department play a very proactive role, working closely with the management and marketing units of the organization, to craft a uniform message to their community.

PRESENT PERSPECTIVES

Sports Journalism

Current insights with regard to sport and media point in particular to the role of sport journalists and sports journalism as having a major impact on the development of the sport industry. Specifically, these individuals, coupled with the increased scrutiny of star athletes and the enhanced style of investigative reporting, have created a magnifying glass approach to the sport media relationship. As such, increased scrutiny and management of sport media are warranted by sport managers. This elevated intensity and reliance on the media is also most apparent in the television outlets, where the ratings game for sport programming has intensified. This is also similar to the impact of the Internet, where increased product extensions and sports information is communicated with sport fans and media alike.

FUTURE CONSIDERATIONS

The future relationship between sport and the media will continue to provide examples of synergies and opportunities for grander levels of importance and influence for sport organizations and sport media outlets. The continued merging of sport and entertainment, including media integration, a number of leading media outlets, and national television companies, will further capitalize on utilizing sport and sport properties to enhance their program lineups. As well, new media will continue to emerge, such as digital media technology, which will generate a whole new genre of communicating with sport fans. A number of factors will contribute to this paradigm shift with regards to sport media, but will include global media convergence of professional sport outlets, sport property ownership by media conglomerates, and global sport markets.

The continued growth and expansion of Internet and wireless services will dramatically change communication strategies employed in the sport industry. The possibilities for interactive consumption of the sport product will expand potential exposure of such goods. These possibilities will present exciting challenges to sport administrators and serve as a continuum for the importance of effective sport communication.

Summary

- Effective communication in sport is one of the most important and pervasive qualities and competencies a sport manager can possess.

- Effective communication requires that sport managers (1) acknowledge the importance of effective communication and (2) demonstrate a willingness to invest the time and effort to improve them.

- The keys to effective communication include effectively planning the message, the integrity of the message, and the credibility of the content.

- Sport managers must consider the type of information being transferred in the message. Messages that contain complex information need to be carefully planned before being issued. Messages that contain information or words that may have an emotional content should also be carefully reviewed before being sent.

- Three major barriers to effective communication are: linguistic barriers, psychological barriers, and environmental barriers.

- The sport manager must appreciate and understand the flow of communication throughout the organization. In an effective communication network, information flows downward, upward, and laterally.

- The major media through which communication typically is transmitted include verbal, nonverbal, and mass.

- *Sport media* is a broad term encompassing many aspects of how sport consumers receive information.

- Mass media communication includes print media, newspapers, radio, television, and the Internet.

- Offices of sports information are important sources of information for the public and for the sport professional.

- The future relationship between sport and the media will continue to provide examples of synergies and opportunities for grander levels of importance and influence for sport organizations and sport media outlets.

DISCUSSION ACTIVITIES

1. Daily, there are a number of media- and sport-related issues occurring in the sport industry. Using current examples, consider how the media influences sport and how sport organizations interact with the media, from both a proactive and reactive perspective.
2. It has been said that the relationship between media and sport is a necessary "synergy," meaning each needs the other to survive in today's marketplace. Discuss.
3. Interpersonal and nonverbal communication are all-important competencies central to the responsibilities and effectiveness of a sport manager and leader. Discuss how these characteristics are intertwined with the other important qualities of a contemporary sport leader.
4. From the chapter, it is noted that the developments in sport media have paralleled those of sport (as an industry and leisure activity). That being said, describe how future developments and expectations in the sport world will affect the delivery and needs of sport media to future sport consumers.

SUGGESTED READINGS

Cosell, H., & Whitfield, S. (1991). *What's wrong with sports?* New York: Simon & Schuster.

Cousens, L., Dickson, G., & O'Brien, D. (2004, June). *Beyond boundaries: A comparative investigation of change in the fields encompassing North American and Australian professional sport organizations.* Paper presented at the 2004 NASSM Conference. Atlanta, GA.

Helitzer, M. (1992). Taming the beast: Riding out a sports crisis. *Sport Marketing Quarterly, 1*(2), 33–42.

Key, M. R. (1975). *Paralanguage and kinesics (nonverbal communication).* Metuchen, NJ: The Scarecrow Press, Inc.

Mahony, D. F., & Moorman, A. M. (2000). The relationship between the attitudes of professional sport fans and their intentions to watch televised games. *Sport Marketing Quarterly, 9*(3), 131–139.

Smith, G. J., & Blackman, C. (1977). *Sport in the mass media.* Ottawa, ON: Canadian Association for Health, Physical Education and Recreation, University of Calgary Press.

Stoldt, C. G., Smetana, G. K., & Miller, L. (2000). Changes in the USA Today's sports coverage patterns during the National Basketball Association lockout: Implications for sport managers. *Sport Marketing Quarterly, 9*(3), 124–130.

Stotlar, D. K. (2000). Vertical integration in sport. *Journal of Sport Management, 14*(1), 1–7.

Turner, P. (1999). Television and internet convergence: Implications for sport broadcasting. *Sport Marketing Quarterly, 8*(2), 43–49.

Anshell, M. (1997). *Sport psychology: From theory to practice* (3rd ed). Menlo Park, CA: Benjamin/Cummings.

Ballard, Chris. (2007, June 25). Step away from the laptop! *Sports Illustrated*, p. 26.

Broadhead, M. B. (2001). Feng shui in the workplace. *Feng Shui Times*. Retrieved January 12, 2005, from http://www.FengShuiTimes.com.

Cosell, H. (1973). *Cosell*. New York: Simon & Schuster.

Cosell, H., & Whitfield, S. (1991). *What's wrong with sports*. New York: Simon & Schuster.

Cousens, L., Dickson, G., & O'Brien, D. (2004, June). *Beyond boundaries: A comparative investigation of change in the fields encompassing North American and Australian professional sport organizations*. Paper presented at the 2004 NASSM Conference, Atlanta, GA.

Gorman, J., & Calhoun, K. (1994). *The name of the game*. New York: John Wiley & Sons, Inc.

Hall, B. F. (2004, June). On measuring the power of communications. *Journal of Advertising Research, 44*(2), 181–187.

Hall, E. (1959). *The silent language*. Garden City, NY: Doubleday.

Helitzer, M. (1992). Taming the beast: Riding out a sports crisis. *Sport Marketing Quarterly, 1*(2), 33–42.

Jacobson, G. (2008). Dallas Mavericks bar bloggers from locker room. Retrieved September 25, 2008, from http://www.dallasnews.com/sharedcontent/dws/spt/stories/031108dnspomavsaccess.2cd1e55.html

Key, M. R. (1975). *Paralanguage and kinesics (Nonverbal communication)*. Metuchen, NJ: The Scarecrow Press, Inc.

Koppett, L. (2003). *The rise and fall of the press box*. Toronto, ON: Sport Classic Books.

Mahony, D. F., & Moorman, A. M. (2000). The relationship between the attitudes of professional sport fans and their intentions to watch televised games. *Sport Marketing Quarterly, 9*(3), 131–139.

Martens, R. (1987). *Coaches guide to sport psychology*. Champaign, IL: Human Kinetics.

Masteralexis, L. P., Barr, C. A., & Hums, M. A. (1998). *Principles and practices of sport management*. Gaithersburg, MD: Aspen Publishers, Inc.

McDonough, P. (2007). Does DVR play-back really hurt advertisers? TV ratings: the new math. Retrieved September 25, 2008, from http://www.nielsen.com/consumer_insight/issue1/ci_story1.html

McErlain, Eric. (2007). When dealing with online rights, bloggers are in a gray area. Retrieved April 20, 2008 from http://sports.aol.com

Nichols, W., Moynahan, P., Hall, A., & Taylor, J. (2002). *Media relations in sport*. Morgantown, WV: Fitness Information Technology.

Rabin, C. (2008). Florida Marlins stadium likely to clear final legal hurdle. Retrieved September 25, 2008, from http://www.miamiherald.com/sports/baseball/florida-marlins/story/697432.html

Riley, Duncan. (2005). A short history of blogging. *Blog Herald*. Retrieved April 20, 2008, from http://www.blogherald.com

Sarthe, S., Olson, R., & Whitney, C. (1973). *Let's talk*. Glenview, IL: Scott & Foreman.

Smith, G. J., & Blackman, C. (1977). *Sport in the mass media*. Ottawa, ON: Canadian Association for Health, Physical Education and Recreation, University of Calgary Press.

Starak, Yaro. (2005). What is a podcast and how can I use one? *Entrepreneurs-Journey.com*. Retrieved April 20, 2008, from http://www.entrepreneurs-journey.com

Steinhart, D. (2002, March 2). Go digital or go home. *The National Post*.

Stoldt, C. G., Smetana, G. K., & Miller, L. (2000). Changes in the USA Today's sports coverage patterns during the National Basketball Association lockout: Implications for sport managers. *Sport Marketing Quarterly, 9*(3), 124–130.

Stotlar, D. K. (2000). Vertical integration in sport. *Journal of Sport Management, 14*(1), 1–7.

Turner, P. (1999). Television and Internet convergence: Implications for sport broadcasting. *Sport Marketing Quarterly, 8*(2), 43–49.

Vasquez, D. (2008). Pondering the DVR effect this season. Retrieved September 25, 2008, from http://www.medialifemagazine.com/artman2/publish/Television_44/Pondering_the_DVR_effect_this_season.asp

What's a blog? (2008). Retrieved April 20, 2008, from http://www.blogger.com

References

Chapter Four

MAMANGEMENT AND LEADERSHIP IN THE SPORT INDUSTRY

JEREMY S. JORDAN • AUBREY KENT • MATTHEW B. WALKER

"May I remind you, Bryant, that we are a corporate management team? Quit hogging the ball!"

> "MANAGEMENT IS DOING THINGS RIGHT; LEADERSHIP IS DOING THE RIGHT THINGS."
>
> —PETER DRUCKER

LEARNING OBJECTIVES

Upon completion of this chapter, the reader should be able to
- Explain the four functions of management;
- Differentiate between the three skills of management;
- Identify the different types of decisions made by managers and how they go through the process of making decisions;
- Discuss the 10 managerial roles and how they are related; and
- Compare and contrast leadership vs. management.

Introduction

"Management is a process of achieving organizational goals with and through other people within the constraints of limited resources" (Chelladurai, 2001, p. 94). Achieving goals is really at the heart of why we form organizations. Thus, management is critical to organizational success, whether through increased operational efficiency or by improving the quality of products and services. Leadership is likewise looked to as a main driver of organizational success. If one has watched the NBC television show *The Apprentice*, it is easy to see that leadership skills are a highly attractive asset for any potential employee to have.

In order for an advantage to be gained by a company, its resources must be valuable, rare, and difficult to imitate or substitute (Barney, 1991). Some companies, nonetheless, conform to or mimic the successful activities of others, thereby hopefully enabling them to become strategically successful—especially in response to uncertainty (DiMaggio & Powell, 1983). Just as a company seeks to differentiate itself from its competition, developing leadership skills can make *you* a source of competitive advantage for organizations as it sets you apart from others. Likewise, one can mimic the activities of successful leaders in order to become more proficient in a leadership role.

As the sport industry continues its prolific growth, visionary leaders as well as competent managers will become increasingly high in demand. Leadership and management skills are always transferable, meaning you will be able to utilize them whether you work in marketing, event management, or any of the areas that the sport industry has to offer. In this chapter, we will explore the core functions, skills, and roles of management, as well as discuss leadership from its theoretical foundations—in order to help you develop your own skills. The many facets of management are more easily understood if divided into the basic functions, skills, and roles that managers are expected to master.

Functions of Management

As mentioned in the introduction, managers can have a significant impact on the success of an organization. Research results have identified different management functions normally fulfilled when one is successfully completing the demands of a particular position. These functions can be classified as (1) planning, (2) organizing, (3) directing, and (4) monitoring. Classification of managerial functions into these four areas helps us understand what managers do and (more importantly) what you can expect when you assume a managerial position in a sport organization. However, because sport organizations are constantly evolving, these four functions do not represent a comprehensive list of responsibilities, but rather a starting point for understanding the complexities of management in sport. Furthermore, these four functions are not always sequential and many times managers must revert to a previous function to make the required adjustments.

PLANNING

The planning function of management involves the establishment of goals for the organization and its members, as well as the identification of the actions necessary to achieve those goals. Organizational goals tend to be general statements that help identify the direction of the sport organization. Because goals are broad in nature, they tend to be difficult to measure and thus have an aspect of subjectivity to them. For example, a minor league baseball team may have the goal of increasing attendance at all of their home games. While this goal helps identify an important issue for the team's management, it does not identify what actions will be implemented in order to achieve the goal and what standards of measurement will be used to assess progress. Therefore, after an organization identifies selected goals, it is important to create measurable objectives that will lead to the successful achievement of established goals.

Objectives, by design, tend to be more specific than goals; however, they are also measurable so subsequent evaluation can take place. A specific objective for the goal of increasing attendance at home games for the aforementioned baseball team could be to increase walk-up attendance (i.e., tickets sold on game day) by 10 percent. This objective is measurable and, if met, allows the team's management to meet, in part, the established goal of increasing attendance. However, what is not known at this point is how the team's management will go about increasing walk-up attendance at their home games.

establish action plans (also called tactics or
...s that will be implemented in order to meet
...team's management may offer special promo-
...r to increase attendance at the games (e.g., t-
...rs). This is an action plan intended to achieve
...tendance at all home games for the team.

...oals, it is important to work within the con-
...nstraints are limitations placed on the organi-
...goals and subsequent organizational activities.
...he organization (internal) or from the environ-
...erates (external). A professional sport team that
...next five years must consider internal and exter-
...rough the planning process. Internal constraints
...t of funding the team is able to put toward the new
...t been able to generate the type of revenue needed to
...stadium, it must seek assistance with the portion of the
...This could mean that the team requests that some of the
...nc new stadium be paid with public funds (i.e., property,
...ity taxes). The willingness of local and state government to
...s to help cover a portion of the construction costs for the new
...resent an external constraint (given the difficulty of passing new
tax legislation). If the public funds have been used for stadiums in the past or for
other sport teams in the area, there may be reluctance on the part of government
officials to allocate the necessary funds for the stadium. Additionally, if the team
has had limited success and by extension does not have a large local fan base, receiving public approval for the funding proposal may be a difficult proposition.
Therefore, when executing the planning function, it is important to understand
both the internal and external constraints placed on the organization. Failure to
identify these constraints could result in the development of goals that are not
likely to be achieved by the sport organization.

The planning function of management normally involves both long-term and
short-term plans. Long-term plans (often called strategic plans) involve goals and
objectives to be achieved in the future. An event management company may have
a strategic plan of hosting a marathon in five years. This plan would have many
components, but one major aspect would be raising the necessary funds through
donations and sponsorships to pay for all of the logistics that go into an event of
this magnitude. The strategic plan may establish goals for securing permits, generating policies, identifying equipment and personnel needs, establishing committees, securing sponsors, securing volunteers, and addressing general marketing and
operational issues needed, over each of the next five years, to plan a marathon race.
In contrast to strategic plans, short-term plans tend to involve goals for the upcoming year and thus are more immediate in nature. In line with the previous example,
event organizers may have a kick-off campaign to introduce the plans for the race
and have the objective of raising 5 percent of the estimated costs at this kick-off
party.

Once the sport organization has established its goals, objectives, and specific action plans, the next function of management that must be executed is organizing.

ORGANIZING

The organizing function of management involves the identification of tasks that must be completed in order to achieve the goals identified in the planning process. In addition, the delegation of these tasks to different work groups or employees is equally as important. In other words, management must decide what things need to be done and who will be responsible for completing these tasks. Not only does this process involve creating individual job responsibilities, but also grouping related tasks together so that they can be accomplished in an efficient manner. Often this grouping of job positions involves the creation of departments that are responsible for certain tasks and responsibilities. A professional sport organization may create a ticket department that is responsible for selling season tickets, mini-packs, and single-game tickets. Achievement of each task may require a slightly different action plan; however, linking them together in one department will allow individuals trained in ticket sales to work on each of the three assigned tasks. The manager's job then is to decide which employees are best qualified for certain tasks and who will be responsible for making sure these tasks are accomplished within a certain timeframe. This point identifies another aspect of organizing, which is the development of an organizational chart. As mentioned previously, part of organizing is grouping job responsibilities and assigning these tasks to individuals who are part of a workgroup. This process is represented in graph form by developing a chart, which identifies different departments in the organization and how these departments are linked. An additional aspect of organizational charts is the identification of management personnel who are responsible for the different departments. For example, figure one identifies the organizational structure of an intercollegiate athletic marketing department.

Organizational charts should be developed for each individual department as well as the organization as a whole. According to Bridges and Roquemore (2004, p. 201), organizational charts should demonstrate the following:

1. Positions of responsibility (who is in charge of what)
2. Lines of authority (who has the power to do what)
3. Manager/employee relationships (levels of management)
4. Formal communication channels (who reports to whom)
5. Lines of responsibility (who is accountable for specific tasks)
6. Grouping of related work activities

Use of an organizational chart helps clarify how an organization is being organized and what responsibilities are being assigned to the different employees and work groups.

DIRECTING

Once managers have completed the planning process and assigned work tasks to different members of the organization, they must motivate and direct employees

Figure 4.1. (UM Organizational Chart)

UNIVERSITY OF MIAMI INTERCOLLEGIATE ATHLETICS

Athletic Director

Community Relations
Associate AD
Program Coordinator

Sports Information
Assistant AD
Assistant SID
Assistant SID
Assistant SID
Dir. of Publications
Administrative Assistant
Administrative Assistant

Sports

Baseball
Head Coach
Assistant Coach
Assistant Coach
Coord. of BSB Ops.
Staff Associate

Men's Basketball
Head Coach
Assistant Coach
Assistant Coach
Assistant Coach
Video Coordinator
Dir of BKB Operations
Staff Associate

Women's Basketball
Head Coach
Assistant Coach
Associate Head Coach
Assistant Coach
Video Coordinator
Administrative Ass't
Staff Associate

Football
Head Coach
Sr. Staff Associate
Defensive Coordinator
Offensive Coordinator
Tight Ends Coach
Wide Receivers Coach
Offensive Line Coach
Defensive Line Coach
Defensive Backs Coach
Line Backers Coach
Running Backs Coach
Graduate Assistant
Graduate Assistant
Director FB Operations
Coordinator/FB Ops.
Staff Associate
Staff Associate

Weight Room
Head Coach
Ass't Strength Coach
Ass't Strength Coach
Ass't Strength Coach
Ass't Strength Coach

Internal Services
Associate AD

Academics
Academic AD
Academic Advisor
Learning Specialist
Academic Advisor
Associate Director
Academic Coordinator

Compliance
Assistant AD
Assistant Director
Assistant Director
Administrative Assistant

Training Room
Head Trainer
Assistant Trainer
Assistant Trainer
Assistant Trainer
Assistant Trainer
Coordinator

External Operations
Associate AD
Staff Associate

Development
Director
Assistant AD
Coord of Special Events
Assistant Director
Staff Accountant
Staff Associate

Capital Campaign
Director
Assistant Director
Assistant Director
Assistant Director

Mktg & Promotions
Director
Assistant Director
Assistant Director
Assistant Director
Staff Associate

Ticket Sales
Director

Internet Communications
Director

Internal Operations
Associate AD & SWA
Staff Assoc

Event Management
Director of Events
Assistant Director of Events

Olympic Sports

Crew
Head Coach
Ass't Coach
Ass't Coach
Rowing Coordinator

Women's Golf
Head Coach

Women's Soccer
Head Coach
Assistant Coach
Assistant Coach

Swimming/Diving
Head Swim Coach
Head Diving Coach
Assistant Coach
Coordinator

Men's Tennis
Head Coach

Women's Tennis
Head Coach
Assistant Coach

Men's Track and Cross Country
Head Coach
Assistant Coach

Women's Track
Head Coach
Assistant Coach
Assistant Coach

Women's Volleyball
Head Coach
Assistant Coach
Assistant Coach

Business Operations
Associate AD and CFO
Staff Assoc

Business Office
Assistant AD
Assistant Director
Assistant Director
Business Office Coord.

Equipment Room
Head Equipment Manager
Ass't Equipment Manager
Ass't Equipment Manager
Ass't Equipment Manager

Facilities, Procurement, and Systems Administration
Assistant AD
Maintenance Mechanic
Assistant Director

Operations and Travel
Assistant AD
Travel Coordinator
Video
Video Coordinator
Ass't Video Coordinator

Ticket Office
Assistant AD
Ticket Operations Coord.
Assistant Ticket Manager
Assistant Ticket Manager
Assistant Ticket Manager

5/9/05 Used with permission of the University of Miami Athletic Department

5/9/05

to achieve established goals. A successful manager will direct employees to put forth their best efforts when implementing the action plans that have been created by the organization. The directing function of management tends to be one of the most difficult to fulfill, because it involves direct interaction between management and employees. Each employee in an organization is likely to respond to managerial direction and motivation efforts differently. This means that a manager cannot use a "best practice" approach to all situations, nor when dealing with all employees. Therefore, successful managers will be able to adapt their style to fit the requirements of a particular situation. Two main elements of the directing function are facilitating task accomplishment for employees and providing motivation for them to perform those tasks to the best of their ability.

Management personnel are responsible for providing support and direction to employees as they complete work tasks. In the majority of situations, the responsibility of management is to delegate appropriate tasks to employees and make certain the assigned tasks are completed efficiently. This could mean that a manager must provide technical assistance to accomplish a task, or evaluate the progress of an employee to make sure the task will be completed in the allotted time. Simply put, the role of management is to provide employees with the resources, skills, and proper assistance necessary to complete assigned tasks. When managers provide these supporting elements to their employees, it likely leads to increased employee productivity and job satisfaction as employees are less likely to encounter "roadblocks" at work, which can lead to frustration (House, 1971). Therefore, in order for managers to successfully direct employees, they must have an understanding of the work that is needed within the organization and be able to facilitate the process by which it is completed.

MOTIVATION

The second aspect of directing involves motivating employees to put forth maximum effort in the workplace. Being an effective motivator includes the ability to identify employee needs and desires, and to provide processes that enable employees to achieve their goals in order to attain desired rewards. While this is sometimes a complicated process, successful managers will understand that effective motivation requires an appropriate balance of tangible, intangible, intrinsic, extrinsic, monetary, and non-monetary rewards. Essentially, different people will be motivated by different things in the workplace. For example, a premium seating sales representative for the Tampa Bay Devil Rays may be motivated by the possibility of receiving a $4,000 bonus if she meets her sales targets for the upcoming season. In contrast, a collegiate marketing director may be motivated by the satisfaction he receives from selling out every home basketball game of the season through various promotions. In yet another setting, a marketing intern for Nike may be motivated because she was recognized as "employee of the month" in her department. The previous three examples illustrate how employees can be motivated in different ways, highlighting the need for managers to accurately discern employee needs and match their motivational strategies to them.

MONITORING

The final managerial function to be discussed is monitoring. This function involves the evaluation of employees, workgroups, or the organization as a whole on the progress that has been made toward achieving established goals and objectives. The performance of employees and workgroups must be periodically monitored to determine if changes are warranted or if current performance levels are appropriate for the achievement of established objectives and goals. The control outlined in this process establishes a set of "checks and balances" for the organization, but it should not be viewed as a replacement for sound planning and organizing. The aforementioned monitoring process involves three critical steps:

1. Developing standards that will be used to evaluate performance.

2. Conducting the evaluation by comparing actual performance to the desired performance identified by the standards.

3. Taking appropriate action to correct a situation when the desired standard of performance is not being met.

The development of performance standards generally takes place before the employee begins working on the assigned task. For example, when you enroll in a sport management course at your university, the instructor spends part of the first day explaining how your performance in class will be evaluated. If this was to occur at the end of the semester it would be impossible for you to make the necessary adjustments to improve your grade. The standards of evaluation must be clearly identified and explained and should be easily measured, in addition to being directly related to the established objectives and goals associated with each task.

The next step in the monitoring process is to evaluate the performance of the organization, workgroup, or employee against previously established standards. Important considerations here are: who will conduct the evaluation, how will the evaluation process occur, and when will it take place? Persons selected to conduct the evaluation should have knowledge of the task being performed and have the authority to make the necessary changes if actual performance does not match a particular standard. It is likely that the evaluation will involve both quantitative and qualitative measures (with the primary mode of evaluation being a quantitative assessment). Quantitative measures involve evaluations of performance based on some type of easily measurable component. For example, if the managers of the Adidas group had an objective to sell more soccer jerseys than the previous year, the evaluation process would involve comparing the previous year's sales with the current year. This evaluation involves the comparison of quantifiable outcomes (number of soccer jerseys sold). Qualitative measures of work performance involve evaluations of work performance that are more difficult to assess accurately and objectively. For instance, employees might be evaluated on their contributions to group projects, attitude at work, or other behaviors that contribute to overall work performance. Additionally, qualitative work evaluations normally involve discussions with employees to determine their feelings about the work experience and the tasks they have been assigned.

After performance evaluations have been conducted, the manager is responsible for making necessary adjustments so that the desired standard can be achieved. This means the manager must determine why a particular performance standard is not being met by the employee's current work performance.

Table 4.1. Factors affecting employee performance
• Deficiencies in employee performance due to effort or motivation to perform the tasks
• Employee not having the necessary technical skills to successfully complete the task
• The performance standard is unrealistic and must be adjusted
• The employee, workgroup, or organization does not have the resources required to complete the task
• Poor planning or organizing
• Unclear task assignment

Once the manager has determined why the performance standard is not being met, the necessary changes must be made and, if required, a new performance standard must be established for the next evaluation period. Generally, this function occurs in three phases: (1) preliminary, (2) concurrent, and (3) feedback monitoring. Preliminary monitoring is a screening mechanism used by the manager in an attempt to prevent problems in performance before they occur. This is an *a priori* process that involves establishing accurate job descriptions that detail the skills and qualifications necessary to successfully complete the tasks assigned to a particular position. Concurrent monitoring takes place during the process of completing assigned tasks. The manager makes periodic checks to determine the progress employees are making on completing assigned tasks. This is a proactive approach to monitoring (as opposed to reacting to a problem), in that managers attempt to make appropriate changes in employee performance or task assignment prior to the project being completed. The final phase occurs when the manager provides feedback to employees regarding their work performance after the project has been completed. This is done for two reasons. First, providing feedback based on evaluations of employee performance helps with employee development and generally improves future performance. This feedback should include specific information on what the employees did correctly as well as areas that are in need of improvement. Second, providing feedback is essential so that formal performance appraisals can be conducted and used for administrative (reward) purposes. Often times, these evaluations are placed in employee files so a record can be kept on each employee's performance as well as the detailed feedback management has provided regarding task performance.

Managerial Skills

Just as an employee develops skills necessary to complete assigned tasks, managers must work on developing their skills in the workplace. Also, managers will have to use these skills at different times and, in certain situations, will have to use a combination of the skills. This point reinforces that being a manager is at times very difficult, due to the many complexities of the work environment. We will explore the skills of management by dividing them into three different categories: (a) technical skills; (b) human skills; and (c) conceptual skills. Like any other activity that requires a certain level of proficiency, managers must work at becoming better at each of the skills outlined and seek opportunities to practice and refine them. The following is a brief description of each skill.

**Skills Needed by
Sport Managers/
Administrators**

Technical skills

Human skills

Conceptual skills

Technical skills involve knowledge of operations, activities, and processes necessary to accomplish organizational goals and objectives. You can think of technical skills as the "know how" in terms of what tasks employees are assigned. For example, an advertiser who designs logos and promotions for professional sport teams must have thorough knowledge of the graphics software used to create "eye catching" stadium signage and other ancillary media items. In addition to understanding the technical aspects of a task, managers must be able to educate and supervise employees on the task and be able to handle any difficulties that prevent employees from completing assigned responsibilities.

A second skill that is critical to being an effective manager is the ability to work with and supervise a variety of different employees—particularly if the manager works with a large organization. Thus, the *human skill* of management involves aspects of leading, communicating, motivating, and, in general, dealing with all aspects of employee relations on a daily basis. The difficult element of this skill is that each employee will be unique and thus respond to managerial influence in a different way. This means that a manager must understand what strategies to use when communicating, motivating, and supervising various employees in their work group.

A final skill required of managers is the ability to conceptualize how all the different parts of the organization fit together so that established goals and objectives can be achieved. The managerial term *synergy* describes this *conceptual skill*, in that a manager must be able to understand how the different departments of the organization are linked. Often you will hear someone say that it is important to understand the "big picture" when establishing a plan of action or organizing employees into work groups. This "big picture" approach requires the manager to abstractly imagine how things would best work together so that the organization can be efficient in its use of resources and be effective in achieving its goals.

One particular management skill that requires a mastery of all of the above-described categories is *decision making*. There is the distinct possibility that as you read this chapter you have already had to make a number of decisions today. These decisions could range from very simple, such as what to eat for breakfast, to difficult decisions such as choosing a career path. When making a decision, whether simple or difficult, you must gather and evaluate necessary information so that your decision can be informed and based on relevant facts.

Decision making is a *primary skill* that a manager will have to utilize when fulfilling the functions of management and executing the different skills necessary to direct employees toward the achievement of established goals and objectives. In fact, the ability to make correct decisions when confronted with organizational opportunities or challenges is one of the main factors that distinguish good managers from bad.

When making decisions, managers will be confronted with issues that are potential problems for the organization, as well as issues that represent opportunities for growth and advancement. Chelladurai (2001) defined a problem as "a situation that reduces or could reduce the effectiveness of the organization, or a situation that disrupts operations" (p. 201). For instance, an athletic director could be confronted with a problem if severe weather forces the cancellation of a home football game, creating the need to reschedule the game at a later time. Solving this problem involves not only rescheduling the game with the other school, but making sure that all groups involved (i.e., media, concessions, transportation, security, EMT's) can be present on the new date. While a problem has the potential to disrupt the operations of an organization, opportunities represent issues or situations that could benefit the organization in terms of profitability, improved production or services, and growth (Chelladurai, 2001).

Decisions that managers have to make can also be simplistically classified as routine or complex. A routine decision is one that could involve clear decision criteria, be repetitive in nature, and involve the application of established rules or policies. An example of a routine decision could be how the Bowl Championship Series (BCS) committee determines the rotation of the college football national championship game. The title game is placed on a four-year rotation and switches between the sites for the Orange, Fiesta, Rose, and Sugar Bowl games. The process of deciding the selection order is a routine decision in that it takes place every year and involves the application of specified parameters created by the BCS and the NCAA. In contrast, complex decisions are those that have more complicated decision criteria, can be difficult to clearly define, and often involve no set policies that can be used in the decision-making process. For example, the Chicago Bulls were awarded the first selection in the 2008 NBA draft. The decision of which player to select first was one that did not involve a set policy and to some degree was difficult to clearly define. The decision to select Derrick Rose with the first pick was a subjective decision by the Chicago Bulls and one that will not be determined as "correct" until after the team is fully able to evaluate the performance of Derrick Rose.

There are no set rules or policies (other than the needs of the team) that dictate which player should be selected, and often teams may not use the same decision criteria as the previous year because there are different players available in the draft. Whether confronted with a complex or simple decision, managers will often use a systematic decision-making approach to gather and analyze information. This process helps ensure that all relevant facts and information related to the decision will be considered, which increases the likelihood that the best decision will be made. While there are a number of different systematic decision-making models that can be utilized by managers, Railey and Tschauner (1993) suggested a basic process that can be implemented by managers in a variety of settings.

In addition to using a systematic process when making decisions, managers must also understand the ramifications of the decisions they make. Managers use their conceptual skills so they can determine the immediate and long-term effects of a decision. Furthermore, managers must consider how different groups or individuals will respond to decisions that are made. Hums, Moorman, and Wolf (as cited in Hums & MacLean, 2004) suggested that managers can develop increased understanding of their deci-

Table 4.2. Problem-Solving Methodology

1. Define and clarify the problem or opportunity.
2. Identify the decision objectives.
3. List, categorize, and analyze all relevant information related to the decision.
4. Identify any issues that may present "roadblocks" to arriving at the correct decision.
5. Generate possible alternatives that solve the problem or capitalize on an opportunity.
6. Select the best two or three alternatives for consideration.
7. Make your decision by selecting the best alternative.
8. Implement the decision by activating policy or rule changes and necessary action steps.
9. Evaluate the effectiveness of the final decision after it has been implemented.

sions and the ramifications of those decisions by applying the SLEEPE principle. Essentially, this model allows managers to evaluate decisions from a number of viewpoints with the end goal being an improved understanding of the impacts a particular decision may have, and further how different groups will respond to that particular decision. Following is a brief description of the different components of the SLEEPE model.

1. **Social**—How will society at large and the local community respond to the decision? Will there be the necessary support from different groups required to effectively put the decision into action? Will public perception of the organization change based on this decision, or is it in line with the mission of the organization?

2. **Legal**—Is the decision in line with organizational rules or policies? Does the decision being made violate any local, state, or federal laws? It is very likely that decisions that violate organizational rules or governmental laws will not be viewed in a positive manner.

3. **Economic**—How will this decision influence the economic situation of the organization? Are there the necessary resources required to carry out this decision? How will this decision affect the local economy?

4. **Ethical**—What are the ethical implications of the decision that is being made? Decisions that violate ethical principles of the organization or society as a whole are likely to meet with some resistance. Hums et al. identified this consideration as the most difficult and complex for managers of all the components of the SLEEPE model.

5. **Political**—The term *political* in the context of the SLEEPE model is not limited to elected officials, but rather includes all groups or individuals that have the ability to exert influence over an organization. If these groups or individuals are opposed to the decision being made, they may be less likely to support the organization in this or other endeavors.

6. **Educational**—This component applies to sport organizations that operate in the context of an educational setting (i.e., intercollegiate athletics). Decisions that are made must be evaluated in terms of whether they are in line with the overall mission of the educational institution.

An additional consideration for managers in decision making is the inclusion of employees in the decision-making process. Chalip (2001) suggested that employees may provide assistance to management personnel in areas such as planning, generating ideas, problem solving, developing organizational polices/procedures, and governance. The benefits of including others in the decision-making process include the following: (a) the ability to gather and analyze a larger quantity of information relevant to the decision that must be made; (b) increased likelihood of members having more comprehensive understanding of the problem/opportunity being considered; (c) improved member support of the final decision because they have been allowed to contribute in the decision-making process; and (d) less difficulty implementing the decision due to the fact that members have increased understanding and are supportive of the decision.

Despite these benefits, there are potential difficulties that also must be considered by managers when evaluating whether to include others in the decision-making process. One difficulty is that group decision making tends to take a longer period of time compared to the manager making the decision alone. A second challenge is that group members may possess limited "on the job" experience thereby hindering their ability to assist in the decision-making process, particularly concerning complex decisions that require certain skills that often take time to develop and refine. Finally, employees may not have access to information that is required when making a decision—for example, employee files or company financial statements. In light of these benefits and challenges, a manager must be able to determine under what circumstances it would be best to include others in the decision-making process and when it would be best to make the decision alone. In order to accomplish this sometimes difficult task, managers can turn to the following three questions about a particular decision.

1. How important is the quality of the decision?

2. How much do others within the organization have to support and commit to the decision?

3. What is the timeframe for making a final decision? (Chalip, 2001)

As the quality required for a decision increases, so do the benefits associated with including others in the process. Remember, including employees in the decision-making process increases the amount of information that is accumulated and also increases the quality of possible solutions. If the execution of a particular decision is going to require support from employees, it may be advantageous to allow group members to provide input, thereby increasing the amount of ownership they have in the final decision. Finally, the amount of time available to make a decision will influence whether others can be included in the process or not.

A final consideration when discussing the appropriate decision style to use is the determination of which employees should be included in the decision-making process. Chalip (2001) suggested that employees should be included in this process when (a) they have information that is relevant to the issues being considered, and (b) the final decision will directly affect them or will require their support when being implemented. Also, decisions that are more complex or risky in nature require individuals that have diverse viewpoints and opinions, which can improve the quality of the solutions and alternatives provided to the manager. This increases the possibility of analyzing a decision from different perspectives (e.g., SLEEPE model, above) and the creation of alternatives that are unique or represent a new approach to solving problems or taking advantage of an opportunity.

Managerial Roles

In addition to understanding the different functions of management and having the ability to implement the skills necessary to achieve organizational goals, managers must often fulfill particular *roles* within the organization. Mintzberg (1975) defined a managerial role as "an organized set of behaviors identified with a position" (p. 54) and established that in most organizations a manager will occupy one of ten different roles at any particular time. These roles can be grouped into three different categories: (1) interpersonal, (2) informational, and (3) decisional.

INTERPERSONAL ROLES

The formal position of the manager within the organization establishes three roles that require the manager to interact with employees. The first of these roles, *figurehead*, involves the manager fulfilling certain ceremonial functions as the result of being in charge of a certain department or the organization as a whole. An athletic director can fulfill this role by presenting an award to a team or individual student-athletes who have won championships in their respective sports. In this situation, the athletic director is not only representing the athletic department but the university as whole in recognizing the accomplishments of teams or individuals. The second role involves the manager being a *leader* to subordinates, directing them toward the achievement of assigned tasks. This role may require the manager to hire, train, supervise, motivate, and evaluate employees in the workplace. When discussing the leader role, Mintzberg (1975) stated that "the influence of managers is most clearly seen in the leader role" (p. 55) and that, by their position, managers have significant power in this regard. However, their ability to use this power is largely dependent upon their capability to lead. The *liaison* role refers to the manager's ability to develop and cultivate relationships with individuals and groups in other departments or from different organizations. For instance, the owner of a professional football team will most certainly have to work with league, city, state, and government officials when seeking funding for a new stadium. In this situation, the team owner is the connection (or liaison) between the various officials and the sport franchise. The type and quality of relationships that managers develop when fulfilling this role can have an impact on departmental or organizational success.

Informational Roles

A manager has access to many different sources of information based on the position occupied within the organization and the number of interpersonal contacts that occur in the workplace. After accessing information, managers must then process what was learned and distribute relevant pieces of information to different groups within the organization. Therefore, the manager can be viewed as an information center and because of this, executes the roles of monitor, disseminator, and spokesperson. As *monitor*, the manager must search the internal and external environment for information that could affect the organization. While in this role, the manager seeks information from liaisons, subordinates, superiors, different media sources, and the network of contacts that a manager develops over time. In addition, managers will rely somewhat on hearsay, gossip, and speculation at times, so that they can be up-to-date on events that are about to occur. Once the manager has accessed and processed the information, the decision must be made regarding which employees need to know the information. As *disseminator*, the manager screens information and passes it along to employees who otherwise would probably not have access to it. Furthermore, a manager acts a bridge between employees who must exchange information but are unable to easily access each other. Finally, as *spokesperson*, the manager communicates information to groups that are outside the organization. For example, in attempts to be the host city for an upcoming Olympic Games, the government, tourism board, and other management and legislative personnel from a given city will have to make a presentation to the International Olympic Committee (IOC) detailing the benefits and challenges of having such a mega-event in their city.

Decisional Roles

As mentioned previously, decision making is a primary skill of management that is used in many of the situations with which a manager will be confronted. Fulfillment of the aforementioned informational roles allows the manager to access the information necessary to make informed decisions. Therefore, the interpersonal and informational roles that a manager occupies, combined with his or her formal position in the organization, place the manager in four decisional roles: (1) entrepreneur, (2) disturbance handler, (3) resource allocator, and (4) negotiator.

Entrepreneur managers look for ways to improve their work group, adapt to internal and external changes, and direct the organization toward opportunities that initiate growth. This means that managers are often on the lookout for new and improved ways to deliver services, provide products, and become more efficient in the use of organizational resources. For example, the concessions manager of a professional stadium who streamlines the inventory and ordering process so he will be better able to track product sales would be fulfilling the managerial role of entrepreneur.

Disturbance handler managers are responsible for reacting to changes affecting the organization that are unexpected and beyond the immediate control of the manager. These are situations that, if not dealt with, could cause significant hardship for the organization and its employees. In 2004, management personnel for the National Hockey League (NHL) and the players' association (NHLPA) had to deal with major changes due to the labor dispute between the league and its players. Managers on both sides functioned as disturbance handlers by reacting to the lockout, which has altered the normal operations of the NHL forever.

When managers distribute organizational resources to different employees or work groups, they are acting as *resource allocators*. Most organizations have a limited number of resources available and therefore allocating the appropriate amount of these resources throughout the organization becomes a very important task for managers. Some professional sport leagues have limits on how much salary money teams can pay to players. The presence of these "salary caps" means management personnel for each of the teams must decide what salary will be paid to each player while making sure to stay within the guidelines of the salary cap restrictions.

The final decisional role identified by Mintzberg (1975) is manager as *negotiator*. In this role, managers are responsible for conferring with employees and work groups located within the organization, as well as those that are on the outside. In order to accomplish organizational goals and objectives, management must often negotiate with other groups with regard to resources or other factors that influence the operations of the organization. Returning to our NHL example, representatives from the league and player's association met to negotiate the terms of a new collective bargaining agreement between the league and players that resulted in ending the lockout that occurred during the 2004–2005 season (which was the first time the Stanley Cup was not awarded since 1919).

A final consideration regarding managerial roles is that they are, for the most part, inseparable. This means that a manager must have the ability to fulfill each role if she is to be successful at directing employees toward the accomplishment of established tasks. Additionally, these roles are often dependent upon each other. For example, an athletic director must be able to fill the liaison role when interacting with the NCAA so that she can have access to information regarding changes in policies that cover student-athlete recruitment. The A.D. must then process this information and, as disseminator, distribute this information to the appropriate employees in the department. Finally, as disturbance handler, the A.D. must deal with any conflict or problems that arise as the result of new recruiting policies.

Management vs. Leadership

A long-standing debate that is sure to arise in most introductory management courses is whether or not there is a difference between a manager and a leader. While there are fairly strong points to be made on both sides of this issue, the consensus of management scholars seems to be forming around the idea that yes, there is a difference between the two. That being said . . . what is the difference? One way to view the difference between management and leadership is to look at the core of their responsibilities, with respect to the skills discussed above. Managers must have developed technical skills primarily, as well as some human skills. Leaders must have a command of all three skill sets and, in order to be truly successful, must have a mastery of the very complex human and conceptual skills.

For some, the manager is the person who is in charge of their daily activities at the workplace. This person is their immediate supervisor, and the person to whom they must be most attentive. For these same people, the person that they identify as the organization's leader might be someone whom they have never met. For example, a person working in an entry-level district sales position for Nike might never meet the company's CEO Phil Knight face-to-face. So the question becomes, how can Phil Knight lead someone whom he has never met? Well, that brings us to the core of the definition between managers and leaders, and also reminds us of the discussion about organization that we had earlier. Phil Knight (or any such organizational leader) is primarily responsible for setting the overall vision, mission, and organizational culture within which workers at Nike function. While people in management positions have much more direct contact with employees, they are functioning within the environment created and maintained by the leadership of the organization. A manager within the organization implements that vision by working with subordinates to achieve multiple goals.

At this point, it is important to note that, while different, there should be no value judgment placed on the management versus leadership debate. While describing the differences between the two, it might be easy to get the impression that leadership attributes are somehow superior and more desirable than management ones, but that is simply not the case. They both have an important role to play in an organization's success, and one cannot prosper in any business without the other. They are not so much different as they are *complementary* to each other within an organization. Additionally, one person can display elements of one or the other at any given time, as they are not mutually exclusive concepts. In this vein, it is more useful to view management and leadership as distinct *processes*, but *not* as different types of people.

LEADERSHIP

Leadership is a phenomenon that has been present and of interest to society for almost as long as civilization has existed. A profound curiosity with leadership has led to a vast amount of research in the past century that has comprised a central part of the social science literature. In fact, many might say that the history of the world is traced through the history of great leaders. From Moses to Mohammed, from Joan of Arc to Napoleon, from Winston Churchill to Ghandi, and from Nelson Mandela to Martin Luther King, we as humans record our history through the chronicling of great leaders. Researchers in the field of sport management have likewise been enamored with the concept of leadership, whether it concerns how coaches deal with their athletes, how athletic director's motivate their employees, or how people create successful sport companies.

As much as leadership has been studied, what it is and how it works has yet to clearly materialize. Within the academic community, a clear definition of leadership has remained elusive, and it has been noted that "there are almost as many definitions of leadership as there are persons who have attempted to define the concept" (Stogdill, 1974, p. 259). However, "most definitions of leadership reflect the assumption that it involves a process whereby intentional influence is exerted by one person over other people to guide, structure, and facilitate activities and relationships in a group or organization" (Yukl, 1998, p. 3). This general definition would be our preferred definition of leadership, because it contains the three elements that we deem critical for leadership to be understood. First, leadership is a complex process. Second, it is *relational*, in that if nobody is following, you are not leading. Finally, it involves *induction.* That is, if your followers would have reached the same destination in your absence, you have not truly led them.

EVOLUTION OF LEADERSHIP THEORY

As noted earlier, research in the area of leadership has been extensive, and as different themes have evolved over time, the definitions of leadership have changed to reflect these themes. Leadership literature has largely focused on theoretical issues that have developed from early trait theories, to behavioral theories, to more recent situational and contingency theories, and finally to the contemporary conceptualizations variously known as visionary, charismatic or transformational, and collectively termed "the new leadership." Also included in this evolution are specific applications of leadership theory appropriate for certain industrial contexts, among them the Multi-Dimensional Leadership model, designed specifically for use in the sport domain.

Some of the earliest systematic attempts to conceptualize leadership were known as the *trait theories.* This approach focused on the characteristics, or attributes, that distinguished leaders from non-leaders. These traits included physical characteristics (e.g., height and appearance), personality traits (e.g., arrogance and self-esteem), and general ability traits (e.g., intelligence, insight, and energy). Hundreds of trait studies were conducted in the early and mid-1900s, but it was ultimately realized that this line of research was not going to yield a consistent relationship to leadership effectiveness. It did, however, become clear to most that while particular traits were not predictors of leader success, certain characteristics would (in some situations) increase the likelihood of a leader emerging. In general, effective leaders appear to be more likely to have traits such as self-confidence, high energy, stress tolerance, integrity, and maturity than will unsuccessful or non-leaders (Yukl, 1998).

As the limitations of the trait theories became evident, many researchers shifted the focus of their studies toward specific behaviors exhibited by leaders. The *behavioral approach* emphasized what leaders and managers actually did on the job, as opposed to their personal characteristics. The behavior leadership theorists focused not only on what leaders would do, but also on how often and at what intensity they would perform certain things to distinguish themselves as leaders. The perceptions of followers to this leader behavior would then, in turn, influence them to act in the manner that they saw fit.

Descriptive research into the leaders' decision making, monitoring practices, and motivating and problem-solving processes would be characteristic of the behaviorist approach (Yukl & Van Fleet, 1992). The major contribution of the behavioral line of research came from Ohio State University in the 1950s, which classified leader behaviors into two independent categories: (1) task-oriented behaviors (i.e., initiating structure) and (2) people-oriented behaviors (i.e., consideration).

From these classifications, certain leader behaviors came to be associated with prescribed follower and organizational outcomes. However, the reliability of such associations was suspect. After a point it became clear that these broadly defined categories were too abstract to provide the basis for understanding the true complexity of leadership and the role requirements of leaders. As Yukl and Van Fleet (1992) stated, "As we found in the trait research, the behavior research suffers from a tendency to look for simple answers to complex questions" (p. 160). As such, the behaviorist view of leadership spurred the emergence of the consideration of time and circumstance alongside leadership traits and behaviors. The results of this development in leadership thinking came to be more commonly known as the *situational leadership theories*.

The *situational approach* to the study of leadership attempted to build upon the foundation that was laid by the study of traits and behaviors. Situational leadership studies (also referred to as "contingency theories") resulted in an understanding that the traits and behaviors identified previously would only be successful to the degree to which any particular situation allowed. Intervening, or moderating, factors were now being brought into the picture by researchers when assessing the overall impact, or appropriateness, of leader behavior. Among the theories that gained recognition in this era were Fiedler's Contingency Model (1967), House's Path-Goal Theory (1971), and Hersey and Blanchard's Situational Leadership Theory (1977).

These models and theories focused on how different moderating variables could affect the outcomes of certain leader behaviors. While these theories provided some deeper insight into the nature of leadership and its effectiveness, many of them were too generally stated and were not empirically testable (Yukl, 1998). As with the behavioral theories, the *contingency approaches* also tended to oversimplify the process of leading by focusing on the "one best way" to behave in certain situations. This lack of flexibility ultimately revealed that these theories had very little utility for improving the effectiveness of practicing managers. Despite their shortcomings, the contingency theories do make a positive contribution for improving the effectiveness of managers in a general sense.

CONTEMPORARY THEORIES

In the past two decades, leadership researchers have developed a broader perspective of the leader-follower relationship as they examined the changes in the followers that came as a result of leader influence. This approach led to the *contemporary theories* of leadership that characterized the leader as charismatic, inspirational, visionary, and/or transformational. Bryman (1992) collectively termed these contemporary approaches "the new leadership" paradigm. Visionary leadership researchers focused on the effectiveness of leaders who were able to extrapolate future goals and successes from the mundane day-to-day activities that consume a leader's time and energy. These leaders are purported to make this a shared vision with others in the group or organization through the leader's heightened communication skills (Bennis & Nanus, 1985).

CHARISMATIC LEADERSHIP

Charismatic leadership theorists have focused on leaders from the perspective that they were perceived to have certain exceptional qualities, which allowed for greater influence over followers in particular situations. German sociologist Max Weber, often cited as the ultimate authority on charisma, saw charismatic leadership as a combination of certain magical qualities that a person would possess that were inaccessible to other, non-charismatic people (Weber, 1947). It is these unique qualities and attributes that compel followers to devote themselves to the leader.

House (1977) was a major contributor to the area of charismatic leadership. He suggested that the personal characteristics of a leader that make up charisma are a high level of self-confidence and a need to influence others, coupled with a dominant personality and a strong conviction in the integrity of their own beliefs. Charismatic leaders have been described as role models for their followers, who build their image so as to create an impression of success and competence. They express ideological goals that serve as ideals for the organization. They are good communicators who can motivate followers to strive toward set goals. In summary, charismatic leaders are believed to be those who have abilities and characteristics that allow them to identify closely with their followers, are able to see clearly into what they want the future to be like, and are able to chart a clear path toward fulfilling that vision.

Conger and Kanungo (1987) introduced Attribution Theory of charismatic leadership, which asserted that follower attributions were responsible for a leader's perceived charisma. This theory suggested that followers attributed charisma to those leaders who acted in an unconventional and sometimes risky fashion, and to those who made self-sacrifices and were confident in their vision, no matter the personal cost. This theory also argued that *facilitating conditions* were needed in order for charisma to be attributed to the leader. These conditions might include having a sense of urgency surrounding a particular situation, having a great deal of follower dissatisfaction with the status quo, or having a group of followers who receive satisfaction from their ability to please and/or imitate the leader.

Transformational Leadership

Charisma is an important component in transformational leadership, another of the "new leadership" paradigm, but is not the only important element. Bass (1985) defined charisma as "a necessary ingredient of transformational leadership, but by itself is not sufficient to account for the transformational process," (p. 31). Combining charismatic and visionary qualities with the ability to persuasively communicate that vision to followers is what constitutes the major components of a transformational leader. Transformational leadership theory has received the most attention among researchers investigating "new leadership" paradigms. This theory focuses on the leader-follower relationship and examines how this relationship can be beneficial to both parties—to the group and to the organization as a whole (e.g., Bass, 1990; Bass & Avolio, 1994). This theory has two parts: (1) transformational leadership and (2) transactional leadership.

Transformational leaders are those people who "seek to raise the consciousness of followers by appealing to higher ideals and moral values such as liberty, justice, equality, peace, and humanitarianism, not to baser emotions such as fear, greed, jealousy, or hatred" (Yukl, 1989, p. 210). These leaders have been purported to heighten follower expectations, and thereby instill in them a greater desire to put forth the effort needed to achieve. Transformational leaders are able to make the followers feel a part of the changing environment by making them feel included and supported, thereby instilling in them higher self-esteem, a willingness to change and put aside self-interest, and to commit themselves to the leader's vision (Bass & Avolio, 1994).

As described by Bass and Avolio (1994), transformational leadership theory has four major components labeled "the Four I's": (1) idealized influence; (2) inspirational motivation; (3) intellectual stimulation; and (4) individualized consideration.

Idealized influence refers to the position of role model that the transformational leader assumes in the eyes of his or her followers. This characteristic closely mirrors the term *charisma* used by other leadership theorists. This leader will be highly respected, admired, and trusted as a result of demonstrating high moral standards and ethical conduct. The leader will put the followers' feelings and needs above his or her own, which will lead to a heightened sense of commitment and a desire to emulate the leader and be leaders themselves.

Inspirational motivation refers to the concept that transformational leaders will inspire and motivate those around them, encouraging others to find challenge and personal meaning in their work, and will thereby foster enthusiasm throughout the organization. This component of transformational leadership involves the leader's ability to communicate clearly with followers, and to demonstrate the commitment and ability to solve problems and achieve set goals. These leaders strive to continually offer positive words of encouragement to provide self-confidence and self-esteem needed to empower, motivate, and inspire their employees.

Intellectual stimulation is the component of the theory that resides in the leader's ability to challenge followers to be more creative and innovative, and to be supportive of follower efforts even when in error. Followers are encouraged in all instances to try new ideas and to question traditional techniques, assumptions, and problem-solving methods. The intellectually stimulating leader also provides followers with the means to follow through on their initiatives. Through this process, followers are enabled to formulate their own methods of problem solving, which encourages them to take on positions of leadership in future situations.

Individualized consideration refers to the role of coach, or mentor, that the transformational leader assumes in the eyes of followers in an organization. Special consideration is given to the unique needs and desires of each individual as they interact with the leader. The leader stimulates followers to achieve higher levels of potential by creating new learning opportunities, increasing responsibility, and recognizing individual differences. The individually considerate leader is an effective listener who keeps open constant and effective lines of communication, and attempts to be physically accessible to all followers.

The other element of transformational leadership theory is called *transactional leadership*. Transactional leaders seek to motivate people by appealing to their self-interests, and by developing a relationship with their followers based on an exchange of effort for reward. This reciprocal relationship can exist comfortably, but the transactional leader would more aptly be classified as a manager *(see earlier discussion)*, as this relationship rarely results in the followers performing beyond the status quo.

Table 4.3. Yukl's (1998) Guidelines for Transformational Leadership
• Articulate a clear and appealing vision, and explain how the vision can be attained • Act confident and optimistic, and express that confidence in followers • Provide opportunities for early success, and celebrate these successes • Use dramatic, symbolic actions to emphasize key values • Lead by example • Empower people to achieve the vision

It is important to note that transactional and transformational leadership are not mutually exclusive concepts (i.e., these types of leadership cannot occur at the same time). Leaders can display varying degrees of either behavior, depending on the situation. However, those leaders who consistently display more transformational behaviors have been shown to be considerably more effective within their organizations than those leaders who are consistently transactional (Bass & Avolio, 1994).

MULTIDIMENSIONAL MODEL OF LEADERSHIP (MML)

Chelladurai attempted to synthesize the earlier approaches to the study of leadership by developing the multidimensional model of leadership (1978; 1993). This model of leadership incorporates the leader, follower, and situational context dimensions of leadership. According to the MML, situational characteristics (such as group size, structure, tasks, and goals, as well as technology, social norms and expectations), leader characteristics (e.g., personality, ability, experience), and member characteristics (e.g., demographics, attitudes, ability) are antecedents (or precursors) of leader behavior.

Leader behavior is further classified as being that which is required, preferred, or actual. Required leader behavior takes into account situational constraints on behavior (e.g., organizational goals, structure, technology, group task, social norms, external regulations, nature of the group). Preferred leader behavior incorporates the type of behavior that followers would like to see in their leader, while actual leadership behavior describes how a leader behaves in a given situation. It is the congruence of these three factors that, in large part, determines the levels of performance and satisfaction that are consequences of leadership in the MML. More recently, elements of transformational leadership theory have been included in the MML to reflect the assertion that these types of leaders will be able to significantly influence the environment within which they function. That is, they will be able to alter the situational and member characteristics in such a fashion that they can essentially create the facilitating conditions needed for them, and their organizations, to succeed (Chelladurai, 2001).

Can You Be a Great Leader?

Until now, we have focused a lot on *what leadership is*, but not on *what leaders do*. It is the actions of leaders that will allow followers to form an opinion of their leaders, for better or worse. Therefore, we will address here the most important actions that you will take as a leader, and discuss how perceptions of your leadership style and effectiveness will be formed by your followers. There are three main criteria that people use when evaluating your quality as a leader. They will take note of (1) your use of power and influence, (2) how you communicate, and (3) how you make decisions. The decision-making options that a leader has at his or her disposal were detailed earlier in the "management skills" section, but now we would like to discuss the other two criteria.

SOURCES OF POWER AND INFLUENCE

To simplistically state what leadership is, we could say that it is the influence over followers. This influence process permeates organizations, and mastering it is a key to being an effective leader. As Yukl (1998) noted, "to understand what makes managers effective requires an analysis of the complex web of power relationships and influence processes found in all organizations" (p. 175). Further, it is your use of these power relationships that will contribute to the perception of your leadership style that others have of you. Managerial power can be defined as a person's potential capacity to influence the contextual elements of an organization, as well as the attitudes and behaviors of others.

French and Raven (1959) identified five primary sources of power for leaders in organizations that were labeled *reward power* (ability to reward), *coercive power* (ability to punish), *legitimate power* (authority to make requests), *expert power* (special knowledge), and *referent power* (charisma). Another source of power in organizations is derived from the political processes that are inherent within them. These political processes are, in fact, merely mechanisms by which an individual can increase his or her power within an organization. As outlined by Pfeffer (1981), *political power* refers to processes such as forming coalitions, keeping control over key decisions, co-optation (i.e., undermining expected opposition), and institutionalization (i.e., filtering information to artificially inflate one's importance).

Ultimately, the opinion that followers form of a leader, and that leaders' success, "depends greatly on the manner in which power is exercised. Effective leaders are likely to use power in a subtle, careful fashion that minimizes status differentials and avoids threats to the target person's self-esteem. In contrast, leaders who exercise power in an arrogant, manipulative, or domineering manner are likely to engender resentment and resistance" (Yukl, 1998, p. 202).

COMMUNICATION STYLES

Most experts and researchers in the areas of management and leadership assert that communication is the foundation for effectiveness in any type of organization (Church, 1994). Moreover, organizational communication is underscored by the importance of several other concepts such as understanding, interpersonal warmth, trust, and openness. Additional organizational experts agree that the key process underlying effective organizational functioning is communication (see Chapter 3). This makes sense when you consider that the word "organization" implies a coordinated effort by a group of people, and that communication is critical for coordination. Without effective communication, people in the organization would not know what to do and would not know what others were doing. The vast majority of a leader's time is spent communicating with others, whether it is speaking or listening to others, emailing, text messaging, writing personal notes, or reading material transmitted from others. As a leader, the communication patterns that you establish will be important in crafting your leadership image in the eyes of others.

Leaders communicate with others in many different ways. However, to be a good leader you must understand that how you communicate sends messages equally as strong as what you communicate. It therefore stands to reason that employees must also be satisfied, not only with the leader's communication, but the more general communication lines that exist within the organization. In today's highly technological workplace, leaders have more communication options at their disposal than ever before. Communication options (i.e., any way you send a message) include but are not limited to: face-to-face discussions, email, handwritten messages, memos posted on a bulletin board, message board postings, texting, etc. Leaders must understand that virtually everything that they do will somehow communicate a message to those who surround them.

Most administrators have a consistent personal communication style that will help to define them as leaders. As you might expect, some methods are more effective than others. McCallister (1994) identified six main ways that people communicate:

The Noble—tend not to filter what they are thinking, and use few words to get their messages across.

The Socratic—believe in carefully discussing things before making any decisions and enjoys the process of arguing their points in detail.

The Reflexive—are concerned with the interpersonal aspects of communicating, and do not wish to offend others, and are therefore often great listeners.

The Magistrate—style is a mix of Noble and Socratic; will tell you exactly what they think, and may make their case in great detail; also tend to have an air of superiority about them, because they tend to dominate discussion.

The Candidate—a mix of the Socratic and Reflexive; tend to be warm and supportive while also being analytical and chatty; base their interactions on a great deal of information and do so in a very likable manner.

The Senator—have developed both the Noble and Reflexive styles, but do not mix the two; rather, they move back and forth between them as needed.

Understanding which of these six styles best describes you will help you to accurately interpret your communication style from the point of view of the "receiver." It should be noted that most of us will often fluctuate among styles, but will more consistently use just one. Also, each style has its own relative strengths and weaknesses and should not be thought of as superior or inferior to any other. The best advice for leaders is to understand your own predominant communication style, but then also endeavor to *match your communication style* with the situation and with those with whom you are trying to communicate.

Summary

- As the sport industry continues to grow and become more complex, the need for effective managers and leaders has increased. Critical to the success of sport organizations are individuals who can direct employees toward the accomplishment of established goals and objectives.

- The many facets of management are more easily understood if separated into the basic functions, skills, and roles that managers are expected to master. The functions of management include: (a) planning (establishment of goals and objectives); (b) organizing (delegation of tasks); (c) directing (leading and motivating); and (d) monitoring (evaluating performance).

- The skills needed to be an effective manager can be separated into three categories: (a) technical (knowledge of operations); (b) human (interpersonal skills); and (c) conceptual skills ("big picture"). A manager will often use a combination of these functions and skills when fulfilling the ten managerial roles identified by Mintzberg.

- Decision making is a primary skill that managers will have to utilize when fulfilling the functions of management and executing the different skills necessary to direct employees toward the achievement of organizational goals and objectives.

- Decision making is a complex activity that involves dealing with problems and opportunities, decisions that are routine or complex, and whether to include others in the decision-making process or make the decision in an autocratic manner.

- One issue that arises in most management courses is the difference between being a manager and being a leader. Managers tend to focus more on technical and human skills while leaders must have competency in all three skills. Furthermore, leaders may be required to deal with more "big picture" issues that affect the organization.

- Successful organizations must have people who are effective managers and leaders, and at times these roles are occupied by the same person. Therefore, it is helpful to consider management and leadership as distinct processes but not as different types of people.

- Study of leadership has evolved from initial examination of leader characteristics to the "new leadership paradigm," which examines the changes in follower attitudes and behaviors that result from the influence of the leader.

- Leadership theory can be separated into (a) trait approach (focus on leader characteristics/attributes); (b) behavioral approach (emphasis on leader actions/behaviors); (c) situational approach (relationship between leader, member, and the situation); and (d) contemporary theories (charismatic, transformational, and transactional leadership).

- The multidimensional model of leadership (MML) has attempted to combine the different approaches and theories into one explanation of effective leadership. This theory explores different antecedents that influence what a leader will do and combines this with the required, actual, and preferred leader behavior.

- The three criteria most often used to evaluate whether someone is an effective leader include: (1) the leader's use of power and influence; (2) ability to communicate; and (3) how the leader makes decisions.

DISCUSSION ACTIVITIES

1. Of the four functions of management, directing is often identified as one of the more challenging responsibilities of being a manager. Discuss why directing employees can be difficult and what you can do to become better at this function.
2. First discuss feedback as it relates to organizational goals and tasks. Second, explain how you would provide feedback to an employee who has not performed up to desired standards. What strategies could you use to improve performance and what could be done to make sure the employee does not become frustrated or discouraged?
3. The owner of a professional football team must decide whether to relocate the team to a new city or remain in the city that has embraced the team for nearly 20 years. This move is being considered because the team has not generated a sufficient amount of revenue to keep the team financially solvent. The team has aging veterans and the drafts have not been particularly helpful to bring the team back to its "glory days." However, this team has some of the most passionate fans in the NFL and is a leader in community outreach and social responsibility. Each year the team hosts numerous fundraising events that benefit different charitable groups in the area. Use the SLEEPE model of decision making to identify the implications of relocating the team or not.
4. First explain the different managerial roles described by Mintzberg. Second, use these roles to provide an illustration of how the general manager of a professional hockey team could fulfill the different managerial roles identified. For example, as a resource allocator the general manager must determine the operational budget for the team for the upcoming fiscal year.
5. Discuss the differences between management and leadership based on the chapter you have just read. Give an example from the sport industry to illustrate these differences. For example, describe someone who you feel is a quality manager but may not be a quality leader and vice-versa.
6. Why should others be included in the decision-making process? As a manager, what challenges would you have to overcome when allowing employees to contribute in decision making? Under what circumstances to you think it would be best for a manager to make decisions using an autocratic decision-making style?
7. Briefly describe the evolution of leadership theory and trace its path to the contemporary theories of today. Within this response, detail why some of the early theories were inadequate and further why the newer theories are more appropriate in terms of the progression of management and leadership theory.
8. In groups of 3–5 students, identify ten individuals you think exhibit good leadership qualities in sport. Which characteristics do they have in common? Which are different?
9. Develop a business plan for a new sport-related company, making sure to address the planning, organizing, controlling, and evaluating functions.

SUGGESTED READINGS

Bennis, W., & Nanus, B. (1985). *Leaders: The strategies for taking charge.* New York: Harper & Row.

Krzyzewski, M., & Phillips, D. T. (2000). *Leading with the heart: Coach K's successful strategies for basketball, business, and life.* New York: Warner Books, Inc.

Summit, P., & Jenkins, S. (1998). *Reach for the summit: The definite dozen for succeeding in whatever you do.* New York: Random House.

References

Barney, J. (1991). Firm resources and sustained competitive advantage. *Journal of Management, 17*(1), 99–120.

Bass, B. M. (1985). *Leadership and performance beyond expectations.* New York: The Free Press.

Bass, B. M. (1990). *Bass and Stogdill's handbook of leadership* (3rd ed.). New York: The Free Press.

Bass, B. M., & Avolio, B. J. (Eds.). (1994). *Improving organizational effectiveness through transformational leadership.* Thousand Oaks, CA: Sage Publications.

Bennis, W. G., & Nanus, B. (1985). *Leaders: The strategies for taking charge.* New York: Harper & Row Publishers.

Bridges, F. J., & Roquemore, L. L. (2004). *Management for athletic/sport administration: Theory and practice* (4th ed.). Decatur, GA: ESM Books.

Bryman, A. (1992). *Charisma & leadership in organizations.* Newbury Park, CA: Sage Publications.

Chalip, L. (2001). Group decision making and problem solving. In B. L. Parkhouse (Ed.), *The management of sport: Its foundation and application* (pp. 93–110). Boston, MA: McGraw-Hill·Higher Education.

Chelladurai, P. (1978). *A contingency model of leadership in athletics.* Unpublished doctoral dissertation. University of Waterloo, Waterloo, Canada.

Chelladurai, P. (1993). Leadership. In R. N. Singer, M. Murphey, & L. K. Tennant (Eds.), *Handbook of research on sport psychology,* pp. 647–671. New York: Macmillan.

Chelladurai, P. (2001). *Managing organizations for sport and physical activity: A systems perspective.* Holcomb Hathaway Publishers, Scottsdale, AZ.

Church, A. H. (1994). The character of organizational communication: A review and new conceptualization. *The International Journal of Organizational Analysis, 2,* 18–53.

Conger, J. A., & Kanungo, R. (1987). Towards a behavioral theory of charismatic leadership in organizational settings. *Academy of Management Review, 12,* 637–647.

DiMaggio, P. J., & Powell, W. W. (1983). The iron cage revisited: Institutional isomorphism and collective rationality in organizational fields. *American Sociological Review, 48,* 147–160.

Fiedler, F. E. (1967). *A theory of leadership effectiveness.* New York: McGraw-Hill.

French, J., & Raven, B. H. (1959). The bases of social power. In D. Cartwright (Ed.), *Studies of social power.* Ann Arbor, MI: Institute for Social Research, pp. 150–167.

Hersey, P., & Blanchard, K. H. (1977). *Management of organizational behavior: Utilizing human resources* (3rd ed.). Englewood Cliffs, NJ: Prentice-Hall.

House, R. J. (1971). A path-goal theory of leader effectiveness. *Administrative Science Quarterly, 16,* 321–339.

House, R. J. (1977). A 1976 theory of charismatic leadership effectiveness. In J. G. Hunt & L. L. Larson (Eds.). *Leadership: The cutting edge.* Carbondale, IL: Southern Illinois University Press.

Hums, M. A., & MacLean, J. C. (2004). *Governance and policy in sport organizations.* Scottsdale, AZ: Holcomb Hathaway.

McCallister, L. (1994). *I wish I'd said that! How to talk your way out of trouble and into success.* New York: Wiley Publishing.

Mintzberg, H. (1975). The manager's job: Folklore and fact. *Harvard Business Review, 53,* 49–61.

Osborn, R. N., & Hunt, J. G. (1975). An adaptive-reactive theory of leadership: The role of macro variables in leadership research. In J. G. Hunt & L. L. Larson (Eds.), *Leadership frontiers.* Kent, OH: Kent State University.

Pfeffer, J. (1981). *Power in organizations.* Marshfield, PA: Pittman.

Railey, J. H., & Tschauner, R. R. (1993). *Man-*

aging physical education, fitness and sports programs. Mountain View, CA: Mayfield Publishing Company.

Weber, M. (1947). *The theory of social and economic organization*. New York: The Free Press.

Stogdill, R. M. (1974). *Handbook of leadership: A survey of the literature*. New York: The Free Press.

Yukl, G. A., & Van Fleet, D. D. (1992). Theory and research on leadership in organizations. In M. D. Dunnette & L. M. Hough (Eds.), *Handbook of industrial and organizational psychology* (2nd ed.). Palo Alto, CA: Consulting Psychologists Press.

Yukl, G. A. (1998). *Leadership in organizations* (4th ed.). Englewood Cliffs, NJ: Prentice Hall.

Chapter Five

AN INTRODUCTION TO SPORT ECONOMICS

MATTHEW T. BROWN • DAVID MATTHEW ZUEFLE

© 2006 Universal Press Syndicate   10-13

www.gocomics.com

"OK, OK, you win! ... Here's 50 grand now, and you'll get another 50 when you get us out of this inning."

LEARNING OBJECTIVES

Upon completion of this chapter, students will be able to
- Appreciate economic theory in sport;
- Understand the laws of supply and demand;
- Analyze competitive balance in professional sport leagues;
- Understand the nuances of economic impact studies;
- Explain the realities and myths of economic impact studies;
- Identify the abuses of economic impact studies; and
- Understand psychic income.

What Is Economics?

Economics is the dynamic study of collective human behavior. Typically, economics involves the study of the market system. Why individuals have money, the determinants of the cost of products, and the examination of the management of resources are all areas of study within economics. In sport, economists examine supply and demand within the sport industry, the market for sports broadcast rights, the relationship between team costs, profit and winning, and the value of sports talent (Fort, 2003). Additionally, economists often examine economic activity benefits accruing to a community hosting sporting events or building new stadia or arenas.

Sport mangers may apply economic theory without realizing so. For example, when calculating price for games, a ticket manager may decide to use a variable pricing model. If she decides to charge $20 for general admission tickets on weekends and $14 for the same ticket Monday to Thursday, she is likely applying the economic principles of supply and demand. In this example, supply is fixed by the general admission seating capacity of the stadium. Demand likely is higher for the product on the weekend versus weekdays. With a static supply and a shift in the demand curve on the weekends, the ticket manger can charge more for the same seat without negatively affecting attendance.

In all, effective sport managers understand key economic principles such as opportunity and marginal costs, supply and demand, competitive balance, and economic impact. Managers with knowledge of these concepts will be able to anticipate the impact of financial decision making on the sport enterprise.

A key belief of economists is that individuals and groups of people choose based on the costs and benefits of their actions. In Arlington, Texas, the city is using $325 million in public funding to help build a new football stadium that will be the home of the Dallas Cowboys and the Cotton Bowl beginning in 2009. The stadium will have the most modern amenities available, including a 120-foot-tall glass-paneled wall that will open to let in fall breezes, a retractable roof, two 60-yard flat screens that hang above the field, and over 200,000 square feet devoted to a club seating luxury area (Hoffer, 2007).

Critics may ask if there was or should have been a better use of taxpayer dollars. A missed chance is an *opportunity cost*. The opportunity cost of a decision is what you must give up to have what you wanted. Those in Arlington wanted a new football venue to attract an NFL team to their city. They gave up $325 million in public funds that may have been used to better community infrastructure or improve public schools. In Washington, D.C., the citizens were asked by Major League Baseball to publicly fund a new stadium for the relocated Montreal Expos. The city lacks a public hospital. Their choice was one of opportunity cost.

Opportunity costs involve either *explicit* or *implicit* expenditures. In Los Angeles, if a fan decides to spend $75 to go to a Lakers game, he then has $75 less to go to a Kings game that week. This is an explicit expenditure, spending money on the Lakers rather than the Kings. If a friend in Phoenix invites you to a Suns game on Monday night and another friend invites you to a Coyotes game that same night, you obviously cannot be in more than one place at the same time. Your choice is an implicit expenditure. The cost is the intangible benefit you would have received by going to the game you chose not to attend.

Opportunity costs also affect owners of sport properties. In the 1990s several profitable National Football League franchises moved. The Rams moved from Los Angeles to St. Louis, the Browns from Cleveland to Baltimore (where they became the Ravens), and the Raiders, from Oakland to Los Angeles and then back to Oakland. While these franchises were making profits in their original locations, they were operating at an economic loss due to the new or renovated stadia and revenue streams available elsewhere.

Sport managers, with an understanding of *marginal costs*, can predict human behavior through the examination of the benefits and costs of doing more. Another key rule of economic behavior is that people think about the marginal impact of their actions. Marginal cost is how much more an individual has to spend to acquire more of what he wants, without worrying about what already has been spent.

For the Texas Rangers, signing Alex Rodriguez to a $25 million per year contract drastically increased their payroll. The Ranger's marginal costs were not changed, however. Baseball teams like the Rangers sell tickets, which allow people to see the players on their roster. The Rangers had to pay Rodriguez $25 million no matter how many people came to see him play in a given year. The team raised ticket prices after signing Rodriguez, not necessarily because they had to, but because they could. Rodriguez's signing excited the Ranger's fans as he was, at the time, one of the best players in the game. With him on the team, Ranger fans were more willing to pay to see the Rangers play. This in turn made them more willing to pay a higher price to see the team play.

Mark McGwire and his agent understood this concept when negotiating his contract with the St. Louis Cardinals. His presence on the team made the fans more willing to pay to see the team play, and seasonal attendance began to increase with McGwire on the roster. McGwire's agent negotiated a bonus for McGwire based on attendance. As a result, his salary increased by $1 for every fan in attendance above 2.8 million.

Supply and Demand

If you are a fan of a baseball team and earn $3,000 a month you can afford to attend a certain number of games during the season based on the price of the team's tickets. If the team were to lower ticket prices suddenly in the middle of the year, you could then go to more games. This is the *law of demand*. The law states that when the price of an item declines the demand for that item increases. When the price goes down enough, people like you can now afford to buy more of the product, which means you can attend additional games.

The relationship between price and the amount of product people wish to consume is called the demand curve (see Figure 5.1). The demand curve slopes down because as price gets higher, the demand for a particular product decreases.

Supply is the quantity of a product that an owner is willing to offer or make available at a given price. The supply curve (see Figure 5.2) charts the relationship between

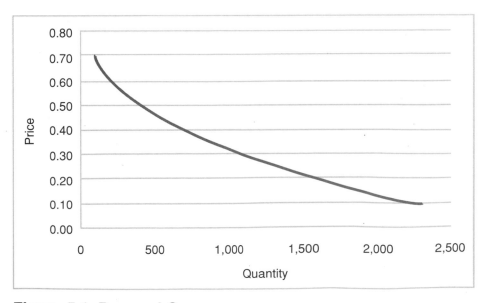

Figure 5.1. Demand Curve.

the amounts of product a company or companies wish to sell and price. Usually, the supply curve slopes upward.

Going back to the example discussed in the opening section of this chapter, a ticket manager determining price could plot the demand and supply curve for her product on one graph (see Figure 5.3). The point where the supply curve and the demand curve overlap is the *equilibrium price*. Here is where the amount of product demanded (tickets) equals the amount of product supplied (seats). Notice the supply curve is vertical. This is because the number of seats in the ballpark is fixed and does not change from game to game.

Figure 5.2. Supply Curve.

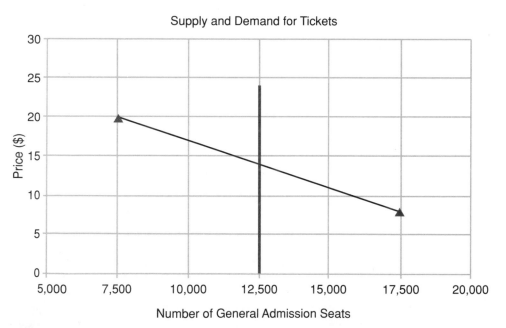

Figure 5.3. Equilibrium Point.

Changes in the demand curve also help explain why the ticket manager can charge $20 for tickets on the weekends and only $14 for those same seats on the weekdays. Figure 5.4 plots the supply curve for general admission seating at the ballpark. Again, the line is vertical as the number of general admission seats is fixed. The demand curve for games Monday to Thursday (D_1) intersects the supply curve at $14. On weekends, the demand for those seats increases and the curve shifts to the right. The weekend curve (D_2) now intersects with the supply curve at $20. Because the demand for the product is greater on weekends, the ticket manager can charge more for seats because supply is fixed.

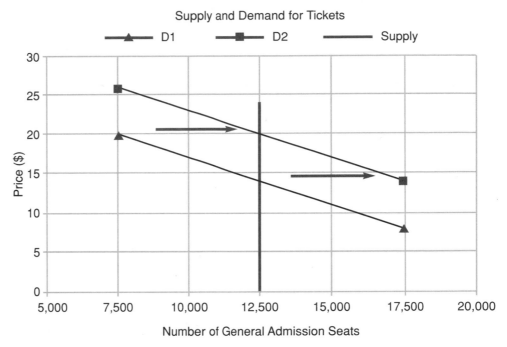

Figure 5.4. Demand Curve Shift for Weekend Games.

Competitive Balance

The National Football League (NFL) is likely the strongest league and sport property in North America. Most analysts attribute the league's strength to parity. In a given year, a last place team from the previous season has a realistic opportunity to compete for the Lombardi Trophy. The St. Louis Rams' and Baltimore Ravens' rise from has-beens to Super Bowl champions are perfect examples. In economic terms, the parity in the NFL is referred to as *competitive balance*.

The NFL is a league that shares a majority of its revenues between owners. These revenues include moneys generated via NFL Properties, NFL Enterprises, and nationwide television packages. Owners keep a vast majority of locally generated revenues from items like stadium naming rights, concessions, parking, local radio, and sponsorship/advertising. Under this structure, the NFL has the highest central-to-local revenue percentage as compared to other professional leagues.

Formerly, the NFL salary cap was set based upon a percentage of nationally shared, or central, revenues. Under the most recent collective bargaining agreement, however, players now receive 59 percent of all league revenues. This change had the potential to affect competitive balance within the league. Small market owners and owners with stadia that did not generate a lot of revenue were at a disadvantage under this new agreement with the National Football League Players Association (NFLPA). Importantly, this could have led to the end of parity within the league.

For example, Team A is a large market team and Team B is a small market team. Both teams receive $110 million from the league's central revenue pool. Team A generates an additional $100 million in local revenues and Team B generates $25 million. Therefore, overall revenues for Team A are $210 million and Team B $125 million. Next, total revenues per NFL team are estimated to be $170 million per team. As players receive 59 percent of total revenues, the salary cap for teams is set at $100.3 million. If both Team A and Team B are paying players at the maximum salary level, Team A spends 47.8 percent of its revenues on player salary while Team B spends 80.2 percent on player salary. With the non-player costs of operating an NFL franchise factored in with salary cap rules regarding the amortization of player signing bonuses, Team B is at a disadvantage in the free agent market. Team B also must worry about profitability as nearly all of its revenues are taken by player salary. This scenario explains, in some part, why the Buffalo Bills are beginning to play games in Toronto. Toronto provides an opportunity for the Bills, a small market team with an older stadium, to generate the additional revenue needed to stay competitive.

The NFL has addressed the problems associated with this new economic model as sharing of local revenues has now begun. Approximately $150 million of local revenue is transferred from the top 15 earning teams to the bottom 15 to offset the salary difficulties presented in the previous example.

The NFL is trying to avoid Major League Baseball's situation. In baseball, where much less revenue is shared, where there is no salary cap, and where owners are willing to spend beyond Major League Baseball's luxury tax threshold (New York Yankees), competitive imbalance exists. Here certain teams consistently win more games over time than the rest of the teams in the league. As an example, the New York Yankees have won approximately one-in-three World Series since 1920. When one team is located in a market where fans will pay more for wins, the more profitable team will win more over time. Therefore, as seen in Major League Baseball, profit variation harms competitive balance (Fort, 2003).

MLB Commissioner Allan H. (Bud) Selig, however, argues that MLB now has the greatest competitive balance of any league. He points to the fact that since 2000 only the Boston Red Sox have repeated as World Series Champions. Foster, Greyser, and Walsh (2006) stated that competitive imbalance at the league level exists when one team dominates the sport over a number of years (dynasties), the same group of teams dominate the sport over a period of time, or the same group of teams remain at the bottom of the standings. According to the data presented in Table 5.1 and Table 5.2, which league, the NFL or MLB, is more balanced?

Competitive Advantage

Within the economic restrictions of a league, teams that are constantly successful understand competitive advantage. For example, to operate within the economic framework of the NFL while signing better players than other teams in the league, it helps to have a thorough understanding of the collective bargaining agreement and league rules. As stated previously, the collective bargaining agreement (CBA) signed with the NFLPA regulates the amortization of player signing bonuses.

The NFL CBA rules state that a signing bonus paid to a player is allocated over the time of the contract (up to seven years). So a player signing a 5-year, $10 million contract with a $10 million signing bonus would be paid $12 million in year one and $2 million per year in years two through five. However, the salary counted

Table 1. NFL Team Wins 2001–2007

#	2007 Team	Wins	2006 Team	Wins	2005 Team	Wins	2004 Team	Wins	2003 Team	Wins	2002 Team	Wins	2001 Team	Wins
1	New England	16	San Diego	14	Indianapolis	14	Pittsburg	15	New England*	14	Philadelphia	12	St. Louis	14
2	Dallas	13	Baltimore	13	Denver	13	New England*	14	Kansas City	13	Green Bay	12	Chicago	13
3	Green Bay	13	Chicago	13	Seattle	13	Philadelphia	13	Indianapolis	12	Tampa Bay*	12	Pittsburg	13
4	Indianapolis	13	New England	12	Jacksonville	12	Indianapolis	12	Tennessee	12	Tennessee	11	Green Bay	12
5	Jacksonville	11	Indianapolis*	12	Cincinnati	11	San Diego	12	Philadelphia	12	Oakland	11	San Francisco	12
6	San Diego	11	N.Y. Jets	10	Pittsburg*	11	Atlanta	11	St. Louis	12	Pittsburg	10	Miami	11
7	Cleveland	10	Philadelphia	10	N.Y. Giants	11	N.Y. Jets	10	Carolina	11	Indianapolis	10	New England*	11
8	N.Y. Giants*	10	New Orleans	10	Chicago	11	Denver	10	Miami	10	N.Y. Giants	10	Philadelphia	11
9	Pittsburg	10	Kansas City	9	Tampa Bay	11	Green Bay	10	Baltimore	10	San Francisco	10	Baltimore	10
10	Seattle	10	Denver	9	Carolina	11	Buffalo	9	Denver	10	N.Y. Jets	9	N.Y. Jets	10
11	Tennessee	10	Dallas	9	New England	10	Baltimore	9	Dallas	10	New England	9	Oakland	10
12	Tampa Bay	9	Seattle	9	Kansas City	10	Jacksonville	9	Green Bay	10	Miami	9	Seattle	9
13	Washington	9	Cincinnati	8	Washington	10	Seattle	9	Seattle	10	Cleveland	9	Tampa Bay	9
14	Arizona	8	Pittsburg	8	Miami	9	Cincinnati	8	Minnesota	8	Denver	9	Denver	8
15	Houston	8	Tennessee	8	San Diego	9	Minnesota	8	Cincinnati	8	Atlanta	9	Washington	8
16	Minnesota	8	Jacksonville	8	Dallas	9	New Orleans	8	New Orleans	8	New Orleans	9	Arizona	7
17	Philadelphia	8	N.Y. Giants	8	Minnesota	9	St. Louis	8	Chicago	7	Buffalo	8	Atlanta	7
18	Buffalo	7	Green Bay	8	Atlanta	8	Houston	7	Tampa Bay	7	San Diego	8	Cleveland	7
19	Carolina	7	Carolina	8	Baltimore	6	Kansas City	7	San Francisco	7	Kansas City	8	New Orleans	7
20	Chicago	7	St. Louis	8	Cleveland	6	Carolina	7	Buffalo	6	Baltimore	7	N.Y. Giants	7
21	Cincinnati	7	Buffalo	7	Philadelphia	6	N.Y. Giants	6	N.Y. Jets	6	Washington	7	Tennessee	7
22	Denver	7	Atlanta	7	St. Louis	6	Dallas	6	Pittsburg	6	Carolina	7	Cincinnati	6
23	Detroit	7	San Francisco	7	Buffalo	5	Washington	6	Cleveland	5	St. Louis	7	Indianapolis	6
24	New Orleans	7	Miami	6	Detroit	5	Detroit	6	Jacksonville	5	Seattle	7	Jacksonville	6
25	Baltimore	5	Houston	6	Arizona	5	Arizona	6	Houston	5	Jacksonville	6	Kansas City	6
26	San Francisco	5	Minnesota	6	N.Y. Jets	4	Tennessee	5	Washington	5	Minnesota	6	Dallas	5
27	Atlanta	4	Washington	5	Tennessee	4	Oakland	5	Detroit	5	Dallas	5	Minnesota	5
28	Kansas City	4	Arizona	5	Oakland	4	Chicago	5	Atlanta	5	Arizona	5	San Diego	5
29	N.Y. Jets	4	Cleveland	4	Green Bay	4	Tampa Bay	5	Oakland	4	Houston	4	Buffalo	3
30	Oakland	4	Tampa Bay	4	San Francisco	4	Miami	4	San Diego	4	Chicago	4	Detroit	2
31	St. Louis	3	Detroit	3	New Orleans	3	Cleveland	4	N.Y. Giants	4	Detroit	3	Carolina	1
32	Miami	1	Oakland	2	Houston	2	San Francisco	2	Arizona	4	Cincinnati	2		

* Won Super Bowl

Table 2. MLB Team Wins 2001–2007

#	2007 Team	Wins	2006 Team	Wins	2005 Team	Wins	2004 Team	Wins	2003 Team	Wins	2002 Team	Wins	2001 Team	Wins
1	Boston*	96	New York (NL)	97	St. Louis	100	St. Louis	105	New York (AL)	101	New York (AL)	103	Seattle	116
2	Cleveland	96	New York (AL)	97	Chicago (AL)*	99	New York (AL)	101	Atlanta	101	Oakland	103	Oakland	102
3	New York (AL)	94	Minnesota	96	New York (AL)	95	Boston*	98	San Francisco	100	Atlanta	101	New York (AL)	95
4	Los Angeles	94	Detroit	95	Boston	95	Atlanta	96	Oakland	96	Anaheim*	99	Houston	93
5	Arizona	90	Oakland	93	Los Angeles	95	Los Angeles	93	Boston	95	Arizona	98	St. Louis	93
6	Colorado	90	Chicago (AL)	90	Cleveland	93	Minnesota	92	Seattle	93	St. Louis	97	Arizona*	92
7	Philadelphia	89	Los Angeles	89	Atlanta	90	Anaheim	92	Florida*	91	San Francisco	95	Cleveland	91
8	San Diego	89	San Diego	88	Houston	89	Houston	92	Minnesota	90	Minnesota	94	San Francisco	90
9	Detroit	88	Los Angeles	88	Oakland	88	Oakland	91	Chicago (NL)	88	Boston	93	Atlanta	88
10	Seattle	88	Toronto	87	Philadelphia	88	San Francisco	91	Houston	87	Seattle	93	Chicago (NL)	88
11	New York (NL)	88	Boston	86	Minnesota	83	Texas	89	Toronto	86	Los Angeles	92	Philadelphia	86
12	Chicago (NL)	85	Philadelphia	85	Florida	83	Chicago (NL)	89	Chicago (AL)	86	Houston	84	Los Angeles	86
13	Atlanta	84	St. Louis*	83	New York (NL)	83	San Diego	87	Philadelphia	86	Montreal	83	Minnesota	85
14	Toronto	83	Houston	82	San Diego	82	Philadelphia	86	St. Louis	85	Chicago (AL)	81	Chicago	83
15	Milwaukee	83	Texas	80	Washington	81	Chicago (AL)	83	Los Angeles	85	Philadelphia	80	Boston	82
16	Los Angeles	82	Cincinnati	80	Milwaukee	81	Florida	83	Arizona	84	Florida	79	New York (NL)	82
17	Minnesota	79	Atlanta	79	Toronto	80	Cleveland	80	Kansas City	83	Toronto	78	Toronto	80
18	St. Louis	78	Cleveland	78	Texas	79	Baltimore	78	Montreal	83	Cincinnati	78	San Diego	79
19	Oakland	76	Seattle	78	Chicago (NL)	79	Cincinnati	76	Anaheim	77	New York (NL)	75	Florida	76
20	Texas	75	Florida	78	Arizona	77	Detroit	72	Pittsburg	75	Cleveland	74	Anaheim	75
21	Washington	73	San Francisco	76	San Francisco	75	Pittsburg	72	Colorado	74	Colorado	73	Texas	73
22	Houston	73	Arizona	76	Baltimore	74	New York (NL)	71	Baltimore	71	Texas	72	Colorado	73
23	Chicago (AL)	72	Colorado	76	Cincinnati	73	Tampa Bay	70	Texas	71	Pittsburg	72	Montreal	68
24	Cincinnati	72	Milwaukee	75	Detroit	71	Colorado	68	Cincinnati	69	Baltimore	67	Milwaukee	68
25	Florida	71	Washington	71	Los Angeles	71	Toronto	67	Cleveland	68	Chicago (NL)	67	Detroit	66
26	San Francisco	71	Baltimore	70	Seattle	69	Montreal	67	Milwaukee	68	San Diego	66	Cincinnati	66
27	Baltimore	69	Pittsburg	67	Tampa Bay	67	Milwaukee	67	New York (NL)	66	Kansas City	62	Kansas City	65
28	Kansas City	69	Chicago (NL)	66	Pittsburg	67	Seattle	63	San Diego	64	Milwaukee	56	Baltimore	63
29	Pittsburg	68	Kansas City	62	Colorado	67	Kansas City	58	Tampa Bay	63	Tampa Bay	55	Tampa Bay	62
30	Tampa Bay	66	Tampa Bay	61	Kansas City	56	Arizona	51	Detroit	43	Detroit	55	Pittsburg	62

* Won World Series

against the team's cap would be $4 million per year (Brown, Nagel, McEvoy & Rascher, 2004). Teams, like Team A above, with a new stadium filled with luxury seating in a large market, have access to unshared revenue that can be used to pay large signing bonuses, creating a competitive advantage on the field. Without revenue sharing between teams in the NFL, too many franchises would gain competitive advantage, thereby leading to competitive imbalance within the league.

Economic Impact

Economic impact is often used to justify the need to build these new stadia with public tax payer dollars.

WHAT IS ECONOMIC IMPACT?

In sport, *economic impact* is defined as the net economic change in a host community that results from spending attributed to a sport event or facility (Turco & Kelsey, 1992). This economic change has both tangible and intangible benefits. The tangible benefits can be seen in Figure 5.5.

Figure 5.5. Tangible Community Benefits.

As Figure 5.5 depicts, the community benefits when the city subsidizes a sporting event or facility if that subsidy leads to new visitors coming to the community. These visitors bring new money into the community, which then leads to job creation. Job creation lowers unemployment and, therefore, the community as a whole benefits from its investment.

Economic impact studies measure the benefits a community receives. The study measures total economic loss or gain after accounting for costs (Agha, 2002). These studies were initially developed by cities to determine the economic impact individual business had on a community. Later they were adapted to measure spending based on a sporting event or a facility. In most communities, sport economic impact studies are conducted by the Chamber of Commerce, or in larger cities, the sports commission.

The first to apply economic impact studies to sport was the Indiana Sports Corporation (ISC). The ISC used its economic impact studies successfully to gain governmental support to build facilities and provide resources for sport in central Indiana. Some of the early events the ISC attracted included the 1982 Olympic Sport Fest and the 1987 Pan Am Games. The ISC's economic impact studies indicated that sporting activities in the state generated 60,000 new jobs and created 7,400 new businesses. The ISC was able to get funding from the state to support its activities because it could prove that its activities created new jobs and brought new money to the region.

TYPES OF SPENDING

Economic impact studies measure three types of spending: direct, indirect, and induced. *Direct spending* measures actual dollars spent in the local community on the event. This spending can be both on site and off site. On-site spending includes items like concessions, tickets, parking, and merchandise. Off-site spending refers to all other spending in the local community such as spending on hotels, for fuel, to shop, and to dine. The key to measuring direct spending is that it has to occur in the local economy as defined in the economic impact study.

Indirect and induced spending develops from direct spending (NASC, 2001). Direct spending creates secondary spending that circulates within the community (see Figure 5.6). This secondary spending includes indirect benefits like additional profits and incomes for local businesses and households. These local businesses then spend some of these dollars on goods and services that support additional local businesses. This is *indirect spending*.

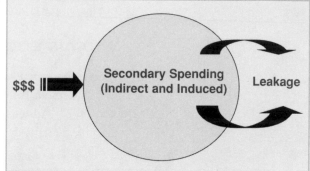

At the same time, household wage earners receive additional income resulting from the increases in business spending. The wage earners spend some of their increased earnings on local goods and services. These expenditures are *induced spending*. Both indirect and induced spending are estimated using a regional multiplier.

The regional multiplier measures how many times money changes hands in the community before it leaves, or leaks out of the region (see Figure 5.6). It is the value multiplied by direct spending to estimate total spending, or economic

Figure 5.6. Community Cash Flow Model.

benefit. The multiplier estimates the secondary spending (indirect and induced) in a region. Figure 5.7 depicts the method by which a multiplier is calculated.

In Figure 5.7, the initial dollar is spent in the local economy. Of that initial dollar, $0.40 is respent in the local economy. Of the $0.40, $0.16 is respent. Then of the $0.16, $0.06 is respent and so on. By adding together the initial $1.00 of spending to the amount of money respent each round, you can calculate the multiplier for the region. For this example, when the initial round of spending is added to the five rounds of respending, the total spending generated in the community would be $1.66; therefore, the regional multiplier is 1.66.

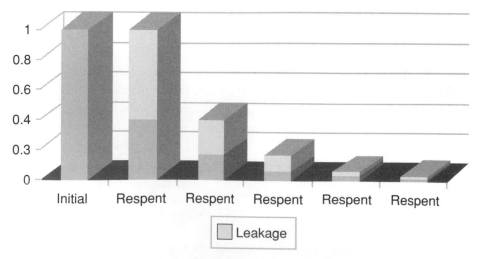

Figure 5.7. Mathematical Multiplier Model.

STEPS TO COMPLETING THE ECONOMIC IMPACT STUDY

To conduct an economic impact study, the first step is to define the local economy. For instance, when conducting an economic impact study on the American Legion State Baseball Tournament held in Athens, Ohio, the researchers had to decide if the economy would be defined as the City of Athens, the area within the zip code of Athens, or Athens County. To define the economy, the researchers must determine where the majority of impact will occur.

Second, the method for collecting data must be determined. In a basic economic impact study, direct spending is measured. Then the multiplier is applied to determine total impact. To measure direct spending, data can be collected directly from participants and spectators or from indirect sources like hotels and restaurants. In some instances, it makes sense to use indirect sources. When hosting a conference tournament, the organizing committee knows where teams are staying. The committee can contact these hotels and collect the exact amounts spent by team for the duration of the tournament.

In most instances, information will need to be collected directly from participants and spectators. Several data-collection tools may be used, including self-administered questionnaires and logs or diaries. Most often, due to costs and efficiency of data collection, self-administered questionnaires are used.

Once the method of data collection is determined, the data must be collected. For an accurate reflection of the impact of an event, it is recommended that at least 350 surveys or diaries be collected. After the data collection, the results can be analyzed and direct spending determined.

USES OF ECONOMIC IMPACT IN SPORT

Economic impact studies are widely used in sport. As noted previously, the Indiana Sports Commission was the first to use economic impact studies to justify taxpayer subsidy. Other examples of the use of economic impact studies in sport vary widely. In the National Football League (NFL), it is estimated by the Maryland Department of Business and Economic Development that the impact of the Baltimore Ravens was $202 million in gross expenditures and $96 million in personal income, with 2,772 full time jobs being created. An economic impact study on the Buffalo Bills indicated that the team's impact was $111.5 million annually. A final NFL team, the Lions, generated $127 in direct spending ("The fans," 2002).

For the Olympics, it was estimated that the economic impact for Atlanta in 1996 was $1.2 billion in direct spending with the total impact over the short term being $5.1 billion (Humphreys & Plummer, 2004). The impact for the 2002 Winter Olympics in Salt Lake was estimated to be $4.5 billion ("2002 Winter," 2003). In NASCAR, one study estimated that a new track would have an annual impact of $221 million (Trevison, 2004).

THE REALITY AND MYTH OF
ECONOMIC IMPACT IN SPORT

Rosentraub (1997) examined several sport economic impact studies. In an era where new stadia were used to lure teams, these economic impact studies were used to justify the use of public funds to build the new sport venues. The Cleveland Browns went to Baltimore when the owner was promised a new stadium to be built and paid for by taxpayers. The same can be said for the Houston Oilers when they moved to Nashville. Even in hockey this can be seen. The Winnipeg Jets moved to Phoenix and played for many years in the publicly funded America West Arena.

Rosentraub noted a problem with many of these studies, however. In several situations, studies were produced that gave the impression that for the right price you could get as large of an impact number as you wanted. For a team moving to a city, two studies could differ by over $100 million.

ECONOMIC IMPACT OF STUDY ABUSES

While economic impact studies are valuable estimates that can aid in planning, development, and the public decision-making process, they can also be misused—sometimes through naïveté and unfamiliarity, and sometimes intentionally.

Professor John Crompton of Texas A&M University identified eleven sources of misapplication in a well-known 1995 article, which appeared in the *Journal of Sport Management*. Crompton's list includes such mistakes as failing to use the correct type of multiplier; failure to correctly calculate the multiplier itself; the inappropriate inclusion of local residents, "time-switchers," and "casuals" (both refer to types of visitors who were not drawn in by the event being studied); and the failure to consider opportunity costs. Along with these categories of mistakes, all of which could be committed unintentionally, Crompton also notes that some mistakes, such as the use of "fudged" multiplier coefficients, can be and are committed willfully (Crompton, 1995).

The problems Crompton pointed out that are associated with multipliers are not minor ones. And within these problems, one of the potentially most profound is that there is no one set of multipliers universally agreed upon and utilized by all researchers and critics. Commonly available commercial options include the RIMS II, IMPLAN, and REIM multipliers. Not only does the availability of competing multipliers contribute to the difficulty of making meaningful comparisons between studies, but it allows for the possibility of intentional misuse.

To illustrate this example, consider the case of a commercial firm with an interest in developing a downtown stadium complex in City A. The firm's best interests in this case would be promoted if an economic impact study demonstrated a large and sustainable return on the initial investment of City A in the project.

Thus in theory, the firm, and perhaps its supporters within City A's government, could contract a researcher to calculate the total economic impact for City A using all common commercially available multipliers. If differences between the estimates existed, the researcher could then select the results that indicated the most favorable outcome for City A. The cost of buying several commercially calculated multipliers could be subsumed into the total project costs and would likely prove to be only a very small percentage of the total study's expense.

While this scenario is hypothetical, and an approach such as the one described in it could be seen as cynical at best and completely unethical at worst, it is clearly possible—and the forces that could promote this kind of questionable decision making are present and powerful.

INTANGIBLE BENEFITS

Many American communities are in transition from more traditional economic bases of support, such as shipping and manufacturing, to new service-oriented industries, such as sport, entertainment, and tourism. And since all politicians must address issues related to employment and the economy, the ability to "create" jobs and wealth are often touted as reasons to support new initiatives and to vote for local tax and rezoning issues related to sport and tourism development.

Through new building, development, and policy changes, local government officials often hope not only to invigorate the private sector but also to increase sport tourism-related revenues through the collection of sales taxes, lodging/hospitality taxes, user fees, and even fines from the visitors who come to their cities. In addition to these multiple streams of revenue, which are often seen as potentially lucrative, many believe that more subtle reasons exist for supporting sport tourism development.

Billy Payne, CEO for the Atlanta Committee for the Olympic Games (ACOG), was one notable proponent of the transformative power of major sport infrastructure development and the hosting of special events. Always a champion of this

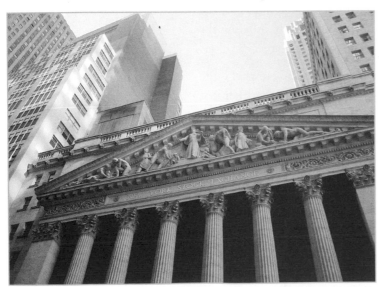

power, his belief appeared to remain unshaken eight years after the 1996 Atlanta Olympics when he noted: "The Games vaulted Atlanta into a very elite group of cities, on a global scale. Naturally, I think it was worth every minute and every dollar that we spent bringing them here and hosting the world" (Yarbrough, 2000).

Not everyone shares Mr. Payne's exuberance, however. In considering the potential return from a proposed new stadium complex for Minneapolis (which has been promoted by Minnesota Governor Tim Pawlenty), financial experts such as Jeff Tollefson of Minnesota Venture Capital Association and Art Rolnick of the Federal Reserve Bank of Minneapolis expressed serious skepticism about the project's financial potential (Horwich, 2004).

Another expert, Mr. David Joy of American Express Financial Advisors, suggested that while the Minnesota stadium project might not be a good investment from the perspective of achieving a real financial return, it might be worthwhile from the perspective of promoting the community's "psychic income" (Yarbrough, 2000).

Psychic income, also sometimes referred to as "psychic capital," is increasingly referred to as a benefit of sport tourism development. This relatively new term refers to the real, yet intangible, qualities associated with community pride, prestige, and competitiveness, which may be associated with major sport and event hosting.

NATIONAL ASSOCIATION OF SPORTS COMMISSIONS

The National Association of Sport Commissions (NASC) in 2000 attempted to address the aforementioned abuses of economic studies when it published guidelines for computation of economic impact. The report stated, "The process of estimating the economic benefit of a sports event can become controversial" (NASC, 2000, p. 1). Because the bidding process on sports events is fairly competitive, owners of events have learned how to market their events in an attractive way. Examples from one event, according to the NASC, had economic impact estimates from $7.5 million to zero. Resulting from many discrepancies similar to this was the need to clearly estimate the return on investment of a host community.

The main problem with economic impact studies is that experts disagree on how to conduct the studies. As a result, economists, using different but legitimate methodologies, can derive far different values of economic impact. Sport organizing committees, wanting to inflate the value of their work, are therefore able to "shop" for the methodology that will show the greatest return on investment. This is affirmed by Crompton (1995) and Noll and Zimbalist (1997). These authors stated that economic impact studies are frequently used to justify a position or to create the appearance of a greater public benefit. Organizing committees, however, need to be cautious. Often bid fees or guarantees promised to an event are partially based upon the economic impact that the event generates. By shopping for an economic impact study with an inflated estimate of the true economic impact of the event, organizing committees and host communities are artificially inflating the cost of bidding for and hosting the event (NASC, 2000).

One of the issues leading to differences in computation of economic impact is the calculation of visitor spending. Visitor spending is defined as the dollars left in a community by persons who came to the community because of the event (NASC, 2000). Upon the examination of this definition, spending by local residents (those who live within the community that hosts the event) is excluded. Only new dollars brought into the community as a result of visitor spending should be counted in an economic impact study. But as Hudson (2001) noted, economic impact studies often include spending by local residents. Thus, the true impact of the event on the local economy is inflated.

The purpose of an individual's visit can also cause variations in the computation of economic impact. For example, an individual may be sent to a conference in Dallas, Texas. The purpose of her visit to Dallas was business—attending the conference. While in Dallas, if she learns that there is a Stars game and decides to go to the game, her money spent at the game would not be counted in the economic impact of that game. The purpose of her trip to Dallas was to attend the conference, not to go to a hockey game. Even if the event has appeal to business visitors looking for entertainment, the spending by that business visitor only would be counted when calculating the economic impact of the conference, not the sporting event.

NASC FORMULA FOR MEASURING ECONOMIC IMPACT

In reaction to the several known shortcomings and abuses common to economic impact studies, the National Association of Sports Commissions (NASC) sponsored a report on the subject. In this report, an overview of economic impacts, visitor spending, classification of visitors, and important issues were discussed. Additionally, the NASC report reviewed the common formulae for calculating economic impact (EI) and proposed a methodology for two versions of a standardized formula.

The standardized formulae were proposed as an attempt to remedy some of the common problems associated with economic impact studies such as misrepresentation of data and the use of "fudged" multiplier values. Worksheets and tables to aid in the calculation of the standardized formulae were also developed. NASC recommended that communities and areas could utilize these tools in-house or in conjunction with outside professional consultants or academic institutions.

The recommended standard formula has three steps, with the first step being essential to all studies and the second two available for utilization to "increase the accuracy" of the EI estimate (NASC, 2001). This potential for choice of methods results in a bifurcation of possible applications that renders the standard formula into two de facto standard formulae.

In the first, and more basic, configuration of the formula, an estimate of Total Visitor Spending (TVS) is calculated by multiplying the Number of Out-of-Town Visitors (OTV) by Average Spending Per Day (ASD) and by the Number of Days (ND). This formula does not utilize a Regional Multiplier and can be represented as:

$$TVS = OTV \times ASD \times ND \quad \text{(Eq. 1)}$$

The second formula configuration includes the other two recommended steps, which results in the calculation of a new base number (Direct Spending) and utilizes a Regional Multiplier. Stepwise, the calculation of this formulation begins with the calculation of Direct Spending (DS) by adding Total Administrative Operations Spending to Total Visitor Spending. This step can be represented as:

$$DS = TVS + TAS \quad \text{(Eq. 2)}$$

Once Direct Spending has been calculated, it can be multiplied by the Regional Multiplier (RM) to calculate the Total Economic Impact (TEI) as so:

$$TEI = DS \times RM \quad \text{(Eq. 3)}$$

Thus, the full version of the second formula can be represented as:

$$TEI = RM \, [TAS + (OTV \times ASD \times ND)] \quad \text{(Eq. 4)}$$

The utilization of both the RIMS Type II Multiplier (available through the Bureau of Economic Analysis, U.S. Department of Commerce) and the IMPLAN Multiplier (available from the Minnesota Implan Group) are discussed in the NASC report and neither value is specified as preferable. A third value, the REIM Multiplier, developed by Regional Economic Models, Inc., is also among those commonly available (Li, Hofacre & Mahoney, 2001), although it is not mentioned in the NASC Report.

While the NASC formula(e) were designed to help standardize calculations in economic impact studies, it seems that these methods may have fallen short of their goal. The most apparent concern is that of the number of permutations of Economic Impact possible through the number of user choices built into the recommendation. The choice of using either the first formula configuration or the second formula configuration will result in an obvious difference in final result (Total Visitor Spending versus Total Economic Impact). Additionally, and perhaps more subtly, if three commonly available multiplier values are available, and a fourth choice of a self-generated or otherwise-selected value is possible, there are up to five different terminal values for economic impact that could be calculated through the NASC formula(e)—even if all of the same estimates for number of visitors, visitor spending, and length of visit are used.

In addition to differences resulting from simple differences in user choice, intentional misuse or manipulation of the NASC standardized formula(e) is also clearly possible. One way this could be accomplished is by obtaining several multiplier estimates and then simply choosing the one with the largest value. There is nothing in the NASC recommendations that would prohibit this, nor is there any proviso that stops users from merely inventing a multiplier value that is much larger than any accepted and calculated values. In all such cases, users could exercise these different manipulations and still maintain that they were operating within all NASC recommendations.

CASE ANALYSIS USING NASC METHODOLOGY

An economic impact study was conducted at a mid-major NCAA Division I school's football games during the 2006 season. The purpose of the study was to estimate the economic impact that these games had on the local community as a result of direct visitor spending within the community.

At each of the five home games during the 2006 season, a survey questionnaire was administered to a random sample of respondents. Information sought on the questionnaire included the amount of money spent (or estimated to be spent) during their time in the local community. The following categories of spending were included: groceries, convenience store, fast food, restaurants, lodging, game expenditures, retail shopping, fuel, bus/taxi/shuttle, rental car, entertainment, and other. An average of 431 surveys were collected from visitors during each of the five home games. Total visitor spending was then calculated.

From Equation 1, we get $TVS = OTV \times ASD \times ND$. Out of town visitor spending averaged \$29.97 per person over the entire season. There was an average of 12,821 visitors to games in the local community in 2006. The number of days was equal to the number of games, five. Therefore,

$TVS = 12,821 \times \$29.97 \times 5$

$TVS = \$1,921,226.85.$

Equation 2, $DS = TVS + TAS$, measures direct spending. As TVS = \$1,921,226.85 (from Eq. 1), we must now determine Total Administrative Operations Spending (TAS). That season, the athletic department calculated that it spent approximately \$90,000 on game operations. So, direct spending for the 2006 football season was:

$DS = \$1,921,226.85 + \$90,000$

$DS = \$2,011,226.85.$

After calculating direct spending, total economic impact can be calculated (Eq. 3). As $TEI = DS \times RM$ and DS = \$2,011,226.85 and the regional multiplier for the local community is 2.0424, total economic impact is

$TEI = \$2,011,226.85 \times 2.0424$

$TEI = \$4,107,729.72.$

Utilizing the full version of the formula (Eq. 4), the equation would take this form:

$TEI = RM \, [TAS + (OTV \times ASD \times ND)]$

$TEI = 2.0424[\$90,000 + (12,821 \times \$29.97 \times 5)]$

$TEI = \$4,107,729.72.$

Utilizing the methodology put forth by the NASC, Equations 2–4 are used as a community option. The report stresses that Equation 1 is a simplified method of reporting economic impact; however, it truly does not measure the economic impact of an event because the secondary effects of visitor spending are ignored. Using only Equation 1 in this study would have led to a calculation of economic impact being \$1.9 million, or \$2.2 million less than the actual impact on the local economy if Equation 4 was used. By providing an option to use Equation 1 or Equation 4 (the stepwise combination of Equations 1–3), the NASC leaves room for confusion over what the true impact is. It is highly recommended that for all events, Equation 4 be used.

It is also important to note that this formula really measures *economic benefit* rather than economic impact. As Crompton (1995) noted, the costs associated with hosting the event must be subtracted from the benefits gained. As Agah (2002) noted, most economic impact studies are actually economic benefit studies, as they fail to make a distinction between economic benefit and economic impact. There is an important difference between economic benefit and impact. Economic benefit measures only the economic gain in the local economy. Economic impact, then, is the total economic gain or loss after accounting for the event's costs. True economic impact studies will account for losses in the local economy due to the studied event.

The NASC methodology actually measures economic benefit because the costs associated with hosting the event are not subtracted from Total Economic Impact. Recall that Equation 4 states that Total Economic Impact equals the Regional Multiplier multiplied by Direct Spending. Local costs associated with hosting the event are not subtracted from the formula. These costs include items like vandalism, police and fire protection, and garbage collection. Equation 4 is not a true measure of economic impact and should be modified. So, prior to calculating Total Economic Impact (TEI), Economic Costs (EC) must be removed:

$$TEI = RM\ [TAS + (OTV \times ASD \times ND)] - EC \qquad (Eq.\ 5)$$

With this equation, economic impact is accurately calculated as it determines net benefits to a community rather than gross benefits.

CONFLICTING STATEMENTS BY ECONOMISTS

It should come as no surprise that within the complex marketplace of ideas there exist conflicting statements by economists as to whether or not sport and sport tourism development projects are worthwhile.

There is certainly no shortage of experts who extol the virtues and benefits of these projects. Increasingly, though, many economists and other scholars are speaking out to challenge these assumptions. Among them, the aforementioned Art Rolnick has flatly stated that "if you want to try to make a case that we should invest public money in sport teams, it really shouldn't be based on what's good for this economy. You're going to lose that debate" (Horwich, 2004).

Still other researchers see questions about the value of sport-related projects as complicated, and not lending themselves to easy answers. One doctoral dissertation on the subject noted that while "mounting evidence suggests that sports stadia have only marginal economic impacts upon the metropolitan economy," economic impact studies have reached these conclusions largely by utilizing the entire metropolitan area as the unit of analysis, rather than the districts and neighborhoods, or "microareas," which are most proximate to these development projects. This study suggests that merely changing the focus, or level of analysis, of these economic studies has far-reaching implications for understanding the value and impacts of sport-related projects (Chapin, 2001).

Economics Is a Social Science

It is worth remembering that the social science of economics has long been jokingly referred to as the "dismal science," perhaps partially because of the pessimistic historical predictions made by early economists such as Thomas Malthus. Malthus became famous for suggesting (over 200 years ago) that unchecked world population growth would accelerate exponentially and would soon result in widespread famine and strife.

Incidentally, most of Malthus' predications have failed to materialize due to what has been commonly seen as his failure to take new and emerging information into account. The lesson of Malthus should not be seen as a general criticism of the science of economics, but rather as a cautionary footnote to understanding the discipline's limitations.

Economic questions most often involve dynamic, rather than static, analyses of collective human behavior—and these analyses are not limited to discrete mathematical formulae, but also should include insights from psychology, sociology, geography, political science, and other fields. The bottom line: economic questions, and the ways in which researchers attempt to address them, are complex and always changing. Studies attempting to gauge the economic impacts of sport development are no exception.

While many researchers work hard to develop, standardize, and advocate appropriate methods for undertaking these studies, it may turn out that there is no one "best way" to design economic impact studies of sport-related developments because of the tremendous diversity of project types and settings. However, if this is a truism, then it is one that imposes very real limitations on our ability to meaningfully compare results between studies, and to think of any study as much more than a "best guess" based on the available information.

With that in mind, the only true problem with these studies may be our failure, unintentional or otherwise, to realize and accept these limitations.

Summary

It should be quite apparent that measuring the economic impact of sport facilities, event operations, and team activities requires a solid understanding of economic theory. In this chapter you were exposed to the laws of supply and demand, opportunity costs, and how these theories are used in the sport industry.

There are many uses of economic impact studies in sport, and many ways in which the results are used. Teams and event organizers use these studies to justify public funding or support. Opponents of public funding can use the results to support their opposition. One must be wary of potential abuses of economic impact studies, and compare the results with previously gathered information.

The study of economic impact in sport is an art, not a science. It is, however, an essential part of the financial makeup of the sport industry.

DISCUSSION ACTIVITIES

1. Select a sport event and try to locate a related completed economic impact study. Look for inconsistencies, common errors, etc.
2. Examine the money you spent on the last vacation you took. Calculate how the money may have been re-spent, both in and out of that community.

References

2002 Winter Olympic games. (2003). Retrieved January 16, 2008, from http://olympicstudies.uab.es/eng/yellow/dir/et.html

Agah, N. (2002). Choosing the optimal area of economic impact. *Sports Economics Perspectives, 1*(2), 1–17.

Brown, M., Nagel, M., McEvoy, C., & Rascher, D. (2004, December). Revenue and wealth maximization in the National Football League: The impact of stadia. *Sport Marketing Quarterly, 13*(4), 227–235.

Chapin, T. S. (2001). *Urban revitalization tools: Assessing the impacts of sports stadia at the microarea level.* Thesis abstract, University of Oregon, Eugene. Retrieved October 5, 2004, from SPORT Discus database.

Crompton, J. L. (1995, January). Economic impact analysis of sports facilities and events: Eleven sources of misapplication. *Journal of Sport Management, 9*(1), 14–25.

Fort, R. D. (2003). *Sports Economics.* Upper Saddle River, NJ: Prentice Hall.

Foster, G., Greyser, S. A., & Walsh, B. (2006). *The business of sports*. Mason, OH: Thompson Southwestern.

Hoffer, R. (2007, July 16). The king of Texas. *Sports Illustrated, 107*, 64–72.

Horwich, J. (2004, April 7). *Financial experts see "psychic income," plenty of risk in stadium deal.* Transcript of Minnesota Public Radio. Retrieved September 30, 2004, from http://news.minnesota.publicradio.org/features/2004/04/08_horwichj_bizstadium

Hudson, I. (2001, February). The use and misuse of economic impact analysis: The case of professional sports. *Journal of Sport and Social Issues, 25*(1), 20–24.

Humphreys, J. M., & Plumber, M. K. (2004). *The economic impact of hosting the 1996 Summer Olympics.* Retrieved January 15, 2008, from http://www.selig.ugs.edu/forecast/olympics/OLYMTXT.HTM

Li, M., Hofacre, S., & Mahoney, D. (2001). *Economics of sport.* Morgantown, WV: Fitness Information Technology.

NASC. (2000, October). *Economic impact study.* Cincinnati, OH: Author.

Noll, R. G., & Zimbalist, A. (1997). The economic impact of sports teams and facilities. In R. G. Noll & A. Zimbalist (Eds.), *Sports, jobs, & taxes* (pp. 55–91). Washington, DC: Brookings Institute.

Rosentraub, M. S., (1997, April). The myth and reality of economic development from sports. *Real Estate Issues, 22*(1), 24–30.

The fans, taxpayers, and business alliance for NFL football in San Diego. (2002). Retrieved January 15, 2008, from http://www.ftballance.org/stadiums/impact.php

Trevision, J. (2004). Racetrack's potential economics effect difficult to gauge. *The Oregonian.* Retrieved October 7, 2004, from http://www.oregonlive.com/motorsports/orgonian/index.ssf?/base/sports/109393538759060.xml

Turco, D. M., & Kelsey, C. W. (1992). *Conducting economic impact studies of recreation and special events.* Alexandria, VA: National Recreation and Park Association.

Yarbrough, C. R. (2000). *And they call them games: An inside view of the 1996 Olympics.* Atlanta: Mercer University Press.

Chapter Six

SPORT FINANCE

TOM REGAN · MATTHEW BERNTHAL

"UNLIKE ANY OTHER BUSINESS IN THE UNITED STATES, SPORTS MUST PRESERVE AN ILLUSION OF PERFECT INNOCENCE. THE MOUNTING OF THIS ILLUSION DEFINES THE PURPOSE AND ACCOUNTS FOR THE IMMENSE WEALTH OF AMERICAN SPORTS. IT IS THE CEREMONY OF INNOCENCE THAT THE FANS PAY TO SEE—NOT THE GAME OR THE MATCH OR THE BOUT, BUT THE RITUAL PORTRAYAL OF A WORLD IN WHICH TIME STOPS AND ALL HOPE REMAINS PLAUSIBLE, IN WHICH EVERYBODY PRESENT CAN RECOVER THE BLAMELESS EXPECTATIONS OF A CHILD, WHERE THE FORCES OF LIGHT ALWAYS TRIUMPH OVER THE POWERS OF DARKNESS."

—LEWIS H. LAPHAM

LEARNING OBJECTIVES

After studying this chapter, the student should be able to

- Understand the relationship between accounting and finance;
- Identify the elements of a balance sheet, income statement, and budgets;
- Understand the relationship between the balance sheet, income statement, and the statement of cash flow;
- Understand the concept of time value of money;
- Understand the type of bonds that are used to fund public assembly facilities; and
- Discuss how to analyze financial information.

Introduction

The financial aspects of the sport industry have grown exponentially in the last 20 years. A sport manager must be able to assess the operations of his or her team, league, conference, municipality, or other organization in order to make informed financial decisions. Consider the following recent developments in the sport industry:

- Liverpool FC agreed to a takeover offer worth 218 million pounds ($431 million) from U.S. sports tycoons George Gillett and Tom Hicks, five days after Dubai's ruler abandoned a bid for English soccer's most successful team.

- Dubai International Capital's later bid for the Liverpool FC Premier League was an offer for $800 million that was turned down, one year after the Hicks and Gillett purchase.

- New York's "Meadowlands Stadium" is expected to cost $1.3 billion.

- The 2012 Olympics is expected to raise the United Kingdom's Gross Domestic Product (GDP) by 1.9 billion pounds (or $374 billion) for the worldwide event.

- *Forbes* reports team values: Dallas Cowboys—$1.5 billion, Manchester United—$1.45 billion, New York Yankees—$1.2 billion, New York Knicks—$608 million, Toronto Maples Leafs—$413 million, Roush/Fenway Racing—$316 million.

- The NCAA announced a $6 billion, 11-year contract with CBS Sports that will expand the network's exclusive right to televise the NCAA Men's Basketball Tournament.

Financial analysis of sport organizations is often very difficult because of their inconsistent structure. The *vertical integration* of current professional sport organizations makes financial analysis very difficult for the casual observer. The degree to which a firm owns its suppliers and its buyers is referred to as vertical integration. Professional sports organizations want to be able to own the team, the media market, and related entertainment outlets.

For example, The Tribune Company owns the Chicago Cubs, super station WGN, and operates extensive television, radio and thirteen newspaper outlets throughout the world. It is often difficult to understand the financial statements relative to the sport-related activities of these multi-national corporations. The Atlanta Braves are owned by Time Warner, the cable and media conglomerate who bought them in 1976 for $12 million.

It is often difficult to find the sport-related financial statements within the filings of these multi-national corporations.

Sport organizations, not unlike individuals, are ultimately concerned with *cash flow*, or the amount of money earned relative to the amount of money paid. For example, consider purchasing a car. Your thoughts may include the following: How much cash do I have on hand? Do I have a car to trade? What are my payments going to be? How much should I borrow, if any? What does my income (cash inflow) need to be in order to make my monthly payment? Should I even buy this car? Do I need it? What benefit is it going to provide? Can I get by with a less expensive car? What if I lose my job? This process is part of *personal financial management*.

The Miami Heat traded Shaquille O'Neal to the Phoenix Suns during the 2007–2008 season. The trade required a significant financial commitment from the Suns' budget-conscious owner Robert Sarver because O'Neal is scheduled to make $20 million in 2007–2008 and $20 million more in the following two seasons. Shaquille O'Neal will change the franchise value of the Phoenix Suns. Robert Sarver purchased the Suns for $401 million in 2004. Before this trade, Forbes estimated the Suns to be worth $449 million, making them the 8th most valuable NBA franchise. But because Shaquille O'Neal is a one-man brand and his name brings such visibility to the team he plays for, *Sport Business Journal* indicated that Shaq's arrival adds anywhere from $25 million—$50 million to the franchise value of Sarver's team. Some experts noted that when Heat owner Mickey Arison acquired Shaq, the franchise value increased by $40 million. Therefore, as a manager, your thoughts might include the following: How much cash do I have on hand? Do we have players to trade? What is my payment going to be? How much should I borrow, if any? What is my income (cash inflow) going to be in order to pay for Shaq? Will season tickets and sponsorship increase? Should we even trade for Shaq? Do we need him? What benefit is he going to provide? Can we get by with a less expensive player? What if he gets hurt? This process is part of *business financial management*.

Importance of Finance in Sport

The goal of this chapter is to introduce basic concepts of business financial management in a sport environment. Sport finance utilizes the same business principles as any organization, except it usually involves players in professional sport as assets. Sport also is highly integrated in the public sector (city, county, state, and federal governments to a degree). The objective is to maximize profit through sound financial decisions.

Professional, college, and amateur sport organizations are borrowing money at record levels. New facilities are being built, remodeled, and expanded at a record pace. It is essential for these organizations to have adequate capital and profit to assure creditors that the assets are secure. Banks, mortgage companies, and insurance enterprises are diligent in lending money, because they certainly do not want to repossess an arena or stadium. What would a bank or other financial lending institution do with a new stadium?

Accounting Is a Partner to Sport Finance

Financial analysis requires useful information. A company's suppliers, creditors, and shareholders have an interest in analyzing a sport organization's financial performance. They need assurances that the sport enterprise has liquidity and solvency to meet short-term debts. Long-term creditors are concerned with projected profitability because they seek assurances that the company will be able to service its debt over several years. Public sport enterprises now must make financial decisions with the aspect of maximizing shareholder wealth. Sport stockholders, like public corporate shareholders, need to assess the potential cash flows and the inherent risks in order to estimate the future price of the common stock.

Analyzing financial performance begins with financial statements. The balance sheet, income statement, and the cash flow statement are the starting point for evaluating the current condition and financial future of the company. Further explanation and examples of the financial statements will occur later in the chapter. A few questions should arise when looking at financial statements:

1. Can the current debts be satisfied from the current liquidity (cash) position?

2. Is the company's long-term debt position overextended, or can the company borrow more money to alleviate liquidity problems?

3. What is the cash flow of the enterprise?

4. What is the debt to cash flow ratio of the company?

5. Why is the sport enterprise more or less profitable than other comparable sport enterprises?

6. Is management aggressive or conservative concerning credit arrangements?

7. How does management's decision to enter the sport business compare to returns gained from non-sport-related business enterprises?

Each of these questions requires information to be gathered in order to make sound decisions. The balance sheet and income statements are essential to initiate an analysis of any business enterprise. Sport managers must exercise caution when reviewing financial statements. Audited financial statements have been compiled by a third party and are independent of the company's accountants and financial officers. Internal financial statements are the product of the financial officers and have not had the scrutiny of an independent auditor. Answers to the questions will involve analysis from financial statements, ratio, trend analysis, and cash flow interpretation.

DATA GATHERING

How does one obtain financial statements for an enterprise that is not a public entity? Professional sport franchises will not provide you with a copy of the financial statements on request. Therefore, you may not be able to obtain the statements for comparison with other teams or franchises. Publicly traded companies will have audited financial statements for shareholders to review and for the potential investing public to access. Sounds great, but the reality is the sport-related business will be part of a larger asset on the balance sheet, such as entertainment division or sport properties. It will not have the baseball or hockey team financial statements broken out for your review.

Gathering data is not a simple process. Public agencies are required by the Freedom of Information Act (FOIA) to provide data if requested. The following is a short synopsis of the FOIA that will assist you in gathering data on public colleges and universities, teams that are publicly traded, and other government agencies.

The *Freedom of Information Act*—"FOIA" or "the Act"—is a law enacted in 1966 that established citizens' statutory right to access government records and information upon request. The basic purpose of FOIA is to ensure an informed citizenry, vital to the functioning of a democratic society, needed to check against corruption and to hold the governors accountable to the governed. Basically, the public or any individual has the right to know or be informed about activities, decisions, and policies of U.S. federal agencies.

The financial statements and related summary material(s) are part of the financial records. A record refers to any document, writing, photograph, sound, or magnetic recording, drawing, computerized record (disks, database), electronic mail, policies, and company decisions or other materials from which information can be retrieved and/or copied. The balance sheet, income statement, statement of cash flows, and other specifically stated financial documents can be reviewed if not a confidential or privileged document.

Can you request such a document? Yes. Corporations, associations, public interest groups, private individuals, universities, and local, state, or foreign governments can all submit FOIA requests. The FOIA is a frequent vehicle for citizens to gain access to public records. You have the freedom to request these documents. Access the site www.aclue.org/library/foia.html to access letters and other legal information that will be helpful in data gathering.

Other sources for data gathering include a request to the Chief Financial Officer for access to the financial information or a written request to the Board of Directors (if available). These requests will probably be unsuccessful. Financial data may have to be gathered from third parties, league contracts that are public (such as television and radio contracts), sponsorships, and revenue sharing. Next, a financial forecast will have to be completed to estimate revenue streams for the team and/or league. You will need attendance figures, ticket prices, merchandise and concessions sales estimates, parking data, luxury and club seating revenues, and other miscellaneous income.

Third party revenue and expense projections may also be available from regional newspapers, trade journals, and sport business journals. *Financial World*, *Sport-Business Journal*, and the *Sporting News* routinely estimate net income and losses for teams, conferences, and leagues. The NCAA produces a document named the "Revenues and Expenses of Intercollegiate Athletics Programs," an analysis of financial trends and relationships. The document is a very good basis for financial comparison of all NCAA division classifications.

ORGANIZATIONAL STRUCTURE

Like any other business, sport has various organizational structures. The structure of the sport organization is vital to the financial analysis necessary to maximize profit. Sport companies exist in three major forms: sole proprietorship, partnership, and corporation. Each differs in legal, tax, and business management, and must be a concern when analysis occurs.

A *sole proprietorship* is a company owned by one person. In sport, many of the original professional franchises were sole proprietorships. This has changed because of

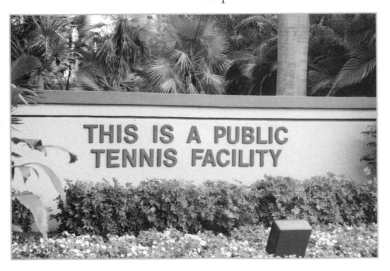

the enormous capital necessary to finance the sport organization. A *partnership* is a company owned by two or more individuals who have entered into an agreement. A partnership agreement will determine how the partners share in the debt and profits of the company. Unless specifically stated in the agreement, all partners will share equally in debt and profit. A *corporation* is a company formed by an agreement between the state and the persons forming the company, with the state requiring legal documentation of the agreement. The agreement must be filed with the Secretary of State. A corporation (called a C Corp) is a separately taxable entity. The profits and losses are taxed directly to the corporation. This can lead to double taxation on dividends that are paid out of corporate profits to the owners.

Special corporations exist in sport business. One special structure is called an *S corporation*, which is simply a C corporation (also known as a standard business corporation) that files IRS Form 2553 to elect a special tax status with the IRS. The articles of incorporation that are filed with the state are the same, whether a corporation is a C corporation or an S corporation. The main difference is a pass-through tax entity—this means that the income or loss generated by the business is reflected on the personal income tax return of the owners. Another special company is called a *limited liability company*, or *LLC*, which is a business entity formed upon filing articles of organization with the proper state authorities and paying all fees. LLCs provide the limited liability to their members and are taxed like a partnership, preventing double taxation. LLCs can be formed in every state. LLCs are now popular company structures in sport organizations.

IMPORTANCE OF ORGANIZATIONAL STRUCTURE

The key to financial management is to structure the sport organization to maximize profit, limit liability, and provide opportunity for infusion of capital for growth. Each company has differences in tax issues, cash flow, and liability. Managing these companies requires knowledge of accounting, finance, and taxation issues. It should be noted that owners of corporations pay taxes twice. They pay taxes as the corporation and, as shareholders, pay taxes on cash dividends they receive from the corporation.

Revenue Sources

Revenue sources for sport franchises have become increasingly diverse in recent years, with teams finding new and creative ways to generate income. Teams generate revenue through sources as standard as ticket sales and facility naming rights, and as creative as advertising on stadium/arena turnstiles, offering fans off-season trips with players, pre- and post-game fan entertainment opportunities and even online auctions of traditional memorabilia and "game experiences" (e.g., retrieving a tee after a kickoff at a football game) (Sold to the Man in Red and Yellow!, 2007). The escalating costs of operating profitable professional sport franchises, seen most visibly in dramatically escalating player salaries, have increased the importance of the generation and maintenance of successful and consistent revenue streams. As standard practice, revenues of franchises are generated through numerous sources, including ticket sales, sponsorships, luxury suites, club seating, media revenue, licensing/merchandising, and concessions and parking. Indeed, a team's annual revenue is linked directly to its market value. For example, NFL franchises are commonly valued at three to four times net revenue, while MLB teams are valued at between two to three times net revenue (CEO Network Chat, 2003). The New York Knicks, the NBA's most valuable franchise, earn over $195 million in annual revenue (NBA Team Valuations, 2007). The purpose of this section is to provide a brief illustrative example of the primary revenue sources for sport organizations. Each of the sources is briefly described below.

TICKET REVENUE

Ticket revenue accounts for a significant portion of revenue for sport franchises, though the proportion that it contributes to total revenue varies by league. The NFL, for example, generates approximately two-thirds of its revenue from media rights and merchandising. Each of the NFL's teams receives an equal share of revenue from these two categories. Other leagues that are less media-rich, such as the NHL, and certainly the numerous minor leagues of professional sports, as well as colleges and universities, rely on ticket sales to generate a larger proportion of their revenue. Ticket revenue is distributed differently among the four major American professional sports leagues. Approximately two-thirds of each NFL team's ticket revenue goes to the home team, while the other third is put into a pool that is shared by all of the other teams. MLB teams also share ticket revenue, with 30 percent of this revenue shared among the teams in the league and 70 percent going to the home team. NHL and NBA teams, on the other hand, keep their ticket revenue, often called the "gate" (CEO Network Chat, 2003).

The significance of the gate can be seen in the steadily increasing ticket prices in sport. The average NFL ticket now costs $62.11, the NBA's $48.83, the NHL's $48.72, and MLB's $22.21 (Team Marketing Research, 2007). Further, many franchises have increasingly turned to *variable pricing* to increase ticket sales and revenue. Variable pricing refers to pricing different events at different levels according to fan demand. Many teams have raised ticket prices for games that have higher demand due to factors ranging from playing a rivalry team, the presence of a superstar on a visiting team, or when the game is played. For example, the New York

Mets charge up to twice as much for tickets when the cross-town rival Yankees are visiting. For the 2008 season, the Seattle Mariners have seven "premium" games on their schedule, including Opening Day and home games against the high-profile Boston Red Sox and New York Yankees. The Mariners add a flat $3 fee to all tickets for these games (Hickey, 2007). The University of South Carolina Gamecocks football team, as a collegiate example, charges significantly higher ticket prices for games against high-profile opponents such as The University of Florida, The University of Georgia, and Clemson University, and lower prices for games against opponents such as Vanderbilt and South Carolina State. The bottom line with this increasingly popular variable pricing is to increase revenue by catering to fluctuating fan demand. Teams boost their revenue by capitalizing on high-demand games and offering lower prices on low-demand games.

SPONSORSHIP

Sponsorship can be broadly defined as a company or brand building equity through association with a specific event, team, athlete, or league (see Chapter 8). Sponsorship marketing represents an enormous revenue source for sport organizations. Even relatively poorly performing teams such as the Houston Texans of the NFL can, and do, generate significant sponsorship revenue. IEG (International Events Group) estimates that North American sponsorship spending will rise 12.6 percent in 2008 to $16.78 billion, which would be the biggest increase since 2000. Of this $16.78 billion, nearly 70 percent, or $11.6 billion, is expected to be spent on sponsorship of sport properties (Klayman, 2008).

As an example of the significant revenue provided by sponsorship, the Beijing Organizing Committee for the 2008 Olympic Games (BOCOG) is likely to garner more than $1 billion in local sponsorships, a figure that prominently factors into the forecast of the Beijing Olympics' being the most profitable Olympic Games in history (Beijing to Set Record, 2008).

Sport organizations sell sponsorship in many forms including, but not limited to, advertising (e.g., venue signage, programs), promotional opportunities tied to the sport property, the right to service the event or facility (e.g., Coors having exclusive beer service rights to Colorado Rockies events), and naming rights to event facilities. Examples of naming-rights deals for big-league, minor league, and NCAA facilities, which provide an increasingly large portion of sponsorship revenue, are provided in Table 6.1.

To an extent, sponsorship revenue is limited only by a sport organization's creativity. For example, sports teams can sell signage alone in numerous categories, including on scoreboards, marquees, the playing surface itself, the facility concourse, turnstiles, game programs, media guides, team newsletters, and the backs of tickets, to name but a few. Further, teams can sell sponsorship of fantasy camps, school assemblies, coach's clinics, and the like. Sponsorship opportunities can range from the relatively small (e.g., $500 for the right to drop coupons from a small blimp hovering just over seats at a minor league baseball game or NCAA basketball game), to the seemingly astronomical, such as the $10 million per year for naming rights to Reliant Stadium in Houston, home of the Houston Texans.

Sponsorship opportunities offered by sport organizations have grown exponentially in recent years, as has the associated revenue. North American-based companies, for example, are projected to spend an estimated $3.5 billion in 2008 to sponsor motorsports teams, tracks, and sanctioning bodies, a nine percent increase from the $3.2 billion spent in 2007, and over twice as much as was spent in 2004 (Motorsports Sponsorship Spending, 2008).

LUXURY SUITES AND CLUB SEATING

Luxury suites and club seating provide another major revenue source for sport franchises, and the percent of team revenue accounted for by this source has steadily increased over the past two decades. Luxury suites are special areas provided for premium seating and entertainment. Club seats provide the patron with special amenities such as wait staff, food and beverage service, and special parking privileges. Indeed, it is the revenue potential of luxury suites and, to a lesser extent, club seating that has been the major catalyst in the boom of new sport venue construction and the upgrading of existing venues.

Table 6.1. Naming Rights

Facility	City/School	Price (millions)	No. of Years	Tenants
Big-League Facilities				
Reliant Stadium	Houston	$300 million	30	Houston Texans, Houston Livestock Show & Rodeo, Houston Bowl
FedEx Field	Landover, MD	$205 million	27	Washington Redskins
American Airlines Center	Dallas	$195 million	30	Dallas Mavericks, Dallas Stars, Dallas Desperados (AFL)
Philips Arena	Atlanta	$185 million	20	Atlanta Hawks, Atlanta Thrashers
Minute Maid Park	Houston	$170 million	28	Houston Astros
Minor League Stadiums				
Raley Field	Sacramento	$15 million	20	Sacramento River Cats (PCL)
KeySpan Park	Brooklyn, NY	$10 million	20	Brooklyn Cyclones (NY-Penn)
PGE Park	Portland	$8.52 million	10	Portland Beavers (PCL), Portland Timbers (USL), Portland State U. football
Fifth Third Field	Dayton, OH	$6.5 million	20	Dayton Dragons (MI)
Fifth Third Field	Toledo, OH	$5.0 million	15	Toledo Mud Hens (IL)
Minor League Arenas				
Qwest Center of Omaha	Omaha, NE	$14 million	15	Creighton U. men's basktball, U. Nebraska-Omaha ice hockey
Wells Fargo Arena	Des Moines, IA	$11.5 million	20	To Be Determined
Verizon Wireless Arena	Manchester, NH	$11.4 million	15	AHL Manchester Monarchs
Allstate Arena	Rosemont, IL	$10 million	10	AFL Chicago Rush, AHL Chicago Wolves, DePaul U. men's basketball
Dunkin' Donuts Center	Providence, RI	$8.3 million	10	AHL Providence Bruins, Providence College men's basketball
NCAA Division I-A Football & Basketball Facilities				
Save Mart Center	Fresno State U.	$40 million	20	
Comcast Center	U. of Maryland	$20 million	25	
Jones SBC Stadium	Texas Tech U	$20 million	20	
Value City Arena	Ohio State U.	$12.5 million	Indefinite	
Cox Arena at Aztec Bowl	San Diego State U.	$12 million	Indefinite	

Source: *Street & Smith's SportsBusiness Journal*, Vol. 6, Issue 36, pp. 10–14

Although the University of Miami football team is neither building a new stadium nor renovating the Orange Bowl, it is moving to Dolphin Stadium where its revenue will increase significantly because of the presence of luxury suites in Dolphin stadium and the lack of such suites in the Orange Bowl. The average Fenway Park suite was leased for $283,000, with a ten-year minimum. When you consider that Fenway Park has 40 such suites, the significance of this revenue stream becomes clear (Reed, 2007). The University of Louisville's basketball team, the most profitable in the country, brought in $10.5 million in the 2006/2007 season from contributions directly tied to premium seating. Its state rival, the University of Kentucky, generated $7 million through 7,000 seats at Rupp Arena during the same season (Schwartz, 2008). Table 6.2 gives the average high and low prices for luxury suites and club seats for venues in MLB, the NFL, the NBA, and the NHL, along with the average quantity of suites and seats for each league.

Table 6.2. Luxury Suite and Club Seat Prices and Quantities

League	Suite Quantity	Suite Low Price	Suite High Price	Club Seat Quantity	Club Seat Low Price	Club Seat High Price
MLB	76	$100,397	$200,072	4,039	$3,456	$5,379
NFL	142	64,061	196,578	7,846	1,955	3,201
NBA	88	137,418	281,053	1,997	6,590	9,121
NHL	96	124,933	261,933	2,096	6,104	8,351

Source: Revenues from Sports Venues, http://www.sportsvenues.info.htm

MEDIA REVENUE

Media revenue is another major source of capital for professional sports leagues and franchises, and new media deals in recent years have increased the proportion of total league and franchise revenue accounted for by broadcasting rights. The importance of media revenue, particularly from television rights, as a source of capital cannot be overstated in today's sports business climate. Indeed, media revenue covers the vast majority of payroll expenses for some franchises with low payrolls, such as the NBA's Los Angeles Clippers. The NFL leads the four major pro leagues in broadcast rights, with ABC, Fox, CBS, and ESPN paying $17.6 billion, or $2.2 billion per season, to broadcast NFL contests from 1998 to 2005.

More recently, Fox signed a $4.27 billion, six-year extension, CBS signed a $3.73 billion, six-year extension, and NBC a $3.6 billion, six-year deal. The NFL also has an $8.8 billion deal with ESPN (through 2013) for "Monday Night Football" rights. Further, the NFL has a $3.5 billion deal with DirecTV that takes them through 2010. The NBA is also heavily supported by broadcast rights revenue, taking in $4.6 billion over the 2002 through 2008 seasons, averaging $766.7 million per season. Over the 2001 through 2006 seasons, Major League Baseball earned $2.5 billion in broadcast rights revenue from Fox, and has a $2.37 billion, eight-year deal through 2013 with ESPN (U.S. Digital Media Rights, 2006). These organizations earn additional media rights revenue from both terrestrial and satellite radio.

Other sports organizations also benefit significantly from media revenue. NASCAR, for example, has a deal with ABC/ESPN, Fox, and TNT for broadcasting rights through the 2014 season. NBC is paying $894 million for all domestic media rights to the 2008 Olympic Games, $820 million for the 2010 Games, and $1.18 billion for the 2012 Games (U.S. Digital Media Rights, 2006). Collegiate sports also benefits from broadcast rights, with the NCAA earning an astronomical $6 billion from CBS alone for the rights to broadcast the NCAA Men's Basketball Tournament as well as 66 other championships for 11 years (through the 2012–2013 season) (*Street & Smith's,* 2004).

LICENSING AND MERCHANDISING

Licensing and merchandising provide yet another source of revenue. Licensing is a contractual agreement whereby a company may use another company's intellectual property in exchange for a royalty or fee (Shank, 2005). Within the sport industry, this most often takes the form of selling the right to use team names and logos to companies (termed the licensee), or selling logoed apparel and other logoed merchandise. Generally, for this right, the licensee pays the sport organization (the licensor) 6 percent to 10 percent of gross sales of the licensed merchandise at wholesale, and this is termed *royalty revenue* for the licensor. Items beyond team names and logos can also be and are licensed. Facility names and designs, advertising slogans, mascots and their nicknames, and even terms or characteristics specifically associated with the sport organization can be licensed in order to generate revenue. As an example of the latter, the NFL secured the rights to the term "Dirty Bird" after it was popularized by the Atlanta Falcons during their Super Bowl season of 1998 (Irwin, Sutton, & McCarthy, 2002). The NFL secured the rights as opposed to the Falcons because the NFL collects licensing revenue for the entire league and distributes it evenly among the league's teams. Sharing of licensing revenue among teams is standard in some form among the four major American pro sport leagues, and each league has a form of a "properties" division that approves licenses and combats trademark infringement (e.g., counterfeiting).

Events and tour sports also generate revenue from licensing. For example, the Kentucky Derby licenses its name and logo to grace products such as bobblehead jockey dolls, steel Derby parking signs, model cars, calendars, mint julep glasses, beer mugs, and paper napkins.

The PGA Tour licenses its brand to a restaurant chain (PGA Tour Grill), cleansing wipes, gourmet food snacks, bracelets, and other products. NASCAR teams benefit from sales of licensed merchandise as well. Dale Earnhardt Jr.'s licensing, for example, is estimated to bring in over $30 million annually, accounting for approximately one-third of all NASCAR merchandise sales (Browne, 2007).

Licensing is big business. According to LICENSE! Global Research, estimated worldwide retail sales of licensed sport products were $19.3 billion in 2006 (Browne, 2007), up from $17.9 billion in 2002. The NFL accounts for more than $3 billion per year of sales of licensed sport products, with more than 100 licensees under contract (Schiller, 2007). The 2007 Super Bowl alone generated $140 million in licensing revenue for the NFL (Schwartz, 2007). The other top licensees in the sport product category are MLB, the NBA, and Collegiate Licensing Co., which as the nation's largest collegiate licensing and marketing organization, handles licensing for more than 180 universities, conferences, the NCAA, bowl games, and the Heisman Trophy. NASCAR and the NHL also contribute significantly to the retail sales figures. These figures represent retail sales of licensed merchandise, of course, and not direct revenue to the sport organizations granting the licenses. However, when again considering the fact that sport organizations generally earn 6 to 10 percent of wholesale sales (sales of licensees to retailers), the impact of licensing revenue is apparent.

Table 6.3. Retail Sales of Sports Licensed Apparel in U.S. and Canada		
YEAR	SALES (in billions)	% +/−
2003	$4.21	18.6%
2002	$3.55	13.6%
2001	$3.125	−9.4%
2000	$3.45	−6.8%
1999	$3.70	−9.8%
1998	$4.10	NA

SportsBusiness Daily, published July 29, 2004

CONCESSIONS AND PARKING

Food and beverage sales account for an additional source of team and venue revenue, and sports teams have taken advantage of the increasing number and variety of concession items available to them to increase their concession revenue. This is the case even for the numerous teams that allow fans to bring food into the stadium, such as the Arizona Diamondbacks, Anaheim Angels, and Philadelphia Eagles. The vast majority of teams contract out their concession services, and, on average, teams retain 35 percent to 45 percent of concession sale dollars. Some industry experts put the average net concession revenue for MLB ballparks, for example, at just over $4 million. Assuming that the teams retain an average of 40 percent of this revenue, this equates to an average of roughly $1.75 million in annual concession revenue for a MLB club. However, with the litany of menu items available to sports fans today, this can mean significant money. Not only do today's fans enjoy the standard fare, such as hot dogs and burgers, they may also choose from seafood items such as crabcake sandwiches and salmon, various wraps, ethnic fare such as Mexican, Italian, and Chinese, and even vegetarian and vegan cuisine now tempt them. Fans also enjoy a much wider range of beverage selections in many venues, from a wide assortment of microbrew beers to premixed alcoholic beverages, such as Bacardi Breezers. Indeed, many of the newer sport venues have food courts that would rival those of the most upscale shopping malls. Odds are if you can find it at a restaurant, you can find it at a stadium or arena.

Teams are also increasingly offering fans easier access to concessions to increase sales. For example, FastBreak cards are offered at many venues through Sportscorp Ltd. ("Not Waiting," 2003). These cards are pre-paid concession and merchandise debit cards that allow fans to use an express line devoted to FastBreak users and "pay with plastic," an ever-increasing consumer preference. At its Joyce Center and Notre Dame Stadium, The University of Notre Dame has followed in the path of many professional and college venues by utilizing "blink" technology, a credit card reading technology offered by Chase Card Services. This technology allows contactless card payment and thus helps speed concession lines, helping fans get back to the action as quickly as possible (Fighting Irish, 2007). By making it easier for fans to purchase concessions, it is likely that the increasing proliferation of this technology across sport venues will lead to increasing concession revenues in the future.

Estimates of per fan spending range from $8–$10 at basketball and hockey games, $10–$12 at baseball games, and $12–$15 at football games (Isidore, 2003). Indeed, for many minor league teams that have relatively low ticket prices and thus a smaller proportion of team revenue accounted for by ticket sales, concession sales can significantly impact profitability (Howard, 1998). Concessions are often accounted for in the same category as parking revenues, and combined, can add significantly to a team's bottom line. Some teams have even begun to use special "concession ticket packages" to entice more fans to games. For example, the Texas Rangers have offered $29 tickets with unlimited concessions for 600 seats at The Ballpark in Arlington (Marta, 2007).

Financial Statements

Financial information is only as good as the statements or detail gathered from the company. Standards are set in most countries to conform to a set of common practices in accounting. In the United States, these common standards are called *generally accepted accounting principles (GAAP)*. GAAP is a combination of authoritative standards (set by policy boards) and the accepted ways of doing accounting. Two private organizations, the American Institute of Certified Public Accountants (AICPA) and Financial Accounting Standards Board (FASB), in addition to the Security Exchange Commission (SEC), an agency of the Federal Government, are the regulatory bodies that help determine GAAP.

BALANCE SHEET

A *balance sheet* is a snapshot of the financial condition of a business at a specific moment in time, usually at the close of an accounting period. A balance sheet comprises assets, liabilities, and owners' or stockholders' equity. Assets and liabilities are divided into short- and long-term obligations, including cash accounts such as checking, money market, or government securities. At any given time, assets must equal liabilities plus owners' equity (A = L + OE). An asset is anything the business owns that has monetary value. Liabilities are the claims of creditors against the assets of the business.

A quick synopsis for the balance sheet will help in your understanding. Assets—items of value owned by a company; total assets equal debt plus shareholder equity. Debt—money a company owes; debt equals total assets less shareholder equity. Equity—Owners' investment in a company; equity equals total assets less debt.

The basic accounting equation is:

Total assets = Total liabilities + shareholder equity

Each time the company enters into a financial transaction, the snapshot of the company changes, demonstrating how the accounting equation is a balance between the separate sections of the equation.

INCOME STATEMENT

An income statement, otherwise known as a profit and loss statement, is a summary of a company's profit or loss during any one given period of time, such as a month, three months, or one year. The income statement records all revenues for a business during this given period, as well as the operating expenses for the business.

Table 6.4. Income Statement	
Gross sales	Revenue from sales and services
Less: Cost of good sold	Cost of goods sold to produce the sales
Gross profit	Gross income or gross earnings
Less: Operating expenses	Selling and administrative expenses
Earnings before interest and taxes (EBIT)	Net operating income
Less: Interest expense	Interest paid on short- and long-term debt
Earnings before taxes	Income, or profit, before payment of tax
Less: Taxes	Federal, state, and local income taxes
Earnings after taxes (net income or loss)	Income, or profit (loss) after taxes

CASH FLOW STATEMENT

The *statement of cash flow* shows the sources and uses of cash for your business over a certain period of time. This period coincides with the reporting period of the income statement. For example, if a cash flow statement covers the 12 months ended on December 31, 2009, the associated income statement covers the same period. A cash flow statement shows how your business performs on a cash basis. An income statement shows how your business performs on an accrual basis. In this respect, a cash flow statement generally supplements the information provided in an income statement.

Financial statement analysis requires understanding the strengths and weaknesses of the company. A student of sport finance should be able to understand where problems may occur and what questions need to be addressed. It is often more important to understand the weaknesses than to focus on the financial strengths of the enterprise.

PRO FORMA STATEMENTS

Data often must be forecasted and *pro forma statements* generated to analyze a situation. *Pro forma* ("as if") financial statements have traditionally been statements based on hypothetical figures used as a means of assessing how assets might be managed under differing future scenarios. The company's financial statements are adjusted to reflect a projected or planned transaction. A "what-if" analysis is applied to consider future asset gains, revenue increases, and related financial activity due to changes that may occur.

A pro forma income statement is similar to a historical income statement, except it projects the future rather than tracking the past. Pro forma income statements are important tools for planning future business operations. If the projections predict a downturn in profitability, you can make operational changes, like increasing prices or decreasing costs, before these projections become reality.

Pro forma income statements provide an important benchmark or budget for operating a business throughout the year. They can determine whether expenses can be expected to run higher in the first quarter of the year than in the second. They can determine whether or not sales can be expected to be above average in June. They can determine whether or not your marketing campaigns need an extra boost during certain months. All in all, they provide you with invaluable information—the sort of information you need in order to make the right financial choices for your business.

To create a pro forma statement, analyze an income statement from the current year. Consider how each item on that statement can or will be changed during the coming year. Ideally this should be done before year's end. You will need to estimate final sales and expenses for the current year to prepare a pro forma income statement for the coming year.

Budgets and Financial Analysis

Budgets affect all aspects of a company. Three types of budgets are commonly found in most companies. They assist the other major departments by providing financial information, but each area is responsible for the accuracy of the budgets. Three types of budgets are commonly found in most companies. They are the *cash*, *revenue*, and *expense budgets*. Each budget has a specific purpose and assists the managers in decision making. Budgeting is about decision making and can provide useful information for important decisions, such as building a new arena, offering player salaries, increasing ticket prices, expanding club seats, moving the franchise, investing in additional marketing activities, etc. These decisions require all departments to work together and provide valuable information for decision making.

CASH BUDGETS

Cash is essential in the sport business because of the seasonality of operations. Cash is often received during season ticket sales and major sponsorship deals. The management of the cash requires timing and planning to estimate cash inflows and outflows.

The management of cash resources holds a central position in the area of short-term financing decisions. Results of investment decisions are estimated in cash terms and the value of a company. In other words, if we are going to expand our arena, how much cash do we have on hand to meet short-term payments, and if we need to borrow money, how much should we borrow?

Cash management is part of the wider task of the business manager, which covers not only the management of the company's cash in the normal course of business—making sure the company always has enough cash on hand to meet its bills and expenses, and investing any surplus cash—but other things as well. Examples include arranging suitable mixes of short-, medium-, and long-term borrowing, and dealing with major fixed asset costs that may include new facilities, upgrades to stadiums, and/or signing bonuses for players and coaches.

The central premise for a cash budget is to record cash when received and record cash when spent. Think of it as your checkbook. You record deposits when made and record expenses when checks are signed and mailed. When the deposits are made, there is a cash inflow; when a check is written, there is a cash outflow.

Though a simple example, the key to successful cash management is timing.

A cash budget is focused on liquidity management. Liquidity means being able to receive cash within approximately ninety days from the sale of assets. These assets are usually current assets and easily transferable to cash. Sources of cash in sport may include but are not limited to the following:

- Ticket sales
- Concessions
- Parking
- Programs
- Club seats
- Luxury boxes
- Signage
- Television and radio sponsorships
- Borrowing money—line of credit
- Sale of assets
- Subsidy from a government agency
- Grants

Uses of cash include many of the major line items in the income statement related to expenses. Operating expenses are the major outflows of cash in a company. Following is a partial list of the major expenses that affect a cash budget.

- Operating expenses
- Payroll and payroll tax patterns
- Purchases of materials/supplies (seasonal factors)
- Debt service (principle, interest and balloon payments)
- Income and other taxes, (EBIT, property tax)
- Capital expenditures, (down payment, retainage)
- Other (bonuses, interest expense, subsidy)

Other factors that are essential when starting a cash budget include an estimated beginning balance for cash, desired or required cash balance at the end of a period, and always the need to forecast borrowing and repaying debt.

REVENUE BUDGETS

Revenue budgets are essential for decision making. Company managers must be able to project future revenue for planning and management decisions. Revenue budgets in sport are usually straightforward. Revenue is recorded when earned. The matching concept states, "Expenses incurred in earning revenues are matched against the revenues." Whatever revenues your company earns during a certain period, you match the appropriate expenses that you incurred in earning those revenues during the same period.

For example, professional football season ticket renewals occur in February and March each year. Millions of dollars are received during these months in cash.

However, the games are played in September, October, November, and December. You receive cash in February and March, but you earn the revenue when the games are played in the September through December timeframe. Revenue is matched against the expenditures related to the players, stadium, and fans.

Sources of revenue will include ticket sales, contributions, dividends, interest earned, sales of company assets, luxury box sales, sales of services, concessions, television, bowl games, playoff games, stadium rental, sponsorship, and promotional activities to name a few. Budgets must address a future decision, as demonstrated by the following questions: Will our team make the playoffs or a BCS game? As these necessary questions reveal, winning does matter and even influences the budgeting process for many organizations.

EXPENSE BUDGETS

Expense budgets must closely identify with the revenue budgets because of the matching concept. Financial managers must be able to analyze expenses in relationship to the cash available to pay for the operational expenses incurred. Expenses are recorded when incurred. This means that professional athletes are paid when they play the game and not before, unless a special contractual arrangement exists.

Operational expenses have fixed and variable cost components. Financial managers must be aware of these expenses when making decisions on financial matters.

- **Expense**—any cost of doing business resulting from revenue-generating activities.
- **Operating expense**—expense arising in the normal course of running a business, such as an office electricity bill.
- **Variable expenses**—unavoidable periodic costs that do not have a constant value, such as electric, gas, and water bills.
- **Non-variable** or **fixed cost**—a cost that does not vary depending on production or sales levels, such as rent, property, insurance, or interest expense.
- **Semi-variable cost**—a cost that has a fixed cost component and a variable expense component.
- **Step cost or discretionary expense**—a recurring or non-recurring expense for goods and services that are either non-essential or more expensive than necessary; examples include entertainment expenses, wellness programs, and speakers.

Each expense item affects the cash outflow of a company, and this determines the need for proper cash management. Cash flow is essential in the sport business because of the nature of when the cash is received and when the expenses occur.

Budgets will help address the following issues. (1) The future is often uncertain. What problem or advantage will tomorrow bring? (2) The prices of goods and services will increase (inflation). A dollar today will buy less in the future. (3) Will an investment today earn a positive return? Budgets are annual events with a three- to five-year projection for planning. That is why cash in hand is worth more than cash in the future.

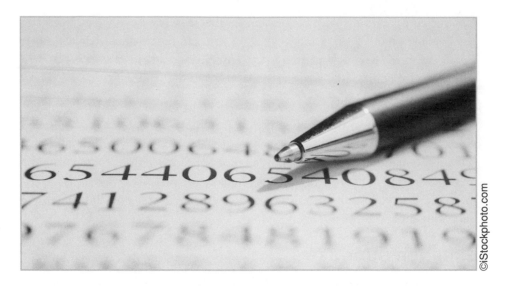

©iStockphoto.com

BUDGETS AND FINANCIAL DECISION MAKING

Budgeting is a planning and controlling activity for the decision maker. Budget preparation prioritizes future company plans in a formalized process. A budget expresses these priorities and plans in financial terms. All departments of the company are involved in budgeting, even though many might believe otherwise. Astute employees can see the company vision by the money allocated to their department or area of interest. Accountability follows money; money is allocated during the budget process and managers must be knowledgeable in accounting and finance in order to attain the company goals.

The time value of money serves as the foundation for all other notions in finance. It impacts business finance, consumer finance, and government finance. Time value of money results from the concept of interest.

Sport Finance Essentials

The introduction to simple interest and compound interest illustrates the use of time value of money tables, shows a matrix approach to solving time value of money problems, and introduces the concepts of intra-year compounding, annuities due, and perpetuities. A simple introduction to working time value of money problems on a financial calculator is included as well as additional resources to help understand time value of money. *Simple interest* is a topic that most people cover in elementary school. Interest may be thought of as rent paid on borrowed money. Simple interest is calculated only on the beginning principle. For instance, if someone were to receive 6 percent interest on a beginning value of $100, the first year they would get: .06 × $100—or—$6 in interest. *Compound interest* is another matter and the preferred way to handle financial decisions. It is good to receive compound interest, but not so good to pay compound interest. With compound interest, interest is calculated not only on the beginning interest, but on any interest accumulated in the meantime. For instance, if someone were to receive 5 percent compound interest on a beginning value of $100, the first year they would get the same thing as if they were receiving simple interest on the $100, or $5. The second year, though, their interest would be calculated on the beginning amount in

Figure 6.1.

year 2, which would be $105; thus .05 × $105 or $5.25 in interest. The following graphs will depict the differences between simple and compounded interest.

Figure 6.1 indicates that simple interest is the same from period to period. However, compound interest increases at a quicker rate due to the process of compounding. You earn more money if investing with compound interest, and have to pay additional money if borrowing with compound interest.

The time value of money concepts will be grouped into two areas: future value and present value. *Future value* describes the process of finding what an investment today will grow to in the future. *Present value* describes the process of determining what a cash flow to be received in the future is worth in today's dollars. The equations for present value, future value, present value of an annuity, and future value of an annuity are shown below.

Table 6.5. Annual Compounding

PV = Present Value	FV = Future Value	CF = Cash flow
R = Interest rate	PMT = Payment	T = Time (years)

Present Value:
$$PV = \frac{CF_t}{(1 + r)^t}$$

Future Value:
$$PV = FV_t = CF_0(1 + r)^t$$

Present Value of a Cash Flow Stream:
$$PV = \sum_{t=0}^{n} \frac{CF_t}{(1 + r)^t}$$

Future Value of a Cash Flow Stream:
$$FV_t = \sum_{t=0}^{n} CF_t(1 + r)^{n-t}$$

Present Value of an Annuity:
$$FVA = PMT \left[\frac{1 - (1 + r)^{-t}}{r} \right]$$

Future Value of an Annuity:
$$FVA_t = PMT \left[\frac{(1 + r)^t - 1}{r} \right]$$

Following is a situational analysis of a golf course. The example will be utilized as a basis for analysis and explanation.

It is necessary to understand accounting to analyze financial information. To assist in this effort, the following case problem describes a start-up sports enterprise. You are to formulate a balance sheet and income statement over a five-year period from the facts given. This is a golf course. The data given is provided to determine your working knowledge of accounting and basic finance.

The facts in the case study are:

1. Borrow $600,000 at 8 percent over 10 years from Bank of America.
2. Investor provides $400,000 to fund your sports enterprise.
3. Long-term assets depreciate on a straight-line basis over 20 years.
4. Short-term assets depreciate over five years using the straight-line basis.
5. Green fees—7,000 rounds at $20 per round. Increases 875 rounds per year.
6. Driving range revenue—3,424 units @ $5 per customer. The units increase at 428 per year.
7. Annual memberships—192 @ $250 per year. Increases by 24 memberships each year with no decrease in initial members.
8. Initiation fees were $14,000 in the first year and increase $1,750 per year.
9. Pro shop revenue was $48,000 and increases $6,000 per year.
10. Bar/lounge grossed $18,400 the first year and increases $2,300 per year.
11. Cost of Goods Sold:
    Pro shop: Year one $35,200 and increases $4,400 per year.
    Bar/lounge: Year one $11,200 and increases $1,400 per year.
12. Other given information:
    Salaries: $115,420—increases $3,463 per year.
    Utilities: $1,000—increases $100 per year.
    Maintenance: $600—increases $75 per year.
13. Spent $800,000 on a building.
    Spent $100,000 on land.
    Spent $7,500 on equipment.
    Spent $16,000 on inventory. Inventory increases by $2,000 per year.
14. Accounts payable is $10,000 in years one through year five.
15. Purchase an additional $750 per year in equipment starting in year two (2).
16. Accounts receivable balance year end $8,040. Increases $1,005 per year (2–5).
17. Don't forget interest expense. Don't forget depreciation expense.

Income tax expense should be calculated at 34 percent.

PREPARE BALANCE SHEET AND INCOME STATEMENTS
FOR A FIVE-YEAR PERIOD.
Use the following format.

SPORT GOLF ENTERPRISES

BALANCE SHEET

Assets:		Year 1	Year 2	Year 3	Year 4	Year 5
Cash	$					
Accounts receivable						
Inventory						
Other current assets						
Total current assets	$					

Property, Plant and Equipment

		Year 1	Year 2	Year 3	Year 4	Year 5
Land	$					
Building						
Equipment						
Accum. Depreciation						
Total PP&E						
Total Assets	$					

Liabilities and Owner Equity:

		Year 1	Year 2	Year 3	Year 4	Year 5
Current installments of long-term debt	$					
Accounts payable						
Total current liabilities.						
Long-term debt	$					
Other L-T liabilities						
Total liabilities						

Owner's equity:

		Year 1	Year 2	Year 3	Year 4	Year 5
Owner's equity	$					
Retained earnings						
Total equity						
Total liabilities & equity	$					

SPORT GOLF ENTERPRISES

INCOME STATEMENT

Revenues:		Year 1	Year 2	Year 3	Year 4	Year 5
Green fees	$					
Driving range						
Annual membership dues						
Membership initiation fees						
Pro shop						
Bar/lounge						
Total revenues	$					
Less: Cost of goods sold						
Pro shop						
Bar/lounge						
Total COGS	$					
Gross profit	$					
Operating expenses						
Salaries	$					
Utilities						
Maintenance						
Depreciation						
Total operating expenses	$					
Earnings before interest expense						
Interest expense						
Earnings before income tax						
Income tax expense						
Net income (loss)	$					

It is difficult to analyze financial information without understanding the relationship of the balance sheet and the income statement. Accounting classes from an applied basis discuss debits and credits and worksheets are prepared. The theoretical concepts are discussed in the context of understanding the practice of accounting. This chapter requires a preparation of financial statements. You need to be able to create a balance sheet and income statement from financial information. This type of exercise will develop business skills necessary for financial analysis, budgeting, and forecasting.

HOW TO INITIATE AND ANALYZE

The income statement is the starting point. You need to record the revenue streams from the example. Calculate the revenue from green fees, driving range, annual membership dues, membership initiation fees, pro shop, and bar/lounge business activities. The next step is to calculate the cost of goods sold in the pro shop and the bar and lounge. The total cost of goods sold will be deducted from total revenues to produce gross profit or gross margin. Then expenses should be calculated and entered into the appropriate categories. Salaries, utilities, and maintenance are common expenses. Then we must calculate depreciation. *Depreciation* is an accounting concept that produces a non-cash expense associated with spreading (allocating) the cost of a plant asset over its useful life.

SPORT GOLF ENTERPRISES

BALANCE SHEET

December 31, 20xx

Assets:	Year 1	Year 2	Year 3	Year 4	Year 5
Cash	$100,058	$134,151	$184,407	$250,715	$333,004
Accounts receivable	$8,040	$9,045	$10,050	$11,055	$12,060
Inventory	16,000	18,000	20,000	22,000	24,000
Other current assets	—	—	—	—	—
Total current assets	$124,098	$161,196	$214,457	$283,770	$369,064

Property, Plant and Equipment

	Year 1	Year 2	Year 3	Year 4	Year 5
Land	$100,000	$100,000	$100,000	$100,000	$100,000
Building	$800,000	$800,000	$800,000	$800,000	$800,000
Equipment	$7,500	$8,250	$9,000	$9,750	$10,500
Accum. Depreciation	($41,500)	($83,150)	($124,950)	($166,900)	($209,000)
Total PP&E	$866,000	$825,100	$784,050	$742,850	$701,500
Total Assets	$990,098	$986,296	$998,507	$1,026,620	$1,070,564

Liabilities and Owner Equity:

	Year 1	Year 2	Year 3	Year 4	Year 5
Current installments of long-term debt	$44,731	$48,309	$52,174	$56,348	$60,856
Accounts payable	$10,000	$10,000	$10,000	$10,000	$10,000
Total current liabilities.	$54,731	$58,309	$62,174	$66,348	$70,856
Long-term debt	$513,851	$465,541	$413,367	$357,018	$296,163
Other L-T liabilities	—	—	—	—	—
Total liabilities	$568,582	$523,850	$475,541	$423,366	$367,019

Owner's equity:

	Year 1	Year 2	Year 3	Year 4	Year 5
Owner's equity	$400,000	$400,000	$400,000	$400,000	$400,000
Retained earnings	$21,516	$62,446	$122,966	$203,254	$303,545
Total equity	$421,516	$462,446	$522,966	$603,254	$703,545
Total liabilities & equity	$990,098	$986,296	$998,507	$1,026,620	$1,070,564

SPORT GOLF ENTERPRISES

INCOME STATEMENT

For the Years Ended December 31, 20xx

Revenues:	Year 1	Year 2	Year 3	Year 4	Year 5
Green fees	$140,000	$157,500	$175,000	$192,500	$210,000
Driving range	$17,120	$19,260	$21,400	$23,540	$25,680
Annual membership dues	$48,000	$54,000	$60,000	$66,000	$72,000
Membership initiation fees	$14,000	$15,750	$17,500	$19,250	$21,000
Pro shop	$48,000	$54,000	$60,000	$66,000	$72,000
Bar/lounge	$18,400	$20,700	$23,000	$25,300	$27,600
Total revenues	$285,520	$321,210	$356,900	$392,590	$428,280
Less: Cost of goods sold					
Pro shop	$35,200	$39,600	$44,000	$48,400	$52,800
Bar/lounge	$11,200	$12,600	$14,000	$15,400	$16,800
Total COGS	$46,400	$52,200	$58,000	$63,800	$69,600
Gross margin	$239,120	$269,010	$298,900	$328,790	$358,680
Operating expenses					
Salaries	$115,420	$118,883	$122,345	$125,808	$129,270
Utilities	$1,000	$1,100	$1,200	$1,300	$1,400
Maintenance	$600	$675	$750	$825	$900
Depreciation	$41,500	$41,650	$41,800	$41,950	$42,100
Total operating expenses	$158,520	$162,308	$166,095	$169,883	$173,670
Earnings before interest expense	$80,600	$106,702	$132,805	$158,907	$185,010
Interest expense	$48,000	$44,687	$41,108	$37,243	$33,069
Earnings before income tax	$32,600	$62,015	$91,697	$121,664	$151,941
Income tax expense	$11,084	$21,085	$31,177	$41,366	$51,660
Net income (loss)	$21,516	$40,930	$60,520	$80,298	$100,281

SPORT GOLF ENTERPRISES

STATEMENT OF CASH FLOW

For the Years Ended December 31, 20xx

	20xx	20xx	20xx	20xx
Cash flow from operating activities:				
Net income	$40,930	$60,520	$80,288	$100,291
Depreciation	$41,650	$41,800	$41,950	$42,100
Accounts receivable	($1,005)	($1,005)	($1,005)	($1,005)
Inventory	($2,000)	($2,000)	($2,000)	($2,000)
Current installment of long term debt	$3,578	$3,865	$4,174	$4,508
Net cash provided by operating activities	$83,153	$103,180	$123,407	$143,894
Cash flow—Investing activities				
Equipment	($750)	($750)	($750)	($750)
Net cash provided by investing activities	($750)	($750)	($750)	($750)
Cash flow—financing activities				
Long term note payable	($48,310)	($52,174)	($56,349)	($60,855)
Net cash provided by financing activities	($48,310)	($52,174)	($56,349)	($60,855)
Net increase (decrease) in cash	$34,093	$50,256	$66,308	$82,289
Cash—beginning of the year	$100,058	$134,151	$184,407	$250,715
Cash balance—end of the year	$134,151	$184,407	$250,715	$333,004

CASH FLOW—THE CONCEPT

The statement of cash flow explains "what happened to the cash?" This cannot be learned solely from the other financial statements (balance sheet and income statement). The statement of cash flows reports the entity's cash receipts and cash payments during a period of time. It answers the questions of where cash came from and where cash was spent. Analysis requires two periods of time, usually two fiscal years or calendar years to compare the balance sheet and income statements. The following flowchart will provide a visual relationship.

The balance sheet is important, but it just reports the cash balance at the end of a period. By comparing two consecutive balance sheets, you can determine the cash increases and or decreases during that specific time period. The curious student will inquire, why has cash changed? The income statement reports revenues and expenses, which results in net income or (loss). The income statement is often referred to as the statement of profit and loss, statement of operations, and the statement of sources and uses. However, the income statement alone doesn't answer why cash increased or decreased. Analyzing the balance sheet and income statement in conjunction with the statement of retained earnings will provide the reader with the information to determine why cash changed and explain the causes associated with this cash adjustment. Cash dominates the sports industry and therefore cash management is essential.

The statement of cash flow is essential for sport managers. They need to be able to make managerial and financial decisions based on cash availability. The purpose of cash flow is to:

1. Predict the future cash flows. Cash, not net income, pays the bills. Net income is not cash.

2. Evaluate management decisions. If general managers make wise investment decisions, the team and organization prosper. If the GM makes poor decisions, the team and organization suffer. For example, should the organization build a new stadium or facility (additions to property, plant, and equipment) with private or public funds? This management decision will impact the financial aspect of the organization for decades. A new facility will impact the ability of the organization to increase revenues. Factors that must be addressed include predicting the economy. If a recession is expected, will the new facility attract these anticipated revenues, or will the economy continue to expand and increase entertainment spending? Management's decisions impact investors' and creditors' cash-flow information.

3. Determine the ability to pay dividends to stockholders and interest and principle to creditors. Return on the stockholders' investment is necessary to maintain stock value, and dividends produce cash to these owners. Creditors (bondholders or financial institutions) want to receive the interest and principle payments on time. The statement of cash flow assists the investors and creditors in determining the capability of management in making these payments.

4. Analyze the business relationship between net income (income statement) and changes in cash (balance sheet). Cash usually increases when net revenues increase; however, sport organizations must make sure the new facility will produce this anticipated result. It should be noted

SPORT GOLF ENTERPRISES

DEPRECIATION SCHEDULE

For the Years Ending, 20xx

Asset Description	Cost/Basis	Method	Useful Life	Depreciation Expense 2008	Accumulated Depreciation 2008	Depreciation Expense 2009	Accumulated Depreciation 2009	Depreciation Expense 2010	Accumulated Depreciation 19 x 3
Building	$800,000	SL	20	$40,000	($40,000)	$40,000	($80,000)	$40,000	($120,000)
Equipment	$7,500	SL	5	$1,500	($1,500)	$1,500	($3,000)	$1,500	($4,500)
Equipment 20 x 2	$750	SL	5			$150	($150)	$150	($300)
Equipment 20 x 3	$750	SL	5					$150	($150)
Total Depreciation expense				$41,500	($41,500)	$41,650	($83,150)	$41,800	($124,950)

that cash could decrease when net income increases and increase when net income decreases. Therefore, the need for accurate cash management is essential for management in the sport and entertainment industry. For example, if a bonus is to be paid to a new free agent, will the organization have the cash on hand to pay the player or will the bonus need to be borrowed from a lending institution?

A TEMPLATE FOR CASH FLOWS:

Indirect Method—Step-by-Step Cash Flows

1. OPERATING SECTION:

➭ Start net income

➭ Add: depreciation

➭ Increase or decrease in current assets

➭ Increase or decrease in current liabilities

2. INVESTING SECTION:

➭ Increase or decrease in long-term assets—usually property, plant, and equipment and/or other long-term assets.

3. FINANCING SECTION:

➭ Increase or decrease in long-term debt and other long-term liabilities.

➭ Increase or decrease in owners' equity—common stock.

➭ Decrease cash for dividends paid.

See Sport Golf Enterprises' Cash Flows to follow template and flow of cash. The key to cash flow is sources and uses of cash. Where did the cash come from and where did it go? Accountants can calculate cash flow. Managers must be able to understand and analyze the details to assist the company in managing cash and other resources.

HOW TO PREPARE THE FINANCIAL INFORMATION

The Sport Golf Enterprises example previously reviewed shows how to prepare financial statements. The case study provided the revenue and expenses necessary to prepare the income statement. You must start with the income statement. Revenue is fairly easy to determine. You must prepare pro-forma estimates for revenue over a five-year period. Historical data and comparison to similar organizations will assist in this area. The organization determines ticket prices, and management must identify the number of paying customers. Calculating gross revenues requires identifying the prices for each round of golf. For example, will you charge green fees and cart fees at the same level during off peak golf times? Are golf carts required? Will you allow non-members to play?

Preparing the income statement requires a careful analysis of the estimated charges for the services rendered. Every revenue stream must be taken into account. In the case previously described you must clearly calculate the green fees, cart fees, driving range revenue, annual membership dues, membership initiation fees, pro shop, and the bar/lounge revenue. Each year stands by itself and requires management to project potential revenue growth per year. Accurate forecasts will lower the potential for miscalculations. Aggressive forecasts can overestimate revenue and therefore produce favorable net income projections.

The next step is to match the expenses with the related revenues in each category. Again, the matching concept is an accounting principle that states that all expenses incurred during the period be matched against the revenues earned during that same span of time. Therefore the following expense items must be forecasted for each year: cost of goods sold, pro shop expenses, bar/lounge expenses, salaries, utilities, maintenance, and depreciation expense. After these expenses are deducted from gross revenue, you must deduct interest expense and income tax to produce net income.

It should be noted that forecasts are produced through the budgeting projections. Forecasting revenue and expenses will not produce the actual numbers utilized to produce the statement of cash flow. Actual numbers will not equal budgeted or forecasted numbers produced from the pro-forma income statements. This is the reality of the financial aspect of the business. Good financial projections will show small variances between the projected and actual numbers by each individual account.

Variances are determined by comparing the forecast or budgeted number to the actual number produced from the operating activities. Variances can be positive or negative. A positive income statement variance occurs when actual revenue is greater than projected or budgeted revenue. A negative variance would be when actual is less than projected. Expense variance would produce a positive variance when actual expenses are less than projected and a negative variance would occur when actual expenses are greater than projected. Variances should be reviewed monthly and analyzed to determine the reason(s) for the variance. Management should determine if the pattern will continue and make adjustments to spending patterns or revenue patterns if necessary. For example, let's review Year 1 revenues:

	Year 1 Actual	Year 1 Budgeted	Year 1 Variance Positive (negative)
Revenues:			
Green fees	$140,000	$145,000	($5,000) actual less than budget
Driving range	$17,120	$27,120	($10,000) actual less than budget
Annual membership dues	$48,000	$42,000	$6,000 actual > budget
Membership dues	$14,000	$12,000	$2,000 actual > budget
Pro shop	$48,000	$48,000	$0 no change
Bar/lounge	$18,400	$20,400	($2,000) actual less than budget
Total revenues	$285,520	$295,520	($9,000) actual less than budget

The financial analysis must review each line item of the revenue section. Overall variance is a $(9,000) negative variance. This means actual revenue was $9,000 less than the budgeted revenue. Prudent financial analysis should identify the reason for each variance. The example uses small dollar amounts, however; identifying the reason is the principle that must be emphasized. Why is the driving range revenue $10,000 less than the actual amount? You should key into the largest variance initially, and then review the smaller variances. Each variance should be addressed in a written explanation. For example, driving range revenues may be $10,000 less than budgeted due to a delay in the construction of the driving range.

Bonds and Other Investment Instruments

An essential element to any sport organization is the facility it utilizes to play the game and entertain the fans in the community. The facility is the cash register and often the key to attract and retain the franchise. Often the financing of the public assembly facility is the most important factor for the community to retain or attract a franchise. College athletics are always expanding stadiums and building new arenas, utilizing public and private monies. Following are the major financial instruments utilized in financing public facilities.

In simple terms, a bond is a "security" that gives the holder a financial claim on the issuer. This claim protects the holder in circumstances in which the issuer is unable to pay the amount due. It is made formal by the "trust indenture," a legal document that specifies all of the bond's features and the legal rights and obligations of all the parties to the agreement. It should be noted that the legal documentation for a bond is required to specify the terms for both interest and principal payments. Interest can be paid monthly, semi-annually, or annually. This makes a difference to the compounding of the interest and will affect the trading of a bond.

Public assembly facilities include large indoor and outdoor stadiums, (50,000–100,000 seating capacity), arenas (12,000–30,000 seating capacity), and other entertainment-related, multi-purpose structures. These facilities become homes for professional, college, and minor league teams. Professional leagues require adequate facilities to become economically beneficial to the owners. Public assembly facilities are typically financed by three types of instruments:

1. General obligation bonds (GO bonds)
2. Revenue bonds
3. Certificates of participation

State and local governments issue bonds in the capital market to finance their capital spending programs for building arenas, stadiums, parking lots, and infrastructure upgrades. Infrastructure improvements often include roads, water/sewer, utility right-of-way, and other utility needs. Investors call these types of bonds *municipal bonds* or *munis*. The bonds are issued by municipalities (subdivisions of states). They are tax exempt because the interest investors receive is exempt from federal taxation. Most states exempt state income tax as well on the interest earned from their bonds. Each state will differ on tax policy and should be addressed on an individual tax basis.

General obligation bonds (GO) are those bonds that will be paid back through the taxing power of the issuing authority. These bonds are typically used to finance traditional capital projects such as highways, roads, and sewers. General obligation bonds are issued against the general full faith and credit of state and local governments. The issuing bodies (state, local, or regional government) generally require the use of *ad valorem taxes*. Ad valorem taxes are property taxes. This means taxes are levied according to the value of one's property; the more valuable the property, the higher the tax, and vice versa. The underlying theory of ad valorem taxation is that those owning the more valuable properties are wealthier, which results in a lower cost of issuance and higher credit rating, and the bond size is often reduced because a debt reserve fund is not always required. General obligation bonds are typically safe investments and are a very dependable source of revenue for municipal budgeting.

Revenue bonds are paid back from revenues generated by the specific project (e.g., stadium). The specific bond is serviced by the cash flows from the project. They are special obligations in public financing that are payable solely from a particular source of funds that may include tax/surcharge revenues from hotel/motel, restaurant sales, liquor/beer, cigarettes, rental cars, and other sources. The "sin taxes" (i.e., alcohol and tobacco taxes) have become very popular. Following are some of the sources utilized to fund public assembly facilities utilizing revenue bonds: hotel tax, meal tax, liquor tax, sales tax, auto rental tax, property tax, tax increment financing districts, business license tax, utility tax, public and private grants, state appropriations, taxi tax, and team tax. The key is that no pledge of state, regional, or local ad valorem tax revenues is required; however, the typical revenue bond does carry a higher interest rate and requires a higher debt services coverage ratio as well as debt serve reserve.

Certificates of Participation (COP's) are public financing instruments that involve the governmental entity creating a corporation to buy (build)—a public assembly facility such as an arena or convention and visitors' center. The corporation then issues certificates of participation to raise money to buy (build) the public facility. The government leases back the building and the lease payments are supposed to pay back the bonds. All this happens without a public vote.

Although certificates of participation seem like traditional bonds, they are not backed by the full faith and credit of the government entity that issues the bonds. In a recession-hammered environment, certificates of participation and lease appropriation financing become popular with local governments looking to fund projects as real estate values decline, and with them property tax collections. These securities are not backed by the full faith and credit of a municipality. Therefore, they are a greater risk than a general obligation bond and are rated lower.

Certificates of participation can be considered a high yield, or "junk," bond by a community or entity that is considered to be a higher credit risk. The credit rating of a high yield bond is considered "speculative" grade or below "investment grade." This means that the chance of default with high yield bonds is higher than for other bonds. Their higher credit risk means that "junk" bond yields are higher than bonds of better credit quality. Studies have demonstrated that portfolios of high yield bonds have higher returns than other bond portfolios, suggesting that the higher yields more than compensate for their additional default risk.

Summary

Good financial planning is a roadmap to success. The revenues produced from facilities and sport events can be significant, but the expense side of the formula cannot be overlooked. Revenue doesn't produce net income or profit. Revenue minus expenses produces net income or net loss.

In this chapter, we discussed the rudiments of financial statements and understanding financial terms and concepts. We discussed the inter-relationship between accounting and finance and how each is a separate course of study in business schools. Accounting and finance work together to produce useful financial information to managers. The chapter identified the importance of organizational structure and the impact on financial statements. Organizational structure is not just a management issue; it is a financial issue with tax implications.

A good financial roadmap will utilize financial statements and cash flow. The chapter discussed cash flow as it relates to sport organizations. Cash flow and budgeting are components of good financial decision making. Budgeting is a major part of decision making. The chapter identifies cash, revenue, and expense budgets and how timing (accrual) affects the budgeting process. During the budget process the time value of money (TVM) and investment of cash produces challenges to the manager to have cash available to pay bills, yet optimize the concept of TVM. The challenge for the manager is to balance cash on hand with good investments.

Sport finance is dependent on fan attendance. The fans produce the cash that transfers to net income or loss for the principals in sport organizations. Sport is a service industry, and sport finance is a key component of the business that assists managers by producing tangible information for decision making.

DISCUSSION ACTIVITIES

1. The authors identified many sources of revenue in professional and intercollegiate athletics. Using the sources provided, identify the main expense categories in college and professional sports.
2. Contact two organizations in the same sport and request their financial documents. Compare and contrast the information, and make a chart of current revenues, expenses, and overall financial position.
3. Using the *Sports Business Daily* (www.sportsbusinessdaily.com), conduct research into the broadcast rights fees of the four major professional leagues in North America. How are they different? What are the similarities?

References

Beijing to set record for Olympics revenue. (2008). *China.org.cn*. Retrieved March 7, 2008, from http://www1china.org.cn/english/sports/153121.htm

Browne, M. (2007, October 15). Sports: Industry annual 2007 report. *LICENSE! Global*. Retrieved February 25, 2008, from http://www.sbrnet.com/Publication.asp?function=detail&magid=163474

CEO network chat on the business of sports.

(2003, February 10). *Forbes.com*. Retrieved March 1, 2008, from http://www.forbes.com/work/2003/02/10/cx_ml_0210sportschat.html

Fighting Irish fans not chasing concessions with new debit card features. (2007, June/July). *Team Marketing Report, 19*(5), 4.

Hickey, J. (2007, December 17). Seattle Mariners raising ticket prices. *Seattle Post-Intelligencer*. Retrieved March 8, 2008, from http://seattlepi.nwsource.com/baseball/343969_maritix18.html

Howard, D. (1998). Financial principles applied to sport management. In L. P., Masteralexis, C. A. Barr, & M. A. Hums, (Eds.), *Principles and practice of sport management*. (pp. 70–71). Gaithersburg, MD: Aspen Publishers Inc.

Irwin, R. L., Sutton, W. A., & McCarthy, L. M. (2002), *Sport promotion and sales management*. Champaign, IL: Human Kinetics, 261.

Isidore, C. (2003, August 8). Life, liberty and hoagies. *CNN/Money*. Retrieved March 11, 2008, from http://money.cnn.com/2003/08/08/commentary/column_sportsbiz/sportsbiz/.

Klayman, B. (2008, January 22). North American sponsorship spending seen up in '08. *Sponsorship.com*. Retrieved March 8, 2008, from http://www.sponsorship.com/About-IEG/IEG-In-The-News/North-American-Sponsorhip-Spending-Seen-Up-In-08.html

Marta, S. (2007, August 22). Rangers test $29 tickets with unlimited concessions. *The Dallas Morning News*. Retrieved March 11, 2008, from http://www.dallasnews.com/sharedcontent/dws/bus/stories/082207dnbusrangers.30b6afe.html

Motorsports sponsorship spending to total $3.5 billion in 2008. (2008, February 16). *Auto moby.blogspot.com*. Retrieved March 10, 2008, from http://automoby.blogspot.com/2008/02/motorsports-sponsorship-spending-to.html

NBA team valuations. (2007, December 6). *Forbes.com*. Retrieved March 6, 2008, from http://www.forbes.com/lists/2007/32/biz_07nba_NBA-Team-Valuations_Revenue.html

NFL team valuations. (2007, September 13). *Forbes.com*. Retrieved March 6, 2008, from http://www.forbes.com/lists/2007/30/biz_07nfl_NFL-Team-Valuations_Revenue.html

NHL team valuations. (2007, November 8). *Forbes.com*. Retrieved March 6, 2008, from http://www.forbes.com/lists/2007/31/biz_07nhl_NHL-Team-Valuations_Revenue_print.html

Not waiting in long concession lines: Priceless. FastBreak cards improve fans' game experi-

ence (2003, December). *Team Marketing Report, 16*(3), 1, 3.

Reed, K. (2007, April 9). Fenway suites are even more luxurious. *Boston.com*. Retrieved March 10, 2008, from http://www.boston.com/business/articles/2007/04/09/fenway_suites_are_even_more_luxurious/

Revenues from sports venues. (2008, March 12). *Sportsvenues.com*. Retrieved March 12, 2008, from http://www.sportsvenues.com/info.htm

Schiller, G. (2007, February 2). Super Bowl drives NFL's rising revenues. *The Hollywood Reporter*. Retrieved March 11, 2008, from http://www.hollywoodreporter.com/hr/content_display/television/features/e3ic9dc7ecac0f2a973f3c4e7cbbafe945f

Schwartz, P. J. (2007, January 31). Super Bowl tops Forbes' most valuable brands. *ESPN.com*. Retrieved March 1, 2008, from http://sports.espn.go.com/espn/print?id=2749584&type=story

Schwartz, P. J. (2008, January 2). The most valuable college basketball teams. *Forbes.com*. Retrieved March 8, 2008, from http://www.forbes.com/sportsbusiness/2007/12/27/college-basketball-valuations-biz-sports_cz_js_0102basketball.html

Shank, M. D. (2005). *Sport marketing: A strategic perspective* (3rd ed.). Upper Saddle River, NJ: Pearson Education, Inc., 235.

Sold, to the man in red and yellow! Iowa State holds online auction to benefit athletic department. (2007, April/May). *Team Marketing Report, 19*(4), 5.

Sports Business Research Network. Prepared by Mediaventures. (2007). Retrieved January 21, 2008, from http://www.sbrnet.com.pallas2.tcl.sc.edu/sbr/directory/directory.cfm?function=search&formType=Form5&MainSport=Football&Sport=Pro%20Teams:%20NFL

Street & Smith's SportBusiness Journal (2004). By the numbers 2004, *6*(36), 10–14, 84.

Team marketing research. (2007, August/September). *Team Marketing Report, 19*(6), 4, 6, 8.

The business of baseball. (2007, April 19). *Forbes.com*. Retrieved March 6, 2008, from http://www.forbes.com/lists/2007/33/07nmlb_The-Business-Of-Baseball_Revenue_print.html

U.S. digital media rights. (2006). *Sports Business Resource Guide & Fact Book*. Retrieved March 3, 2008, from http://www.sportsbusinessjournal.com/images/random/resource2006_E-116,117.pdf

Chapter Seven

SPORT MARKETING

JOHN CLARK

"I used to nag him about being a world-class couch potato. But that was before he landed a lucrative endorsement contract."

LEARNING OBJECTIVES

Upon completion of this chapter, students will be able to
- Define marketing and its role in sport;
- Distinguish between marketing and promotions;
- Understand the need for market segmentation; and
- Identify the need for market research.

Introduction

Think about the last time you attended or watched a professional sporting event on television. In addition to the game, you likely observed signs of companies throughout the arena or stadium, cheerleaders or a dance team, or a mascot roaming the sidelines or stadium rows entertaining fans. You may have heard the public address announcer talking about special offers or upcoming events and noticed entertaining elements on the scoreboard. If you were attending a professional baseball game and a hometown player hit a home run, there may have been a fireworks display. If you attended a baseball game in Milwaukee or Pittsburgh, in the middle of the game you may have seen sausages or pierogies racing in the park. If you attended a National Basketball Association (NBA) game in Indianapolis, you may have seen "Boomer," the Pacers mascot, repel from the rafters at the beginning of the game, or don a mask of the Grim Reaper and stand behind the opposing team's bench late in the game.

Most things seen or heard at a professional sporting event are specifically designed to enhance our experience at that game. The same holds true for sporting events we watch on television or the Internet. Technological advances have allowed broadcast networks and production companies to enhance our viewing experience, making it easier to follow the action by providing the viewer with more information, increasing the number of cameras, and taking the viewer "into the action" with enhanced audio/visual capabilities. The end result, whether the game is viewed in person or from the comfort of a living room, is an elaborate strategy designed to keep the fans coming back. In essence, that is what sport marketing is all about—compelling customers to consume the sport product once, knowing that if they have a good time and are more than satisfied with their experience, they will keep coming back.

Ask several industry experts what sport marketing is exactly, and several different answers will emerge depending on the area of the industry in which the respondent works. Any all-inclusive academic definition of sport marketing would certainly include something about each of the four Ps (product, price, promotion, and place) as they relate to the target consumers' behavior. It is beyond the scope of this chapter to tackle such a daunting task as creating *the* perfect definition for sport marketing; therefore, we will use a two-part definition from Mullin, Hardy, and Sutton (2000):

> Sport marketing consists of all activities designed to meet the needs and wants of sport consumers through exchange processes. Sport marketing has developed two major thrusts: the marketing of sport products and services directly to consumers of sport, and marketing of other consumer and industrial products or services through the use of sport." (p. 9)

"SPORT IS THE TOY DE-PARTMENT OF HUMAN LIFE."

—HOWARD COSELL

The latter portion of the definition—marketing other products or services through sport—refers to promotional licensing or sponsorship, and will be dealt with extensively in the following chapter. As for the part of the definition that deals with the marketing of sport products and services, it bears exploring *why* the sport marketing specialty is needed. In other words, how is sport marketing different from traditional marketing?

Purpose of Marketing

An important caveat must be stated at this point. The primary purpose of marketing, both in the traditional and sport context, is ultimately to increase revenue for an organization. Certain marketing strategies may not lead to immediate sales (e.g., brand awareness strategies), but even these strategies have as their ultimate goal increased revenue. Aspiring sport marketers must remember that their efforts should pursue the objective of increasing revenue either in the short or long term.

SPORT CONSUMERS

In professional sport, all conceivable marketing strategies would not amount to a penny were it not for consumers. Both core and ancillary products in spectator and participatory sport rely on consumers for success. Sport is woven into the fabric of society—locally, regionally, nationally, and internationally. In the words of NBA Commissioner David Stern, as he watched the Houston Rockets and Sacramento Kings play a preseason game in China, "Fans are fans" (ESPN, 2004). As such, we learn to consume sport at a young age, both as participants and as spectators. For a sport marketer, two basic consumer characteristics exist that help differentiate types of sport consumers. These two characteristics are *involvement* and *commitment*. According to Mullin, Hardy, and Sutton (2000), involvement can be behavioral (the actual doing of a sport activity), cognitive (seeking out information and knowledge about a sport), and affective (the feelings and emotions a sport consumer has for a particular activity or team).

Meanwhile, commitment refers to the frequency, duration, and intensity of involvement in a sport, or the willingness to expend money, time, and energy in a pattern of sport involvement (Mullin et al., 2000, p. 57). Sport is rife with examples of both of these consumer characteristics. For example, fans of the Boston Red

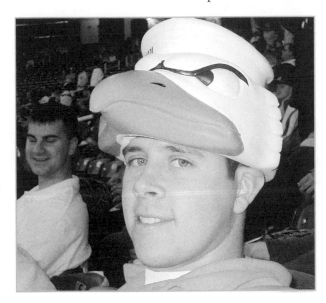

Sox continued to pack Fenway Park and drive up the ratings for Red Sox games on the New England Sports Network despite enduring over eighty years without a World Series title—that is, until recently. It seemed as if each October brought heartbreak to the Red Sox nation, as when the team was ousted from the American League playoffs by their hated rivals, the New York Yankees, in the year prior to their sweep of the World Series. Despite disappointments like this, each spring Red Sox fans would well up with optimism in anticipation of the upcoming season and the end of the "Curse of the Bambino." Red Sox fans were highly committed to their franchise and were heavily involved with each up and down of the season. One could tune into a Boston sport radio talk show on any day between February and October to hear the Red Sox fans complain, suggest trades, disparage poor play, and of course, deride the Yankees. Researchers contend that highly committed and highly involved sport consumers are more loyal than casual consumers; therefore, the sport marketer who can foster these characteristics in a consumer base will derive the benefits of a loyal customer base.

Involved and committed customers are important tenets of relationship marketing—a theory gaining increasing popularity in the sport world. According to Gordon (1998), relationship marketing is

> the ongoing process of identifying and *creating new value* with individual customers and then *sharing the benefits* [italics added] from this over a lifetime of association. It involves the understanding, focusing and management of ongoing collaboration between suppliers and selected customers for mutual value creation and sharing through interdependence and organizational alignment. (p. 9)

Howard Schultz, chairman and CEO of the Starbucks Coffee empire and the former owner of the NBA's Seattle SuperSonics (now the Oklahoma City Thunder), along with Anaheim Angels' owner Arturo Moreno, are two excellent examples of professional sport managers who went to great lengths to ensure their customers were an integral part of the franchise by incorporating value-added strategies throughout the franchise operations. Both of these owners created mechanisms to communicate directly with fans. More importantly, Schultz and Moreno incorporated customer feedback into the franchises' operations to improve the overall consumer experiences. These men understand that each game attended by a customer is a vote of confidence for the franchise, as well as a product trial.

The fans are spending their disposable income on event tickets and ancillary products and have certain levels of expectations about what their money will get them. Efficient, friendly service, comfortable seating in a clean facility, certain types of concessions, and an entertaining two to three hours are just some of these expectations. The key for a sport marketer to remember is that consumer expectations are unique to the individual, and whatever the consumer's individual perceptions may be, they are correct—at least for that individual consumer.

CONSUMER EXPERTISE AND IDENTITY

One other important aspect of sport consumers is the familiarity that most consumers have with their chosen pastimes. Many consumers have actually participated with their favorite sport on some level—whether that level was during their formative years, in high school or college, or in some recreational capacity. Having played the game, consumers are better able to identify with the action on the field, court, or track. For example, Bill France, founder of NASCAR racing, was adamant that early racers drive stock cars available to the average person. Early racing fans actually witnessed drivers race the same model of car they would drive to church or to the grocery store (Hagstrom, 1998).

Of course, this level of familiarity is a double-edged sword for a sport marketer. In Pittsburgh, Sunday afternoons during the football season find thousands of people second-guessing every move the Pittsburgh Steelers make—from play selection to player personnel issues. Of course Western Pennsylvania is a hotbed of high school football, so the level of familiarity with the sport makes it more likely that fans feel qualified to critique the Steelers organization. Whether the fans are actually qualified or not is irrelevant. It is each person's own perception of being qualified that heightens the individual and collective levels of commitment and involvement with the team. So, when a team starts to lose, these fans will voice their opinions.

The following section explains the four Ps of marketing: product, price, promotions, and place. Each of these areas is common to every product or service, but in the sport industry, each requires the sport marketer to consider the unique aspects of sport when determining what marketing strategy to use.

The Four Ps of Marketing

THE SPORT PRODUCT

Imagine that immediately after class, you and your classmates go to the school gym to play basketball. You play for one hour and then go on with the rest of your day. Exactly one week later, after the same class, you and your classmates go to the gym to play basketball again. Imagine the weather is exactly the same, everyone is wearing the same clothes, and you have all had the exact same breakfast food as the week before. You do everything within your control to replicate the conditions of that basketball game you played one week earlier. Even with all the efforts to ensure the game will be the same—will it? In the words of the famous John Wayne movie character Jacob McCandles (*Big Jake,* 1971), "Not hardly." Each and every sporting activity or game is different from one consumptive episode to the next.

This is part of sport's appeal, but this characteristic is problematic for the sport marketer because the core product is largely out of the marketer's control.

What if you had a job marketing Dial soap? To be more specific, say your job was to market the bath size, unscented bars of Dial soap. Due to production mechanisms and quality control programs, it is fairly certain that each bath size, unscented bar of Dial soap is the same as the next. The same cannot be said for a marketer of the Minnesota Vikings. One week, the Vikings may play flawless football, and the next, the Vikings offense may turn the ball over seven times. The crux of the issue is that the sport product is inconsistent and is largely out of the sport marketer's control.

Sport Production and Consumption

The next important difference between the sport product and traditional products deals with "when" the sport product is produced. Go back to the earlier example of the class playing basketball. The ball, the gym, the baskets, and the clothes people wear were all "produced" at a time before the actual game; yet those things combined do not create the experience. It is the actual game that produces the experience or product. Sport activities, similar to hotel rooms and plane flights, are produced in the same moment that they are consumed. Consequently, there is no inventory of the core product once the game is over. You cannot take empty seats and add them to the arena or stadium capacity the next home game; likewise, no one will buy tickets to yesterday's game or fight. That is why there is such a great emphasis in the industry to pre-sell the contest.

Core Product

If one were to list sport products, the first things to spring to mind would be spectator sporting events at all levels, participatory activities such as playing tennis or jogging, instructional lessons like karate or a session with a personal trainer, sporting goods (e.g., balls, golf clubs, equipment), and sport-related apparel (e.g., jerseys, hats). Most of these are usually considered part of sport's *core* product—the essential component to a sporting activity or event. These are all important aspects of the sport product, yet there are many more. Ticket stubs, programs, brochures, luxury suites, club seating, mascots, promotions, spirit squads, cheerleaders, broadcasts, and web pages are other components of the core product. In reality, a sport product can be anything related to a sport organization that has consumer demand, and in an industry where the ability to create new revenue streams is at a premium, sport marketers are always searching for new products to sell.

PRICING SPORT

Potentially one of the most controversial issues facing a sport marketer is how to price an activity, event, or sponsorship. Compounding this problem, at least for spectator sport, is the previously mentioned fact about the inconsistent nature of the core product. For example, a Michigan–Ohio State football game will almost always be more attractive to a majority of the country than a Michigan–North Dakota game. Even so, sport marketers must devise a pricing strategy that appears fair to the paying public, while at the same time being careful not to set the price too low, thereby leaving the proverbial money "on the table." In addition, a wrongly priced product could potentially lower the perceived value of the product. It was previously mentioned that perceptions by individual consumers, be they correct or incorrect, often dictate consumption patterns. Similarly, consumer perceptions about the cost of an event or activity relative to its value also dictate consumptive behavior. The benefits for a sporting event or activity range from health benefits to psychological benefits or sociological benefits. In the fall of 2004, Master Card International extended its "Priceless" ad campaign to include the Major League Baseball (MLB) playoffs by running a commercial asking Boston Red Sox fans what it would be worth to see the Red Sox in the World Series. Fans' responses ranged from "my first born" to "my right arm." The spot ends with the Master Card catch phrase, "Seeing the Red Sox win the World Series—Priceless." Clearly for Red Sox fans, seeing their team win the World Series had a value far beyond any monetary figure.

Price vs. Total Cost

Conversely, the cost of a particular event or activity reaches beyond the actual dollar figure paid for a ticket or equipment rental. Also factored into the equation is the time it takes to travel to and from the activity or event, the cost of giving up something else to partake in the sporting activity or event, or the psychological or social cost of participating in an activity or event. In addition to these factors, a sport marketer also has to consider how frequently a particular activity or event is offered. NASCAR can charge more for a Nextel Cup race than a MLB franchise can charge for a regular season contest because the Nextel Cup race is only once a year, as opposed to the 81 home regular season dates for a MLB franchise. The National Football League (NFL) also enjoys the benefit of having a limited supply of home games when it comes to pricing strategy. The eight regular season home games in the NFL allow member franchises to charge, on average, higher ticket prices across the league, compared to their other professional league counterparts.

Additional Benefits

Another factor in pricing strategy is the amenities offered as part of the activity or event. Most professional sport franchises offer premium services and graduated benefits to season ticket holders, depending on how many games are in the season ticket package and where the seats are located. An NFL season ticket holder purchasing club seats will receive access to a special area in the stadium with premium food, more luxurious surroundings, special parking privileges, the ability to purchase discounted merchandise at the team store, invitations to special season ticket holder parties, and other benefits. Meanwhile, the NFL fan who purchases season tickets in the upper level of the stadium may receive only the discounted merchandise and parking privilege benefits. Naturally, the club seating ticket package will cost more, as there are consumers who value those types of benefits and have no problem paying extra for them.

Variable Pricing

A recent pricing trend in the spectator sport industry has seen franchises and athletic departments incorporate variable pricing strategies into their marketing efforts. Variable pricing refers to charging higher amounts for more desirable games, and charging lesser amounts for the least desirable games. For example, assume the University of Wisconsin football team was to play Prairie View A & M one week, and the University of Michigan the following week. The Badgers would be expected by their fans to beat Prairie View handily, which would impact the demand for tickets. On the other hand, the University of Michigan game, along with being a Big 10 match-up, would also be perceived as a "big game" by the Badger fans, which would drive demand for tickets. If the University of Wisconsin were to implement a variable pricing strategy, it would charge a lesser price for tickets to the Prairie View game than it would for the Michigan game.

Competition

A final consideration when determining a pricing strategy is the sport organization's competition in the marketplace. By setting a much higher price than the competition, a sport organization may create a perception of a high-quality product; however, this could occur only if the core product and ancillary product components were of high quality as well. For instance, the Green Bay Packers, the only major professional sport franchise in their market, can set prices much higher than the University of Wisconsin-Green Bay athletic program or local high school athletic programs, without experiencing any detrimental effect on attendance. This is due to the Packers' storied history of success and the affinity Wisconsin residents statewide have for the Packers franchise. In this case, the higher price is consistent with the image and value consumers place on the Packers.

On the other hand, in a market with many affordable entertainment options for consumers to choose from, a high price may have a negative impact on consumption levels, especially if there are not enough affluent consumers in the marketplace who value the core product offering. In this sense, a pricing strategy should consider the disposable income levels of both current and future primary consumer segments. To illustrate, consider the fans of the NBA. On average, NBA season ticket holders hold white-collar jobs and possess higher than average household income and education levels—in short, people who can afford to pay for tickets that may cost on average between $20 and $50. Yet, the NBA has many fans that are younger and live in urban areas with below average household income and education levels. From a long-term perspective, the NBA may have to develop alternative pricing strategies that will enable these customers to consume NBA basketball with more financial ease.

In conclusion, there is no universally accepted formula for pricing sport products. The shrewd sport marketer must consider all of the factors described above as well as conduct a thorough examination of the marketplace to ensure that the pricing strategy employed will generate sufficient levels of revenue without driving away large groups of consumers who are unwilling or unable to pay the price.

PROMOTIONS

While attending a minor league baseball game, fans, during the break between half innings, are likely to see some sort of contest involving fans on the playing field. This may be a contest requiring contestants to place their forehead on a bat and spin around for several seconds before running to first base, or it may require the contestants to throw a baseball through a target to win a prize. These contests are promotional contests. In general, the term *promotion* encompasses advertising, publicity efforts, personal selling, and sales promotion in all of their varied forms. Promotions can be categorized in two ways: *price promotions* and *non-price promotions.* To determine which type of promotion to use, sport marketers must first understand what they hope to achieve through the use of promotions. Once these objectives are clear, then the appropriate promotional strategy can be employed.

Price Promotions

As its name implies, a price promotion manipulates the actual cost of consuming a sport activity or event. Two-for-one ticket promotions are a popular promotional strategy used by many sport organizations on both the professional and amateur levels. Other popular price promotions involve coupons, a donation of canned goods in exchange for free or discounted tickets, children gaining free admission with the purchase of an adult ticket, and family packages in which a family of four receives four tickets and discounts at the concession stand for one packaged price. Price promotions are used to increase attendance and are most effective when a sport organization is in a market where consumer demand for the core product is not strong or the customer base is price-sensitive. Used properly, price promotions can increase attendance for activities or events that would usually not have great appeal to the public.

However, a sport marketer must exercise caution when contemplating the use of price promotions. If discounted tickets or admission through the use of price promotions becomes the standard fare for the sport organization, the danger exists of cheapening the core product as perceived by consumers. For example, if a minor league hockey team has a buy-one-get-one-free price promotion for every Friday home game, consumers in that market may consider attending a hockey game only on a Friday, when they can get the tickets cheaper, as opposed to considering attending a hockey game on another night when the cost of admission is full price. Also, price promotions can anger full-paying season ticket holders who have already purchased their tickets and cannot take advantage of the discounted offer.

Non-Price Promotions

The other type of promotions—non-price promotions—include all other activities designed to make the activity or event more attractive and enjoyable to con-

Table 7.1. Top 15 promotional giveaway items and their impact on attendance in MLB, NBA, and NHL teams

Giveaway	Change from Average (%)	Total Attendance	Additional Tickets Sold	Number of games
Jack-in-the-box	20.7	89,957	15,407	4
Travel Mug	19.8	156,828	25,939	6
Ring	14.3	142,653	17,863	4
Bobblehead	12.5	1,532,414	170,400	53
Stuffed Animal	11.3	127,344	12,920	4
Puzzle	10.8	172,369	16,805	5
Backpack	9.7	193,133	17,057	8
Notebook	9.1	304,391	25,292	8
Clock	8.9	98,085	8,035	4
Figure	8.3	659,520	50,460	22
Batting Helmet	7.2	187,479	12,590	5
Rally Towel	6.8	357,775	22,831	10
Cap	6.2	1,780,670	104,209	52
Ball/Puck	5.7	604,558	32,628	19
Wristband	4.9	138,778	6,441	4

This list does not include giveaways held by fewer than four teams, fan activities (e.g., fireworks, concerts, etc.) or discounted ticket deals.

Source: Street & Smith's *SportsBusiness Journal*, October 18th-24th, 2004

sumers. Giveaways, fireworks, autograph-signing sessions, and concerts are examples of non-price promotions used to increase interest and attendance at sporting events. Table 7.1 lists some of the more popular and successful non-price promotions used in professional sport.

From a sport marketing perspective, the question that must be answered is *how many people will we draw with this promotion and will the revenue generated from the additional people more than cover the cost of staging the promotion?* For instance, if a franchise were to contract with Justin Timberlake to perform after a game, would the attendance spike cover not only the cost of paying Timberlake's appearance fee, but also the advertising that will promote the concert, the cost of paying staff for the extended time at the event, and any other costs that accompany staging the promotion? Ideally, a promotion like this example will not only break even financially, but generate a profit for the franchise as well. One way to improve the chance for financial success is to have a third party (sponsor) pay for some or all of the costs associated with the promotion (see below, and chapter 8).

Of critical import to the sport marketer is the question of *when* to use this type of promotion. One school of thought suggests that larger non-price promotions (including historically successful giveaways like bobblehead dolls) should be used on a date that the sport organization is not expecting a very large crowd. If used at this time, the non-price promotion should provide the desired spike in attendance, creating at least some business on a date that was anticipated to have very little business. The conflicting viewpoint is that larger non-price promotions should be used on more desirable dates in an effort to reach the capacity of the stadium or arena. Proponents of this view would argue for placing the concert on a Saturday evening (usually a well-attended date for most spectator sport franchises) against a good opponent in hopes of having a sell-out crowd. Sport teams have experimented year-by-year with these types of non-price promotions with varying degrees of success. Each marketplace is different, which underscores the need for sport marketers to understand their consumers so they might know what type of promotion will work at what time.

Fireworks and concerts are only one part of non-price promotions. The activities that occur during the down time in a game are also non-price promotions. Having a mascot shoot hot dogs into the crowd or deliver a pizza to a randomly chosen fan, or having sausages race around the ball park are also non-price promotions. These types of promotions add to the overall atmosphere and experience of attending a sporting event, especially for attendees who are only casual fans and are looking at the event more for its entertainment value. Moreover, these types of promotions are saleable. In other words, they can be built into a sponsorship package and generate revenue for the sport organization. The sausage race mentioned earlier is actually done by the Milwaukee Brewers franchise of MLB. This promotion has four people dressed up in over-sized sausage costumes race from the centerfield wall to home plate, and is sponsored by Usinger's—a maker of bratwurst and other processed meats in Milwaukee.

Clever and memorable non-price promotions of this sort help a sponsoring company as much as the franchise, as attendees to the event link the promotion back to the sponsor, which will ideally remain with consumers until it is time for them to make a purchase from the sponsor's category of products/services. Minor league sport franchises are often the testing ground for novel promotions of this sort, which, if successful, often make their way to the major league level.

PLACE

In traditional marketing, place refers to distribution of the product as well as the "place" of consumption. In that sense, sport marketers also consider the final "P" both place and distribution, since the physical setting (e.g., stadium, arena, health club) *is* where the sport product is distributed. Place can be an important factor in the purchase decision for many sport consumers. A facility that is both physically and aesthetically appealing enhances the core product and improves the overall sport consumptive experience. The place also is a major factor in consumers' initial perception of a sport organization. For instance, if a consumer walks into a stadium or club and is met with rude workers, litter, and poorly marked directions, they are most likely to have a negative perception toward the sport organization. It takes twelve positives to cancel out one negative in a consumer's mind. If a sport organization does not cancel out the negatives, it may lose the consumer's business.

Today, newly constructed sport facilities are designed with amenities that provide additional revenue-generating streams for the sport organization, such as club seating, luxury suites, in-stadium retail stores, and a varied assortment of concessions and restaurants. Newer stadiums like the Pittsburgh Pirates' PNC Park and the Seattle Mariners' Safeco Field serve as attractions in and of themselves, which aid in driving attendance when the core, on-field product is perceived as substandard. The construction style is reminiscent of sport's Golden Age, evoking nostalgic emotions in older fans, while catering to fans' tastes for updated amenities. Even older facilities, with or without an update, can serve as attractions, drawing fans regardless of franchise performance. Wrigley Field in Chicago, Fenway Park in Boston, and Lambeau Field in Green Bay all are excellent examples of how a stadium exemplifies an experience and a franchise. Annually, thousands of fans visit these stadiums to experience the rich history associated with each one.

In sport, the amount of input a marketer has on the construction of a newer facility varies across the industry; however, every effort should be made in both new and existing facilities to accommodate fans and facilitate customer service. Such issues as the appropriate number and placement of restrooms, concession stands, customer service stations, and entrances should be thoroughly planned to anticipate the ideal customer experience. Merchandise kiosks, food stands selling locally flavored concessions, and in-stadium restaurants serve as other revenue-generating sources for the sport organization, while offering more choices for the consumer base. Interactive zones are also commonplace in sport stadiums featuring activities for fans that tie entertaining activities with an organization's history to provide a richer experience for the consumer. Additionally, these areas serve as a mechanism to attract consumers with low involvement who may otherwise grow weary of just the core product. However you view it, the place in sport is an integral component of the marketing mix, and should be managed if a sport organization desires to stand out from the competition.

The Role of Research in Sport Marketing

Earlier in this chapter, the involvement and commitment of sport consumers was discussed as a means of determining the best consumers of a sport organization. That discussion brings up the question, "How do you get that type of information?" Furthermore, in order to make calculated, strategic marketing decisions, a sport marketer requires additional information about the market, the competition, and the consumers. These issues can be addressed by incorporating a systematic marketing research agenda into the business practices of a sport organization. Market research is a topic with such sufficient depth that one semester of study barely touches all the issues involved in designing and analyzing research. Needless to say, a portion of a chapter can only introduce the aspiring sport marketer to the utility of research. Therefore, in this section, we will touch on consumer market research and its applicability for the sport marketer.

Sound market research helps the sport marketer understand who comprises the customer base, what characteristics are similar among customers, how they prefer consuming the sport product or service, when they are most likely to consume, and where the consumers reside. Once compiled, this information can be analyzed to divide the consumers into similar groups. This process is called *segmentation*. Segmentation is the process of dividing large, unlike groups of consumers into smaller, more defined groups of people who share similar characteristics (Mullin et al., 2000). The smaller groups of consumers allow a sport organization to communicate more effectively and efficiently because marketing communication messages can be constructed that appeal to the unique characteristics of the small groups. Two popular segmentation methods use *demographics* and *psychographics* to group consumers. Demographics describe consumers' state-of-being, including such factors as income level, education level, zip code, marital status, age, race, religious affiliation, occupation type, number of children in the home, and gender. Psychographics refer to consumers' state-of-mind, exploring the likes and dislikes of consumers and using the similarities to create the segments. Exhibit 7.1 at the end of this chapter displays a survey with both demographic and psychographic items from a minor league baseball franchise. Once collected, this information will allow the franchise to develop marketing strategies aimed at specific segments that appeal to the characteristics used in segmenting the consumers. For instance, if a sport organization conducts research and discovers a segment of its customer base is married with two children under the age of twelve, they may approach a local Chuck E. Cheese restaurant and develop a family package whereby consumers purchasing the package receive tickets to a game and discounted dinner at Chuck E. Cheese. This example brings up another important use of research: the ability to use the information not only to increase consumption levels of consumers, but also to sell corporate sponsorships.

When used correctly, market research helps the sport marketer make decisions that improve customer service, the type of merchandise or concessions sold, the number and type of promotions staged, as well as where marketing communications messages should be placed for maximum efficiency. Increasingly, sport organizations of all sizes and types are utilizing market research to improve their businesses, both from a revenue-generating and a customer service standpoint. As you progress through your academic career, you will be wise to learn as many market research techniques as you can, as they will be instrumental in your sport marketing career.

Developments in the Field of Sport Marketing

As one could imagine, the task of marketing a sport organization involves constantly altering the marketing mix to adjust to internal and external changes facing the organization. The caliber of team play, the state of a fitness facility, a downturn in the economy, or a new competitor entering the marketplace are but a small sample of events that force a sport organization to revisit and adjust its marketing strategy. In this section, we will briefly examine a few developing strategies sport organizations have employed to face such challenges.

EDUSELLING

Eduselling, a term first introduced by Sutton, Lachowetz, and Clark in 2000, refers to a process by which sport professionals approach new users of their products or services more as "teachers" than salespeople. Viewed primarily as a method to enhance sponsorship sales, the nine-step eduselling framework moves beyond the traditional transactional exchange between organization and consumer, instead focusing on building a long-term relationship that benefits both parties. To that end, eduselling advocates that the sport organization work with the potential sponsor in understanding all of that potential sponsor's wants and needs, as well as the particular objectives for entering into the sponsorship.

With that clear understanding in hand, the sport organization then develops a comprehensive sponsorship plan utilizing the relevant pieces of sport organization inventory to ensure successful achievement of the sponsor's objectives. Since many potential corporate sponsors may not fully comprehend all of the uses of certain pieces of team sport inventory, eduselling calls for the sport organization to develop "how to" guides detailing exactly how the sponsor could best use aspects of their deal. Once the sponsor decides to commit to a deal with the sport organization, the sport organization must monitor the sponsor's activities and collect feedback from the sponsor to make the necessary adjustments to the deal. When carried out well, the sponsor will achieve its objectives and the sport organization will have a corporate customer for many years to come.

To illustrate the eduselling concept, let us examine a hypothetical situation involving a Major League Baseball franchise and a regional bank with headquarters in the franchise's market. According to the eduselling framework, before the baseball franchise can present the bank's marketing manager with a sponsorship proposal, the franchise should learn as much as it can about the bank's current business (market position, customer base, current marketing activities, etc.) and future business

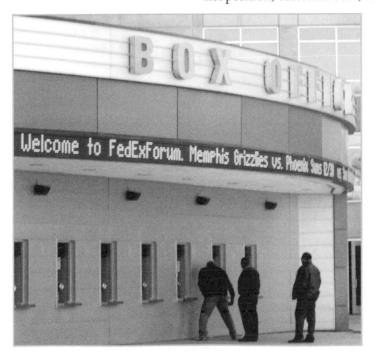

plans. The next step requires the franchise to meet with the bank's marketing manager to learn detailed information that will augment the research already conducted. Only then will the franchise be able to structure a sponsorship proposal that is likely to meet the wants and needs of the bank. Of course, some of the components of the proposal may be unfamiliar to the bank's marketing manager; therefore, the franchise should allow the marketing manager an opportunity to "sample" those components with the goal being the bank's marketing manager will have a better understanding of how the various components fit together in the overall plan.

Once the deal is signed in our hypothetical situation, the franchise should not only schedule periodic meetings to gather feedback from the bank, but the franchise should also monitor the various components of the sponsorship to identify and correct any problematic issues before they are brought to the bank's attention. Then, after the annual sponsorship cycle is completed, the franchise will sit down with the bank's marketing manager and discuss the sponsorship program in detail, gaining valuable feedback for the next year.

Today, the eduselling concept is being used by sport franchises not only in the sale of sponsorship agreements, but also in the sale of premium seating, broadcast contracts, and ticket packages. As the competition for customers' disposable income and a portion of businesses' marketing budget increases, the relational nature of eduselling is an effective method to create partners for the sport organization, instead of just one-time, transactional customers.

LOADED TICKETS

Another recent development in the field of team sport marketing is the concept of "loaded tickets" utilizing stored-value technology. The loaded ticket is actually a normal ticket with an additional dollar amount "stored" into that ticket's bar code, which allows users to scan their tickets for purchases instead of paying cash or using their credit cards. In this sense, the ticket is all a fan would need to enter into the stadium and enjoy the game.

One of the first team sport franchises to use the technology was Major League Baseball's Philadelphia Phillies as a means to increase the per capita consumption levels of fans (Muret, 2008). The additional cost of the loaded ticket is packaged into the total ticket price, and most franchises using the concept today offer the packages in special seating sections. The upside for the franchises is the increased spending by fans—the Phillies franchise claims fans with loaded tickets spend 70 percent more than fans without loaded tickets (Muret, 2008). The benefit for the fans is a hassle-free way to purchase concessions and merchandise without searching for an ATM or using a high-interest-rate credit card. In certain instances where loaded tickets are purchased by a company and then given to employees or customers, the additional monetary value stored in the bar-code allows for a convenient, expense-free evening of entertainment.

While the loaded ticket concept has mostly been used in specially branded season ticket sections, additional uses are being explored by sport organizations in all of team sport. The loaded ticket may be a desirable feature for fans purchasing group tickets, or even for fans enjoying just an individual game.

ALL-INCLUSIVE

Convenience for customers also is the focus of yet another sport marketing development; the all-inclusive concept. Common in the restaurant (think "buffets"), retail (Wal-Mart), and resort industries (Sandals resorts), the concept is being seen more in both spectator sport and the fitness industry. At its root, the all-inclusive package means providing customers with everything they need or may want to ensure that they have the most enjoyable experience possible.

Spectator sport organizations have long had a similar concept in luxury suites where wealthy customers were sequestered from the masses while enjoying wine, veal medallions, and crème brulee. But today, the hoi polloi can also experience the all-inclusive concept without breaking the bank. For instance, in the 2008 season, Major League Baseball's Pittsburgh Pirates unveiled a new seating section where for $30 ($40 if you purchased your tickets the day of the game), you not only received a game ticket, but license to an unlimited, all-you-can-eat game experience (alcohol not included). For the Pirates, the addition of this ticket option was most certainly in response to waning attendance due to poor team play, but the fact that the roll-out of the program coincided with a downturn in the economy certainly made the offer more attractive to cost-conscious fans. Since the Pirates unveiled the program, other team sport organizations both within MLB and without have announced they would offer a similar ticket.

In the fitness industry, the all-inclusive trend has also taken hold as a response to varying consumer wants and ever-changing fitness fads. For the fitness industry, the all-inclusive concept takes the form of providing one-stop health and fitness shopping for the club's members. These offerings range from the traditional (e.g., weight rooms, cardio equipment, fitness classes) to the latest developments (e.g., holistic healing, massage therapy, nutritional counseling). In these types of facilities, it would not be uncommon to find an area for members to enjoy a nutritious snack or light meal as well as a full-blown spa staffed by trained and registered professionals. According to the International Health, Racquet and Sportsclub Association (IHRSA), approximately one-quarter of the 41.3 million Americans belonging to some type of fitness club are members of one of these all-inclusive facilities (IHRSA/American Sports Data 2005 Health Club Trend Report). The obvious benefit for members of these clubs is that they are able to take care of all their health and fitness needs without traveling to various locations. For the club owners, the added amenities allow them to gain a larger share of their customers' health and fitness dollars. Of course, with new fads in the industry always on the horizon, the club owners have to carefully monitor the wants and needs of the membership so that the club is providing what the members desire.

PLACE: BIGGER AND BETTER

The new millennium seems to have ushered in a new gilded age of sport stadium construction, and the race is on between storied sport organizations to create the most fan-friendly, revenue-friendly facility. At the forefront of this race are the Dallas Cowboys and New York Yankees organizations. Both entities are in various stages of construction on facilities that will cost over one billion dollars. The push to build new stadiums is linked back to the revenue a sport organization can generate—revenue that is oftentimes excluded from any league-wide revenue-sharing agreements. The new stadiums boast the latest technology that supposedly will make the fans' experience better, but that experience will come at a price. For example, the Dallas Cowboys new stadium will be home to the world's largest video screen (over 11,000 square feet); approximately 200 luxury suites (some only twenty rows from the field!); 15,000 club level seats; approximately ten acres of space in the end zones for gatherings; 280 concession areas; 1,600 toilets; and both the Dallas Cowboys Hall of Fame and Ring of Honor (Dallas Cowboys.com, 2008). The roughly 80,000-seat venue (with the capacity to add another 20,000 seats in the future) will be easier to get to as well, since the Cowboys and the City of Arlington, Texas, are working to upgrade the interstate highway system leading to and surrounding the stadium. Experts contend that this grand stadium may set a record with its naming rights deal, with some experts predicting the Cowboys will receive over $20 million a year (Marta, 2008) (see Table 7.2). By all accounts, attending a Dallas Cowboys game in the near future will be a trip into sport luxury, but if you plan on going, you had better make sure to bring lots of money. For those Cowboys fans who desire season tickets to the new stadium in one of the club levels, they must first purchase a 30-year seat license, which will cost them anywhere between $16,000 and $150,000. In addition, the fan must then pay for the actual game ticket, which will cost $340 (Exorbitant Prices, 2008). Revenue generation indeed!

The Cowboys and Yankees are not the only two sport franchises in pursuit of new stadiums. In the metropolitan New York area alone, MLB's New York Mets, the

Table 7.2. Top 10 Naming Rights Deals for Major League Sports

THE PRICE OF A NAME				
Venue, City	Total	No. years	Annual	Exp.
1. *Barclays Center, Brooklyn, N.Y Sponsor: Barclays PLC	$400 million	20	$20.0 million	2029
2. *Citi Field, Queens, N.Y. Sponsor: Citibank N.A.	$400 million	20	$20.0 million	2028
3. **Reliant Stadium, Houston Sponsor: Reliant Energy Inc.	$310 million	31	$10.0 million	2032
4. FedEx Field, Landover, Md. Sponsor: FedEx Corp.	$205 million	27	$7.59 million	2025
5. American Airlines Center, Dallas Sponsor: AMR Corp.	$195 million	30	$6.5 million	2030
6. Philips Arena, Atlanta Sponsor: Royal Philips Electronics N.V.	$185 million	20	$9.25 million	2019
7. Minute Maid Park, Houston Sponsor: The Coca-Cola Co.	$178 million	28	$6.36 million	2029
8. University of Phoenix Stadium, Glendale, Ariz. Sponsor: Apollo Group Inc.	$154.5 million	20	$7.72 million	2025
9. Bank of America Stadium, Charlotte, N.C. Sponsor: Bank of America	$140 million	20	$7.0 million	2023
10. Lincoln Financial Field, Philadelphia Sponsor: Lincoln National Corp.	$139.6 million	20	$6.98 million	2022

SOURCE: *SportsBusiness Journal*
* Under construction
** Reliant has the naming rights to the entire Reliant Park, which also includes Reliant Arena.

NFL's Giants and Jets, and Major League Soccer's New York Red Bulls all are in the process of building new stadiums that will allow fans to be closer to the action in more comfortable seats as they nibble on a more varied food selection—all of which will cost the fan more money. While franchises that have high demand for their product (e.g., the Cowboys and the Yankees) have little worry they will be able to sell the pricey seats in their new stadiums, other sport franchises that have a weaker brand must be careful they do not alienate their fan base and appear as if they are gouging their loyal customers.

Summary

Any successful sport organization relies on its customers for stability and solvency. Sport marketing plays the primary role in acquiring and keeping customers. While the task may seem daunting at times, the great asset that many sport marketers enjoy is that they are marketing sport. As we have discovered, sport holds a special place in our society, where consumers' emotions are heightened and their involvement exceeds that in many other products or services. By utilizing sound market research to incorporate the proper mix of the marketing elements, sport marketers will be able to generate the revenue necessary to operate the organization, while creating fun and exciting experiences that will keep consumers returning game after game, season after season.

DISCUSSION ACTIVITIES

1. Describe how the 4 Ps of sport marketing can be inter-related by developing a marketing plan for a new minor league baseball team in your hometown.
2. Explain relationship marketing and provide an example of how marketers from your university's athletic department could do a better job creating a relationship with the student body.
3. Describe some of the main unique aspects of sport marketing and apply them to the sport with which you are most familiar.

SUGGESTED READINGS

D'Alessandro, D. F. (2002). *Brand warfare.* New York: McGraw-Hill Education.
Earls, M. (2002). *Welcome to the creative age—Banana, business and the death of marketing.* New York: John Wiley & Sons.
Grant, J. (2002). *After image: Mind-expanding marketing.* London, UK : Profile Business.

References

Dallas Cowboys new stadium. (2008). Retrieved August 11, 2008, from http://stadium.dallascowboys.com/

ESPN SportsCenter interview with NBA Commissioner David Stern. Aired October 17, 2004.

Exorbitant prices at new Dallas Cowboys Stadium haven't hurt sales one bit, says Dallas Cowboys management. (2008, February 3). Pegasus News Wire. Retrieved August 11, 2008, from http://www.pegasusnews.com/news/2008/feb/03/exorbitant-prices-new-dallas-cowboys-stadium-haven/

Gordon, I. (1998). *Relationship marketing.* New York: John Wiley & Sons.

Hagstrom, R. G. (1998). *The NASCAR way.*

New York: John Wiley & Sons.

IHRSA/American Sports Data 2005 Health Club Trend Report. Retrieved August 8, 2008, from http://cms.ihrsa.org/index.cfm?fuseaction=Page.viewPage&pageId=18890&nodeID=15

Marta, S. (2008, March 31). Dallas Cowboys stadium naming rights may top record deal. *Dallas Morning News*. Retrieved August 11, 2008, from http://www.dallasnews.com/sharedcontent/dws/spt/football/cowboys/stories/033008dnbusnamingrights.2b2caec.html

Mullin, B., Hardy, S., & Sutton, W. A. (2000). *Sport marketing* (2nd ed.). Champaign, IL: Human Kinetics.

Muret, D. (2008, March, 10–16). Loaded tickets catch on among MLB teams. *SportsBusiness Journal*, 12.

Normann, R. (2000). *Service management* (3rd ed.). New York: John Wiley & Sons.

Sutton, W. A., Lachowetz, T., & Clark, J. (2000). Eduselling: The role of customer education in selling to corporate clients in the sport industry. *International Journal of Sports Marketing and Sponsorship*, *2*(2), 145–158.

Exhibit 7.1: Attendee Survey of Lake County Captains

LAKE COUNTY CAPTAINS 2004 FAN SURVEY

Thank you for taking this survey about attendees of Lake County Captains games. Please carefully read each question, and mark the correct answer that is closest to your opinion about your experience at Captains' games. This is not a "test." There are no "correct" or "incorrect" answers. Most questions simply ask for your opinion and the results will be anonymous. Work quickly and record your immediate thoughts. Some of the questions may seem similar to you, or may not be worded exactly the way you would like them to be. Even so, give your best estimate and continue working through the survey. It is important that you answer all the questions. Your best response is far more valuable than an incomplete response.

Below are some statements regarding how you feel about the Lake County Captains. Please read each statement, and then circle the appropriate number printed on the right to indicate your level of agreement or disagreement with the statement.

	Strongly Disagree				Strongly Agree		
The Captains' stadium is a clean, comfortable facility.	1	2	3	4	5	6	7
There is ample parking around the Captains' stadium.	1	2	3	4	5	6	7
The ushers are courteous and friendly.	1	2	3	4	5	6	7
It is enjoyable to visit the Captains' stadium.	1	2	3	4	5	6	7
I enjoy going to the stadiums for Captains games.	1	2	3	4	5	6	7
To me, the Captains are the same as other franchises.	1	2	3	4	5	6	7
On most nights, the Captains provide quality entertainment.	1	2	3	4	5	6	7
Captain ticket-takers are courteous.	1	2	3	4	5	6	7
I consider myself a loyal customer of the Captains.	1	2	3	4	5	6	7
I enjoy the in-game promotions at Captains games.	1	2	3	4	5	6	7
There are many items to choose from at the concession stands.	1	2	3	4	5	6	7
I think the price of concession items is fair.	1	2	3	4	5	6	7
If I had to do it over again, I would not come to a Captains game.	1	2	3	4	5	6	7
I follow the Captains because they are my hometown team.	1	2	3	4	5	6	7
It is important for me to support the Captains as my hometown team.	1	2	3	4	5	6	7
The Captains are an important part of the community.	1	2	3	4	5	6	7
I come to Captains games because it is the best choice of entertainment for me.	1	2	3	4	5	6	7
The Captains provide a rallying point for the community.	1	2	3	4	5	6	7
The Captains do not have adequate in-game entertainment.	1	2	3	4	5	6	7
I am proud to attend Captains games.	1	2	3	4	5	6	7
I care about the long-term success of the Captains.	1	2	3	4	5	6	7
I am a loyal fan of the Captains.	1	2	3	4	5	6	7
I feel a sense of belonging at Captains games.	1	2	3	4	5	6	7

Please provide answers to the following questions about the Captains and other area entertainment options.

1. Approximately how many Captains games do you go to each season? _____

2. Please tell us how you hear about Captains games and promotions.
   A. Newspaper / Circulars   B. Radio
   C. Television
   D. Internet website
   E. Word-of-Mouth
   F. Pocket Schedule
   G. Other (please specify) _____

3. Your decision to attend *today's game* was made within the past:
   A. 24 hours
   B. 2–7 days
   C. 8–14 days
   D. 15–30 days
   E. 31+ days

4. How did you purchase / receive your ticket for today's event?
   A. Mail order
   B. Bought it today at the box office upon arriving
   C. Telephone order
   D. Ticket was given to me
   E. I have season tickets

5. For the following organizations, please indicate how many times a year you attend:
   _____ Cleveland Indians games
   _____ Movies at a theater
   _____ Swimming at a public pool
   _____ Amusement Park
   _____ Eating out at a restaurant
   _____ Other Minor League Baseball games
   _____ Other Amateur baseball games
   _____ Plays / Symphony / Ballet

6. Please rank the following sport organizations according to your personal preference. Use #1 for your favorite organization, #2 for your second favorite organization, and so on.
   _____ Lake County Captains
   _____ Cleveland Indians
   _____ Cleveland Browns
   _____ Cleveland Cavaliers
   _____ Cleveland Barons
   _____ Cleveland Force

7. Are you at today's game as a member of a group? YES   NO

8. Are you a Captains season ticket holder? YES   NO

Below are some more statements about the Captains. Please circle number the best describes your opinion about each statement.

I feel the Captains franchise is . . .

	1	2	3	4	5	6	7	8	9	10	
Very Undependable	1	2	3	4	5	6	7	8	9	10	Very Dependable
Very Incompetent	1	2	3	4	5	6	7	8	9	10	Very Competent
Of Very Low Integrity	1	2	3	4	5	6	7	8	9	10	Of Very High Integrity
Very Unresponsive to customers	1	2	3	4	5	6	7	8	9	10	Very Responsive to customers

I feel the EMPLOYEES of the Captains are . . .

Very Undependable	1	2	3	4	5	6	7	8	9	10	Very Dependable
Very Incompetent	1	2	3	4	5	6	7	8	9	10	Very Competent
Of Very Low Integrity	1	2	3	4	5	6	7	8	9	10	Of Very High Integrity
Very Unresponsive to customers	1	2	3	4	5	6	7	8	9	10	Very Responsive to customers

For the prices you pay at a Captains game, would you say the experience at a Captains game is a . . .

Very Poor Deal	1	2	3	4	5	6	7	8	9	10	Very Good Deal

For the time you spend in order to get to the game, would you say attending a Captains game is . . .

Highly Unreasonable	1	2	3	4	5	6	7	8	9	10	Highly Reasonable

For the effort involved in coming to a Captains game, would you say attending a game is . . .

Not at all worthwhile	1	2	3	4	5	6	7	8	9	10	Very Worthwhile

How would you rate your overall experience at a Captains game?

Extremely Poor Value	1	2	3	4	5	6	7	8	9	10	Extremely Good Value

Please provide us with some demographic information about yourself.

1. Gender   A. Male   B. Female

2. Marital Status   A. Married   B. Single   C. Divorced   D. Widowed

3. How many children are living at home with you? _____

4. What is your race?
   A. African American   B. Asian
   C. White   D. Hispanic
   E. Other

5. What is the highest level of education you have completed?
   A. High School Graduate   B. Trade School / Technical School Diploma
   C. Some College   D. College Graduate
   E. Graduate Degree

6. What is your annual household income level?
   A. less than $25,000   B. $25,001–$40,000
   C. $40,001–$60,000   D. $60,001–$80,000
   E. $80,001–$100,000   F. $100,001–$120,000
   G. More than $120,000

7. What is your age?
   A. 18–24   B. 25–34
   C. 35–44   D. 45–54
   E. 55–64   F. 65 or older

8. What is your occupation? _____

9. What is the zip code of your primary residence? _____

Thank you for completing the survey! Please use the space below to share any additional comments or opinions with the Lake County Captains.

Case Study

What does a one-year-old minor league baseball franchise do to continue the success from its inaugural season into year two? How do they ensure that the fans continue to have a good experience, and develop new revenue streams? The answer for the Lake County Captains, a Class A affiliate of the Cleveland Indians organization, is to use market research. The Captains organization plays games in a new stadium located in Eastlake, OH, just minutes from the parent club's home in downtown Cleveland; yet, the franchise routinely fills its stadium to near capacity. They do it with a mix of family entertainment off the field and quality, developing players on the field. The first year of the franchise's existence was a success, but like any other business, the Captains' management felt they needed to keep a pulse on their consumers' wants and needs pertaining to their experience, so the Captains could alter their marketing strategy to meet those changing wants and needs. How did they know what the customers wanted? They asked them.

Exhibit X-1 shows the survey the Captains disseminated to their customers. Because they already had information about ticket package holders, the vast majority of respondents were individual game attendees. Standard demographic questions (age, income levels, education levels, number of children at home, etc.) were asked of respondents to allow Captains management to obtain a clearer picture of their non-ticket plan holding fan base. These demographic questions, along with select psychographic questions (e.g., how many times a year do you eat out at a restaurant) help the franchise determine business categories that should be pursued for sponsorship opportunities or other strategic partnerships.

Finally, certain survey items ask the respondents to indicate their opinion of the franchise's performance on several different elements. These items allow the franchise to gauge customers' attitudes toward operational and procedural elements of the franchise. If a particular area turns up lacking (based on fan responses), the franchise management can then make changes designed to improve fans' experience at a Lake County Captains game.

As you can see, market research plays an important role in the operation of a minor league baseball organization, as well as any sport organization. From an organizational perspective, it is important to regularly plan to collect data from your customer base. Survey research is only one method. Focus groups, stadium intercepts, and secret shoppers are other methods that allow a franchise to collect valuable information about their organization and fans. The important point to remember is that you cannot meet the wants and needs of your customer base, if you do not know what those wants and needs are.

Chapter Eight

SPONSORSHIP AND SALES IN THE SPORT INDUSTRY

NANCY L. LOUGH

"OK, listen up. Pack the gear. Bob's decided to move the team to a neighborhood with a more lucrative fan base."

LEARNING OBJECTIVES

Upon completion of this chapter, the student will be able to
- Define and describe the use of corporate sponsorship in sport;
- Describe how "fit" is determined between a sport property and potential sponsor;
- Discuss the product adoption process and relationship to sponsorship;
- Identify the three levels of branding and importance of brand equity;
- Identify two primary reasons sponsors defect, and how activation and leveraging can prevent sponsor defection; and
- Describe methods of evaluating and measuring sponsorship

Introduction

Sport, as we have come to know it, could not exist without the financial support provided by corporate sponsorship. This practice of seeking a cash and/or in-kind fee paid to the property (typically in sports, arts, entertainment, or causes) in return for access to the exploitable commercial potential associated with the sport property, was once thought to be the antithesis of all that was good about sport (Ukman, 1995). Yet, throughout the last two decades, corporate investment in sponsorship became a key indicator of a sport property's legitimacy. Sponsorship can make a sport, as is the case with NASCAR. Lack of sponsorship can contribute to the dissolution of a sport entity, as was the indication from WUSA officials when the league initially ceased operations.

SPONSORSHIP

Sponsorship has many definitions and many potential benefits. The essence of any quality definition includes reference to a relationship between a business and a sport entity in which the business provides funding, resources, and/or services to the sport property in exchange for rights and privileges provided as a result of the association and/or affiliation with the sport entity. Pope (1998) provided the following definition:

> Sponsorship is the provision of resources (e.g., money, people, equipment) by an organization (the sponsor) directly to an individual, authority or body (the sponsee), to enable the latter

to pursue some activity in return for benefits contemplated in terms of the sponsor's promotion strategy, and which can be expressed in terms of corporate, marketing, or media objectives.

Primary *benefits* sought by sponsors who invest in a sport relationship include generating brand awareness, image enhancement, improved trade relations, increased market share, client acquisition, hospitality, product trials, and sales opportunities (Howard & Crompton, 2004; Stotlar, 2002; Gwinner & Eaton, 1999). Given the prospect for achievement of the aforementioned benefits, a sponsorship may appear to be an easy sell. Yet, the bottom line for the majority of businesses that invest in this type of communication vehicle is *return on investment* (Lough & Irwin, 2001).

> Corporation bosses are increasingly having to justify their marketing investments to their shareholders and can no longer just say being associated with the Olympics is good for a company—they will have to prove it with hard facts. (Keeping the Olympics, 1997, p. 32)

Every business should have its own marketing plan that incorporates each of the Ps of sport marketing: product, price, place, and promotion. In order for a sport sponsorship to deliver a positive return on the investment made by the business, consideration must be made regarding the integration of the sponsor's *marketing objectives* and the benefits provided via the sport affiliation. For example, the New York City Marathon signed ING, the Amsterdam-based financial services company to become the title sponsor in 2003. ING opted for sponsorship of major marathons because of the fit between the services (product) they offer and the participants in major markets, such as New York City. With more than 13.4 million U.S. adults identifying as avid runners, ING research found that brand awareness was 15 percent higher among avid runners. The same study also indicated that 70 percent of avid runners own an investment and prefer to make informed financial decisions (Kaplan, 2007). Thus, the value (price) of the services offered may be of greater interest to marathon participants. To communicate with these potential consumers, the ING sponsorship activation plan starts with turning the event orange, through signage and cheering zones in quarter-mile stretches. Fans are provided orange thunder sticks and signs. Meanwhile, street teams of ING employees also engage the "place" by offering refreshments to the crowd and generating excitement. Other promotional aspects of the sponsorship include exposure to the ING brand hundreds of times, from race registration to email updates in the months prior to the race, to race-day signage and water stops. Added promotion is available in the two-day race expo in which ING has a booth that showcases their financial services. Runners competing in the race receive orange "pace bands" to track themselves during the race. Still the communication and brand leveraging continues after the race with follow-up emails and the quintessential race "goody bag." Lastly, when publications such as *SportsBusiness Journal* and the *New York Times* publish articles (public relations) regarding ING's sponsorship of the race, all of the Ps suggested for a successful strategic marketing plan are addressed. This type of relationship illustrates the *symbiotic*, or win-win, nature of effective sponsorship in sport. Will ING gain more investors as a result of this deal? Properly conducted research would indicate whether New York City marathoners will be more likely to consider ING for their financial services provider. An increase in sales is one of the most common methods to measure return on investment and sponsorship effectiveness.

Advertising ≠ Sponsorship	Advertising may appear to serve the same purpose as sponsorship. Yet upon analysis of the components of a sponsorship relationship, the limitations of advertising can be illuminated. In promotions such as advertising, one of the most common approaches is referred to as the *AIDA* concept. The goal of the AIDA (awareness, interest, desire, and action) approach is to move consumers along in the progression toward actual product purchase. Yet, this model stops short of acquiring the ensemble of benefits available via sponsorship. In advertising, little opportunity exists in a thirty-second televised spot to gain access to a specific target market segment, and even less opportunity is available to create trust or enhance employee morale via an element such as hospitality. Still the most convincing argument for sponsorship versus advertising may be the potential for building loyalty and, thereby, *brand equity*. Dedicated marathoners and true running fans may perceive the success of major races such as the New York City Marathon as hinging on the success of the sponsors. In many cases, sport fans have become loyal consumers of the products and companies that support their sport. They understand that without sponsors, they might not be able to compete or see their favorite athletes compete whether on television or in person.

SPONSORSHIP GROWTH

Sponsorship prior to the late 1980s was typically simplistic in nature. Often the primary rationale for a company to sponsor a sport was the CEO's intent to "rub elbows" with elite athletes. However, the 1984 Olympic Games changed the landscape of sport sponsorship dramatically. After years of debt accruing to host cities for the Olympic Games, the Los Angeles Olympic Organizing Committee set out to prove that hosting this one-of-a-kind world-class event could prove profitable for the city and others involved. A total of 32 companies agreed to pay between $4 million and $13 million in cash, goods, and services. At the previous Olympic Games in Montreal, 628 sponsors were involved for a total of $4.18 million. The result of the shift to category-specific sponsors and enhanced contributions was a net profit reported to be $222 million.

Today, corporate sponsors can be involved at various levels with the Olympic Games. For example, the sponsorship fee to be one of the 11 TOP (The Olympic Partner Program) sponsors has been reported to be approximately $70 million for the 2008 Beijing Olympics. *TOP sponsors* sign up for a four-year contract that includes both the Summer and Winter Games. They are granted the right to Olympic affiliation in every participating country with worldwide *exclusivity* in their product category. Overall, sponsorship growth has been phenomenal following the example set by the success of the 1984 Olympic Games.

Additionally, recent corporate scandals have created an enhanced need for demonstration of responsibility in all facets of a company's financial matters. Accountability for sponsorship investment is more often required in today's business environment, including some validation of the potential for increasing company profitability as a direct result of the sport sponsorship. The process of *evaluation* and servicing has taken on a new level of importance with regard to the likelihood of *renewal*. Those sport entities that fail to evaluate and/or quantify for the sponsor the value received will likely find a higher rate of *defection* (current sponsors that decide not to renew).

Competition in the sport marketplace has proliferated at a rate commensurate with the growth of sponsorship in the sport industry. More sport products exist today in the form of tours, leagues, special events, professional sport properties, and intercollegiate athletics, so one can quickly appreciate the need for more sophisticated approaches to sponsorship and selling within the sport industry. As the sport marketplace splinters, the opportunity to address specific target segments via lifestyle and affinity marketing opens the door for new and more creative sponsorship opportunities. Similarly, growing sophistication resulting from competition and marketplace fragmentation has necessitated the growth of inventory that may be offered to potential sponsors.

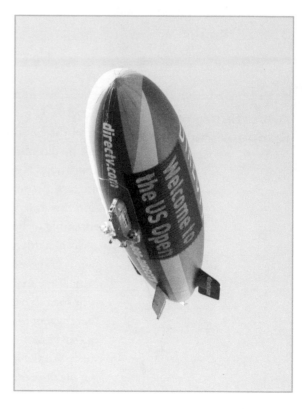

Sport Legitimatization

The 1999 Women's World Cup of soccer proved to be one of the most successful sport events ever held on U.S. soil. Yet, few realize the struggle event organizers experienced as they sought corporate involvement. Women's soccer had received needed exposure leading up to and following the 1996 Olympic Games. However, convincing corporate decision makers that investing in the Women's World Cup would provide substantial return on their investment was a hard sell. Few decision makers understood the value of associating with a women's sport property. Many companies who had committed to support the Men's World Cup, when the U.S. hosted the event, experienced disappointing results.

Two risks were apparent. First, the sport was soccer, which had yet to achieve significance in the U.S. sport marketplace. Second, it was women's sport, often considered outside the mainstream for appealing to typical sport fans. Yet, prepared with research suggesting that an enormous untapped market was available for those willing to sign on, event organizers managed to secure sufficient sponsorship dollars. This premier women's soccer event achieved unprecedented results including record crowds, unparalleled television ratings, and considerable media exposure. For the potential sponsors who neglected to sign on, what appeared to be a once-in-a-lifetime opportunity was missed.

Fortunately, the learning curve was short. In 2003, FIFA moved the Women's World Cup to the U.S. due to an emergency situation. The SARS epidemic caused World Cup Officials to realize that China could not serve as the host. In less than four months, the US Soccer Federation, with the help of corporate partners, created a tournament that turned a big profit. The $7.5 million generated was more than triple the earnings from the 1999 World Cup.

Sport Failure and Sponsorship

The Women's United Soccer Association was launched as a direct result of the phenomenal success of the 1999 Women's World Cup. Corporate backers saw potential and committed to building a league that would capitalize on the unprecedented interest. Organizers created the league with a solid vision and financial base of support. Yet, the long-term plan included increasing levels of corporate sponsorship as the years progressed. Concern mounted as time wore on, due to unfulfilled goals. In today's hypercompetitive sport marketplace, setting realistic, attainable goals is crucial. Missing an established target market often results in the need to return to the drawing board. As sponsors' needs went unmet, it became apparent that the WUSA was missing its mark.

Three primary concerns contributed to the defection of sponsors and ultimately dissolution of the league:

1. Diminished television ratings
2. Decreased on-site attendance
3. Pricing that did not equate to the market delivered

Delivery of a realistic market estimate is vital to continued sponsorship. With teams competing in only eight markets, average attendance below 7,000, and television ratings of 0.1 (approximately 100,000 households), it was unrealistic to expect sponsors to contribute $2.5 million to sustain the league. As the WUSA works to answer the difficult questions and arrive at a new launching point, we can all learn valuable lessons from this promising sport property. Finding the fit between all the sport property has to offer and the image/goals of the corporate sponsor will lead to satisfaction and continued involvement for both parties.

Hot or Not? X Games vs. Gravity Games

While sponsorship—through affiliation—can often establish a level of credibility for a sport, a lack of credibility in a sport product rarely can be altered, even with significant sponsors. For example, the X Games were created by ESPN to provide a venue for competition among the world's elite action or extreme sport athletes. Initially, the idea was considered a gamble or a fad, at best. Yet, as the success of the X Games became apparent, so too did the absence of any competitor in the same class. The Gravity Games were created to compete directly with the X Games for the action/extreme sport market. Multiple attempts have been made, yet the Gravity Games have not achieved the status of the original extreme sport competition, the X Games. In 2007, after seven years in existence, an announcement was made that Gravity Games H20 would be suspended. To keep the brand alive and maintain a fan base, *Versus* created a Gravity Games weekly 30-minute television show that features top extreme sport athletes from around the world.

The image of Mountain Dew, as a drink presumably chosen by extreme-minded opinion leaders, illustrates the magnitude of effectiveness the X Games has provided for their top tier sponsors. Without the X Games, Mountain Dew would have continued to struggle for a place in the soft drink market. Instead, Mountain Dew (the brand) has become synonymous with the "extreme" image and action sports. In 1999, the brand became the third most popular soft drink in the US, surpassing Diet Coke, and in 2005, Mountain Dew was the only carbonated soft drink to increase its volume. In a survey conducted by ESPN Research, 96 percent of respondents recognized Mountain Dew as a sponsor of the X Games and Winter X Games (Case study: Mountain Dew). The Gravity Games has not provided the same level of *image enhancement* for sponsors, largely due to the event's lack of credibility among the target audience. A surprising relationship to evolve from the success of the X Games was the US Navy sponsorship. The US Navy became a top tier sponsor of ESPN's X Games because of the fit between its target market for recruitment for the once secretive branch known as the Seals, and this unique sport product. Spectators who enjoy an extreme physical challenge and happen to have an age range of 17–24 years were exposed to the message and image crafted by the US Navy Seals. Given the elite status of the Navy Seals among all military branches, affiliation with the Gravity Games would not have provided the same level of credibility.

Creating "Buy in"

To create "buy in" for potential sponsors, the cost and value of a sponsorship deal must be equitable for both parties. The primary factor that contributes to the value for sponsors is the fit between the sport property and the corporate partner.

Fit is determined by the following criteria: (a) the sport property's image should be compatible with the desired image of the brand, and (b) a match needs to exist between the target market of the sport entity and the target market of the brand. The value of a sponsorship often is created by the sport entity's need for funding or resources. However, problems can arise when the value associated with a sponsorship is lower than the associated cost.

In sport marketing, myopia is a common problem. In essence, myopia is the result of sport personnel focusing solely on the sport product and not considering the needs and wants of consumers. In sponsorship relationships, myopia occurs when sport representatives focus solely on the offerings associated through the sport sponsorship, yet neglect to consider the fit criteria that essentially establish the value or worth for the potential sponsor.

In a college town where an NCAA Division I program garners the majority of the sport media's attention, the concern for creating a fit between local sponsors and the athletic team or program is often neglected. The environment is one in which businesses commit to sponsorship deals more for the benefits associated with being perceived as a community leader or contributor to the university. Typically, sponsorships such as this lack the sophistication necessary in a more competitive marketplace and put the athletics marketing personnel in the dangerous position of becoming lulled into complacency. The creation of arbitrary sponsorship levels, which commonly occurs in these situations, results in a rigid menu of benefits available, with little room for focusing on the needs and wants of the sponsor. Thus, there is often a poor "fit," and, therefore, many of these types of sponsorships are ineffective at meeting the marketing needs of the sponsors. The only benefactor in this situation is the athletic program. Without a fair exchange of value and benefits, the sponsorship is at risk for non-renewal at any time.

FOCUS ON TARGET MARKETS

When considering the aspect of buy-in for sponsors that relates to their desired target market, a recognizable example can be seen in the relationship between FedEx and the PGA Tour's new playoff points system. FedEx has experienced the benefits of communicating with a specific target market of golf fans, many of whom possess an average income over $75,000. The FedEx sponsored playoff format was initiated in 2007 with tremendous success. Reportedly, 50 percent of avid and casual PGA fans said they were more likely to try FedEx products or services because of the sponsorship relationship. Similarly, about 56 percent reported they were more likely to have a favorable opinion of FedEx products, while 45 percent indicated they were likely to increase their use of FedEx. This first-year deal exemplified the ideal fit between a target market for a company and the audience of a sport property. With a fit this clear, the effort needed to create buy-in is reduced, therefore allowing more time to focus on enhancing communication platforms and promotional campaigns.

Beyond the cost and value factors, there remains the need to protect companies who commit to sport sponsorship. Increasing competition to get a promotional message across has resulted in diminished value in certain situations. The three primary concerns that arise from competition in the marketplace include clutter, noise, and ambush marketing. *Clutter* is the result of too many sponsors being associated with a sport entity. No single brand image stands out as the sponsor. Spectators are less able to distinguish competing brands in this instance, thereby diminishing the value for all. Clutter commonly occurs when no specific sponsorship categories are designated. Consider the typical 5k road race t-shirt. On the back is a conglomeration of company names and tag-lines. Yet, no single brand stands out or gains significantly from association with race participants.

Noise can be considered very similar to clutter. The average person is exposed to as many as 5,000 selling messages a day. Whether they are radio, television, Internet, billboard, or print advertisements, the "noise" from each begins to desensitize the consumer to all messages. This explains the yelling car salesman who is trying to break through the noise by being the loudest, or most annoying. Yet, the result is often a consumer who tunes out the message. Public address, or PA, announcements at stadiums and arenas come complete with sponsor mentions. Yet, very often these messages go unnoticed because of the "noise" factor.

Still the most challenging element of competition to handle in sponsorship is the deliberate attempts to ambush another sponsor's association with a sport entity. Take for example Coca-Cola's decision to race eight cars complete with Coca-Cola branding to launch their new "low carb" product, C2. The race chosen was the Pepsi 400. Obviously, Pepsi had paid a premium to be the title sponsor of the race. Coca-Cola officials insisted there was no intent to ambush, yet this example exhibits the very definition of *ambush marketing*: a direct competing brand in the same product category, staging a presence to create confusion in the mind of the consumer regarding who is the official sponsor. Clearly, new or non-seasoned race fans may have confused the title sponsor of the race (who paid millions for the official rights) with the ambush company who bypassed the official payment to circumvent the event with their own branded race cars.

Increasingly, sponsors are requiring some assurance that ambush will be prevented by the sport property.

EMOTION AND LOYALTY

Just as the Pepsi/Coke scenario points out, when creating buy-in for potential corporate partners, nothing appeals quite as strongly as the example of NASCAR fans.

It is not by accident that NASCAR has been one of the fastest growing sports in the industry. In this sport that incorporates sponsorship into every conceivable element, fans are famous for their degree of emotional commitment to each of their favorite driver's sponsors. Some fans have gone so far as to say that they will buy only the products from companies that sponsor "their" driver. This may seem logical if the sponsor happens to be involved in auto parts or a similarly linked product; however, products such as *Tide* laundry detergent have also been cited as chosen for purchase directly due to their sponsorship involvement with a race car driver. Few sports can claim this degree of emotional commitment and loyalty, yet it remains the ultimate goal of all who create sponsorship deals.

Sponsor Rationale

The most desirable strategies are those that create a win-win situation. A win for both the sponsor and the sport entity can best be achieved by meeting sponsors' objectives, including those that replace direct funding or dollar allocation with trade-outs or in-kind services. A familiar model in which this strategy is evident is the gift-in-kind of shoes and apparel to a collegiate sport team by a company such as Nike or Adidas. The company in many instances provides little or no financial contribution to the athletic program. Instead, a trade is made in which the company agrees to provide their branded product for the right to be affiliated or directly associated with the team or program. The benefit for the shoe company is reaped when local fans become consumers and possibly develop loyalty to the brand as a result of the sponsorship for their favorite team. Additionally, if the team happens to receive significant media coverage, the brand then benefits from the university's success. When a university team appears on ESPN, in March Madness on CBS, or in a football bowl game on network television, then the return on investment is significantly increased. Recruits and the general public often judge coaches and teams as legitimate if they have a significant sponsorship deal.

EMPLOYEE MOTIVATION

While return on investment is arguably always a primary motivation, other motives can impact sponsorship decisions and lead to the accomplishment of many of the same objectives. Consider the sponsorship involvement of Safeway grocery stores and the LPGA. Safeway serves as the host (and title sponsor) for a sanctioned tournament at Superstition Mountain in Arizona, at which one of the primary benefits is the delivery of every tournament attendee directly to a tent, where product trials and samples for Safeway brands and partner brands who sell in Safeway stores are given out freely. The most direct path to the first tee box is through the Safeway tent, because very few sports fans will turn down free samples of food, drink, candy, and similar grocery store items. These fans are treated well and are aware of the sponsor before they have reached the actual tournament. Add to this the opportunity for Safeway employees to be a part of this premier professional sport event by performing the many volunteer duties, and one can see how value becomes more than monetary for both parties involved.

The final perk from this exemplary relationship in 2003 and 2007 was the participation of Michelle Wie, the 13-year-old golf prodigy and later the 17-year-old golf phenomenon. Due to Wie's decision to compete in the tournament during her high school spring break, the media attention resulted in coverage by local and national newspapers, as well as television exposure. Based on this example, the assortment of benefits available to the sponsor and the ensuing rationale for involvement with the sport event/property become clear.

AWARENESS

Most often companies engage in sport sponsorship to create brand awareness and enhance their brand image. The Lance Armstrong/Subaru sponsorship has been most effective in illustrating aspects such as lifestyle and affinity marketing. In *lifestyle marketing*, the company is attempting to cut through all the other selling messages by appealing to consumers who have or desire the lifestyle depicted in the sport sponsorship relationship. Lance Armstrong represents many facets of the ac-

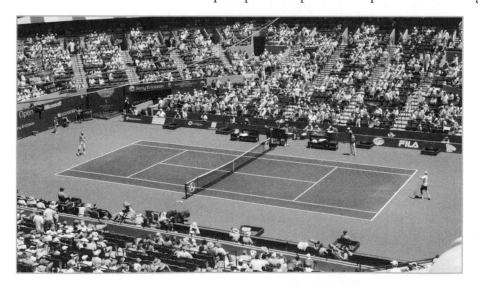

tive adult lifestyle considered to be attractive to a large target market. Lifestyle marketing often cuts across demographic lines, appealing to people who already have an affinity for the activity or lifestyle represented by the sport sponsorship. This is not to say that those who comprise this target market have an ambition to ride or win the Tour de France. However, the appeal of a winner who has overcome great odds and survived, and who competes in a sport that more people can participate in recreationally, certainly speaks to the value in creating brand awareness for the sponsoring company. Throw in a recognizable link such as the tag-line "driven by what's inside," and this becomes an exceptional example of a win-win relationship.

IMAGE

There can be a negative side to sponsorship relationships, however, when ethical concerns are not addressed. Phillip Morris's Virginia Slims brand was the title sponsor of the women's professional tennis tour for nearly 20 years. The positive image of active, healthy elite women tennis players effectively transferred to the Virginia Slims brand. "There is a link between the word 'slim' and the activity of tennis as a means of becoming slim. Tennis champions are in peak physical condition, and since endurance is important, their hearts and lungs are particularly strong and healthy. The obvious implications of the linkage are that sport and smoking are desirable for women" (Howard & Crompton, 2004, p. 483). This type of relationship illustrates the ethical challenge that can arise when companies want to provide significant funding for association with a sport product, with the intent of using the sport image to improve their company or product image.

Clearly, opportunities arise in which the sport entity would be wise to back away from sponsorships that create ethical dilemmas. An example that better illustrates a positive link of brand image with a sport that has a lifestyle all its own would be Roxy and surfing. The brand Roxy was created by Quicksilver to appeal to the women's surf market. Roxy has been so successful in associating with top women surfers and surf competitions that Roxy is synonymous with the surfing lifestyle among women.

SALES OBJECTIVES

Perhaps the most clear, rational, and measurable benefit in a sport sponsorship is meeting sales objectives. The case of the FIFA World Cup in South Korea illustrates this rationale well. Product purchase intentions are most often considered a key sales objective that can be measured. When consumer purchase intentions were examined, as influenced by the 2002 FIFA World Cup in Korea/Japan, a significant relationship was found. Consumers felt more positively about the image of the companies that sponsored the event, they were more accurate at recognizing the actual sponsors, and they indicated that they would be more likely to buy the products of the sponsors (Shin, 2002). To the companies involved, this indicates a successful sponsorship relationship because of the likely return on investment.

SELLING SPONSORSHIPS

One of the most important factors to recognize relative to sponsorship in sport is that those who can sell well advance quickly. With this in mind, a focus on a few of the methods that enhance success in sales is provided. There are seven rules for effective personal selling according to Mullin, Hardy, and Sutton (2007):

1. The utilization of a marketing database generates leads that are likely to have a greater interest and/or ability to become consumers.

2. Communicate with consumers based on a shared interest in the sport product. Consider the potential consumer as a potential friend.

3. The LIBK rule needs to be adhered to. This means to "let it be known" that you are proud and enthusiastic to be selling a product you believe in.

4. Be prepared for the most common objections used. Be flexible in your approach and capable of providing examples that show how current consumers once had similar objections.

5. Be an effective listener, then be prepared to react with points that address the consumer's concerns.

6. Take the consultant approach. Approach the consumer as though you are proposing possible solutions to the consumer's needs and wants, not just trying to make a sale.

7. Just as "fit" is critical to success in sponsorship, "fit" is key to success in sales. Match the consumer to a product that is appropriate for his or her budget and lifestyle.

When selling sponsorship, the most desirable measure from a sponsor's perspective is a return on investment (ROI). The impact that a sponsorship investment has on sales is the best indicator that the sponsorship was a success. Sales objectives are most often expressed in three ways:

• Increase in traffic at retail points of purchase

• Resulting number of new sales leads

• Actual increase in sales connected with a sponsorship

Actual sales can be measured by tracking coupon redemptions or ticket discounts given with a proof of purchase of the sponsor's product. Similarly, a comparison of sales during a three-month period corresponding with the event and the sales for a comparable period can be calculated to measure actual increases.

The AIDA concept for promotions was previously discussed relative to meeting sponsor's objectives. Yet, this concept can be extended to assist in the enhancement of sales. The *product adoption process* is an extension of the AIDA concept that awareness builds interest and knowledge of a brand's associated benefits, which in effect, creates an image in the mind of the consumer. When the image is congruent with an image the consumer desires, then a product trial is likely. Evaluation is being conducted in the mind of the consumer both before and after the product purchase. The goal is to move the consumer to purchase the product. Following the consumer's experience with the product, the option exists to repeat the purchase, re-evaluate and consider alternate brands, or discontinue the process.

If the consumer chooses to repeat their purchase, then product adoption has been attained. At this point, the levels of branding suggest that consumers have progressed from *brand recognition* to *brand preference*. Once brand preference has been achieved, loyalty builds as the consumer refuses to purchase any other company's product in that category. Ultimately, the consumer then moves into *brand insistence*, which is the creation of *brand loyalty*. As we have seen from NASCAR and other similar examples, sponsorships are often sold because of the potential for brand loyalty as exemplified in sport.

Take, for example, the recent sponsorship between Lexus and the Atlanta Braves.

One of the attributes of the Lexus sponsorship was the provision of parking spaces at Atlanta Braves games free of charge for Lexus owners. This approach was intended to reward Lexus owners and encourage their loyalty to the brand, while also creating an opportunity to expose Atlanta Braves fans to new Lexus models. This strategy illustrates another important concept in selling, which is the *consumer escalator*. With the consumer escalator model, the goal is to move consumers from non-aware/non-consumers onto the consumption escalator and ultimately up each level from light to medium to heavy users. Heavy users are known to be responsible for up to 80 percent of all purchases. This is significant, especially considering that heavy users may represent as few as 20 percent of all consumers. This *80/20 principle* suggests that a focus be made on moving consumers up the escalator while keeping the existing heavy user segment content.

In sales, finding new consumers or leads is far more difficult than assisting the existing consumers to increase their level of consumption. In addition, existing consumers provide invaluable promotion through word of mouth. Many consumers step onto the escalator as a direct result of influence by a friend or colleague who happens to be a consumer.

Why Sponsors Defect

Sponsors defect or discontinue their relationship with a sport entity for two primary reasons: (1) their goals and objectives were not met, and/or (2) they have chosen a new marketing approach that may focus on a new target market or a different direction altogether. Little can be done when the second rationale is given; however, failure to meet objectives or company marketing goals rests with the company as well as the sport entity. The key strategy that must be incorporated is a leveraging or activation plan. *Leveraging* involves developing an integrated plan that specifies the role promotional tools will play and the extent to which each will be used. Unless a company invests in these additional means to amplify the intended message, its initial sponsorship fee will likely be a wasted investment. Sponsorship offers a unifying theme that needs to be exploited to communicate with a specific target market through the use of a full array of promotional tools. *Sponsorship activation* means that for every dollar spent on a sponsorship fee, an equivalent dollar is typically spent in the promotion of the sponsorship. This 1:1 ratio was once considered an industry standard. Thus, one of the surest ways to see a sponsorship fail is to neglect allocating funding to activate the sponsorship. Today, many elite sponsors say the ratio is more likely to be 1:5 for a sponsorship that will be short term (1 year or less). When the contract includes multiple years, the ratio can be closer to 1:2 or 1:1, with an extended period of time to create a strong association between the sport entity and sponsor to build the message and enhance loyalty.

Take, for example, Subaru and Lance Armstrong. Subaru spent significantly more money promoting its association with the seven-time Tour de France winner than it paid initially to become an official sponsor. The tag line "Driven by what's inside" became synonymous with Lance and Subaru. His success was their success. Yet, waiting for media coverage to catch a glimpse of Lance with a Subaru support vehicle behind him in a competition would be foolish. Instead, Subaru created television, print, and web campaigns that utilized the association to communicate the message consistently and effectively over time. In contrast, when Subaru was a sponsor of the LPGA, little to no actual promotion of the LPGA sponsorship was created. Instead, at the end of the single-year contract, Subaru opted out of its relationship with the LPGA. This shows the need to build into the contract a clear understanding of activation, leveraging, and servicing of the sponsorship.

Sponsorship Evaluation and Measurement

Generally, the one aspect in which many sport entities fall short in regard to corporate sponsorship is the area of measurement and evaluation. Commonly, the only means for communicating with sponsors following the event ends up being a quickly written thank-you note with a picture of their sign or logo at the event. Seldom are sponsors informed of the *impact* of their sponsorship. For example, how many people were in attendance, and who were they? What was the extended audience reach? The profile of the audience reach incorporates the media outlets that covered the event and the amount of coverage/publicity given by each. Most media outlets have data on their audiences that can assist in determining if the target market was reached. Yet, as simple as this type of feedback may seem, many of the best means for providing information can be acquired with equally simple recognition and recall techniques.

Recognition occurs when a spectator can correctly identify the brand of a sponsor from a list. *Recall* equates to a higher level of effectiveness. In recall, a spectator can remember and correctly identify a sponsor's brand without input or prompting. The downside to recognition measuring is that oftentimes consumers identify brands that were not official sponsors, indicating ambush has occurred. In the case of the 2002 FIFA World Cup, most spectators surveyed indicated that Nike (63.7 percent) was an official sponsor. In reality, the official partner was Adidas. Nike had contracted to supply uniforms for the Korean team, in addition to Brazil, Portugal, Russia, and Nigeria. Nike also had several well-planned promotions that confused consumers as to who was the official sponsor. Nonetheless, on a similar measure, the sponsorship by Adidas proved to be effective. Purchase intentions toward the sponsoring company's products increased 41.5 percent for Adidas due to their sponsorship of the FIFA World Cup. Purchase intention has been found to have a significant relationship with corporate image, prior use experience, and sponsor recognition accuracy (Shin, 2002).

Given the common omission of feedback provided by sport entities, specialized companies have emerged for the sole purpose of evaluating sponsorship effectiveness. One such company, Joyce Julius and Associates, created a model in which each and every second that a sponsor's brand was recognizable during a television broadcast was counted. An accumulation of hours and seconds that the brand was visible then was utilized to calculate the equivalent dollar amount that such visibility would have cost if the corporate sponsor had chosen to simply buy advertising time on that station, at that time, on that day. Surprisingly to some, the accumulation of minutes often equated to hundreds of thousands of dollars. More often than not, the cost paid by the sponsor was significantly less than the equivalent "value" attributed by this evaluation technique. Similar measurements can be calculated in print media coverage by measuring column inches (size), number of company mentions, and location within the print publication (e.g., newspaper sports section). A photo with the brand of the sponsor prominently displayed often is attributed a higher value than being mentioned in the text of an article.

Overall, sponsorship evaluation should be designed to meet two primary purposes: (1) measuring the accomplishment of the sponsor's objectives and (2) generating information that can be utilized when selling future sponsorships.

Summary

There are five primary concerns that need to be addressed to create success when selling sport sponsorships:

1. Benefits sought by potential sponsors are framed as specific, measurable objectives.

2. A good "fit" equates to a shared image between the corporate sponsor and the sport property with target market access.

3. Integration with other communication vehicles around a unifying theme should be incorporated with promotional actions that reinforce the sponsor's desired message.

4. Protect clients from ambush, clutter, and noise (perceptual distortion).

5. Time/longevity of a sponsorship relationship contributes to improved recall, recognition, and product purchase intentions among consumers, thereby improving sponsorship effectiveness.

Sponsorship is one of the most valuable tools sport managers have to work with. Future sport professionals will need to understand and be capable of utilizing this essential tool.

DISCUSSION ACTIVITIES

1. Consider for a moment the sport events you have attended or consumed through some form of media. Next consider recent purchases you have made. Did sponsors of the sports you consumed influence these purchases? If so, why?

2. Look through some recent issues of *Street and Smith's SportsBusiness Journal*. Based on what you've learned in this chapter, select a few sport properties and match them with potential corporate sponsors.

SUGGESTED READINGS

Howard, D. R., & Crompton, J. L. (2004). *Financing sport* (2nd ed.). Morgantown, WV: Fitness Information Technology.

Lagae, W. (2005). *Sport sponsorship & marketing communications: A European perspective*. London, UK: Financial Times Prentice Hall.

Martin, P. (2003). *Made possible by: Succeeding with sponsorship*. London, UK: Jossey-Bass Wiley.

References

Fuse Marketing. (n.d.). *Case study: Mountain Dew*. Retrieved February 25, 2009, from http://www.fusemarketing.com/modules.php?name=CaseStudies&ServiceID=1&TacticID=1&CaseID=19

Gwinner, K. P., & Eaton, J. (1999). Building image through event sponsorship: The role of image transfer. *Journal of Advertising, 28*(4), 47–67.

Kaplan, D. (2007, October 29–November 4). Running up big numbers. *Street & Smith's SportsBusiness Journal, 10*(27), 18–23.

Keeping the Olympics Ideal. (1997, April). *Sport Business*, 32–33.

Lough, N., & Irwin, R. (2001). A comparative analysis of sponsorship objectives for U.S. women's sport and traditional sport sponsorship. *Sport Marketing Quarterly, 10*(4), 202–211.

Mullin, B., Hardy, S., & Sutton, W. (2007). *Sport Marketing* (3rd ed.). Champaign, IL: Human Kinetics

Pope, N. (1998, January). Overview of current sponsorship thought. *The Cyber-Journal of Sport Marketing*. Retrieved July 21, 2004, from http://www.cad.gu.edu.au/cjsm/pope21.htm

Shin, H. (2002). The effects of sport sponsorship on consumer purchase intentions. Unpublished master's thesis, Illinois State University, Normal, IL.

Stotlar, D. (2002). Sport sponsorship: Lessons from the Sydney Olympic Games. *International Journal of Applied Sports Sciences, 14*(2), 27–45.

Ukman, K. (1995). *The IEG's complete guide to sponsorship: Everything you need to know about sports, arts, event, entertainment and cause marketing*, Chicago, IL: IEG.

Chapter Nine

SPORT FACILITY AND EVENT MANAGEMENT

BERNARD GOLDFINE • TOM SAWYER

"THE OLDEST STANDING BUILDING IN ROME IS THE COLOSSEUM."

—RED SMITH

LEARNING OBJECTIVES
Upon completion of this chapter, the student should be able to • Discuss the skills necessary for event and facility management; • Identify models used in the management of facilities; • Understand the importance of operational philosophies and mission statements regarding the management of venues; • Address the elements of public and media relations; • Explain the risk management considerations in the management of venues; • Identify revenue streams in facility management; • List the elements of event planning; • Describe how events can be most effectively organized for success; and • Recognize the role of marketing and budgeting in event and facility management.

Introduction

Have you ever been a spectator at a sporting event or concert and left with the feeling you had just experienced something that was incredibly special? Conversely, have you ever had a miserable experience at a highly anticipated event? Your experiences could very easily have been influenced by the manner in which the event and/or facility was managed. If you have ever wondered how you would plan an event differently, perhaps facility and event management might be a career path to consider.

To embark upon such a career, you have to be someone who likes organization, order, advanced planning, leading others, and does not mind being assertive and aggressive (Solomon, 2002). Specifically, some of the attributes that successful facility and event planners must possess are (1) interpersonal and leadership skills (i.e., inspiring others to perform effectively and calmly under pressure); (2) proactive thinking (i.e., anticipating problems and having contingency plans ready when obstacles present themselves) (Walker & Stotlar, 1997); (3) organizational skills (such as when and how to delegate tasks); and (4) the ability to think quickly on one's feet when crises emerge. Also, this field calls for individuals who do not mind working nontraditional and extended hours.

There are many opportunities for sport management graduates to use facility/venue and event management skills, including working for a large, prominent organization that specializes in event management, such as Jack Morton Worldwide (www.jackmorton.com). Or you could work for a worldwide venue management company like Ogden Entertainment, which oversees concessions, merchandising, ticketing, maintenance, security, sponsorships, and complete venue management in over 125 entertainment venues internationally. However, this skill set can also be used in smaller boutique event or venue management firms.

The skills required for event and venue management are also advantageous for individuals seeking employment in sport-related organizations that manage their own facilities or run their own events. For example, sport organizations that do not outsource their operations need individuals whose focus is game-day operations or event management. In *participant-oriented organizations*, individuals with very specialized skill sets often manage municipal parks, YMCAs, recreation departments, collegiate recreation settings, and special events. The aforementioned organizations' facilities, in addition to some *public assembly facilities* that are often run by the municipalities themselves, require competent personnel to operate them in the most cost-effective and safe manner.

Facility management and event management often go hand-in-hand; certainly most events require a venue in which to be held. There are, however, distinct differences in each job that will be spelled out in the following sections.

Sport Facility/Venue Management

"WHATEVER YOU DO, DO IT WITH ALL YOUR MIGHT. WORK AT IT, EARLY AND LATE, IN SEASON AND OUT OF SEASON, NOT LEAVING A STONE UNTURNED, AND NEVER DEFERRING FOR A SINGLE HOUR THAT WHICH CAN BE DONE JUST AS WELL NOW."

—P. T. BARNUM

Facility/venue management is a coordinated and integrated process of utilizing an organization's resources to achieve specific goals and objectives through the managerial functions of planning, organizing, leading, and evaluating. Venue management also includes effective booking and scheduling, provision of security and safety for fans and participants, and maintenance of the venue.

Planning for events and getting the details right is also an essential part of facility/venue management. When things don't go correctly, chaos ensues. For example, in a recent NBA professional basketball overtime game featuring the Atlanta Hawks and the Miami Heat, the NBA—in a stunning move—took away a victory from the Atlanta Hawks and ordered the team to replay the end of the overtime. What led to this bizarre ending? The Atlanta Hawks' statistician crew, charged with keeping the statistics and running the game clock, incorrectly disqualified then–Miami Heat center Shaquille O'Neal with too many fouls and was ruled "grossly negligent" by the NBA. Additionally, the Atlanta Hawks organization was fined $50,000 (Smith, 2008).

Sport facility venues can be classified into sub-categories. Examples of outdoor venues could include

- aquatic centers,
- baseball and softball parks,
- football and soccer stadiums,
- motor sport tracks,
- golf courses and practice facilities,
- tennis stadiums and complexes,
- recreational sport fields, and
- parks and playgrounds.

Indoor venues could include

- basketball arenas,
- bowling alleys,
- domed stadia,
- field houses,
- gymnastic venues,
- fitness centers,
- family centers,
- soccer facilities,
- water parks,
- ice hockey and skating rinks, and
- natatoriums.

VENUE OWNERSHIP AND MANAGEMENT

Venues are either publicly or privately owned. Public ownership requires management to operate the venue within regulations and procedures established by the governing body. Recently, both publicly and privately owned venues have moved toward private management companies, yet their different objectives have a direct impact on a facility and event manager's decision making process.

Table 9.1 depicts four eras and shows that there has been a substantial shift over time in responsibility for funding these types of facilities. (Crompton, 2004)

Public Ownership

The local government and/or government entities operate publicly owned venues such as Shea Stadium in New York and Soldier Field in Chicago. The objective of these governmental agencies is to provide a service to the community while generating enough revenue to break even. All revenue beyond expenses goes back into operation of the venue.

Private Ownership

A number of individuals privately own venues (e.g., Forum Arena, Pro Players Stadium, Texas Stadium, Wrigley Field); others are owned by corporations (e.g., Green Bay Packers, Green Bay, WI). The primary objective of a privately owned facility is to deliver a profit for the owners and/or stockholders. The management focuses on maximum return on investment.

Sports Authorities

These are not-for-profit entities generally operated by a commission or board of directors appointed by a governmental body. Sport authorities control a number of venues, such as Bank One Ballpark (Arizona Diamondbacks), 3 Com Park (San Francisco Giants), Coors Field (Colorado Rockies), ThunderDome (Tampa Bay Devil Rays), Turner Field (Atlanta Braves), U.S. Cellular Field (Chicago White Sox), and Camden Yards (Baltimore Orioles), among others.

Table 9.1. Comparison of Public and Private Sector Financing by Funding Era

Combined Costs for Stadiums and Areas

Era	% Public	% Private
Gestation (1961–69)	88	12
Public Subsidy (1970–84)	93	07
Transitional Public-Private Partnerships 1985–94	64	36
Fully-Loaded Public-Private Partnership 1995–2003	51	49
Future Partnership (2004–2015)	33	67

Modified from Crompton, J. L. (2004). Beyond economic impact: An alternative rationale for the public subsidy of Major League sports facilities. *Journal of Sport Management, 18*(1), 41.

NAMING RIGHTS IN PUBLIC ASSEMBLY VENUES

One of the major sources of finance for sport facilities is sponsorship through naming rights in large, public assembly venues. This phenomenon was referred to in Chapter 6 (Sport Finance) and in Table 6.1. To determine the extent to which primary naming rights (naming of the facility) and secondary naming rights (parts of the venues—such as clubs levels, hospitality suites, etc.) are being used in today's sports venues, examine the following tables:

Primary Naming Rights—MLB

Category	Amount	Percent of Total
Financial*	5	31%
Food & Beverage	4	25%
Communications	3	19%
Insurance	2	13%
Software	1	6%
Retail	1	6%
Total	16	100%

Primary Naming Rights—NHL

Category	Amount	Percent of Total
Financial	7	44%
Insurance*	2	13%
Automotive	1	6%
Communications	1	6%
Technology	1	6%
Online	1	6%
Conglomerate	1	6%
Media	1	6%
Energy	1	6%
Total	16	100%

Table 9.2. Primary Naming Rights of Professional Sport Venues

PRIMARY NAMING RIGHTS—MLB

Facility	Location	Teams	Sponsor	Sponsor HQ	Category	Inception	Price	Term	Price/Year	Exp.	Other Events/ Tenants
AT&T Park	San Francisco, CA	San Francisco Giants	AT&T Inc.	San Antonio, TX	Communications	2000	$50,000,000	24	$2,083,333	2024	NCAA Emerald Bowl
Chase Field	Phoenix, AZ	Arizona Diamondbacks	JPMorgan Chase & Co.	New York, NY	Financial	1998	$66,000,000	30	$2,200,000	2028	—
Citi Field*	Flushing, NY	New York Mets	Citigroup, Inc.	New York, NY	Financial	2006	$400,000,000	20	$20,000,000	2026	—
Citizens Bank Park	Philadelphia, PA	Philadelphia Phillies	Citizens Financial Group Inc.	Providence, RI	Financial	2004	$95,000,000	25	$3,800,000	2029	—
Comerica Park	Detroit, MI	Detroit Tigers	Comerica Inc.	Dallas, TX	Financial	2000	$66,000,000	30	$2,200,000	2030	—
Coors Field	Denver, CO	Colorado Rockies	Molson Coors Brewing Co.	Golden, CO	Food and Beverage	2005	$15,000,000	Indefinite	NA	Indefinite	—
Great American Ball Park	Cincinnati, OH	Cincinnati Reds	Great American Insurance Co.	Cincinnati, OH	Insurance	2002	$75,000,000	30	$2,500,000	2032	—
McAfee Coliseum	Oakland, CA	Oakland Raiders	McAfee Inc.	Santa Clara, CA	Software	1998	$11,800,000	10	$1,180,000	2008	Oakland A's
Miller Park	Milwaukee, WI	Milwaukee Brewers	Miller Brewing Co.	Milwaukee, WI	Food and Beverage	2000	$41,200,000	20	$2,060,000	2020	—
Minute Maid Park	Houston, TX	Houston Astros	The Coca-Cola Co.	Atlanta, GA	Food and Beverage	2001	$170,000,000	28	$6,071,429	2029	—
PETCO Park	San Diego, CA	San Diego Padres	Petco Animal Supplies Inc.	San Diego, CA	Retail	2003	$60,000,000	22	$2,727,273	2025	USA Sevens (Annual Rugby Tournament)
PNC Park	Pittsburgh, PA	Pittsburgh Pirates	The PNC Financial Services Group Inc.	Pittsburgh, PA	Financial	2001	$40,000,000	20	$2,000,000	2021	—
Rogers Centre	Toronto, Canada	Toronto Blue Jays	Rogers Communications	Toronto, Canada	Communications	2004	$17,736,000	10	$1,773,600	2014	Toronto Argonauts (CFL) Int'l Bowl (NCAA)
Safeco Field	Seattle, WA	Seattle Mariners	Safeco Corp.	Seattle, WA	Insurance	1999	$40,000,000	20	$2,000,000	2019	—
Tropicana Field	Tampa, FL	Tampa Bay Devil Rays	Tropicana Products Inc.	Bradenton, FL	Food and Beverage	1996	$46,000,000	30	$1,533,333	2026	—
U.S. Cellular Field	Chicago, IL	Chicago White Sox	U.S. Cellular Corp.	Chicago, IL	Communications	2002	$68,000,000	23	$2,956,522	2025	—

Sources: Collected by Adam Powell from *SportsBusiness Journal*, Wikipedia.com, Ballparks.com, and company websites.
*Not yet opened

Table 9.2. *Continued*

PRIMARY NAMING RIGHTS—NHL

Facility	Location	Teams	Sponsor	Sponsor HQ	Category	Inception	Price	Term	Price/Year	Exp.	Other Tenants
BankAtlantic Center	Sunrise, FL	Florida Panthers	BankAtlantic	Fort Lauderdale, FL	Financial	2005	$27,000,000	30	$2,700,000	2035	—
Bell Centre	Montreal, Canada	Montreal Canadiens	Bell Canada	Montreal, Canada	Communications	2002	$60,000,000	20	$3,000,000	2023	—
Sommet Center	Nashville, TN	Nashville Predators	Sommet Group	Franklin, TN	Conglomerate	2007	NA	NA	NA	2018	Nashville Kats (AFL)
General Motors Place	Vancouver, Canada	Vancouver Canucks	General Motors	Detroit, MI	Automotive	1995	$18,500,000	20	$925,000	2015	—
HP Pavilion at San Jose	San Jose, CA	San Jose Sharks	Hewlett-Packard Co.	Palo Alto, CA	Technology	2001	$47,000,000	15	$3,133,333	2016	San Jose SaberCats (AFL) San Jose Stealth (NLL)ATP SAP Open
Honda Center	Anaheim, CA	Mighty Ducks	Honda	Tokyo, Japan	Automotive	2006	$60,000,000	15	$4,000,000	2021	—
HSBC Arena	Buffalo, NY	Buffalo Sabres	HSBC USA Inc.	Hong Kong	Financial	1996	$22,500,000	30	$750,000	2026	Buffalo Bandits (NLL)
Jobing.com Arena	Glendale, AZ	Phoenix Coyotes	Jobing.com	Glendale, AZ	Online	2006	$25,000,000	10	$2,500,000	2016	—
Mellon Arena**	Pittsburgh, PA	Pittsburgh Penguins	Mellon Financial	Pittsburgh, PA	Financial	NA	NA	NA	NA	NA	—
Nationwide Arena	Columbus, OH	Columbus Blue Jackets	Nationwide Insurance	Columbus, OH	Insurance	2000	$135,000,000	Indefinite	NA	Indefinite	Columbus Destroyers (AFL)
Pengrowth Saddledome	Calgary, Canada	Calgary Flames	Pengrowth Mgmt.	Calgary, Canada	Financial	2000	$20,000,000	20	$1,000,000	2020	—
Prudential Center*	Newark, NJ	New Jersey Devils	Prudential Financial	Newark, NJ	Financial	2007	$105,300,000	20	$5,265,000	2027	Seton Hall (basketball)
RBC Center	Raleigh, NC	Carolina Hurricanes	RBC Centura Banks Inc.	Halifax, Canada	Financial	2002	$80,000,000	20	$4,000,000	2022	NC State (basketball)
Scotiaban Place	Ottawa, Canada	Ottawa Senators	Scotia Bank	Toronto, Canada	Financial	2006	$200,000,000	15	$1,330,000	2021	—
St. Pete Times Forum	Tampa, FL	Tampa Bay Lightning	St. Petersburg Times	St. Petersburg, FL	Media	2002	$30,000,000	12	$2,500,000	2014	Tampa Bay Storm (AFL)
Xcel Energy Center	Minneapolis, MN	Minnesota Wild	Xcel Energy	Minneapolis, MN	Energy	2000	$75,000,000	24	$3,125,000	2024	Minnesota Swarm (NLL)

Sources: Collected by Adam Powell from *SportsBusiness Journal* research, Wikipedia.com, Ballparks.com, and company websites.
* Not yet opened
** Will be razed after the 2009 NHL Season

Secondary Naming Rights

Category	Amount	Percent of Total
Food & Beverage	17	23%
Spirits	14	19%
Automotive	9	12%
Financial	9	12%
Communications	5	7%
Media	4	5%
Airlines	3	4%
Retail	3	4%
Attorney	1	1%
Building Products	1	1%
Casino	1	1%
Energy	1	1%
Online	1	1%
Real Estate	1	1%
Software	1	1%
Tobacco	1	1%
Travel	1	1%
Total	73	100%

Table 9.3. Secondary Naming Rights of Professional Sport Venues

NFL STADIUMS (SECONDARY)

Facility	Team	Sponsor	Category	Branded Area
Jacksonville Municipal Stadium	Jacksonville Jaguars	Crown Royal	Food and Beverage	Crown Royal Touchdown Club (Luxury Suites)
		Budweiser	Food and Beverage	Bud Zone (Sports Bar)
		Pepsi	Food and Beverage	Pepsi Plaza (Entertainment Zone)
Edward Jones Dome	St. Louis Rams	Budweiser	Food and Beverage	Budweiser Brew House
Ford Field	Detroit Lions	Comcast	Media	Comcast Family Fun Zone
Gillette Stadium	New England Patriots	Fidelity Investments	Financial	Fidelity Investments Clubhouse
		Bank of America	Financial	Bank of America access ramp
		uBid.com	Online	uBid.com access ramp
Heinz Field	Pittsburgh Steelers	Coca-Cola	Food and Beverage	Coca-Cola Great Hall (retail/entertainment area)
		McDonalds	Food and Beverage	McDonalds Steelers KidZone Show
INVESCO Field at Mile High	Denver Broncos	Budweiser	Food and Beverage	Budweiser Champions Club
		United Airlines	Airlines	United Club Level (Suites)
M&T Bank Stadium	Baltimore Ravens	Budweiser	Food and Beverage	Backyard Bash (Hospitality)
		Miller Lite	Food and Beverage	Beer Garden Tents
Monster Park	San Francisco 49ers	Budweiser	Food and Beverage	Bud Light Goldmine (entertainment)
		Coca-Cola	Food and Beverage	Coca-Cola Red Zone (exclusive ticket package)
Qwest Field	Seattle Seahawks	Wells Fargo	Financial	Club Wells Fargo Lounges
		Fox Sports Net (FSN)	Media	FSN Lounge
Reliant Stadium	Houston Texans	Miller Lite	Food and Beverage	Miller Lite Entrance
		Ford	Automotive	Ford Entrance
		Coca-Cola	Food and Beverage	Coca-Cola Entrance
		Gallery Furniture	Retail	Gallery Furniture Entrance
U of Phoenix Stadium	Arizona Cardinals	Insight Enterprises	Software	Insight Club East

Table 9.3. *Continued*

NBA ARENAS (SECONDARY)

Facility	Main Teams	Sponsor	Category	Branded Area
Air Canada Centre	Raptors Maple Leafs	TD Waterhouse	Financial	TD Waterhouse Platinum Club (Restaurant)
American Airlines Arena	Miami Heat	Dewar's	Spirits	Dewar's 12 Lounge
American Airlines Center	Dallas Mavericks Dallas Stars	AT&T	Network	AT&T Plaza
		Jack Rouse Associates	Energy	TXU Concourse
US Airways Center	Phoenix Suns	Bud Light	Food and Beverage	Bud Light Paseo (Venue and Bar)
		Lexus	Automotive	Lexus Club (Lounge and Seating)
		Levy Restaurants	Food and Beverage	Levy Restaurant
		Verizon Wireless	Communications	Verizon Wireless Jungle (Jungle gym and Arcade for kids and families
AT&T Center	Spurs	AT&T	Communications	The AT&T Center "Star" (East entrance)
		AT&T	Communications	AT&T Center FAN SHOP and "Atomic Spur"
		Ashley Furniture	Retail	Ashley Furniture Saddle and Spurs Club
		Frost Bank	Financial	Frost Bank Saddle and Spurs club
		HEB	Retail	HEB Fan Fiesta
BankAtlantic Center	Florida Panthers	Lexus	Automotive	Lexus Club Level/Lexus Lot
		Spirit Airlines	Airlines	Spirit Gateway
		WCI Communities	Real Estate	WCI Communities Private Club
		BankAtlantic	Financial	BankAtlantic Chairman's Club
		Patron Tequila	Spirits	Patron Tequila Platinum Club
Bradley Center	Milwaukee Bucks	Cambria	Quartz Surfaces	Cambria Club (Premium seating and Lounge)
Continental Airlines Arena (Meadowlands)	Nets, Devils	Marquis Jet	Airlines	Marquis Jet Locker Room
		Vonage	Communications	Vonage Press Club
Conseco Fieldhouse	Indiana Pacers	Krieg DeVault	Attorney	Kreig DeVault Club Level (Premium Seats)
Energy Solutions Arena	Utah Jazz	Lexus	Automotive	Lexus Club
		All Star Catering	Food and Beverage	All Star Catering
Jobing.com Arena	Phoenix Coyotes	Lexus	Automotive	Lexus Level
Madison Square Garden	New York Knicks	WaMu	Banking	WaMu Theatre
Nationwide Arena	Columbus Blue Jackets	Bud Light	Food and Beverage	Bud Light Arena Pub

Table 9.3. *Continued*

NBA ARENAS (SECONDARY)

Facility	Main Teams	Sponsor	Category	Branded Area
Oracle Arena	Golden State Warriors	Smirnoff	Food and Beverage	The Plaza (Smirnoff) Club (Lounge and cocktails)
		Corona	Spirits	880 (Corona) Club (Lounge and cocktails)
Palace of Auburn Hills	Detroit Pistons	Jack Daniels	Spirits	Jack Daniels Old No. 7 Club (Restaurant)
		Captain Morgan	Spirits	Captain's Quarters (Restaurant)
Pepsi Center	Denver Nuggets Colorado Avalanche	Lexus	Automotive	Club Restaurant
		Denver Post	Media	Lounge
Philips Arena	Atlanta Hawks	Absolute	Spirits	Absolute Martini Bar
		First Horizon	Banking	First Horizon Club (Suite and Club seats)
Rose Garden	Trailblazers	Lexus	Automotive	Lexus Level
St. Pete Times Forum	Lightning	Absolute	Spirits	Absolute Experience Lounge
Staples Center	Lakers	Fox Sports	Media	SkyBox Restaurant
Target Center	Timberwolves	US Bank	Financial	US Bank Theater
TD BankNorth Garden	Celtics	New Balance	Apparel	Sports Museum
United Center	Bulls	Ketel One	Spirits	Ketel One Club (Club and Banquet)
		Jose Cuervo	Spirits	Jose Cuervo Cantina
		Budweiser Select	Food and Beverage	Budweiser Select Brew Pub and Carvery
Verizon Center	Washington Wizards	Lexus	Automotive	Lexus Suite Level
		Acela Express	Travel	Acela Club Seating
		Johnny Walker	Spirits	Johnny Walker Coach's Club
		Dewar's	Spirits	Dewar's 12 Clubhouse
		Crown Royal	Spirits	Crown Royal Suite
Wachovia Center	76ers	Holt's Cigars	Tobacco	Holt's Cigars Club
		Bud Light	Food and Beverage	Bud Light Zone
		Lexus	Automotive	Lexus Club (Restaurant)
		Cingular	Communications	Cingular Pavilion (Food and Beverage)
Xcel Energy Center	Minnesota Wild	Treasure Island	Casino	Treasure Island Resort and Casino Club Level

Sources: Collected by Adam Powell from the *SportsBusiness Journal* research, Wikipedia.com, Ballparks.com, and company and facility websites

PRIVATE MANAGEMENT (PRIVATIZATION OR OUTSOURCING)

When venue operations are privatized or outsourced, the owners pay a private organization to manage the day-to-day operation of the facility. There are five major private venue management companies including Centre Management, Global Spectrum, Leisure Management International (LMI), Ogden Allied, and Spectator Management Group (SMG). These companies manage venues worldwide. The first venue to be privatized or outsourced was the Louisiana Superdome. This type of management enables the owner to maintain control over the venue and at the same time (1) reduce or eliminate an operating deficit, (2) improve services, (3) increase the quality and quantity of the events scheduled, (4) join a larger na-

tional and international network of venues, which will expand opportunities for future booking of events, (5) provide greater flexibility concerning policies, procedures, and overall operational structure, (6) improve concessionaire (food service and pouring rights) and full-service restaurant agreements, and (7) expand the sale of licensed merchandise (Mulrooney & Farmer, 2001; Sawyer, Hypes, & Hypes, 2004). According to the *International Association of Assembly Managers (IAAM)* and the International Facility Management Association (IFMA), there are six easy steps in selecting a private management company. The steps include (1) preparing a *request for proposal (RFP)*, (2) distributing the RFP to all major management groups, (3) providing venue tours for all prospective bidders, (4) reviewing proposals, selecting the top five, and interviewing the top five bidders, (5) selecting the finalist and negotiating the contract, and (6) gaining final approval from both sides (Mulrooney & Farmer, 2001).

Types of Venues

A simple and effective way to classify facilities is by the types of events held within them. Table 1 describes the various venues based on events. Most of the facilities below include administrative and staff office; bars, ballrooms, concession and merchandising spaces; day care facilities; dressing, locker, and shower areas; lobby, lounge, and reception spaces; maintenance areas; parking, press, and interview spaces; public restrooms; restaurants; spectator seating (e.g., general admissions, club seats, private license seats [PSLs], and luxury [VIP] boxes); and ticket sales spaces.

Arenas, centers, coliseums, field houses, pavilions, palaces, and domes are indoor facilities that can be utilized for a variety of activities and events including circuses, concerts, shows, graduations, political rallies, and sporting events. Other specialized facilities include adventure areas, fitness centers, ice arenas, natatoriums, and skate parks. An adventure area might provide a ropes course (high and low), challenge (or confidence) course, and/or a rock-climbing wall. A fitness center might include activity spaces for cardiovascular exercises, free weights, gymnastics, martial arts, walking or jogging, racquetball courts, strength training, tennis, swimming, and aerobics. Ice arenas have been constructed for figure skating competitions, ice hockey, curling, and instructional and recreational skating. A natatorium is an aquatic center constructed to provide for swimming and diving, synchronized swimming, and water polo competition, and for instructional and recreational swimming and diving. Finally, skate parks have been designed as safe areas for kids to practice and compete in skateboarding activities. The number of parks nationwide has grown dramatically over the past decade.

Venue Organization

All successful venues have an established organization model to guide operations. The model outlines the personnel required for operations, an organizational philosophy, a mission statement, and goals and objectives based on the organization's philosophy and mission statement.

THE MANAGEMENT TEAM AND PERSONNEL

A venue director, general manager, chief executive officer, or executive director heads the management team for a venue. The head of the management team is ultimately responsible for venue planning and management. Further, he or she is responsible for negotiating major contracts pertaining to the venue, often including events being scheduled in the venue. Other members of the management team oversee marketing, public relations, customer relations, advertising, sales, and operations (Mulrooney & Farmer, 2001).

The number of personnel needed to manage a venue depends on the size of the venue and the number of events scheduled annually. Commonly, the following positions are present within a venue:

Venue Director/General Manager/Chief Executive Officer/Executive Director

Director of Operations
   Concessionaires
   Parking Attendants
   Ticket Takers
   Ushers
Coordinator of Maintenance
   Housekeepers
   Maintenance Workers
Coordinator of Events
Coordinator of Security (Emergency Management, Risk Management and Safety)
   Security Officers
   Emergency Medical Technicians

Director of Marketing
   Coordinator for Advertising
   Coordinator for Sales
      Ticket Sellers
      Retail Sales Associates

Director of Finance
   Accountants

Director of Customer and Public Relations

Figure 9.1. Typical Venue Personnel

The *director of operations* is the primary assistant to the head of the management team. This individual has a wide variety of departmental responsibilities, including event coordination; engineering; security, safety, and medical services; and maintenance and housekeeping. The *director of marketing* is responsible for market planning, advertising, and sales (i.e., sponsorships, merchandise, and tickets). The *director of finance* is responsible for fiscal accountability, budgeting, cost control, contract negotiations, and financing.

MISSION STATEMENT

The *mission statement* provides guidelines that outline the parameters for operating the venue and is the basis for the development of goals and objectives for the venue. *Goals* are achievable statements provided by management, ideally developed through consultation with all stakeholders in the venue. The goals are based on the mission statement and are used to justify the fiscal resources requested in a budget document. *Objectives*, sometimes called action strategies, are the activities to be implemented to reach the overall goal. Each objective should be measurable using assessments to evaluate whether or not the outcome has been met. A mission statement should be purposefully broad and vague, with more specific goals and objectives in support of the mission. Following is the mission statement of the Sports and Exhibition Authority of Pittsburgh and Allegheny County:

> The Sports & Exhibition Authority (SEA), formerly known as the Public Auditorium Authority, of Pittsburgh and Allegheny County was incorporated on February 3, 1954 pursuant to the Public Auditorium Authorities Law Act of July 29, 1953. As a joint authority for the City of Pittsburgh and Allegheny County, the SEA's mission is to provide venues for sporting, entertainment, educational, cultural, civic, and social events for the benefit of the general public. The SEA currently owns and operates the Civic Arena, leases the Benedum Center to the Pittsburgh Cultural Trust, and is responsible for the management of the David L. Lawrence Convention Center.

Source: http://www.pgh-sea.com/The_Authority/the_authority.html

POLICIES AND PROCEDURES

Policies should be developed with the mission statement in mind. A policy, although formal in nature, should be designed with some flexibility. Policies are general statements that serve to guide decision making and prescribe parameters within which certain decisions are to be made. Policies set limits but are subject to interpretation because they are broad in nature (Sawyer & Smith, 1999).

Procedures are a series of related steps that are to be followed in an established order to achieve a given purpose. Procedures prescribe exactly what actions are to be taken in a specific situation. They are similar to policies, as both are intended to influence certain decisions, but differ in that they address a series of related decisions (Sawyer & Smith, 1999).

All policies and procedures should be written and compiled into a policy and procedures manual or operations manual. This manual should be revised regularly to reflect changes or current practices within the organization. Finally, the manual should be provided to all employees so that they may familiarize themselves with all aspects of the operation.

Venue Operations

Operating a sport facility is challenging and complex, requiring knowledge of all managerial functions. There are important operational areas critical to the successful functioning of the venue, including booking and scheduling; customer and public relations; security, safety, and medical services; maintenance and housekeeping; retail sales; financial management; and risk management.

BOOKING AND SCHEDULING

Revenue generated from holding events is the main source of income at most venues. The mission of the venue will determine what types of events are booked and scheduled. Facilities that are home to an NFL franchise often utilize the facility for other events beyond the ten home football games per year. Each venue relies on shows, concerts, and events to shape its image. A public facility is obligated to provide for the scheduling of community events (e.g., charitable activities, home and garden shows, non-profit functions, or political rallies) whereas a private venue, depending upon its formation agreement, may limit charitable and non-profit activities. Ticketing activities often fall under the auspices of the booking and scheduling departments.

Booking is the act of engaging and contracting an event or attraction. The mechanics of booking include reserving a specific space, within a specific venue, for a specified date, at a specific time, for an agreed-upon amount of money. *Scheduling* is the reservation process and coordination of all events to the venue's available time. The reservation process involves scheduling a series of events and providing the best possible event mix to fit the venue's usage. Written contracts, with specific penalties for cancellation, revenue sharing, and other concerns are part of booking and scheduling.

Tickets are sold through the box office, one of the most important areas in the venue. It is the first contact the public has with the venue. Tickets account for a large amount of revenue for the facility. There are many ticketing variables, including venue capacity, types of seating (e.g., reserved and general admission), and type of ticket (e.g., computerized tickets or rolled tickets). Finally, there are specialized seating contracts, including luxury boxes, club seats, and *private seat licenses (PSLs)*.

PUBLIC AND MEDIA RELATIONS

"PUBLIC SENTIMENT IS EVERYTHING. WITH PUBLIC SENTIMENT, NOTHING CAN FAIL; WITHOUT IT, NOTHING CAN SUCCEED."

—ABRAHAM LINCOLN

A *public relations* program is designed to influence the opinions of people within a target market through responsible and acceptable performance, based on mutually satisfactory two-way communication. In order to gain public sentiment, sport venue managers must be in touch with a wide variety of constituents, including booking agents, promoters, sponsors, risk management experts, fans and patrons, employees, government officials, and the public in general. An effective public relations program will open communication lines with various publics and effectively utilize the media in a manner that competently presents the objectives of the organization to the public at large. Further, it will modify the attitudes and actions of the public through persuasion and integrate them with those of the organization.

In modern society, with its sophisticated communications media, citizens are virtually bombarded by thousands of messages per day. It is critical for the venue operator to make his or her message stand out among all the "noise."

SECURITY, SAFETY, AND MEDICAL SERVICES

The security, safety, and medical services usually are under the jurisdiction of the department of operations. Larger venues generally have some full-time safety personnel, but generally hire part-time help—usually police officers and EMS personnel to assist with particular events. Often, private crowd management firms like Contemporary Services Corporation (CSC), Tenable, and Landmark are retained to help with crowd control at events. All employees should be trained in CPR and first aid. The venue should also have an emergency response plan. Examples of potential emergency situations are bad weather, fire, bomb threats, medical emergencies, terrorism, an airplane crash, loss of power, and hazardous material leakage.

The majority of patron problems involve excess consumption of alcohol. This problem can be minimized by enforcing strict guidelines pertaining to alcohol distribution during events (e.g., no beer sales after the seventh inning in baseball or halftime in football). The quantity of beer sold to any one patron at a time (e.g., no more than one beer per patron per sale) should be regulated. Finally, all beverage sellers and other staff should be taught to recognize signs of unacceptable intoxication and the steps to be followed to limit further abuse.

MAINTENANCE AND HOUSEKEEPING

Studies have shown that a well-maintained venue encourages repeat patronage. Maintenance and housekeeping are functions designed to keep a venue clean, safe, and appealing for patrons. The maintenance and housekeeping staff work together cooperatively to keep the venue clean and in good repair. The housekeeping crew is responsible for all seats, stairways, stairwells, restrooms, offices, tile, concrete, carpet floors, walls, ceilings, elevators, upholstered seats, and much more. The maintenance crew is responsible for setup and breakdown of events, replacing filters, maintaining the seating area, and operation of equipment, restroom facilities, doors, HVAC, and much more.

RETAIL SALES

This area is responsible for food services, pouring rights, and merchandise sales.

An opportunity for you to learn more about facility management is also a great way to raise money for your sport management student organization. Sport management students at Slippery Rock University in Pennsylvania work for Landmark Event Services at Pittsburgh Steelers and University of Pittsburgh games to raise money for the Sport Management Alliance. These funds offset some of the costs associated with annual sport management trips to Ireland, Costa Rica, Italy, and other international sites.

The food service is the business operation that prepares, delivers, and sells food to customers. A concessionaire provides the food service. Various teams manage their own food and beverage service, but often venues contract with a private vendor. The main concessionaires in the sport industry are Ozark Food and Beverage, Inc., Ovation Food Services, Aramark, Levy Restaurants, Sportservice (Delaware North Company), and Centerplate. Sport venues may have two concessionaires working the same event, including one servicing the fans in the general concourse areas and a premium concessionaire servicing the club level and luxury suites.

Revenue from concessions and pouring rights plays a vital role in the success of any venue. Coca-Cola and Pepsi regularly compete for the pouring rights in professional and collegiate sport venues. *Pouring rights* are the exclusive ability to sell soft drinks, bottled water, and beer in a facility. Pouring rights in multi-purpose venues, with upwards of 250 event nights per year, can be very lucrative.

Merchandise sales are another vital revenue stream for any venue. Gift shops, team stores, and vendors sell novelties and licensed products including tee-shirts, jerseys, sweat shirts, caps, blankets, cups, pens, pins, players cards, autographed balls or bats, disposable cameras, and more to patrons. Concessions, pouring rights, and merchandise sales can generate at least 60 percent of a venue's operating revenue.

PARKING

Fees generated from selling parking spaces can be another source of revenue, even when it is shared with local parking vendors. Parking fees can range from $5 per vehicle for minor league stadiums to $35 per vehicle at downtown major league stadiums. Additional sources of parking revenue can be generated from selling preferred, personalized parking spaces, like the Atlanta Braves did in 2004 by creating Lexus-only parking spaces (sponsored, of course, by Atlanta-area Lexus dealers) for season ticket holders driving Lexus vehicles. Premium parking spots are often sold to season ticket holders at professional venues and major athletic donors at colleges and universities. Parking lots can also be rented for new or antique car shows, carnivals, food festivals, driver's safety school, and other events.

FINANCIAL MANAGEMENT

Efficient financial management is essential to the successful operation of a sport facility. Large venues have an in-house staff and smaller venues outsource fiscal duties. Financial managers are concerned with developing and monitoring the operational budget, ordering equipment and supplies, paying accounts payable, collecting accounts receivable, developing a capital budget, seeking financing when necessary, managing all internal accounting, working with internal and external auditors, establishing and maintaining bank accounts, and payroll.

RISK MANAGEMENT

Risk management is a process to reduce or limit risk exposure in a venue. The goal of risk management is to reduce or eliminate all types of risk the venue could be exposed to during operation. Every venue, large or small, should have a risk management committee and a person on staff directly assigned to risk management. The risk management committee should establish policies and procedures for identifying and assessing foreseeable risks faced by the venue. The risks should be classified into (a) high, moderate, or low loss potential and (b) high, moderate, or low frequency of exposure. After the risks are classified, an action strategy should be developed for each risk ranging from avoidance to modification to transferring a portion of the risk to a third party

(e.g., insurance company). Finally, the risk management committee and the risk management director or coordinator should annually conduct a risk audit to identify progress made and new risks that surface.

Sport Event Security Management

There is a major concern regarding sport event security issues existing in today's society. These can include the concern of potential natural disasters (e.g., earthquakes, hurricanes, and tornadoes) and man-made (e.g., fan/player violence, spectator injuries) emergencies. Further, weapons of mass destruction (e.g., chemical, biological, radiological, nuclear, and explosive) and the identified lack of training and education of key scholastic and collegiate personnel responsible for sport security operations have resulted in The Department of Homeland Security identifying high-profile sporting events in the United States as potential terrorist targets (Lipton, 2005). Terrorist incidents in the sporting world, such as Munich 1972, Atlanta 1996, and more recently, when an Oklahoma University student prematurely detonated a bomb strapped to his body outside the 84,000-seat stadium in October 2005 (Hagmann, 2005), are examples of events with the potential for catastrophic consequences.

All sport event security management personnel should be trained in alcohol, crowd, and emergency management. The manager of this area should be concerned about all personnel being able to

- Understand sport terrorism activity,
- Explain homeland security national strategies and principles,
- Identify federal, state, and local roles in the event of a terrorist incident, natural disaster, or crowd management issue (e.g., alcohol management, fan/player violence, or spectator emergency),
- Detect critical infrastructure protection systems,
- Identify key assets as a sport venue,
- Analyze sport business preparedness, continuity, and recovery systems,

- Demonstrate the importance of organizing and building a multi-disciplinary vulnerability assessment team and assessing local sport venues,
- Evaluate potential threat elements,
- Determine local vulnerable targets,
- Identify potential countermeasures and strategies to improve security at a sports venue,
- Assess the importance of contingency planning,
- Identify and analyze components of an emergency response plan,
- Develop an emergency response plan for a sporting venue,
- Appraise physical security measures,
- Evaluate perimeter and access controls,
- Analyze incident/crisis management processes, and
- Evaluate vendor and contractor management strategies.

Alcohol Management

The focus on patron safety relating to alcohol consumption began in 1983 with the *Bearman v. University of Notre Dame* case. This was a landmark case because the court determined that intoxicated persons could pose a general danger to other patrons. This determination flew in the face of previous decisions that placed the responsibility of duty of care on the individual or group, not on the event organizers. The court determined that foreseeability dictated that Notre Dame had a duty to protect its patrons from the potentially dangerous actions of intoxicated third parties. This case set the standard for duty of care for the management of alcohol at events (Sawyer, 2005).

In a number of states, there are dram shop statutes that allow injured plaintiffs to bring suit against restaurants, bars, and other establishments that allow the defendant to become drunk. In some states, the court allows recovery through common negligence actions. There are a few states that allow recovery using both methods. In addition to the dram shop statutes, there is another statute known as the social host liability. This statute provides the injured plaintiff an opportunity to sue based on a social host knowingly serving alcohol to individuals who become intoxicated and cause injury or damage to property (Sawyer, 2005).

Venue managers should have in their liability tool bags an alcohol management plan. This plan should be coordinated with the crowd control management plan. The plan should include procedures to check age restrictions, restrictions on the number of beers served, terminating beer sale at a specific point during the event (e.g., basketball, end of third period; football, beginning of third quarter; ice hockey, end of the second intermission; and baseball, end of the seventh inning), deploying trained personnel to watch for trouble, and incorporating a designated-driver program (Sawyer, 2005).

Miller Brewing Company, in combination with previous research and encouragement from its legal department, provided the following suggestions regarding an effective alcohol sales strategy:

1. Decide whether or not to sell alcohol, and if the decision to sell alcohol is made, then an alcohol management plan must be developed.

2. Develop procedures to stop outside alcohol from entering the venue.

3. Establish crowd management procedures for alcohol management for day and evening events and for weather.

4. Install appropriate signage to enlightened patrons about responsible and irresponsible drinking and its consequences.

5. Establish a strong ejection policy.

6. Do not promote or advertise drinking during the event.

7. Make sure that security personnel are aware of the demographics of the crowd in each section of the venue (e.g., gender, white-collar, blue-collar, families, senior citizens, under 21, etc.).

8. All staff (not just security and servers) should complete regulated alcohol management training.

9. Establish consumption policies (e.g., number of beers per patron at one time, termination of sales prior to conclusion of the event).

10. Permit tailgating in parking lots only under strict supervision of security personnel.

11. Establish non-alcohol sections within the venue (i.e., family sections).

12. Develop a designated-driver program. (Modified from Ammon, Southall, & Blair, 2004, pp. 188–189)

Crowd Management

Crowd management is an organizational tool that can assist venue directors and/or event coordinators in providing a safe and enjoyable environment for patrons. The crowd management plan is an integral part of the larger risk management plan and includes training programs for staff; drills and procedures to be used to in an emergency; procedures to eject disruptive people; a proper signage system; an efficient communication network; a security response plan; and measurable performance objectives. The personnel are either in-house or outsourced by the venue. Smaller venues often utilize on- or off-duty police in uniform. Larger venues have an in-house security force composed of part- and full-time officers. A number of venues have outsourced the security function.

Medical Emergencies

The venue should have as part of the larger risk management plan an emergency management plan. Emergencies can range from localized medical emergencies (e.g., slips and falls, heart attacks, diabetic complications) to mass casualty situations (e.g., collapse of bleachers, roof, or walkway) and large disasters (e.g., hurricane, tornado, earthquake, or fire). The plan should include training programs for staff (e.g., CPR, first aid, AED), drills, and communication links with outside emergency agencies. Evacuation strategies, security procedures, and measurable performance objectives should also be included.

Table 9.4. Common Traits of Sport Event Managers

- Prepares and manages a checklist of activities
- Projects a positive attitude
- Works independently or as a team member
- Accurate and quick at details
- Articulate on the telephone and in written and oral communication
- Creative, flexible
- Works under extreme pressures for long hours
- Works with all levels of people, including volunteers
- Effective at balancing multiple projects simultaneously
- Excellent time manager
- Effective negotiator
- Finance and budget conscious
- Possesses good typing, word processing, and other office skills
- Leadership ability
- Quick problem solver
- Good motivator
- Desire to learn and grow

PARKING MANAGEMENT

Management of a parking operation can be profitable, but it has liabilities. The manager, before charging for parking, must be sure to accomplish the following:

- Purchase adequate liability insurance,
- Provide adequate surfacing for the proposed traffic,
- Ensure safe entrance and exit areas,
- Provide adequate lighting,
- Plan for immediate snow and ice removal,
- Establish an emergency plan for the space,
- Ensure that adequate supervision and security is available,
- Provide for the safety of the pedestrians,
- Plan a graphic system that makes it easy to find customers' cars at the conclusion of the event, and
- Provide an adequate number of cashiers and attendants.

After the manager has accomplished the above, it is time to decide how many spaces will be allocated for the handicapped (i.e., review state and federal handicapped guidelines for actual number of spaces), VIPs, and regular customers (Sawyer, 2005).

According to Russo (2001), the following controls should be implemented to ensure a smooth operation: "(1) sensors or loops buried in each entrance line, (2) a single pass lane, (3) a cashier or checker watching the sellers and authorizing passes, (4) spot checks on sellers, (5) different colored tickets for different events, days, or hours, (6) cash registers, (7) TV monitors, and (8) clean graphics and signs indicating special entrances."

The parking operation is second only to the box office in terms of direct contact between the facility and the patron. A well-designed and managed parking operation will ease crowd tension and allow for sufficient time for patrons to buy a snack, enter the venue, and still be in their seats on time. There is no question that the ease of access and parking is a major factor in increased public acceptance and attendance at events (Sawyer, 2005).

Event Management —The Process

Event management, like any other form of management, is directing, working with, and overseeing human resources and motivating professional spirit and cooperative efforts toward fulfillment of goals (Horine & Stotlar, 2003). Any event, regardless of scope, requires more than one person to be successful. Therefore, effective leadership is an essential element in the production of events. All individuals, including volunteers, interns, and paid staff, need to be treated with respect and encouraged to do whatever is necessary to make the event a success.

While creating and managing an event can be viewed as a linear process where exact steps are followed, the reality is that many issues occur simultaneously, requiring managers to handle multiple tasks proficiently (Solomon, 2002). Event managers must not only be able to anticipate problems and have contingency plans in place, they need to be able to think quickly on their feet when unforeseen crises arise. A student who pursues event management as a career option must also be flexible and adapt to setbacks or changes.

The scope of events that are executed are as varied as one's imagination. However, event management authority and educator Julia Rutherford Silvers has created an excellent classification scheme for categorization of the events, based upon their respective purposes:

Types of Events

Table 9.5. The Event Genre of Event Management

Business and Corporate Events	Any event that supports business objectives, including management functions, corporate communications, training, marketing, incentives, employee relations, and customer relations, scheduled alone or in conjunction with other events.
Cause-Related and Fundraising Events	An event created by or for a charitable or cause-related group for the purpose of attracting revenue, support, and/or awareness, scheduled alone or in conjunction with other events.
Exhibitions, Expositions and Fairs	An event bringing buyers and sellers and interested persons together to view and/or sell products, services, and other resources to a specific industry or the general public, scheduled alone or in conjunction with other events.
Entertainment and Leisure Events	A one-time or periodic, free or ticketed performance or exhibition event created for entertainment purposes, scheduled alone or in conjunction with other events.
Festivals	A cultural celebration, either secular or religious, created by and/or for the public, scheduled alone or in conjunction with other events. (Many festivals include bringing buyer and seller together in a festive atmosphere.)
Government and Civic Events	An event comprised of or created by or for political parties, communities, or municipal or national government entities, scheduled alone or in conjunction with other events.
Marketing Events	A commerce-oriented event to facilitate bringing buyer and seller together or to create awareness of a commercial product or service, scheduled alone or in conjunction with other events.
Meeting and Convention Events	The assembly of people for the purpose of exchanging information, debate or discussion, consensus or decisions, education, and relationship building, scheduled alone or in conjunction with other events.
Social/Life-Cycle Events	A private event, by invitation only, celebrating or commemorating a cultural, religious, communal, societal, or life-cycle occasion, scheduled alone or in conjunction with other events.
Sports Events	A spectator or participatory event involving recreational or competitive sport activities, scheduled alone or in conjunction with other events.

(From: Silvers, J. R. http://www.juliasilvers.com/embok.htm#Event_Management_as_a_Profession)

Planning: A Must

The primary issue in planning an event is determining its purpose (Walker & Stotlar, 1997). When the mission or goals of an event are clearly delineated, the event manager and his or her team have a framework within which to operate. Examples of common event goals are

1. profitability;

2. raising awareness, sensitivity, or money for a particular cause or charity; and

3. improving organizational image and visibility.

Another consideration is whether or not an event will be a regularly scheduled occurrence (e.g., an annual road race) or simply a one-time affair (e.g., a visit by a candidate for political office). Obviously, an event that may be run on a regular basis will be managed quite differently (e.g., long-term sponsorships agreements may be sought).

Once a mission and goals have been established, a timetable must be established for an event. The *timetable* can also be seen as a countdown to an event that provides the schedule of tasks and when they need to be completed. It is more difficult to plan a timeline with first-time or one-time events, but this should not deter event managers from developing a basic schedule. In addition to a timetable, written operational guidelines and responsibilities should be created to clarify roles and expectations for the management team (Walker & Stotlar, 1997). Regardless of whether an event is annual or one-time, such documentation helps to avoid duplication of effort and increases the likelihood of intra-group cooperation and a more smoothly run event.

Personnel

Event managers need to address recruitment, selection, training, motivation, and evaluation of both paid personnel and volunteers. Being able to get the right people placed in key roles is essential to delegating responsibility. Also, *job descriptions* need to be clearly stated so people know their roles and responsibilities. Can you, as Jerry Solomon—one of the leading sport event managers in the country—asks, "create a team atmosphere and a sense of camaraderie that energizes others to go any length in making the event a success" (Solomon, 2002)?

Media and community outlets can be used to advertise for volunteers; additionally, volunteers can be recruited from local community service organizations such as the Rotary Clubs or university groups. Volunteers must be treated well and shown appreciation, especially if an event is going to occur on a regular, annual, or semi-annual basis. Creative gifts of recognition such a mugs or T-shirts and good food (which can be garnered from a sponsor) can be very motivating. In fact, if volunteers enjoy their experience, they can become informal recruiters in persuading others to volunteer the next time the event is held. Organizers of large-scale events, such as the USGA's U.S. Open Golf Championship, utilize well over 5,000 volunteers to help manage their events.

Members of the event management team must possess leadership skills, knowledge of small-group dynamics, excellent communication skills, the ability to motivate, and a talent for organizing committees. Team leaders and their committees need to know their responsibilities and keep an updated timetable regarding completion of tasks that is in concert with the master calendar for the event.

"THE DOCTOR CAN BURY HIS MISTAKES, BUT AN ARCHITECT CAN ONLY ADVISE HIS CLIENT TO PLANT VINES."

—FRANK LLOYD WRIGHT

Location, Facilities, and Equipment

In order to draw participants or spectators, get commitments from athletes and/or performers, solicit sponsors, or, in some cases, negotiate a television deal, you must be able to have a location/venue secured. However, it is important to consider all your choices based on predetermined criteria before committing. Certain venues may seem perfect at first glance but have major drawbacks when analyzed more thoroughly. For example, Manhattan Beach, California, may seem like the perfect venue for a pro beach volleyball tournament until you consider that the number of tickets you can sell is restricted by the California Coastal Commission to 25 percent of the total of spectators attending. In other words, if there are 4,000 seats, 3,000 must be given away for free (Solomon, 2002). Contracts need to be carefully analyzed so you know the restrictions to which you must adhere.

After you have decided where to hold your event, the venue must be staged. One of the best ways to be certain a venue is ready to use is to develop facility and equipment checklists. Walker and Stotlar (1997) developed a comprehensive list of items to include in these checklists:

- Cleaning the facility
- Providing adequate parking and special areas for emergency vehicles
- Testing the public address system and lighting
- Assuring proper signage for pedestrian and vehicular traffic
- Providing adequate ticket sales areas
- Examining first aid facilities

- Addressing the needs of participants
- Making proper provisions for concessions and merchandise stands or vendors
- Making special arrangements for sponsors
- Inspecting the permanent and/or temporary seating
- Addressing the needs of the media
- Developing a system for on-site communications among personnel

An area that is often overlooked when planning an event is meeting the needs of individuals with disabilities. A common misconception is that disabled individuals are confined to wheelchairs; event managers need to consider disabilities in a broader sense to include individuals who are hearing, visually, or mentally impaired.

Marketing and Budgeting for an Event

Event marketing includes determining if the potential event matches customers' interests. Will the target market of spectators or participants be attracted to an event and be available during the timeframe you select? Budgeting, advertising, recruitment, and developing promotions to inform the public about the event are key components of event marketing. Figure 9.2 illustrates elements of event marketing.

Being able to attract customers requires research to determine if an event has appeal. Ideally, marketing research specialists can help determine an event's marketability; however, as a graduate from a sport management program, you will be able to collect your own data. Regardless of how this research is conducted, you ultimately need to be able to gain information that accurately portrays a picture of the potential customers' socio-demographic (i.e., age, income, gender, zip code) and psychographic (interests, attitudes, etc.) profile.

Most, but not all, events are set up to make a profit; therefore, it is of the utmost importance that the budgeting process be handled diligently. Someone on the event management team needs to oversee the accounting function so that the event's financial status can be determined at any given time. Also, it must be clear who is to pay the bills, authorize purchases, oversee petty cash, and handle contingency funds.

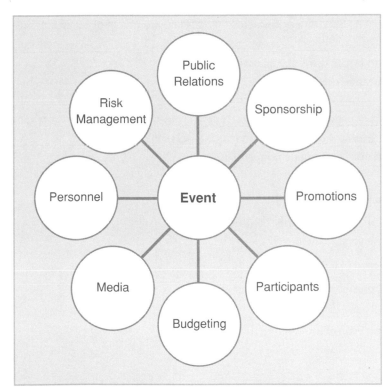

Figure 9.2.

The Event and Post-Event Evaluation

On the day of the event, assuming everything has been staged properly, the focus of all personnel should be making sure that all spectator, participants, the media, and special guests have a wonderful experience. The courtesy and friendliness of event staff cannot be overemphasized. Everyone from parking attendants, concession stand workers, ticket-takers, ushers, and bathroom attendants needs to be as helpful, enthusiastic, and friendly as possible. In the area of risk management, when there are emergencies or problems that arise, there needs to be medical personnel and security in place and ready to act, as mentioned previously in the section on facility management.

A final evaluation plan for the event should be in place well before the event takes place and a timetable for completing the evaluation should be developed. This is especially critical for regularly occurring events. Establishing a baseline measurement for fan, participant, and media satisfaction is essential for continued improvement and suc-

Without consistent assessment and evaluation, facilities are at risk of becoming outdated and destined for demolition.

cess. The post-event evaluation process allows you to figure out what you did well and what you can improve upon the next time you stage the event.

Summary

The purpose of this chapter was to introduce the segment of the sport management field dealing with sport and facility management. The major concepts presented in this chapter include

- the skill set necessary for facility and event management;

- the differences in public and private ownership of public assembly facilities, in addition to approaches to management (in-house versus outsourcing);

- an overview of the wide array of participant-oriented facilities;

- the management and personnel required in facility management and execution of events;

- the concepts of planning, organizing, leading, and evaluating relative to facility and event management;

- the importance of risk management;

- the use of timetables in event management;

- marketing, budgeting, and public relations in facility and event management; and

- post-event evaluation.

DISCUSSION ACTIVITIES

1. If you had to initiate, organize, and oversee a four-person team co-ed volleyball tournament, what steps would you take to ensure its success?

2. As director of operations for women's basketball at Eagle University (a Division I program), you are charged with running the end-of-the-season conference tournament. The college does not outsource any of the facility functions. How will your manage this process? What considerations have to be made as far as preparing and managing the facility? What will you do to enhance the entertainment value, minimize the risk, and market the tournament?

SUGGESTED READING

Howard, D. R., & Crompton, J. L. (2004). *Financing sport* (2nd ed.). Morgantown, WV: Fitness Information Technology.

References

Ammon, R. Jr., Southall, R. M., & Blair, D. A. (2004). *Sport facility management: Organizing events and mitigating risks*. Morgantown, WV: Fitness Information Technology.

Crompton, J. L. (2004). Beyond economic impact: An alternative rationale for the public subsidy of major league sports facilities. *Journal of Sport Management, 18*(1), 41.

Hagmann, D. J. (2005, October 30). Black hole in America's heartland. *Northeast Intelligence Network*. Retrieved December 28, 2007, from http://www.homelandsecurityus.com/site/modules/news/article.php?storyid=16

Horine, L., & Stotlar, D. (2003). *Administration of physical education and sport programs* (5th ed). Boston: McGraw-Hill.

Lipton, E. (2005, March 16). U.S. report lists possibilities for terrorist attacks and likely toll. *New York Times*, Sec. A, p. 1.

Mulrooney, A., & Farmer, P. (2001).Managing the facility. In B. Parkhouse (Ed.), *The management of sport: Its foundation and application* (3rd ed). Boston: McGraw-Hill.

Russo, F. (2000). Marketing events and services for spectators, 151–162. In H. Appenzeller & G. Lewis, *Successful sport management* (2nd ed.) Durham, NC: Carolina Academic Press.

Sawyer, T. H. (2005). *Facility design and management for health, fitness, physical activity, recreation, and sports facility development*. Champaign, IL: Sagamore Publishing.

Sawyer, T. H., Hypes, M. G., & Hypes, J. A. (2004). *Financing the sport enterprise*. Champaign, IL: Sagamore Publishing.

Sawyer, T. H., & Smith O. R. (1999). *The management of clubs, recreation, and sport: Concepts and applications*. Champaign, IL: Sagamore Publishing.

Silvers, J. R. (2003, October 26). *Event management body of knowledge project*. Retrieved December 28, 2007, from http://www.juliasilvers.com/embok.htm#Event_Management_as_a_Profession

Smith, S. (2008, January 12). Hawks lose win over Heat to statistical error. Teams forced to replay last minute of December game. *Atlanta Journal Constitution*, Sec. A, p. 1.

Solomon, J. (2002). *An insider's guide to managing sporting events*. Champaign, IL: Human Kinetics.

Walker, M. L., & Stotlar, D. K. (1997). *Sport facility management*. London, UK: Jones & Bartlett, Inc.

Chapter Ten

SPORT INDUSTRY AND THE LAW

PAUL J. BATISTA

"Aaaaah! Dewey's exercised an escape clause in his contract!!"

© 1998 Universal Press Syndicate

www.uexpress.com

LEARNING OBJECTIVES

After reading and studying this chapter, the student should be able to

- Define "the law";
- Identify three primary ways to resolve disputes;
- Describe the philosophical basis for American law;
- Determine if "sport law" is an existing and readily identifiable field of study within the law;
- List the three general classifications of law;
- Explain the four main sources of law in the United States;
- Identify the eight content areas of sport law, and the manner in which each affects the sport manager or organization; and
- Understand the obstacles facing students seeking to become an agent for professional athletes.

Introduction

A glance at the local newspaper or just a quick look at ESPN's SportsCenter demonstrates that sports and law are inextricably connected. We read and hear of athletes involved in criminal activities, illegal drug use, and domestic violence. There are free agents to sign and contracts to negotiate, collective bargaining agreements to finalize to avoid strikes by players, or lockouts by management. Amateur and professional athletes, as well as spectators, file personal injury lawsuits. Other athletes sue claiming they are victims of discrimination based on race, gender, religion, age, or disability.

We look for the day's scores, but instead find that today's game takes second billing to the activities of judges, mediators, arbitrators, prosecutors, defense attorneys, investigators, and police officers. R. K. Smith in 1986 noted that "attorneys and judges are more than idle spectators at sporting events" (Appenzeller, 1998). More than 20 years later, that observation has become even more accurate.

Most Americans became enamored with the pleasures of sports as youngsters, but as adults, we see that law permeates sports as much as it does other areas of society. As this book went to press, the media was reporting on these items:

- Barry Bonds was indicted on charges of perjury in the investigation of performance-enhancing drugs in Major League Baseball;
- The Michigan High School Athletic Association was ordered to pay $7.4 million in legal fees to the successful attorney in a Title IX case;

- A high school student injured by a "schoolyard bully" during a pick-up game of football was awarded $4 million in damages for his injuries;

- While Atlanta Falcons quarterback Michael Vick was in prison for his criminal activities, a federal court in the civil case ruled that the terms of the NFL Collective Bargaining Agreement prohibited the team from seeking repayment of millions of dollars in roster bonuses he had received;

- Gambling on professional tennis matches is being investigated by numerous authorities;

- Federal courts are establishing guidelines on First Amendment free speech and religion for students, coaches, and athletic directors; and

- Lawsuits have been filed by coaches alleging they were fired because of gender or race discrimination.

But how much have times really changed? In a speech in 1987, Bart Giamatti, the late Commissioner of Major League Baseball, discussed the pervasive influence both law and sports have on American society: "The fact is, American culture, American daily life is soaked in the law, in legal and legalistic nuance, in mythology, anxiety, gossip, awe, resentment, impatience, admiration before, about and for the law . . . [i]t governs obtrusively and unobtrusively the culture's daily life" (Giamatti, 1988).

He continued by making an interesting analogy about law and sport: "Sport is about energy and action within rules, boundaries, codes; it has a vast body of internal law and regulation and officials to dispense judgment, if not justice, quickly and in public."

Clearly, despite internal rules such as the "chin music" delivered when a hitter digs in, or the unwritten rules enforced by the "goon" in hockey, law has permeated sport in the same manner that it has affected society as a whole. It is not surprising, then, that the sport management curriculum includes a study of the legal aspects of sport. You will note that the subject is called both "sport law" and "sports law," depending on the preference of the individual author. In this chapter, it will be referred to as "sport law," except when used in direct quotations.

©iStockphoto.com

What Is "The Law"?

While virtually every student will have an idea what "the law" is, most likely the student's perception developed through the media—reading newspapers and magazines, or watching television or movies. The study of any subject, and particularly law, should begin with a discussion of the basics.

Although there are hundreds of definitions of *law*, a reasonable description would be a body of enforceable rules, established by the lawmaking authorities of a society, governing the relationships among individuals, and between individuals and their government. The New Jersey Legislature has defined law as "all the official rules and codes that govern citizens' actions, including the Constitution, statutory laws enacted by the Legislature, case laws established by court decisions, and administrative law as set forth by executive branch agencies" (Glossary of Terms, 2008).

Deciding on a definition, however, fails to answer the basic philosophical questions: What makes laws necessary, and why do we have laws?

WHAT MAKES LAWS NECESSARY?

The fundamental purpose of laws is to resolve (or avoid) conflicts. In ancient days, and indeed in parts of the world today, law was defined by the phrase "might makes right," where the strongest person/group made the laws and enforced them. As we have become more civilized, society has generally agreed that mortal combat is not the appropriate manner of resolving disputes. Therefore, laws have been established to resolve conflicts without the necessity of physical battle.

There are three primary methods of resolving conflicts. The first (and most widely used) is negotiation. While most people do not stop to think about how they resolve disputes, it is true that most disputes are resolved through negotiation. *Negotiation* is a process involving formal or informal discussions in order to reach an agreement. The collective bargaining agreements of the various professional sport leagues are examples in which negotiation was used to reach a contractual agreement.

> THE LAW IS REASON
> FREE FROM PASSION.
>
> —ARISTOTLE

The second way to resolve disputes is through *alternative dispute resolution* (ADR). ADR may be defined as resolving a dispute through any means other than litigation or negotiation. The primary forms of ADR are mediation and arbitration.

Mediation is the submission of a dispute to a disinterested third person who intervenes between the parties in an attempt to settle their dispute without going to court. In mediation, the third party (*mediator*) communicates with all parties to the dispute, presents proposals from each party to the other, and facilitates resolution of the dispute, if possible. The mediator makes no ruling, and has no authority to enforce his or her judgment on any party.

Arbitration is the submission of a dispute to a neutral third party (*arbitrator*) who listens to all parties, considers the legal position of each, then renders a decision to resolve the dispute. The arbitrator acts much like a judge. The arbitrator's decision may not be binding on the parties, or may be binding if there is a prior agreement of the parties, or required by applicable law. Disputes in major league baseball are resolved by specially appointed arbitrators under the sport's collective bargaining agreement.

The final manner of resolving disputes is *litigation*, which is the process of filing a lawsuit so that a court can resolve the disagreement. In the U.S., all citizens have access to the court system and have the right to petition courts to settle disputes.

In his article in *the Marquette Sports Law Review*, Professor Timothy Davis used the title to ask the pertinent question "What is sports law?" (Davis, 2001). Although students frequently have a preconceived idea that sport law primarily involves agents and the statues of player representation, the question is not so easily answered by lawyers and academicians.

Does "Sport Law" Exist?

Professor Davis presented the three prevailing views of sport law in order to allow the reader to form his or her personal answer to the question. He described the first view as the traditional view, which holds that sport law does not exist, but "represents nothing more than an amalgamation of various substantive areas of the law that are relevant in the sports context," and that "sports law is a misnomer, given that sport represents a form of activity and entertainment that is governed by the legal system in its entirety" (Davis, 2001). The recent steroid investigations of BALCO and various athletes is a classic example. The court did not decide the case differently because it involved a sport setting, but followed traditional criminal law principles. The second alternative is called the moderate position, and presents a middle ground between the other two perspectives. This view argues that a body of law related to sport has not yet fully developed to the extent to be clearly recognized, but "factual peculiarities residing in sports . . . require the unique application of generally applicable legal doctrine(s) . . . (producing) results that would not occur in other contexts" (Davis, 2001). Therefore, according to the moderate position, the area of sport law is inevitably developing into a separate substantive area of law. This outlook points to the development of concepts such as the *limited duty* rule (baseball teams have a limited duty to protect spectators from foul balls, thus providing teams with protection from liability) and *assumed risk* by participants (participants injured by an inherent risk of the activity cannot recover for injuries).

Finally, the third alternative is the belief that the field of sport law already exists. This perspective emphasizes the "growing body of case and statutory law specific to the sports industry as evidence of the existence of a separately identifiable body of law" (Davis, 2001). This argument contends that most, if not all, identified areas of law are not entirely separate, but overlap with other areas. Therefore, according to this theory, cases emerging from sport settings create an "increasing body of judicial and legislative law specific to sports" (Davis, 2001). For example, professional athletes may need representation in various legal disciplines such as contract law (to negotiate contracts or endorsements), tort law (injury or death of player), constitutional law (drug testing or religious accommodation), intellectual property law (right to use player's name or likeness in advertising), international law (work visas for foreign-born athletes), probate (settling player's estate after death), labor and antitrust law (management and players' unions collectively bargain for terms and conditions of employment), tax law (to file tax returns), and perhaps family law (divorce, paternity, or child support) and criminal law. Examples supporting this view are found in various statutes regulating athlete agents.

Regardless of the reader's viewpoint, Davis aptly noted that a lawyer practicing sport law is the "ultimate general practitioner," contradicting the idea of many "law students, novice practitioners and lay persons who equate the practice of sports law to the representation of players in their contract negotiations" (Davis, 2001).

The Study of Law

In most law schools in the U.S., the curriculum is based on the *case study method*, which is significantly different than how you have been taught in your undergraduate studies. The case study method presents students with the opportunity to read previous cases in order to learn how courts make legal decisions by applying relevant law to the facts of the case. In this manner, law students not only learn "the law" but also gain an understanding of the reasoning courts use in deciding disputes.

While you are not law students, this is still the best method to "learn" the law. It gives you the vicarious experience of being involved in the resolution of disputes arising out of actual situations involved in the real world. By acquiring the ability to understand courts' reasoning, and to learn basic legal principles, you will gain at least a rudimentary basis for decision making.

As you progress through your career in sport management, you will undertake a more detailed study of the legal aspects of sport. Undoubtedly, you will be required to read court cases and thereby be exposed to this case study method of learning. The purpose of case study is to equip you with the knowledge you need to (hopefully) avoid situations that put your participants, your employer, or you at risk. Further, it will give you the vicarious experience of being involved in the dispute. Finally, it should alert you to the situations that need the intervention of your attorney. While you might not have an attorney whispering advice into your ear all the time, you will have basic legal principles that should create "red flags" when you are getting into dangerous legal territory.

Note: Professor Davis's article contains an outstanding bibliography of books, journals, law reviews, and other publications that contain a wealth of information and articles relating to virtually every aspect of the study of the legal aspects of sports.

Although law affects every person sitting in college classrooms, most students have a limited exposure to, and understanding of, how the legal system works. In an effort to simplify and distinguish the differences among various types of law, it is helpful to divide law into three general classifications, and distinguish the characteristics within each of the three classifications.

SUBSTANTIVE V. PROCEDURAL

All court cases involve both of these types of law. *Substantive law* is the law that defines, describes, or creates legal rights and obligations—it is *what* the law is. In contrast, *procedural law* is the method of enforcing rights and obligations given to citizens by substantive law—it is the step-by-step mechanics concerning *how* the rights are enforced.

PUBLIC V. PRIVATE

Generally, *public law* governs the relationship between citizens and their government, while *private law* governs the relationship among private citizens. In many cases, these categories are not always easily distinguishable. Generally, public law includes areas such as criminal, tax, environmental, constitutional, and administrative, as well as protection of rights of the general public. Private law includes most other areas of law including contracts, property, personal injury, products liability, insurance, etc.

> **Example:** The First Amendment to the U.S. Constitution states that "Congress shall make no law respecting an establishment of religion, or prohibiting the free exercise thereof." In Santa Fe Independent School District (ISD) v. Doe (2001), the U.S. Supreme Court held that Santa Fe ISD's policy authorizing prayers before high school football games violated this clause, but also acknowledged an individual student's right to engage in religious activities at public schools. Both the Constitutional provision and the Court's interpretation as it relates to the facts in Santa Fe are substantive law because they declare what the law is.
>
> However, before the Supreme Court could hear and rule on the case, the plaintiffs were required to comply with the procedural prerequisites, such as filing the case in the proper court, giving notice of the suit to the school, completing discovery, engaging in alternative dispute resolution, trying the case before a judge and jury, properly appealing it to the appellate court, then ultimately asking the Supreme Court to resolve the dispute. In order to enforce rights given by substantive law, parties must comply with the rules of procedural law in the respective courts.

CRIMINAL V. CIVIL

Criminal law deals with unlawful acts committed against the public as a whole, in which a defendant is accused of violating a statute defining a criminal act, thereby committing a *crime*. Congress and the individual state legislatures create these criminal statutes, which authorize the government to punish the violator by either a fine or incarceration. It is the government seeking to impose the penalty that defines the violation as a criminal act. *Civil law* includes everything that is not criminal law. It should be noted, however, that a single situation could include both criminal and civil cases, e.g., the Michael Vick case, in which the government sought to send him to prison for dog fighting, while the Falcons sued for return of his roster bonuses.

> **Example:** There is a federal statute governing workplace safety that is enforced by the Occupational Safety and Health Administration (OSHA), a regulatory agency established by the U.S. Congress. The workers in professional sport stadiums are provided certain protections by this law and have the right to file claims with OSHA for violations. Enforcement of this statute would be considered in the "public" domain. On the other hand, although the professional athletes are also workers, they are represented by unions who collectively bargain terms and conditions of players' work with the owners and ultimately enter into a contract called a collective bargaining agreement (CBA). In the event that either party violates this agreement, the parties have the "private" right to enforce its provisions, without government intervention.

Example: As this book goes to press, the U.S. government is investigating allegations that Roger Clemens committed perjury (the criminal act of lying under oath) when he testified to Congress during the BALCO investigation. Clemens has also filed a civil suit for defamation (libel and slander) against Brian McNamee, alleging that he lied about Clemens' drug use, thereby harming Clemens' reputation.

Although these categories seem to create a clear distinction among the classifications, it is important to note that the divisions are not always as simple as they may appear. It is also important to note that most cases have one of the characteristics from each category. For example, the Clemens' case includes not only substantive and procedural law, but also criminal and civil law, and public and private law.

Sources of Law in the United States

All law in the U.S. comes from one of four sources: (1) Constitutions, (2) statutes, (3) administrative rules and regulations, and (4) court cases. If you will review the definition of law by the New Jersey legislature cited above, you will see that it includes all these sources in the definition.

CONSTITUTIONS

The "Supreme Law of the Land" is the United States *Constitution*. It takes precedence over any other law. Each state also has a constitution, but it is subordinate to the U.S. Constitution. If the terms of a state constitution violate a provision in the U.S. Constitution, the state provision will be declared unconstitutional. Constitutional questions raised in sport settings include issues relating to religion, criminal search and seizures, due process, equal protection, drug testing, and persons with disabilities.

STATUTES

Statutes are particular laws passed by the U.S. *Congress*, or a state *legislature*, which declare, command, or prohibit some conduct, or require citizens to act in a certain manner. Violation of these statutes normally creates various kinds of penalties for acting in a manner contrary to the law, such as going to jail for driving while under the influence of drugs or alcohol. Legislatures can essentially institute whatever statutes they desire, so long as they do not violate provisions of an applicable constitution. Examples of statutory enactments include Title IX, Americans with Disabilities Act, the Sherman and Clayton Antitrust Acts, Bankruptcy Act, and state Athlete Agent Acts.

ADMINISTRATIVE RULES AND REGULATIONS

When Congress or state legislatures pass statutes regulating some industry or activity, frequently they will also establish administrative agencies to oversee enforcement of the legislation. These agencies are granted authority to establish directives in order to carry out the legislative body's intent in passing the statute. These directives are known as *Administrative Rules and Regulations*. They generally carry the force of law as if they were passed by Congress or the state legislature, and violators of the rules and regulations are subject to the penalties provided in them. Examples of Administrative Agencies that establish such Rules and Regulations include the

Federal Communications Commission (FCC), which regulates television and radio, the Occupational Safety and Health Administration (OSHA), which regulates workplace safety, and the Office of Civil Rights (OCR), which administers Title IX.

CASE LAW

The final source is law established within the court system. The U.S. adopted the *common law* system from England, which allows courts to create rules of law. Under this system, appellate courts announce a rule of law that applies to the facts of a particular case. The rules established in this manner are called *case law*. Once case law is established, other courts will usually adhere to the opinion of the original court and follow its holding, citing the original case as a *precedent*.

Courts are not required to follow precedent unless it is announced from a higher court within the same court system. For example, a California intermediate appellate state court must follow a precedent established by the California Supreme Court, but is not required to follow a precedent of the Florida Supreme Court. Further, appellate courts on the same level may have different opinions on the same issue, with the issue remaining unresolved until a higher court establishes the precedent for all inferior courts.

Courts may also change their precedent and issue a new opinion changing the previous rule, although this is not a routine occurrence. An example of this is the 1954 U.S. Supreme Court decision in *Brown v. Board of Education*, which desegregated public schools. The existing educational system was based on a Supreme Court decision in an 1896 case which established the principle that a "separate but equal" system segregating races was constitutional. In *Brown*, the Court changed its precedent and held that such systems violated the Equal Protection clause of the 14th Amendment.

Each of these areas supplies various laws affecting sport. Let's take a look at some specific examples of the legal aspects of sport.

Practice Areas in Sport Law

As the study of sport management has exploded during the last 20 years, with sport management programs being established in hundreds of colleges and universities, there has been concern among sport management professionals that there were no standards in place to assure that all students were being taught the essential subject matter of the discipline. Too often, a sport management program was created within another department, when an interested faculty member decided it was time to offer sport management to students at the institution. Unfortunately, this led to programs that provided degrees modeled after the curriculum of the original department. Programs in business departments were business based, while programs in kinesiology or exercise science were primarily science based.

Although a discussion of all legal subjects related to sport law would be appropriate, the sheer volume of such a discussion makes it unrealistic. Therefore, discussion of content areas within the legal aspects of sport will be limited to the most commonly addressed areas in sport management curricula nationwide.

LEGAL SYSTEM

Although the legal system encompasses law from all four sources discussed earlier in this chapter, this portion will be limited to the court system and litigation. You will remember that one of the ways to resolve disputes is through litigation, or filing a lawsuit. Court systems have been established to handle these lawsuits.

There are two court systems in the United States—one federal system and 50 independent state systems. The U.S. Constitution established the federal system, and the state systems are created by the respective state constitutions or statutes.

State Court Systems

State court systems generally hear matters that occur within the boundaries of the state, and involve disputes that involve state (as opposed to federal) law. Examples of cases normally heard in state courts are cases involving personal injury and other negligence claims, contracts, family disputes, defamation (libel and slander), products liability, workers' compensation, and state criminal matters.

Most state court systems have three levels. The first level where the case is initially filed is the *trial court*. This is the court where the parties actually "try" the case, pre-

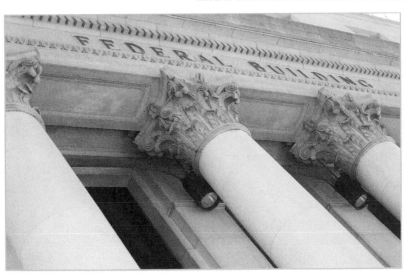

senting evidence to a jury and legal arguments to a judge. This is the type of court that is shown in most movies and television shows. The jury will render a *verdict*, then the judge will enter a ruling, or *judgment*, in favor of one party or the other.

If one of the parties thinks the judge made a mistake in the way he or she tried the case (such as applying the wrong law), that party can *appeal* to the next court level, the *intermediate appeals court*. Most of these courts are called "Courts of Appeals," although they have different names in various states. Litigants are not required to seek permission of these courts to process the appeal to the intermediate appellate level. The function of these courts is to determine if the judge followed the law (both substantive and procedural) when trying the case.

Appellate courts normally enter one of three results in a case:

- *Affirmed*—The trial court made no significant mistakes, and the ruling stands.

- *Reverse and remand*—The trial court made a significant mistake and the case should be tried again, but correctly this time. If the court allowed testimony that should not have been heard, the appellate court will order the case tried again, this time without the improper testimony.

- *Reverse and render*—The trial court made a significant mistake, but there is no need for another trial because when the correct law is applied, the winning party cannot prevail. If a court entered a judgment holding a state university liable for negligence, even though that state's sovereign immunity law protects the state from liability in negligence cases, the appellate court will reverse and "render" the judgment that should have been entered (that the plaintiff cannot recover from the university).

After the Court of Appeals has rendered its judgment, any of the parties (but typically the losing party) may take an appeal to the highest appellate court in the state, usually called the Supreme Court. In order to have a case heard, the litigant must file an application with the court asking that the case be heard. In most states, the Supreme Court can hear or refuse to hear any case it chooses, at its sole discretion. If the court refuses the application, the case is finished, with the result in the intermediate court being the final ruling in the case. If the Supreme Court accepts and decides the case, it will enter one of the same rulings as the intermediate appellate court.

Federal Court System

The federal system is established in Article III, Section 1, of the U.S. Constitution, which states, "The judicial power of the Unites States shall be vested in one Supreme Court and in such inferior Courts as the Congress may from time to time ordain and establish." Congress has established a court system similar to the state systems.

In order to file a case in a federal court, the litigant must establish that a law specifically allows for such a case to be filed in federal court. The four categories primarily used to establish that cases should be heard in federal court are (1) when a litigant is seeking to enforce rights created under the U.S. Constitution or a federal statute (this is called a *federal question*), (2) when the dispute is between two states, (3) when the United States is a party to the lawsuit, and (4) when there is *diversity of citizenship*, meaning that the parties are citizens of different states and the amount in controversy is above $100,000.

The *federal trial courts* are called *U.S. District Courts*, followed by a geographical description of the location of the court (e.g., United States District Court for the Western District of Pennsylvania). There are 94 throughout the country, with at least one located in every state. These courts operate essentially the same as state trial courts, providing a trial of the case before a judge and jury. When a judgment has been entered, either party has the right to pursue an appeal to the federal intermediate courts, called Courts of Appeals.

The Courts of Appeals are divided into 11 regional groups, called *circuits*, as well as a circuit for the District of Columbia and a specialized federal Court of Appeals. These courts are normally referred to by their circuit number, so that cases from Louisiana, Mississippi, and Texas are heard in the 5th Circuit, while cases from Alabama, Florida, and Georgia are decided in the 11th Circuit, etc.

In the event that a litigant wants to appeal a decision of a Circuit Court, the appeal would be taken to the United States Supreme Court by filing an application for a *Writ of Certiorar*i. If the Court grants the application, the Supreme Court will issue a Writ of Certiorari, ordering the lower court to forward the case to the Supreme Court for its consideration. It takes a vote of four justices to issue the Writ and hear a case.

The Supreme Court is not required to hear any case, and may refuse to hear a case for any reason. A refusal to hear the case is not considered a decision by the Supreme Court. Therefore, the ruling of the Circuit Court becomes final. Further, a refusal by the Supreme Court to hear a case is not considered a comment on the Circuit Court's opinion.

In the most recent Supreme Court reporting period, the 2006–2007 Term of Court, 8,857 applications were filed, 78 cases were argued before the Court, and the court issued 67 written opinions (2007 Year End Report, 2007). If a litigant is dissatisfied with the result in the Supreme Court, there is no other avenue of appeal in the court system.

CONTRACT LAW

Of all the elements of sport law, the most publicized subject deals with issues related to player contracts. Think of the regularity with which sportscasters talk about free agency, trades, contract extensions, bonuses, suspensions, options, and other contractual matters. When you discuss sport law with your friends, most will immediately think of these contractual issues. With the amount of money involved in professional and amateur sports, contracts are common in every facet of sport.

Simply stated, a *contract* is an agreement, or exchange of promises, that creates legally enforceable duties and obligations for all parties to the contract. Except under certain circumstances, contracts are not required to be in writing to be enforceable. However, it is wise to remember the words of movie producer Samuel Goldwyn: "A verbal contract isn't worth the paper it's written on." Reducing a contract to writing not only establishes proof of an agreement, it also provides reliable evidence of the terms of the contract.

Four elements are required to form a valid contract: legal capacity, agreement, consideration, and legality.

Legal Capacity

Each party to a contract must be legally competent to enter into the contract. The courts are concerned with the relative strength of bargaining power, and if there is a great discrepancy among the parties, the courts will protect the party with much lower mental capacity. In this manner, contracts with *minors* (persons under age 18) and people with significant mental disabilities are normally not enforceable against them, and courts will allow those parties to avoid the terms of the contract. Recognizing the proliferation of world-class athletes under 18 (such as Freddy Adu in soccer and Michelle Wie in golf), sport managers should be especially vigilant when seeking to enter into contracts with minors. An experienced lawyer is essential in negotiating the terms of such contracts.

Agreement

The very essence of a contract is the agreement among the parties, and there can be no contract without an agreement. Normally, an agreement is reached through a process called *offer and acceptance*, which involves the parties making a series of proposals to the other until the negotiations culminate with an agreement. The normal pattern for negotiating player contracts is a classic example of the offer and acceptance scenario. The team will make a contract proposal to a player, who then presents a *counteroffer* to the team, and this process continues until the parties reach agreement on the terms of the contract. The final component of agreement is that all of the essential terms of the contract must be agreed upon, so that the parties have a "meeting of the minds" on all aspects of the contract.

Consideration

Once the parties have agreed to the terms of the contract, there must be an exchange of something of value for the contract to be valid. The purpose of consideration is to provide some agreed benefit to both parties of the contract. Each party must get and give consideration. In most instances, *consideration* is the payment of money by one party to the other, who in turn provides something of value. However, promises to perform an act or service, or even refrain from performing acts or services, will be sufficient to establish consideration. When a baseball player signs a contract with a team, the team promises to pay the player for performing, and the player promises to perform, follow team and league rules, refrain from dangerous activities, etc.

Legality

Courts will not enforce contracts that require performance of an illegal act. If the contract is the subject of an illegal act, the contract is void. If a person supplies an athlete with an illegal controlled substance (steroids, cocaine, etc.), then sues the player for not paying for the substance, the courts will not require the athlete to honor the contract.

CONSTITUTIONAL LAW

Many provisions contained in the U.S. Constitution (and to a lesser degree, state constitutions) have become the focus of litigation in sports. Among the constitutional issues that have been raised are

- establishment or expression of religion in public schools (locker room or pregame prayer),
- free speech (wearing items of clothing as a political protest),
- search and seizure (drug testing),
- due process (right to notice and a hearing prior to suspension),
- equal protection (discrimination based on race, ethnicity, gender, religion, age, etc.), and
- freedom of association (discrimination by private clubs or societies).

This list could continue indefinitely, but the examples listed above are representative of the issues sport managers and participants have dealt with in the past.

The first topic to consider in constitutional issues is to determine if the plaintiff has been deprived of his or her rights by *state action*. The U.S. Supreme Court has said state action means that "the State [federal or state government] is *responsible* for the specific conduct of which the plaintiff complains" (*Brentwood Academy v. Tennessee Secondary School Athletic Association*, 2001), meaning that the state has caused the harm suffered by the plaintiff. Virtually all of the rights established in the U.S. Constitution are designed to protect citizens from actions by the government. Under most circumstances, if the state is not involved, there is no violation of the Constitution.

Clearly, statutes passed by Congress or state legislatures, ordinances passed by city governments, or policies of public schools are state action, and subject to the provisions of the Constitution. In *Santa Fe ISD v. Doe* (2001), the public school district established a policy that enabled a student chosen by the student body to say a prayer over the public address system before a high school football game. The Supreme Court held that the school was a state actor, and that the school's policy violated the *Establishment Clause* of the First Amendment.

ADMINISTRATIVE AND STATUTORY LAW

As discussed in the sources of law section, Congress and state legislatures create law by passing "statutes." Frequently, these laws establish agencies to enforce the laws that have been passed. Many agencies are more commonly known by their acronyms. Some of the agencies that sport managers are most likely to encounter during their careers, and the matters they regulate, are listed below.

- Equal Employment Opportunity Commission (EEOC)—workplace discrimination issues
- Occupational Safety and Health Administration (OSHA)—workplace safety
- Office of Civil Rights (OCR)—Title IX
- National Labor Relations Board (NLRB)—labor laws
- Internal Revenue Service (IRS)—tax
- Social Security Administration (SSA)—retirement

This is a representative list of federal agencies, but there are hundreds more. Additionally, sport managers should be familiar with state agencies in the state in which they are employed.

As previously stated, statutory laws are generated from both Congress and state legislatures. As sport management students, you will complete a more thorough examination of many of the applicable statutes later in your studies. However, a cursory exposure to some of these statutes is appropriate in an introductory course. (Note: The descriptions are for general informational purposes only, and are not an exhaustive coverage of the particular statute. Detailed study will come in later courses.) Federal statutes dealing with sport include, in no particular order, the following:

1. **Title IX of the Education Amendments of 1972 ("Title IX").** (20 U.S.C. § 1681 et. seq.) Probably the most discussed statute relating to sport is Title IX. When it was passed in 1972, it was a one-sentence law that stated, "No person in the Unites States shall, on the basis of sex, be excluded from participation in,

be denied the benefits of, or be subjected to discrimination under any education program or activity receiving Federal financial assistance." The intent of Congress was to prohibit *gender discrimination* in educational activities. There was no mention of sport or recreation in Title IX. However, this is a good example of Congress authorizing an administrative agency to enforce the laws it has passed. The *Office of Civil Rights* (OCR) division of the *Department of Education* has been charged with enforcing Title IX. OCR has passed administrative regulations governing the implementation of Title IX, and has determined that both interscholastic and intercollegiate athletics is an educational activity subject to Title IX.

2. **Title VII of the Civil Rights Act of 1964 ("Title VII").** (42 U.S.C. § 2000e, et. seq.) The Civil Rights Act of 1964 is a comprehensive set of laws that address discrimination issues in a wide range of circumstances. Title VII of the Act protects employees (and prospective employees) from discrimination by making it unlawful for an employer to discriminate against a person in employment activities (i.e., hiring, firing, compensation, promotion, classification), based on "race, color, religion, sex, or national origin." Courts are given wide-ranging powers to address and remedy violations of this Act.

3. **Americans with Disabilities Act of 1990 ("ADA").** (42 U.S.C. § 12101, et. seq.) The purpose of the ADA is "to provide a clear and comprehensive national mandate for the elimination of discrimination against individuals with disabilities." The ADA not only encompasses issues of accessibility to facilities, but also prohibits discrimination against disabled persons in employment, subject to some specific exceptions. The overriding feature of this law requires "reasonable accommodation" of disabled persons.

4. **Sherman Antitrust Act.** (15 U.S.C. § 1, et. seq.) As American business developed during the Industrial Revolution, the advances in manufacturing, transportation, and communication created a model of business operation that effectively created monopolies. This was accomplished by consolidating all existing companies in an industry into a single business entity called a *monopoly*, and allowing all former companies to have an ownership interest in the new, single entity. The effect of removing all competition was deemed detrimental to American citizens. In response, Congress passed the Sherman Antitrust Act, which declared any contract, combination, or conspiracy "in restraint of trade or commerce" to be illegal. Although the U.S. Supreme Court, in the 1922 case of *Federal Baseball Club v. National League*, has held that Major League Baseball was not involved in commerce and was not an interstate business enterprise, and, therefore, was not subject to this Act, all other major sports are subject to antitrust laws. In your later studies, you will find out that this Act (coupled with later legislation called the *Clayton Antitrust Act*) ultimately caused a change in the relationships between management and players, resulting in familiar scenarios such as unions, free agency, strikes, lockouts, and collective bargaining agreements.

Individual states have also passed legislation that affects sport managers. It is impractical to list all, or even a small percentage, of state statutes. However, there are a few subjects that are appropriate to mention.

1. **Athlete Agent statutes.** In 1981 California became the first state to adopt a statute attempting to regulate athlete agents. Since that time at least 32 states have adopted laws seeking to protect prospective professional athletes (Wolohan, 2003). Because of the differences in the various state statutes, there was no consistency among the acts in those states that attempted to regulate athlete agents. The NCAA and other organizations sought to standardize the various state provisions, ultimately culminating in the passage of the *Uniform Athlete Agents Act* on November 30, 2000, by the National Conference of Commissioners on Uniform State Laws. It should be noted that this is not a federal statute, but merely a model for states to use in passing legislation.

2. **Sovereign Immunity.** The theory of *sovereign immunity* has existed for thousands of years, and can best be summed up by the maxim that "the king can do no wrong." Under this theory, the state cannot be held liable for any act, unless it agrees to accept liability. While some states retain this protection, other states have *waived* or given up the right to be immune from liability. Most of these statutes are referred to as *tort claims acts*, indicating that the state has agreed to accept liability for certain tort claims. The state laws vary widely, from states that have waived liability in all cases, to those that have waived liability only under limited circumstances.

3. **Recreational Use statutes.** Acknowledging the social benefits of recreational activities, state legislatures became concerned by the upsurge in lawsuits against owners of recreational facilities by injured participants. Reacting to the threat that lawsuits would cause these facilities to close, state legislatures passed laws that provide liability protection to the owners and operators. The statutes protect them by placing responsibility for injury on the participant who voluntarily assumed the risk. Generally, as long as the assumed risk is inherent to the activity, the injured party cannot sue for damages.

4. **Charitable Immunity.** In addition to the benefits of recreational activities, legislatures have recognized the value of charitable organizations, such as youth sport programs that provide services and activities to citizens. Many states (and the federal government) have passed statutes that provide liability protection for *charitable organizations* that operate sports or recreational activities. For states that do not have such statutes, the federal *Volunteer Protection Act* (42 USC § 14501, et. seq.) provides protection (for individuals, only, not organizations) unless the state has specifically chosen not to be covered by the Act. Most of these statutes provide protection to volunteers, employees, and the organization, so long as the organization has insurance in the amount required by the statute to cover losses sustained by injured participants.

TORT LAW

A *tort* is a civil wrong—other than a breach of contract—for which an injured party can recover damages. The basic premise of tort law is that a person who is damaged by the unlawful acts of another is entitled to recover his or her losses (*damages*) from the person causing the harm. In other words, the person responsible for the harm bears the financial loss. There are three categories of torts: intentional torts, negligence, and strict liability.

Intentional torts occur when the party acting wrongfully (called the "tortfeasor") intends to cause the harm by committing the act that causes the injury. For example, a group of experienced players engage in hazing activities to initiate their new teammates. A team member who sustains an injury has grounds to file a lawsuit against those who caused his or her injury. (Incidentally, not only is *hazing* an intentional tort, but most states have enacted statutes making hazing a criminal offense.) Other intentional torts include assault, battery, defamation (i.e., libel and slander), and invasion of privacy.

Negligence is described as the failure to exercise ordinary care, or the degree of care that the law requires, by acting differently than a person of ordinary care would have acted under the same or similar circumstances. Negligence is an unintentional tort, where the responsible party acted without the intent to commit the act, or to cause harm or injury to the plaintiff. Most tort lawsuits are prosecuted under this theory, by alleging that the defendant has acted negligently, thus causing harm or injury to the plaintiff.

To decide whether the defendant has acted with ordinary care, the court will apply the *standard* known as the "reasonably prudent person" standard. The court will determine if the defendant acted as a reasonably prudent person would have acted under the same or similar circumstances. If so, then there is no negligence. If not, then the defendant acted negligently (assuming the other elements of negligence are present). For example, when a player is injured by lightning when a coach fails to end soccer practice after several nearby lightning strikes, the coach has not acted as a reasonably prudent coach would have acted under those circumstances. Even though being struck by lightning is normally considered an "act of God," the coach is negligent and is liable for the injuries the plaintiff sustained.

In addition to negligence, you will study gross negligence, which falls somewhere between the standards of intentional torts and negligence. *Gross negligence* is acting in such a reckless manner that the court will consider that the defendant exhibited a conscious indifference toward the safety of the plaintiff, even though the defendant did not intend to injure the plaintiff. Driving while under the influence of alcohol or drugs is the classic example of gross negligence.

Strict liability is the tort theory of liability without fault. This theory is usually associated with products liability discussed below.

You will also study various defenses to tort liability, including the concepts of assumption of risk, waivers and agreements to participate, indemnification agreements, procedural noncompliance, sovereign immunity, charitable immunity, and recreation and Good Samaritan statutes protections.

RISK MANAGEMENT PROCEDURES

Risk management includes identifying and reducing potential risks for participants, spectators, owners, operators, and organizations. Successful organizations incorporate various liability concerns into a risk management plan, which may include policies regarding employment and personnel practices, supervision, security, emergency care, crisis management, insurance, transportation, and legal issues involved in the operation and administration of the organization. There is a more detailed discussion of risk management including crowd control and event security may be found in the facility and event management chapter of this book (Chapter 9).

PRODUCTS LIABILITY

A person who is injured by an object may be allowed to recover for his or her injuries under the concept of *products liability*. The theory is that a person who places a defective product into use is liable for the harm it causes. Virtually everyone involved in the design, manufacture, distribution, or sale of the product might be held liable.

Products liability encompasses three distinct concepts: Negligence, breach of warranty, and strict liability. The first theory asserts negligence in the manufacture or design of the product, or negligence for failure to warn purchasers of the dangers associated with the product. One case held the manufacturer liable for injuries sustained by a baseball player when his sunglasses were hit by a ball and shattered, causing loss of his eye, because the lenses were designed and manufactured to be too thin (*Filer v. Rayex Corp.*, 1970).

The second concept involves a *breach of warranty* by the defendant. A *warranty* is a promise or guarantee that products will comply with a certain standard. In such a case, the plaintiff alleges that the goods do not comply with the guaranteed standards. The "Golfing Gizmo" (a golf ball attached to an elasticized string) included in the instructions the statement "completely safe ball will not hit player." While hitting the ball, a 13-year-old suffered head injuries. The court held that the plaintiff should recover because the manufacturer/seller was liable for breaching its warranty that the gizmo was completely safe (*Hauter v. Zogarts*, 1975).

The Supreme Court of New Mexico has described the purpose of strict liability "to allow an injured consumer to recover against a seller or manufacturer without the requirement of proving ordinary negligence. Its goal is to protect the injured consumer" (*Aalco Manufacturing Co. v. City of Espanola*, 1980). In this case, the plaintiff was injured by a falling volleyball net standard, and the court held that the manufacturer was liable even though it did not negligently cause the injury. The strict liability theory also applies to the manufacture and sale of items that are unreasonably dangerous to the user of the product.

Summary

There is no area of sport management that is not impacted by "the law." For every category within the discipline, there is a special set of rules and regulations that impact virtually every decision you will make. This chapter is designed to introduce you to general principles of law involved in sport management, including:

- a basic understanding of "the law" and how it works,
- the sources of law in the United States,
- the different methods of resolving disputes, and
- the body of law that applies to sport in America.

Neither this chapter nor your further study of the legal aspects of sport will make you a lawyer. The purpose of this chapter is to make you aware of legal issues when (or before) they arise, not to teach you to make legal decisions. Each fact situation is unique and may involve many rules of law or exceptions to the general rules you will learn. If in doubt, get a legal opinion from your lawyer. The best money you will ever spend is the cost to avoid problems before they arise.

Post Script— Representing Professional Athletes

"Show me the money!" has become the mantra of agents and those who dream of representing professional athletes in negotiating their contracts, coordinating their business and financial dealings, and basically acting as a clearinghouse of information for the player. An *agent* is a person who is authorized to transact business or manage some affair for another person. The perceived glamour, prestige, and financial reward of being an agent attract many students, who envision themselves as a real-life Jerry Maguire.

When asked their career goal, a substantial percentage of sport management students express an interest in being an agent or working for an "agency." These students have seen the cinematic *Jerry Maguire* and have read the exploits of agents in newspapers, books, and magazines. As an introduction to sport management, this book is designed to assist students in making appropriate career choices. Accordingly, it is appropriate to discuss the challenges and realities involved in becoming a player agent.

In *The Agent Game*, one of the earliest books examining the agent business, author Ed Garvey highlighted the criteria to become an agent: "How does someone become an agent? The answer is simple: find a client. If you have an athlete as a client who wants to play professional football, basketball, soccer, tennis, baseball, or hockey, *you are an agent*. Congratulations" (Garvey, 1984). Unfortunately, while a student may eventually become certified as an agent, successfully recruiting a client or securing employment with a player representation firm is extremely unlikely.

As the Executive Director of the National Football League Players Association at the time, Garvey wrote his book in an effort to educate prospective professional athletes about the perils of dealing with agents. He outlines some of the realities of dealing with agents ("each agent has to out-promise the competition"), and some of the unethical tricks-of-the-trade used to sign players, then reaches the conclusion that for agents, "recruitment, not performance, is the key" (Garvey, 1984).

In the 20-plus years since Garvey's book was published, all of the professional players' associations have adopted strict rules regulating the actions of agents representing players, but recruitment of clients remains the most important aspect of being an agent. It is unrealistic to expect that a recent college graduate would be able to out-recruit established agents, with their impressive client lists, previous experience, and financial investments in the recruiting process.

The opportunity to secure employment with an established firm is also rare for newly graduated students. One well-known agent, who represents dozens of clients in various sports, has said that he and his partner received an average of more than

200 letters a month from students—including undergraduate, graduate, and law students—seeking a job or internship with his firm. In over 20 years, this two-man firm had hired only secretarial employees, and not a single prospective agent.

Taking into account the perils of seeking employment as an agent, students should proceed at their own risk, acknowledging that the odds against them are monumental. One Internet source asserts that there are over 25,000 individuals who act as sport agents in the U.S., and about 3,500 of those agents are certified (Sports Agency Directory, 2008). As Garvey said, "The number of agents is astounding . . . How can so many agents make a living in this business? The answer is, they can't."

Follow your dreams, but understand the challenges ahead. The purpose of this section is not to discourage you, but to present relevant information so that you can make educated choices.

SUGGESTED READINGS

Champion, W. (2000). *Sports law in a nutshell.* St Paul, MN: West Group.

Cotten, D., & Wolohan, J. (2003). *Law for recreation and sport managers* (3rd ed.). Dubuque, IA: Kendall/Hunt Pub Co.

Dougherty, N., Goldberger, A., & Carpenter, J. (2002). *Sport, physical activity, and the law* (2nd ed.). Champaign, IL: Sagamore Publishing.

Suggs, W. (2005). *A place on the team: The triumph and tragedy of Title IX.* Princeton, NJ: Princeton University Press.

Weiler, P., & Roberts, G. (2004). *Sports and the law: Text, cases and problems* (3rd ed.). St. Paul, MN: West Group.

Wong, G. (2002). *Essentials of sports law* (3rd ed.). Westport, CT: Praeger Publishers.

References

2007 Year End Report on the Federal Judiciary. Retrieved February 26, 2009, from http://www.supremecourtus.gov/publicinfo/year-end/2007year-endreport.pdf

Aalco Manufacturing Co. v. City of Espanola, 618 P.2D 1230 (NM 1980).

Appenzeller, H. (1998). *Risk management in sport.* Durham, NC: Carolina Academic Press.

Brentwood Academy v. Tennessee Secondary School Athletic Assoc., 531 U.S 288, 295 (2001).

Brown v. Board of Education, 347 U.S. 483 (1954).

Davis, T. (2001). What is sports law? *Marquette Sports Law Review,* 211.

Federal Baseball Club v. National League, 259 U.S. 200 (1922).

Filer v. Rayex Corp., 435 F.2d 336 (7th Cir. 1970).

Garvey, E. (1984). The agent game. Washington, DC: Federation of Professional Athletes, AFL-CIO.

Giamatti, A. B. (1988, Summer). Morality strikes out: Address before the Justinian Society, Chicago. *The Sports Lawyer, 6,* 1–3.

Glossary of Terms. (2008). Retrieved February 26, 2009, from: http://www.njleg.state.nj.us/legislativepub/glossary.asp#L

Hauter v. Zogarts, 534 P.2d 377 (CA 1975).

NCAA. (2008). Uniform athletes agent act (UAAA) history and status, Retrieved February 26, 2009, from http://www.ncaa.org/wps/ncaa?ContentID=427

Santa Fe ISD v. Doe, 530 U.S. 290 (2000).

Sports Agency Directory (2008). Retrieved February 26, 2009, from: http://www.prosportsgroup.com/SportsAgentDirectory/features.htm

Chapter Eleven

SPORT GOVERNANCE

DENNIS PHILLIPS

www.gocomics.com © 2008 Universal Press Syndicate

"And remember, Timmy: Along with the status of being a star athlete comes a responsibility to act as if the law does not apply to you."

LEARNING OBJECTIVES

After studying this chapter the student will have an understanding of
- The origin and purpose of governing bodies;
- Differences between governing bodies;
- Benefits of membership in a governing body;
- The governance legislative process in sport;
- The principles and bylaws of the NCAA; and
- Legal issues associated with governing bodies.

Introduction

As you race to the cafeteria to grab a quick bite of breakfast before your morning class, you notice the headline in the local newspaper stating that an Olympic athlete lost his or her medal because of a positive drug test for a banned performance-enhancing substance. Between classes you hear two athletes discussing a new financial aid rule passed by the National Collegiate Athletic Association (NCAA). Walking across campus you see a bulletin board flyer announcing an organizational rules meeting for all teams interesting in participating in the intramural flag football league. After class you go to the swimming pool for a workout and see signs on the wall from the Red Cross explaining mandatory safety procedures and CPR techniques. At dinner you flip the remote to ESPN's Sports Center and hear about a new National Football League (NFL) disciplinary rule governing touchdown celebrations. In one day you have seen several indications of governance and policy development at work within the sport industry.

It is difficult to imagine the world of sport without organization or rules. What would sport be like without referees, league officials, commissioners, event managers, sport medicine personnel, scoreboard operators, or timekeepers making policy, enforcing rules or following guidelines? Even children playing wiffleball in a backyard establish an agreed-upon set of rules and boundaries to enjoy play. The sport continuum runs from relatively unstructured recreational play, through the various levels of club and youth sport leagues, to the more highly controlled contests of interscholastic and intercollegiate competition, and finally the elite level of amateur and professional athletic achievement. As different as the participants and goals may be, they all share at least one thing in common; their actions are governed by someone or a group with authority, control, and power.

A practice used by some sports reporters when writing a game summary is known as the "5 W's and an H" methodology. A report of "Who," "What," "When," "Where," "Why," and "How" will "cover all the bases" of content needed to explain the story. That same technique may be used to explore the importance of governance in sport.

THE "WHAT"

Let's first start with the "what." What is meant by the term *governance*? The Merriam-Webster Dictionary (2004) definition of governance is "to control and direct the making and administration of policy" (p. 313). Other descriptors could include "direct," "influence," "determine," "regulate," and "restrain." Authors Hums and MacLean (2004) operationally defined sport governance:

> Sport governance is the exercise of power and authority in sport organizations, including policy making, to determine organizational mission, membership, eligibility, and regulatory power, within the organization's appropriate local, national, or international scope (p. 5).

Governance is usually recognized in terms of the power and authority vested in amateur and professional sport organizations at the municipal, state, national, and international levels. Local sport groups such as the Hattiesburg, Mississippi, Youth Soccer Association (HYSA), and Oak Grove, Mississippi, Dixie Youth Baseball Association administer youth sport programs in the local community. The Pennsylvania Interscholastic Athletic Association, Inc. (PIAA) is an example of a state-level organization that develops policy and enforces rules governing athletic competition among nearly 350,000 athletes at approximately 1,420 public and private schools.

At the national level, amateur sport agencies such as the Amateur Athletic Union (AAU), the National Federation of State High School Associations (NFHS), USA Track and Field (USATF), and the National Intramural-Recreational Sports Association (NIRSA) regulate sport and recreational activities. Examples of professional sport organizations include Major League Baseball (MLB), the Professional Golf Association (PGA), the Women's National Basketball Association (WNBA), and the National Association for Stock Car Auto Racing (NASCAR). International governing organizations include the International Olympic Committee (IOC), the Federation Internationale de Football Association (FIFA), which governs soccer (football), and the Federation Internationale de Gymnastique (FIG) the organization for international gymnastics competitions.

THE "WHY"

It is apparent, then, that governing agencies are a common and extremely important part of the sport industry, but "why" study it? For those who wish to engage in sport as their vocational pursuit there are many reasons why knowledge of organizational governance will prove beneficial. A sport manager at the community level will need knowledge of local government structures and politics in order to effectively achieve budgetary approval for community recreational programs. An athletic administrator involved in intercollegiate athletics will need to know the legislative process of the National Collegiate Athletic Association (NCAA) in order to enact new rules and regulations. Detailed knowledge of the rules and regulations regarding eligibility, financial aid, and recruiting will enable the organization to act ethically in the pursuit of competitive excellence and to avoid costly and embarrassing rule violations.

Awareness of governing principles of organizations will promote a smooth working relationship with your superiors and an understanding and appreciation of the functions of various committees and departments within your company. You will also appreciate the "big picture" of how various agencies within and outside of your industry segment relate and effectively interact with one another.

THE "WHO"

The "who" of sport governance focuses on leadership positions within an organization. Sport governing agencies, like all businesses, rely heavily on top-level management leadership to strategically plan for the future, formulate and implement policy, and communicate the mission and goals of the organization. The leadership methods used by governing bodies of sport come in a variety of packages; however, there are some common practices familiar to most sport organizations. All organizations have membership requirements with specific dues, application documents, regulations, and minimal qualifications for acceptance in good standing with the group. When the large group of members gathers together for meetings, conventions, or special events (e.g., conference tournaments, The Final Four, College World Series, etc.), the body is frequently called a General Assembly, General Business Meeting, or Congress. Organizational business is conducted and policies are developed and voted upon by the membership after a "quorum," or majority, of available attendees has been established.

The membership representatives are selected according to the by-laws and constitution guidelines of the organization, and the sessions are conducted under a set of established procedures common to most "official" business meetings called "Robert's Rules of Order." These procedures assure legislative fairness, maximum participation, and an orderly process by participants, while protecting individuals from domination by certain vocal subgroups. Membership can revise the by-laws or constitution by an overwhelming 2/3 vote of the assembly.

"Sport is best governed autonomously. Like universities and theatres, sports are intermediate social institutions which need protection from day-to-day partisan political pressures—but their autonomy is only valuable in so far as it helps them to promote and protect the public good which they govern."

—Katwala, 2000: 93

While most General Assemblies are composed of volunteer members of the organization, there is often a need for permanent, paid staff to conduct the business of the organization in between convention and business meetings. These full-time staff members are often referred to as the Executive Staff. The Executive Staff is frequently led by a person with a title such as Executive Director, Chairman of the Board, President, Chief Executive Officer (CEO), or Chief Operating Officer (COO). The staff assisting the leader usually consists of functional managers in charge of such areas as membership services, eligibility, marketing and sponsorship, finance and budgeting, publications and printing, media and public relations, administration, conference and special event planning, legislative advocacy, and educational services. These individuals are paid employees, located at a centralized headquarters to perform the tasks of the daily organizational business. Generally they work through committees comprised of selected membership with specific expertise and responsibilities, who gather together periodically to conduct particular tasks.

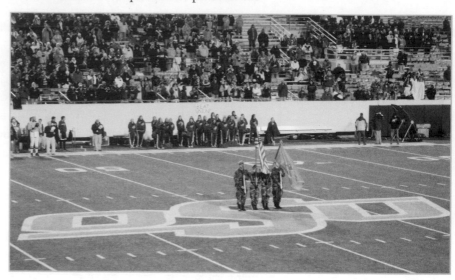

Annual or continuous tasks are completed by permanent "standing" committees. Finance, budget, championship, enforcement, legislative action, and appeals committees usually fall under the "standing" category. Single use, temporary committees assigned with a specific responsibility are frequently called "ad hoc," "single-use planning," or "task force" committees. Tasks that require special problem solving for non-programmed events, such as dealing with recruiting scandals, Internet gambling abuse, penalties for distribution and use of an illegal performance-enhancing substance, or security plans for a sport venue following terrorist threats, are examples of directives assigned to a task force. Upon completion of the assigned responsibility, the committee will permanently disband.

THE "HOW"

By now, the question of "how" may be surfacing in your thought patterns. How do sport groups get things done? How are they structured in order to be effective and efficient? We may have leaders and staff who guide the organization, and membership who participate and financially support it, but how is it all organized? Are there management principles that help organize a sport unit in the process of delegating, coordinating tasks, and distributing human, financial, and informational resources to achieve objectives? The answer, of course, is yes. These principles guide the governance of a sport body by establishing the scope of authority, clarification of an individual's responsibility, coordination in task completion, and supervision of employees. The principle of *Unity of Command* states that an employee should only have one boss to which he or she reports. The *Scalar Principle* refers to the chain of command that denotes a clear line of authority from top to bottom of the organization. This principle shows who your immediate boss is, as well as those who you supervise. Another principle is the *Division of Labor*, a directive that shows the separation of departments by function or specialization such as Marketing, Finance, Accounting, Event Management, Media Relations, or Athletic Training. The *Span of Management* principle refers to the number of employees reporting to a specific manager. Factors that affect this principle include the complexity and safety of the task, the experience and competence of the employees, the experience and competence of the manager, and the size of the organization. The greater the *Span of Management*, the broader the organizational chart. Lower-level managers tend to supervise a larger number of employees, with a narrower span of management the higher one ascends (Lussier, and Kimball, 2004).

An organizational chart is generally used to represent a business structure. Lussier and Kimball (2004) defined an organizational chart as "a graphic illustration of the organization's management hierarchy and departments and their working relationships" (p. 152). "How" can organizational charts help sport management graduates entering their first job, or starting a new job in the sport industry? Organizational charts can provide great insight into the kind of organization environment in which you are employed. For example, if the chart appears to be very steep, with many levels of management, then it is probably a "tall" organization with a bureaucracy that involves many levels of managers or committees and decision-making centralized at the top levels of leadership. If, however, the chart appears to be shallow and broad, it is probably a "flat" structure, characterized by few levels of management and de-centralized decision making. Immediate and effective response to customer service is critical in today's sport industry, and "flat" organizations are often able to respond more quickly to the needs of their sport customers.

A recent example of this occurred during a "mystery shopper" adventure conducted by a consulting firm at a National Football League game. The "mystery shopper" played the role of a fan claiming to have lost his ticket and needing help from the guest services personnel to find a seat for the game. The NFL team customer service employee had the authority to make rapid decisions without going through many management channels in order to best serve the customer. The "shopper" was pleased at the rapid resolution to his problem and gave a positive report to executives of the team (R. B. Crow, personal communication, September 2, 2004).

Sport governing bodies can be organized in a variety of ways, the most common of which are

- By function,
- By geographic location,
- By product line, and
- By customer segment.

For example, Benjamin Russell founded the Russell Corporation in 1902 in Alexander City, Alabama. From humble beginnings with only eight knitting machines and ten sewing machines, the company has grown to become the largest supplier of athletic team uniforms in the United States. Today, with annual sales of over $1 billion in team uniforms and active-wear, the company employs over 15,000 people worldwide. Russell is best known for it apparel brands of *Russell Athletic* team uniforms, *JERZEES* casual-wear, *Mossy Oak* hunting and outdoor-wear, *Cross Creek* and *Three Rivers* promotional clothing, *Moving Comfort* high performance athletic-wear for women, and *DeSoto Mills* socks (Russell, 2004). There are several ways the Russell Corporation could be organized:

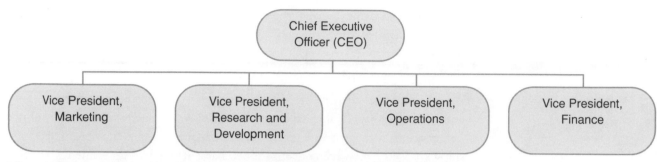

Figure 11.1. Sport Governing Bodies Organized by Function.

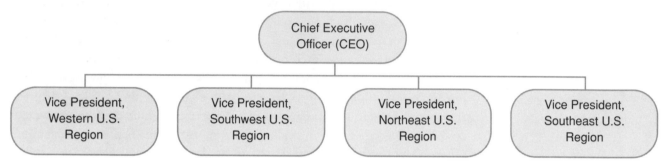

Figure 11.2. Sport Governing Bodies Organized by Geographic Location.

Figure 11.3. Sport Governing Bodies Organized by Product Line or Brand.

Figure 11.4. Sport Governing Bodies Organized by Customer Segment.

Each method of departmentalization can become a separate entity in itself and can lead to various management styles, work force division, formal or informal authority lines, and line and staff chain of commands. *Line employees*, like those shown in the above charts, issue orders and relate directly to the objectives of the organization. *Staff employees* assist and support line employees and relate indirectly to the organization's objectives. Staff employees can have titles such as *secretary, administrative assistant, equipment manager, athletic trainer, academic adviser,* or *assistant strength and conditioning coach.* They are often shown under or on the side of the supervision authority of line employees. If they have an "informal" relationship to another line employee or different departmental unit, they may have a "dotted line" attached to their position within the organizational chart.

THE "WHEN"

The question of "when" governance began in American sport can be answered only by going back to the historical foundations of organized amateur sport in the U.S. Organizations like the Young Men's Christian Association (YMCA), the Amateur Athletic Union (AAU), the National Collegiate Athletic Association (NCAA), and the National Federation of State High School Associations (NFHS) were extremely influential in the development of amateur sport in the United States. Each association faced challenges in developing rules, regulations, and policies during the early stages of its organizational life. Eligibility, amateurism, financial support, administrative and coaching leadership, equipment conformity and safety, and legislative control were just a few of the issues these early governing bodies had to face during their infancy. It became apparent that each organization needed a statement of its core values and operating philosophy in order to provide a compass for the direction the group would take.

For many sport associations, a "Mission or Vision" statement helped provide that direction. A "Mission Statement," according to Bridges and Roquemore (2000), "is the broadest of objectives and defines the purpose and uniqueness of the organization regarding its products, services, markets and revenues" (p. 124). Every governing body of sport has a purpose for its existence and a unique quality that makes it unique. A brief summary of a few of the early governing bodies of sport and their origins, mission, growth, and present day influence will help us discover "when" sport governance began.

The Young Men's Christian Association (YMCA)

George Williams founded the YMCA in London, England, in 1844 in response to declining moral, social, and cultural changes in society following the industrial revolution. The organization, which mixed an emphasis on spiritual principles with athletic fitness and competition, rapidly grew and opened in the U.S. in 1851. The YMCA began to develop a fourfold purpose, "The improvement of the spiritual, mental, social, and physical condition of young men" (YMCA, 2008, p. 1). The successful formula of combining "inspiration and perspiration" led to a growth in fitness and sport programs as swimming pools and gymnasiums were built. By the 1890s the mission had been narrowed to include the present-day symbol of the inverted triangle representing the unification of "mind, body, and spirit." The organization was blessed with gifted young leaders and inventors like James Naismith (basketball—1891), William Morgan (volleyball—1895), and Joe Sobek (racquetball—1950). The network of national and international YMCAs provided an easy vehicle for the spread of such sports and activities to a worldwide audience. Today, the 2,663 YMCAs make it one of the largest not-for-profit community service organizations in America, working to meet the health and social service needs of 20.2 million men, women, and children in 10,000 communities in the United States. YMCAs stretch beyond the United States and are located in more than 120 countries around the world (YMCA, 2008).

The YMCA Mission statement is:

> To put Christian principles into practice through programs that build healthy spirit, mind, and body for all. (YMCA, 2008, p. 1)

The Amateur Athletic Union (AAU)

The Amateur Athletic Union is one of the oldest and largest multi-sport governing bodies in the United States. Formed in 1888, its original purpose was to bring uniformity and standards to amateur sport. The AAU quickly became the dominant sport organization in America and the driving force in representing our country in all international sport competitions including the Olympic Games. The role of the AAU changed, however, following the enactment of the Amateur Sports Act of 1988, which established an official governing body for international sport, The United States Olympic Committee (USOC). The AAU then focused on the programming of the largest grass roots venture for sport competition with over 50,000 volunteers helping administer over 30,000 age division events, and 250 national championships for over 500,000 participants. In 1996, the Disney Corporation and the AAU formed a strategic alliance to further the goals of each organization. The outgrowth of their partnership was *Disney's Wide World of Sports* complex, which is home to more than 40 national AAU events each year (AAU, 2008). The AAU mission is:

> To offer amateur sports programs through a volunteer base for all people to have the physical, mental, and moral development of amateur athletes and to promote good sportsmanship and good citizenship. (AAU, 2008)

National Federation of State High School Associations (NFHS)

The National Federation is a prime example of an organization formed to meet the needs of a growing program of interscholastic athletic competition. Interscholastic sport developed quickly in America during the late 1800s. Football became a very popular spectator and participant sport in the 1890s, but suffered from some of the same ills as its intercollegiate counterparts. Problems such as increasing violence and injury, the overemphasis of winning, the use of ineligible players, and financial mismanagement were rampant (Rader, 1999). The need for adult supervision and a centralized organization with the authority to set minimum, consistent standards was apparent to many state association leaders. In 1902, the Fifteenth Conference on Academies and High Schools met and issued basic recommendations to initiate faculty and state association control of interscholastic sports. Upper Midwest states such as Illinois, Wisconsin, and Michigan had already organized state associations by the first decade of the 1900s, and rules governing minimum course loads, satisfactory progress, participation standards, and even basic rules controlling play were enacted to ensure fair and equitable competitions (Covell, 1998).

In 1920, the Midwest Federation of State High School Athletic Associations was formed when representatives of Illinois, Indiana, Iowa, Michigan, and Wisconsin met to discuss high school athletic competitions. Student-athlete welfare issues were discussed as well as consistent rules for competitions across state boundaries. By 1923, the organization changed its name to accommodate new state associations, and the group became known as the National Federation of State High School Athletic Associations. The name remained unchanged until fine arts were added during the 1970s and the word "Athletics" was dropped from the organizational title. (NFHS, 2008a).

Today, the organization represents 50 state associations and the District of Columbia. The NFHS works with over 18,500 high schools and almost 11 million students. The organization promotes educational programs in areas such as sportsmanship, citizenship, gender equity, sexual harassment, hazing prevention, drug and alcohol prevention, academic eligibility and participation standards, and eating disorders. The NFHS also publishes sports and rules books for over 16 interscholastic sports (NFHS, 2008a).

The governance power of high school sports, according to Wong (1994), rests in state and local agencies. School boards, state education associations, state legisla-

©stock.xchng iv

tures, and coaching associations yield regulatory power over the conduct of sport programs. The NFHS is a service provider that assists state associations with programs, rather than a sanctioning body with enforcement personnel and penalty provisions. High school extracurricular programs are voluntary and therefore participation is legally and financially viewed as a *privilege* rather than a *right*.

The NFHS organizational chart consists of several committees that determine the direction of the governing body. At the top is the membership represented by each state association. The *National Council* is the equivalent to a Senate legislative governing body, as it consists of one member from each state association meeting twice each year to enact legislation and, consider by-law and constitution revisions. The *Board of Directors* is composed of one member from each one of the eight geographic sections of the country, and four additional at-large members for a total of twelve members. The Board conducts the business and financial affairs of the organization, approves committees, and oversees the annual budget. The *Executive Director* and *Executive Staff* support the daily activities of the Indianapolis headquarters including marketing, publications, information and member services, convention planning, certifications, educational training, and financial services. The organization has several member associations that strongly influence the state of interscholastic sport and activities: The Coaches, Officials, Spirit, Music, Speech/Debate/Theatre Associations help develop rules and regulations that govern the extracurricular competitive experience for young men and women.

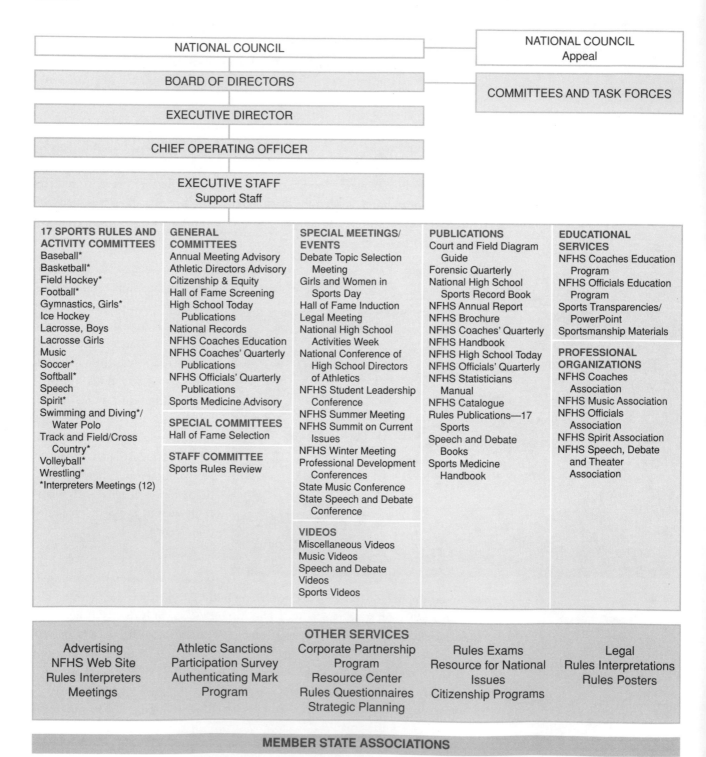

Figure 11.5. NFHS Organizational Chart.

The National Interscholastic Athletic Administrators Association (NIAAA) is another group under the National Federation umbrella that has a tremendous impact on high school and junior high sports. One of the most important roles of the NIAAA is to provide management and leadership skill development through continuing education opportunities in their more than 30 Leadership Training Courses (LTC's). Graduate-degree programs specializing in Interscholastic Athletic Administration at Ohio University, Indiana University, Purdue University at Indianapolis, and the University of Southern Mississippi utilize LTC materials to further the professional growth of present and future interscholastic athletic administrations. The rest of the organizational structure consists of the standing and special committees that administer the various programs and professional organizations of the NFHS. The mission of the NFHS is to

> serve its members and its related professional groups by providing leadership and national coordination for the administration of interscholastic activities which will enhance the educational experiences of high school students and reduce risks of their participation.

The NFHS will promote participation and sportsmanship to develop good citizens through interscholastic activities that provide equitable opportunities, positive recognition and learning experiences to students while maximizing the achievement of educational goals" (NFHS, 2008b).

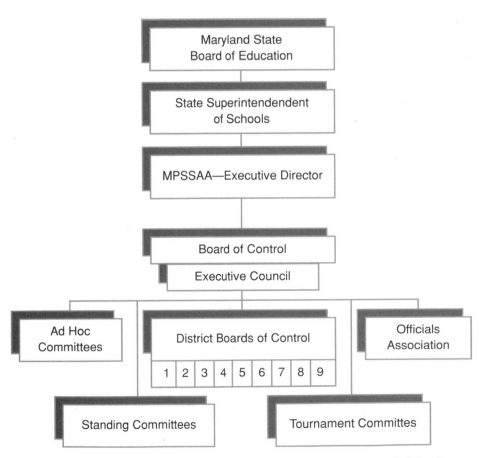

Figure 11.6. Maryland Public Secondary Schools Athletic Association Organizational Chart.

State Governing Body of Interscholastic Sport

The Maryland Public Secondary Schools Athletic Association (MPSSAA) was founded in 1946 and consists of 184 public high schools. The MPSSAA is under the authority of the Maryland State Department of Education and 24 local school systems, which are divided into 9 districts. The legislative powers of the association are entrusted to a *Board of Control* made up of one delegate from each county, three superintendents, and representatives from each of the counties based on school enrollment in grades 9–11. The structure of this Board is similar to the House of Representatives in Congress as the number of representatives (1–5) is based on the enrollment of students in the member schools in that county. The elected officers of the association include a President and a President-Elect. Standing Committees include Nominating, Finance, Constitution, Tournaments, Classification, Appeals, and Officials (MPSSAA, 2008). The purpose of the MPSSAA is to

> promote and direct public high school interscholastic activities in order to assure that those activities contribute toward the entire educational program of the state of Maryland. (MPSSAA, 2008)

National Collegiate Athletic Association (NCAA)

One of the most powerful sport governing agencies in the United States is the National Collegiate Athletic Association. Prompted by the numerous injuries and deaths occurring in football during the early 1900s, President Theodore Roosevelt called 13 college presidents and athletic leaders to the White House in 1905 to discuss needed reforms in the game. The outgrowth of that and subsequent meetings was rule reform and the formation of a group to organize college athletics. The Intercollegiate Athletic Association of the United States (IAAUS) was founded in

1906 with 62 members. Four years later, the association changed its name to the present-day name of the National Collegiate Athletic Association (NCAA, 2008).

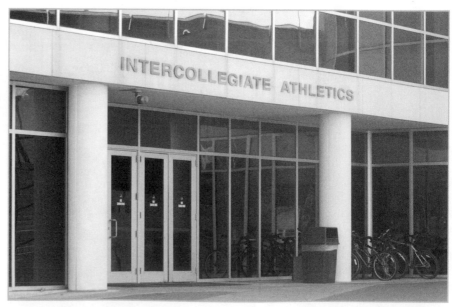

The organization evolved over time from a service-oriented, facilitative group based on the philosophy of "Home Rule," or local college control of all aspects of the athletic program, to a sanctioning body with enforcement and policy-making authority and responsibility. Factors that prompted the philosophical change in governance included eligibility and academic fraud, recruiting scandals, financial aid abuse, and amateurism violations. Following World War II, a "Sanity Code" was adopted to try to regulate and prevent further abuse in those areas. By 1973, the organization divided into three divisions of competition in order to promote unity of like-minded institutions in athletic contests. The NCAA began to administer championships and programs for women in 1981–82, and the organization grew dramatically (NCAA, 2004).

The organization took a major step forward in 1997, when it reorganized the governance structure. Upon recommendations by the Knight Foundation *Commission on Intercollegiate Athletics*, more autonomy was given to each division for specific division-only matters, and presidential authority was required at all levels of policy making. The new Division I chart included a Board of Directors composed of 18 college or university presidents charged with the responsibility of dealing with all legislative proposals. A Division I Management Council, comprised of 49 members, most of whom were athletic directors, received reports from special cabinets beneath them, and recommended policy to the Board of Directors (NCAA, 2008).

Further reorganization of the NCAA structure was proposed in October 2007 and was approved in January 2008 for implementation in September of 2008. The revised organization replaced the Management Council with two, 31-member bodies: The Leadership Council, and the Legislative Council. The Legislative Council

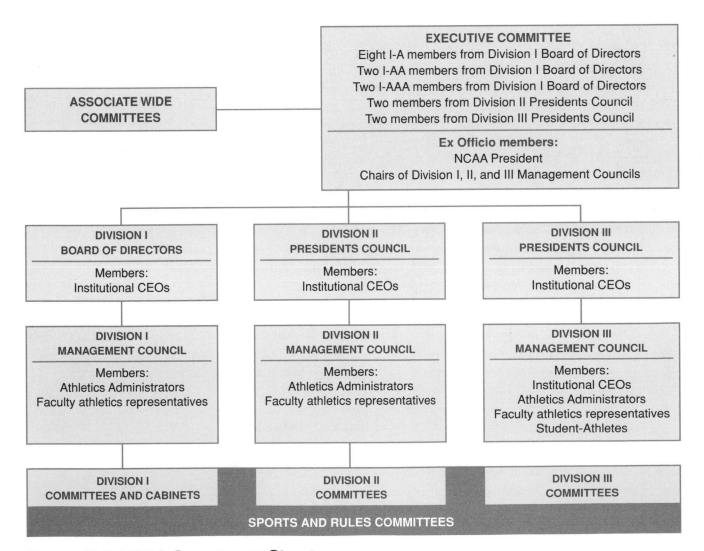

Figure 11.7. NCAA Governance Structure

is straightforward in name and deed. It will be responsible for final action on more routine legislative matters. The Leadership Council is expected to have a national focus on current and emerging issues in intercollegiate athletics. It will be the primary advisory group to the Board of Directors on strategic and policy issues (Hosick, 2008). The current Academics/Eligibility/Compliance Cabinet and the Championship Cabinet were eliminated and replaced by six, 21-member Cabinets focused on Championships; Administration; Academics; Student-Athlete Awards, Benefits, and Financial Aid; Recruiting; and Amateurism (Philippi, 2008)

The NCAA is devoted to

> the expert administration of intercollegiate athletics for its member-ship. The purpose of the NCAA is to provide programming and deliver national championships for intercollegiate athletes. (NCAA, 2008)

The United States Olympic Committee (USOC)

One of the most visible sport competitions in the world is the Olympic Games. What is the governing body that administers the team and individual programs that compete for the United States in major international events?

The International Olympic Committee (IOC), headquartered in Lausanne, Switzerland, was founded in 1894 and is the umbrella organization that organizes the summer and winter Olympic Games. The IOC is comprised of National Olympic Committees (NOC) from each country that sends athletes to the Games. The NOC of the United States is *The United States Olympic Committee* (USOC).

The USOC was formed in 1978 when the U.S. Congress passed the Amateur Sports Act (now called the Ted Stevens Olympic and Amateur Sports Act), and gave it overall authority to manage and promote the Olympic, Pan American, and Paralympic Games. The USOC is composed of over 78 member organizations categorized by Olympic Sport, Pan American Sport, Affiliated Sport, Community-Based Multisport, Education-Based Multisport, and the Armed Forces. Headquartered in Colorado Springs, Colorado the USOC employs more than 500 staff, but also relies heavily upon additional volunteers to run their extensive activities (USOC, 2008).

The USOC underwent the most sweeping changes in its history because of allegations of Code of Ethics violations, infighting within the organizational leadership, the forced resignation of the President due to résumé misstatements, and scandals involving illegal payments to IOC members. An independent commission was appointed by the U.S. Congress, as well as an internal Governance and Ethics Task Force created to investigate actions that had tarnished the image of the USOC.

The process began in 2003, as Bill Martin was named acting president and charged with leading the organization through a difficult time of reform, and culminated in recommendations to develop a more efficient governance structure. Peter Ueberroth, former President of the Los Angeles Olympic Organizing Committee (LAOOC) 1984 Olympic Games, will Chair the new Board of Directors for the USOC. Ueberroth developed the financial and organizational model currently used by the USOC, by managing the first privately financed games in Los Angeles that netted over $238 million profit. He later became Commissioner of Major League Baseball.

Ueberroth presides over a structure that accomplished the following: (1) reduced the size of the Board of Directors from an unwieldy 125 to 11; (2) reduced the number of standing committees from 23 to 4; (3) eliminated an Executive Committee from the governance structure; (4) refined the Mission Statement to emphasize support for the U.S. athletes; and (5) created an Olympic Assembly (USOC, 2008a). According to Acting Secretary General Jim Scherr, "The new governance structure will enable the USOC to better fulfill its mission while reaffirming for the American public that its confidence and trust in our organization is well-placed" (2004, p. 5).

The USOC Mission Statement is to

> support United States Olympic and Paralympic athletes in achieving sustained competitive excellence and preserve the Olympic ideals, and thereby inspire all Americans. (USOC, 2008b)

Professional Sport Organizations

Professional sport in America has a long and varied history beyond this chapter's discussion. The governance structures of the four major U.S. professional organizations, Major League Baseball (MLB), The National Football League (NFL), The National Basketball Association (NBA), and The National Hockey League (NHL), have many similarities. All four have a storied history, with MLB's National League the earliest to form in 1876 (Scully, 1989).

The first professional football league was the American Professional Football Association, created in 1920, which later became the National Football League (NFL) in 1922. The American Basketball League (ABL) was the first professional basketball league and was founded in 1924. After the ABL went out of business, two rival leagues, the Basketball Association of America (BAA) and the National Basketball League (NBL) came into existence, only to join together to become the NBA in 1949. The NHL began in 1917 with four Canadian teams. It expanded to the United States in 1924 (Quirk & Fort, 1992). All of the established leagues have withstood challenges by rival leagues such as the Players and Federal Leagues in Baseball, American Basketball Association, the American Football League and XFL, and the World Hockey League.

The "Big 4" professional leagues all have a number of teams divided into conferences and divisions of competition, usually based on geographical location. MLB has 30 teams divided into the National and American Leagues, each with East, Central, and West Divisions. The NFL has 32 teams divided into the American

Football Conference (AFC) and the National Football Conference (NFC). The teams are further divided into North, South, East, and West Divisions. The NBA has 29 teams in Eastern and Western Conferences that are further divided into Atlantic, Central, Midwest, and Pacific Divisions. The NHL has 30 teams in the Eastern and Western Conferences. Northeast, Southeast, Atlantic, Central, Northwest, and Pacific Divisions provide competitions based on proximity (Hums & MacLean, 2004). Further similarities abound in the central governance of these leagues. All of the leagues have a league commissioner, a Board of Governors made up of team owners, a central office to administer daily business, a player's association, and individual teams—each with their own unique structure. All four leagues are headquartered in New York City.

Centralized league functions include security, marketing, policy development, dispute resolution, rule-making, disciplinary actions, licensing, public relations, officiating, media coordination and production, and international business operations. De-centralized team functions cover some of the same areas, but with a local orientation. Teams usually have departmental units that focus on individual and group sales, facility security and management, marketing and promotions, concessions and merchandise sales, player development, finance and business operations, community outreach, and legal services.

THE "WHERE"

The "where" can be addressed in two ways: *Location* and *Future*. Where is the location of the "governance of sport"? A simple answer is, it is *everywhere*! It is impossible to imagine organized sport without "organization." Governance gives us consistency with the past and guiding principles for the future. However, where does that future lead us?

Each level of governance has current and future challenges to overcome. Local, state, and national levels of amateur sport face issues of increasing costs of participant health care, increased insurance and product costs involved with the demands of a litigious society, unethical behavior by management, spectators, and players, and the safety of athletes. In interscholastic sport, fund raising and sponsorship issues, hazing, funding for extracurricular activities, facility renovation and improvement, home school athlete eligibility, sportsmanship and character development, and a shortage of qualified coaches and officials present hurdles to overcome.

In intercollegiate athletics, issues include

- Maintaining (and in some cases establishing) academic integrity,
- Reducing operational costs,
- Title IX compliance,
- Meeting the increased demands of television,
- Justifying runaway coaching salaries,
- Combating the use of illegal performance-enhancing substances,
- Dealing with financial aid and amateurism issues,
- Curtailing athletes' involvement with agents,

- Increasing awareness about gambling and point shaving scandals, and
- Reducing early entrance into professional leagues by student-athletes.

Issues confronting competitive equity, revenue sharing, big market vs. small market team revenues, contraction of teams, free agency spending, facility enhancement and revenue generation, naming rights, and spending caps and luxury taxes dominate the business landscape.

Summary

Sport as we know it today would not exist without the formal organizational structure under which teams, leagues, conferences, and governing bodies operate. There are many career opportunities within governing bodies in sport, all of which can be both financially and personally rewarding. As you've undoubtedly read elsewhere in the text, the best way to prepare yourself for these jobs is through volunteering and performing internships. Developing an understanding of the complexities of these various governing bodies will assist you as you prepare for a career in the industry.

DISCUSSION ACTIVITIES

1. Locate the mission statement from your local university and compare it to the mission statement of the athletic department. What are the similarities? What are the differences?
2. Visit the NCAA website (http://www.ncaa.org) and examine the organizational structure of the Association. Determine why it is structured in this manner.

SUGGESTED READINGS

Juico, P. (2000). *Sports & governance: Pole-vaulting into the 21st century*. Malate, Manila: De La Salle University Press.

Kluka, D., Stier, W., Schilling, G., & Smyth, A. (Eds.). (2003). *Perspectives: Sport governance*. Berlin, GM: Meyer & Meyer.

Quirk, R., & Fort, R. (1999). *Hard ball*. Princeton, NJ: Princeton University Press.

References

AAU. (2008). *About the AAU*. Retrieved April 24, 2008, from http://www.aausports.org/

Bridges, F. & Roquemore, L. (2004). *Management for athletic/sport administration: Theory and Practice* (4th ed.). Decatur, GA: ESM Books.

Covell, D. (1998). High school and youth sport. In L. P. Masteralexis, C.A. Barr, & M. A. Hums (Eds.), *Principles and practice of sport management* (pp. 137–163). Gaithersburg, MD: Aspen Publishing.

Hosick, M. B. (2008, Winter ed.). *Governance split adds value. Champion Vol. 1*(1), 63. Indianapolis, IN., NCAA Publishing.

Hums. M., & MacLean, J. (2004). *Governance and policy in sport organizations*. Scottsdale, Arizona: Holcomb Hathaway Publishing.

Lussier, R., & Kimball, D. (2004). *Sport management: Principles, applications, skill development*. Mason, Ohio: Thomson Learning South-Western Publishing.

The Merriam-Webster Dictionary, Eleventh Ed. (2004). Springfield, MA: Merriam-Webster Inc.

MPSSAA. (2008). *MPSSAA Organization*. Retrieved April 24, 2008, from www.mpssaa.org/intro/organization

NFHS. (2008a). *About the NFHS*. Retrieved

April 25, 2008, from http://www.nfshsa.org/about.htm

NFHS. (2008b). *National Federation of State High School Associations 2007–2008 handbook*. Indianapolis, IN: NFHS.

NCAA. (2008). *About the NCAA. Purposes and goals*. Retrieved April 23, 2008, from http://www.ncaa.org

Philippi, R. (January 16, 2008). *Division I governance changes*. Conference USA Memorandum to Directors of Athletics.

Rader, B. C. (1999). *American sports: From the age of folk games to the age of televised sports* (4th ed.). Upper Saddle River, NJ: Prentice Hall.

Russell Athletic Corp. (2004). *About Russell Athletic*. Retrieved February 24, 2004, from http://www.russellathletic.com

USOC. (June 14, 2004). *USOC Pressbox*. Retrieved April 26, 2008, from http://www.usolympicteam.com

USOC. (2008a). *About the United States Olympic Committee*. Retrieved April 26, 2008, from http://www.usolympicteam.com

USOC. (2008b). *United States Olympic Committee Bylaws, Article II*. Retrieved April 26, 2008, from http://www.usolympicteam.com

Wong, G. M. (1994). *Essentials of sport law*. Westport, CT: Praeger.

YMCA. (2008). *YMCA History*. Retrieved April 24, 2008, from http://www.ymca.net/index.jsp

Chapter Twelve

ETHICS IN THE SPORT INDUSTRY

LYNN L. RIDINGER • T. CHRISTOPHER GREENWELL

"Quit stalling! Now do I get the million bucks, or do I fill this record-setting home run ball full of lead?!"

LEARNING OBJECTIVES

Upon completion of the chapter, the student will be able to
- Define and understand key terms associated with ethics;
- Demonstrate a basic knowledge of ethical theories;
- Examine his or her personal value system;
- Acquire an appreciation of the role that personal values and professional ethics play in the management of sport organizations;
- Identify the progressive stages of moral development and reasoning;
- Apply the steps of ethical decision-making to help resolve ethical dilemmas;
- Understand the role of codes of ethics and understand how codes of ethics are formulated; and
- Gain an appreciation for the impact socially responsible organizations have on key stakeholder groups.

Introduction

In 2007, several events unfolded that illustrated some of the questionable decisions made by athletes, coaches, and administrators. Here are a few of the more notorious examples:

- The Mitchell report was released describing widespread use of performance-enhancing drugs in Major League Baseball.
- Shortly after breaking the all-time home run record, Barry Bonds was indicted for perjury.
- Atlanta Falcons quarterback Michael Vick was sentenced to prison for his role in a dog-fighting scandal.
- Track star Marion Jones had to relinquish her Olympic medals after pleading guilty to two counts of obstruction of justice related to inquiries of illegal steroid use in sports and a check-cashing scheme.
- Referee Tim Donaghy pled guilty to charges related to gambling on NBA games.
- Despite telling owner Arthur Blank otherwise, Atlanta Falcons head coach Bobby Petrino walked out on his Atlanta Falcons team to take a job at the University of Arkansas, having several games left on his contract.
- Florida State suspended a large number of players for their bowl game against Kentucky due to an academic cheating scandal.

In sport, we see numerous other incidents such as teams using ineligible players, hiring discrimination against women and minorities by sport organizations, coaches cheating to gain a competitive advantage, professional teams circumventing salary caps, and boorish behavior of athletics both on and off the playing field. These incidents are problematic as the sport industry prides itself on providing wholesome entertainment, promoting positive values, building character, and creating good role models, but unethical behavior threatens all of the positive benefits.

Ethics and Morals

The terms *ethics* and *morals* are sometimes used interchangeably, but they are different. Ethics deals with theories or principles whereas morals have a more practical base and take into account social values, motives, and attitudes (DeSensi & Rosenberg, 2003). *Ethics* can be defined as a set of principles or values that are used to determine right and wrong. *Morals* are the fundamental baseline values that dictate appropriate behavior within a culture or society (Solomon, 1992). For example, most societies have the moral value that murder is wrong. Other types of conduct, however, may not be as clear. Providing a token of appreciation as a means to gain favor may be viewed simply as a gift in some societies whereas that same token might be considered a bribe in another culture.

Billington (1988) identified six characteristics of ethical or moral questions:

1. Dealing with questions of ethics and morals is unavoidable. As long as one lives among and interacts with others, moral issues will arise and ethical decisions will need to be made.

2. Moral decisions involve other people; there is no such thing as a private ethics.

3. Not all decisions have ethical implications. Moral decisions are reserved for those ideals that matter most to a society such as honesty, fairness, respect, and integrity.

4. Ethical decisions offer no final answers. Philosophers usually do not provide definitive right or wrong answers. Some ethical theories and actions may be shown to be more reasonable and correct than others, but rarely can a completely satisfactory solution be achieved.

5. A central element of morality is choice. Ethical dilemmas are associated with a variety of options or actions that can be taken.

6. The aim of moral reasoning is to discover the right or correct form of behavior. Because there are a variety of competing ethical theories and none without some weakness, no action can be declared as absolutely correct or incorrect. Nevertheless, through moral analysis, an appeal to ethical principles can be made and certain decisions may be deemed more justifiable than others.

Ethical Theories

The most widely accepted ethical theories are either teleological, deontological, or some combination of the two (Branvold, 2001). Theories based on *teleology* (from the Greek meaning "end") focus on the consequences of an action and weigh the benefits against the costs. A popular teleological theory is utilitarianism. Morality is assessed by whether or not the action creates the greatest good for the greatest number of people. In applying utilitarian to decision making, the good of the group supersedes the good of the individual. For example, a coach may decide to play a star athlete to increase the chance of victory for the team despite the fact that the player is not fully recovered from an ankle injury.

Deontology (derived from the Greek for duty) is based on the idea of absolute rules of moral behavior. Immanuel Kant provided the foundation for this approach with his categorical imperative statements. According to Kant, moral action is: (1) universalizable and would make sense to everyone in a similar situation, (2) demonstrates respect for the individual, and (3) is acceptable to all rational beings. Critics feel that this theory is too vague and it does not address the issue of conflicting individual rights. In the previous example, would the action be considered moral under Kant's theory? Would all coaches in a similar situation keep the injured star in the game? Was respect shown for the individual? Would all rational beings agree that this was the appropriate action? For a more detailed discussion of ethical theories, refer to DeSensi and Rosenberg (2003).

Values

It is often said that sports builds character, provides positive role models, and teaches valuable lessons in teamwork, discipline, and sportsmanship, but there is little evidence to support this belief. Participation in sports does not automatically produce better or worse people (Weinberg & Gould, 2003). Character development is a learned process that involves the adoption and application of various virtues such as compassion, fairness, sportsmanship, and integrity (Shields & Bredemeier, 1995). These virtues are based on values that are instilled by socializing agents such as parents, teachers, coaches, and friends. Societal influences such as culture, religion, educational institutions, and the media also contribute to the formation of values, character, and moral development.

Values provide the foundation of ethics. A description of a person's ethics would revolve around his or her set of values (Hitt, 1990). According to Rokeach (1973), values are enduring beliefs that provide guidance for personal goals and behavior. He classified values into two categories: (1) *terminal values* that relate to end-states of existence (goals), and (2) *instrumental values* that relate to one's mode of conduct (behavior). Terminal values can be viewed as the ends toward which one is striving whereas instrumental values are the means that one will use to achieve the ends. The ends and the means would be consistent and mutually reinforcing in a unified value system (Hitt, 1990).

Values in Sport

There has been a growing concern that the value system of some sport participants, managers, and spectators is in decay. In an effort to combat moral transgressions and emphasize the important role that sports can play in contributing to positive values of society, nearly 50 influential sport leaders gathered for a conference in May of 1999 and issued the *Arizona Sports Summit Accord*. The Accord encourages greater emphasis on the ethical and character-building aspects of athletic competition. The goal of formulating this document was to establish a framework of principles and values that would be adopted and practiced widely by those involved with sport organizations. According to the Accord, "the essential elements of character-building and ethics in sports are embodied in the concept of sportsmanship and six core principles: trustworthiness, respect, responsibility, fairness, caring, and good citizenship" (Arizona Sports, 1999, p. 2). A sample of the declarations of the Accord are listed below:

- It is the duty of sports leadership, including coaches, athletic administrators and officials, to promote sportsmanship and foster good character.

- Sports programs must be conducted in a manner that enhances the mental, social, and moral development of athletes.

- Participation in sports is a privilege, not a right. Athletes and coaches have a duty to conduct themselves as role models on and off the field.

- The academic, emotional, and moral well-being of athletes must be placed above desires and pressures to win.

- Coaches and athletes must refrain from disrespectful conduct such as verbal abuse, taunting, profane trash-talking, and unseemly celebrations.

- Sports programs should adopt codes of conduct for coaches, athletes, parents, spectators, and other groups that impact the quality of athletic programs.

- Relationships with corporate sponsors should be continually monitored to ensure against inappropriate exploitation of the sport organization's name or reputation and undue interference of influence of commercial interests.

Following are some questions to consider related to the above list of the declarations of the Accord:

- Do these ideals apply only to youth sports or are they applicable to all levels of sport?

- What strategies could sport managers implement to promote these ideals?

Go to http://www.charactercounts.org/sports/strategies.htm to see how your answers compare to the strategies suggested on the website.

Personal and Professional Ethics

Personal values and professional standards of right and wrong do not exist in a social vacuum, nor are they mutually exclusive (Beauchamp, 1988). All organizations, including sport organizations, are guided by beliefs or values that communicate what is important to the organization. A healthy organizational culture is characterized by congruence between the organization's statement of values

VALUES CLARIFICATION EXERCISE

Listed below are a set of terminal values and a set of instrumental values from *The Nature of Human Values* by Milton Rokeach. To help clarify your own values, analyze the lists in terms of *their relative importance to you.* Choose the five most important values and the five least important values from each list.

Terminal values

1. A comfortable life—a prosperous life
2. An exciting life—a stimulating, active life
3. A sense of accomplishment—lasting contribution
4. A world at peace—free of war and conflict
5. A world of beauty—beauty of nature and the arts
6. Equality—brotherhood, equal opportunity for all
7. Family security—taking care of loved ones
8. Freedom—independence, free choice
9. Happiness—contentedness
10. Inner harmony—freedom from inner conflict
11. Mature love—sexual and spiritual intimacy
12. National security—protection from attack
13. Pleasure—an enjoyable, leisurely life
14. Salvation—saved, eternal life
15. Self-respect—self-esteem
16. Social recognition—respect, admiration
17. True friendship—close companionship
18. Wisdom—a mature understanding of life

Instrumental values

1. Ambitious—hard-working, aspiring
2. Broadminded—open-minded
3. Capable—competent, effective
4. Cheerful—lighthearted, joyful
5. Clean—neat, tidy
6. Courageous—standing up for your beliefs
7. Forgiving—willing to pardon others
8. Helpful—working for the welfare of others
9. Honest—sincere, truthful
10. Imaginative—daring, creative
11. Independent—self-reliant, self-sufficient
12. Intellectual—intelligent, reflective
13. Logical—consistent, rational
14. Loving—affectionate, tender
15. Obedient—dutiful, respectful
16. Polite—courteous, well-mannered
17. Responsible—dependable, reliable
18. Self-controlled—restrained, self-disciplined

Discussion Questions

1. Do you have a unified value system? In other words, do your instrumental values support your terminal values?

2. Do you have a good understanding of your own value system? Was it easy for you to determine which values are most and least important? Why or why not?

3. Compare your value selection with one or two of your classmates. Do you agree on which values are most and least important? Why or why not?

and the daily behavior of its members (Hitt, 1990). Sound professional ethics begins with good moral behavior of the people associated with an organization. An individual's personal values of honesty, fairness, and integrity will have a social effect through the decisions that he or she makes as a member of an organization. It is important for leaders within sport organizations to clarify the parameters of professional conduct and set the tone for merging personal and professional ethics through their own words and actions. Sport managers should express expectations about ethical and moral conduct in the workplace and define for members what is considered acceptable and unacceptable behavior (DeSensi & Rosenberg, 2003).

Moral Development and Reasoning

Even when guidelines for ethical behavior have been established, real-life ethical dilemmas are often complex and require some degree of moral reasoning. The capacity for moral reasoning is dependent upon an individual's level of moral development. *Moral development* refers to a process of growth in which a person's capacity to reason morally is developed through cognitive maturation and experiences. *Moral reasoning* is the decision process in which an individual determines whether a course of action is right or wrong. *Moral behavior* is the execution of an act deemed right or wrong (Weinburg & Gould, 2003).

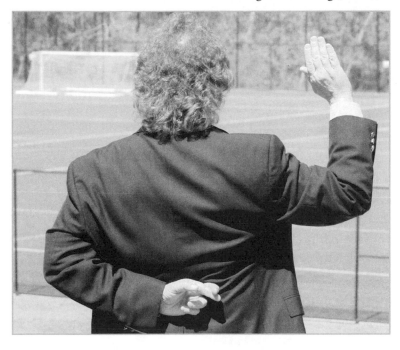

According to Kohlberg (1987), a leading scholar on moral development, children and adolescents progress through distinct stages of moral reasoning. Kohlberg's model, comprising three levels, each with two stages, is based on the relationship between the individual and the rules and expectations of the society. Level I, preconventional, is characterized by a separation between conventions and the individual. This is the moral level of most children under age 9 and many adolescent and adult criminals. Level II, conventional, is based on a person's conformance to society's rules and is the level of most adolescents and adults in societies. Level III, postconventional, is where the individual's values are formed independently of social norms. This final level is reached by a minority of adults and is usually attained only after age 20 (Kohlberg, 1987).

LEVEL I: PRECONVENTIONAL

Stage 1—*Heteronomous Morality.* At this stage, what is right is to avoid breaking rules that will lead to punishments. Individuals at this stage have a very egocentric point of view and do not consider the interests or intentions of others.

Stage 2—*Individualism, Instrumental Purpose, and Exchange.* What is right is to follow rules only as a means to achieve one's own interests and let others do the same. At this stage, the person is aware that others may have different interests so sometimes a deal or agreement must be reached. What is right in this case is a fair or equal exchange.

LEVEL II: CONVENTIONAL

Stage 3—*Mutual Interpersonal Expectations, Relationships, and Interpersonal Conformity.* What is right is to be good, to have others recognize this goodness, to show concern for others, and abide by the Golden Rule. An individual at this stage moves beyond self-interest to recognize the feelings and expectations of others.

Stage 4—*Social System and Conscience.* What is right is to perform duties, adhere to laws, and contribute to groups, institutions, and society. Someone at this stage views individual relations in terms of their place in the social system.

LEVEL III: POSTCONVENTIONAL OR PRINCIPLED

Stage 5—*Social Contract or Utility and Individual Rights.* What is right is being aware that others may hold different values, accepting those differences, and upholding basic fundamental rights like life and liberty in all societies.

Stage 6—*Universal Ethical Principles.* Right is based on self-chosen ethical principles such as justice, equality, and respect for the dignity of individuals. These principles are universal; they are comprehensive, consistent, and can be justified to any moral rational individual. A person at this stage believes that most laws and social agreements are valid because they rest on such principles; however, when laws violate these principles, one acts in accordance with the principles.

In her work on teaching sportsmanship and values, Weiss (1987) outlined five levels of moral development that progress in similar fashion to Kohlberg's model. Keep in mind that not everyone reaches the highest level of moral reasoning and oftentimes adults operate at lower levels of moral reasoning despite their cognitive capacity to think at higher levels. Level 1, the lowest level of moral reasoning, is based on external control. In other words, "It's okay as long as I don't get caught." At this stage, a child determines whether an action is right or wrong based on self-interest and the outcome of his action. If Billy is penalized for tripping his opponent, then the action must be wrong. On the other hand, if the official does not see the intentional trip, then the action is deemed okay.

In Level 2, one will compromise and rationalize to maximize self-interest. This "eye for an eye" orientation is often used in defending questionable actions. For example, Billy may feel justified in tripping his opponent because the opponent had previously tripped him. This type of moral reasoning is evident when athletes think that it is okay to use performance-enhancing drugs because everyone else is using them.

In Level 3, the child begins to take a more altruistic view and treats others like he or she would like to be treated. Billy may choose to not intentionally trip his opponent because he does not want to be tripped. A coach may insist that his players not taunt the other team because he wants his team treated with respect.

Level 4 of moral reasoning involves following external rules and regulations. At this stage, a child realizes that rules were made for the common good because not everyone can be trusted to do the right thing. Self-interest is no longer the driving force because the child can now understand the bigger picture and the importance of everyone playing by the same rules. In this case, Billy would not trip his opponent because it is against the rules.

Level 5 focuses on doing what is best for everyone involved whether or not it is in accordance with the official rules and regulations. This is considered the most mature level of moral reasoning because a person seeks to maximize the interests of the group by taking action that does not violate anyone's fundamental rights as a human being. Thus, Billy would reason that he should not trip his opponent not just because it is against the rules, but because it would create a unsafe playing environment and could cause harm.

Ethical Dilemmas

An *ethical dilemma* occurs in situations where the course of action is not clear due to the presence of: (1) significant value conflicts among differing interests, (2) real alternatives that are equally justifiable, and (3) significant consequences on stakeholders in the situation (McNamara, 1999). Sport managers face ethical dilemmas on a regular basis. Examples of situations associated with ethical dilemmas are reported in the sports media everyday. For each of the following situations, decide if an ethical dilemma exists and discuss what, if any, action should be taken by sport managers.

- An athlete is under investigation for the use of performance-enhancing drugs and has just qualified for the Olympic team.
- You are interested in joining a private golf club, but you learn that club policies ban women from becoming members and restrict their tee times on the course.
- Sales of luxury suites in a new ballpark are slow so the owner attempts to create an incentive to buy by falsely advertising that there are only a few suites left to purchase and they are selling fast.
- A star player is accused of sexual assault just prior to the playoffs.
- A college basketball coach has been very successful in leading her team to the NCAA tournament for the past several seasons, but the graduation rate of her players is 0 percent.
- A NASCAR driver intentionally spins out to bring out a caution flag.
- In a search for a new coach, qualified minority candidates are excluded from the interview pool.
- The parents of players in a youth soccer league have become increasingly verbally abusive toward officials and opponents.
- A baseball pitcher intentionally hits a batter in retaliation for his teammate being hit by a pitch in the previous inning.
- The highest bid for naming rights for a new sports facility at a university is a beer company.
- During the last few seconds of a high school football game, there is confusion

and the home team ends up winning on 5th down. The mistake is not detected at its occurrence, but becomes apparent the next day during a review of the game film.

- The team mascot, an Indian chief, has caused controversy. Some people are offended by this symbol, but most of the alumni and financial donors associate the symbol with school pride and do not want the mascot changed.

Ethical Decision Making

Trying to decide on the best alternative to resolve an ethical dilemma can be a challenging task for sport managers who often deal with various stakeholders with different interests. Ethical analysis and decision making should incorporate a systematic process of reasoning. McNamara (1999) recommended that organizations develop and document a procedure for handling ethical issues. He suggested that organizations form an ethics committee comprised of top leaders, board members, and staff to resolve ethical dilemmas. There are various models for ethical analysis that are built on the foundations of basic ethical theories. They are not designed to provide absolute answers, but they do provide guidelines for assessing ethical issues and evaluating alternatives.

An adaptation of a model suggested by Zinn (1993) and presented by Crosset and Hums (1998, p. 129) outlines the following steps in the ethical decision-making process:

1. Identify the correct problem to be solved.
2. Gather all the pertinent information.
3. Explore codes of conduct relevant to your profession or to this particular dilemma.
4. Examine your own personal values and beliefs.
5. Consult with your peers or other individuals in the industry who may have experience in similar situations.
6. List your options.
7. Look for a "win-win" situation if at all possible.
8. Ask the question, "How would my family feel if my decision and how and why I arrived at my decision were printed in the newspaper tomorrow?"
9. Sleep on it. Do not rush to a decision.
10. Make your best decision, knowing it may not be perfect.
11. Evaluate your decision.

While this may seem like a tedious process, keep in mind that ethical dilemmas and ethical decisions involve complicated problems. The decisions of sport managers are often publicly scrutinized and may receive more media attention than other types of businesses. It is therefore important to have a logical approach to deal with ethical issues and to develop a sound game plan for managing ethics in the workplace.

Managing Ethics

Considering the importance of protecting the integrity of their respective sports, many sport organizations and governing bodies have developed *codes of ethics* to guide the actions of their constituents. By providing guidelines, organizations hope to both encourage ethical behavior and discourage unethical behavior by assisting individuals in making the right ethical choices.

Sport organizations and governing bodies incorporate codes of ethics to meet a variety of needs; therefore, the content and purposes of these codes of ethics will vary from organization to organization. For example, the purpose of the International Olympic Committee (IOC) Code of Ethics is to stress commitment to the fundamental principles of the Olympics and the Olympic ideal (IOC, 2004). Its code focuses on four key themes: dignity, integrity, use of resources, and relations with states. The National Association of Sport Officials (NASO) publishes a code of ethics for the purpose of guiding the professional conduct of its members. Its code covers themes such as impartiality, conflict of interest, professional courtesy, and other themes that are important to sports officials. The USA Gymnastics Code of Ethics is written with the intent to "guide and to affirm the will of all of USA Gymnastics' members to safeguard the best interests of the sport by acting ethically at all times" (USA Gymnastics, 1996, p. 1).

> "The integrity of college sports has always been first priority. If it weren't for the integrity of the sport, no one would be interested—players, fans, media." (NCAA President Myles Brand, as cited in *Barnhouse*, 2004, p. 1D)

Codes of ethics will target different stakeholder groups depending on the organization or governing body. For example, The New Jersey Sports and Exposition Authority is a state agency operating sports and convention venues. Therefore, their code of ethics has been written to define acceptable behavior for their members and employees. The National Youth Sports Coaches Association has a much different mission; therefore, they publish three codes of ethics: one for coaches, one for players, and one for parents. Some organizations take their codes a step further and address their fans. This is the case at the University of Florida where they produce the Gator Fans' Code of Conduct designed to prohibit inconsiderate or dangerous behavior from their fans.

Ideally, these codes are developed in advance to promote positive behavior and prevent problems. However, sometimes codes of ethics are developed in response to growing controversies. Recently, members of the National Association of Basketball Coaches (NABC) agreed to adopt codes of ethics for their basketball programs. This movement stemmed from unethical incidents involving basketball coaches at St. Bonaventure, Georgia, Baylor, Fresno State, and Iowa State that tarnished the image of the coaching profession (Moran, 2003). Similarly, the International Skating Union (ISU) adopted a code of ethics in 2003 in response to the judging scandal at the 2002 Olympics, where French judge Marie-Reine Le Gougne voted in favor of Russian skaters under suspicious circumstances ("ISU adopts," 2003).

CRITERIA FOR GOOD CODES OF ETHICS

Considering the importance of encouraging good conduct, it is important to take care in developing a code of ethics to ensure the code will be effective in meeting its stated purpose. Mahony, Geist, Jordan, Greenwell, and Pastore (1999) identified several factors related to constructing an effective code of ethics.

- Codes of ethics should avoid being too vague or too specific. When codes are too vague, individuals are provided little guidance on how to make ethical decisions. However, codes that are too specific are limited in that they may not apply to a wide variety of situations. For example, think of what happens when a new performance-enhancing drug is introduced that is not expressly prohibited by a governing body's code of ethics. Athletes may be tempted to use it because it is not expressly prohibited, event though it gives the athlete an unfair advantage.

- Effective codes of ethics are founded on a few themes that can be used to guide individuals' decisions in a variety of situations. These themes represent the organization's values and will vary from organization to organization. In a study of intercollegiate conference codes of ethics, several themes emerged as being important. *Sportsmanship, welfare* of participants, *compliance* with institutional and conference rules, *equitable treatment*, and professional *conduct* of employees were themes commonly found in codes of ethics (Greenwell, Geist, Mahony, Jordan, & Pastore, 2001).

- Organizations developing codes of ethics should communicate what is in the code of ethics to those individuals addressed in the code. The NCAA realizes this as they call for each member institution to continuously educate their stakeholders about policies related to sportsmanship and ethical conduct (NCAA, 2003). The NBA and NFL do this by hosting orientation events for rookies that focus, in part, on ethical behavior (Broussard, 2003).

- Codes should be clear as to whom they apply. This can be especially challenging in sport contexts due to the large number of stakeholder groups affected. The behavior of coaches, administrators, athletes, and fans can all impact the organization.

- Consequences for violating ethical standards should be established (DeSensi & Rosenberg, 2003; Lere & Gaumnitz, 2004). Without some sort of penalty, the code is simply a suggestion and is not likely to influence behavior. These penalties should be clear, should identify who is in charge of enforcing penalties, and should identify methods of appeal. In terms of common penalties, Greenwell et al., (2001) found intercollegiate conferences included penalties ranging from reprimands and probation to player and team suspensions. For the most serious violations, penalties included institutional fines and institutional expulsion.

- Finally, in order for codes to be effective, codes must be relevant to the stakeholders addressed in the code (Wood & Rimmer, 2003). In order to encourage increased acceptance, codes should be developed with input from those who will be impacted by the standards (DeSensi & Rosenberg, 2003; Stead, Worrell, & Stead, 1990). This type of participatory approach to developing codes of ethics should lead to better understanding of what coaches and athletes desire from each other, which should ultimately lead to effective codes of ethics.

Select a sport organization. Who should be addressed in its code of ethics? What values should be highlighted in their code? How should those participants be encouraged to follow what is in the code?

Social Responsibility

> "THE PUBLIC IS FOCUSED NOW MORE THAN EVER ON WHAT FIRMS ARE SAYING ABOUT THEIR CORPORATE SOCIAL RESPONSIBILITY."
>
> —SNIDER, HILL, & MARTIN, 2003

Sport organizations often impact multiple stakeholder groups including employees, coaches, athletes, spectators, the business community, and the local community in general. Further, sport organizations often rely on these stakeholder groups for the resources they need to operate successfully. For example, organizations may utilize government money to fund programs like city recreation leagues or tax revenue to build stadiums and arenas. They may require other resources from the community such as volunteers to staff an event or local media to promote events. Similarly, the actions of sport organizations impact the community in many ways, both positively and negatively. On the positive side, sport organizations contribute to the local economy, and citizens are provided opportunities to participate in activities or enjoy sports performances. Negatively, bad acts by an organization can harm the reputation of the community, and bad acts by athletes can provide poor role models to the youth of the community. These points illustrate an inextricable relationship between the organization and its stakeholders; therefore, sport organizations' responsibilities toward their stakeholders is an important issue.

CORPORATE SOCIAL RESPONSIBILITY

Corporate social responsibility is the term most often used to refer to the role an organization has within the community. Because of the media exposure sport organizations receive and the celebrity of their athletes, sport often has greater opportunities to impact their communities than other organizations (Babiak & Wolfe, 2006). Smith and Westerbeek (2007) stated "sport offers a bridge across social and economic gaps, an opportunity to improve the quality of life, and a stimulus to encourage large and profitable businesses to share a little of their prosperity" (p. 43).

According to Carroll (1999), socially responsible businesses have four main responsibilities: economic, legal, ethical, and philanthropic, and responsible organizations will seek to achieve each.

Economic responsibilities require organizations to produce goods and services and sell them at a profit, because that is how a capitalist society operates (Carroll, 1999). At first this definition seems to imply that organizations should act in their self-interest without regard to other stakeholder groups, but Carroll (1999) argued that economic viability also influences other parts of society. For example, professional sports teams have a responsibility to make wise fiscal decisions, since the local economy may benefit from jobs, tourist dollars, and tax revenue generated by the existence of a team. In intercollegiate athletics, administrators are entrusted with funds from the university, donors, and corporate sponsors. These administrators have a responsibility to use these funds efficiently to maximize the experience of the student-athletes and contribute to the university.

Under this definition, socially responsible professional teams should strive to produce the best product. This would seem to be the goal of every team, but it is not always the case. After the Florida Marlins won the World Series in 1997, team owner Wayne Huizenga, frustrated by a lack of profits, dismantled the team by trading away many of the team's star players and not re-signing others in order to cut costs (Useem, 1998). This resulted in the Marlins becoming the first team to win the World Series and then lose over 100 games the next year, and attendance dropped dramatically over the next six years. Considering how much the community had invested, both economically and psychologically, into the team, was Huizenga justified in his actions?

Legal responsibilities require organizations to reach goals within legal constraints. Sport organizations are often under the scrutiny of contract laws, labor laws, criminal laws, etc., and socially responsible sport managers are expected to adhere to these laws. Further, legal responsibility also applies to organizational rules and procedures. For example, Olympic athletes have numerous eligibility and anti-doping rules to adhere to, and colleges are expected to adhere to rules in the NCAA manual.

The competitive nature of sport often provides challenges to organizations, coaches, and athletes who are tempted to "bend the rules" for their advantage. For example, the New England Patriots were caught using video to spy on the New York Jets, and Formula One's McLaren team was caught with secret technical data from rival Ferrari (Powers, 2007). In both cases, the offending parties argued they really had not done anything against the rules of their respective sports. We also see this in college sports where coaches bend recruiting rules to land top athletes. These coaches may feel that winning is what is important, and that they should win at all costs. Socially responsible coaches also want to win, but they see more value in "winning within the rules."

Ethical responsibilities require organizations to operate by established norms defining suitable behavior. In other words, ethical responsibilities represent what organizations are expected to do above the rule of law. A good example of acting within the law but breaking ethical standards comes from the University of Colorado. The Buffaloes' football program admitted to hiring exotic dancers to entertain prospective recruits. Although this activity was not prohibited by law or by NCAA rule, it shocked many who felt it deviated from suitable behavior (Kluger, 2004). In professional sport, the Chicago Cubs have been accused of scalping their own tickets. The Cubs, in an effort to capitalize on high demand for tickets, set up their own brokerage service where they sell their own tickets at dramatically inflated prices. Whereas many Cubs fans have claimed it is unethical to "scalp" their own tickets, the team argues they are acting within the law (Ciokajlo, 2002). These two examples illustrate that even though an organization is working within the law, it may not necessarily be acting responsibly.

Philanthropic responsibilities require organizations to give back to their communities. Bill Veeck, who owned the Cleveland Indians Baseball team in the 1950s, exemplified philanthropic responsibilities. Contrary to most baseball owners at the time who felt the city owed them something, Veeck surmised that his team was dependent on the facilities of the city and the goodwill of the citizens (Veeck & Linn, 1962). Due to this belief, the Indians were active in philanthropy, inviting community groups to attend for free and contributing gate receipts to community charities and youth sports programs. This trend continues today as many professional sports teams have established charitable foundations to contribute to their communities. In addition to financial contributions, many sport organizations contribute other resources to their communities. Many universities create programs like the University of Louisville's Cards Care program. The Cards Care program organizes activities for student-athletes to donate their time to various community projects such as pen pal programs with local schools, visits to children's hospitals, shifts serving food at soup kitchens, etc.

INDIVIDUAL SOCIAL RESPONSIBILITY

Social responsibility applies to individuals as well as organizations. Individual athletes, coaches, and administrators have a responsibility to their communities and to their peers. Administrators bear the weight of knowing their decisions affect many stakeholder groups ranging from owners, employees, athletes, to fans. Coaches are often responsible for teaching values in addition to skills, and these coaches often hold a high public profile in the community. Tony Dungy, former coach of the Indianapolis Colts, is one of many coaches who actively used his stature in the community to make a positive impact. Dungy was actively involved with Big/Brothers/Big Sisters, Boys and Girls Clubs, and several faith-based initiatives. Conversely, negative incidents involving coaches can send entirely different messages to their athletes and to the people who follow their teams. Two recent examples involved high-profile coaches. New York Knicks head coach Isiah Thomas was entangled in a sexual harassment scandal, and St. Louis Cardinals manager Tony LaRussa was arrested on drunk-driving charges. In both cases, the coaches' actions were starkly opposed to the values they tried to communicate to their athletes and their fans.

In addition to coaches, athletes impact their communities in many ways. Like it or not, athletes serve as role models, for young kids often emulate their heroes. This is why brands such as Nike and Sprite are willing to pay LeBron James millions of dollars in endorsement deals. They do this knowing kids will want to wear what LeBron wears and drink what LeBron drinks. This influence can be both positive and negative. On one hand, role models such as Mia Hamm and Lisa Leslie have encouraged girls to get involved in sports and to lead healthier lives. Many kids have taken up golf to be like Tiger Woods. On the other hand much of the boorish behavior seen in youth sports can be attributed to kids emulating professional athletes such as Roger Clemens throwing at a batter or Manny Ramirez charging the mound. What do children learn about sportsmanship when they see athletes like Carmelo Anthony brawl with opposing players or Terrell Owens spit in the face of an opponent? Although many athletes may want to shun this responsibility, high-profile athletes have to realize they are always being watched and emulated.

Many athletes feel a responsibility to use their fame to have a positive impact on their communities. For example, professional football player Warrick Dunn established the Homes for the Holidays program, which assists single mothers in purchasing homes. According to the Warrick Dunn Foundation, Dunn has helped 74 single parents and 192 children with affordable homeownership. The majority of these homes are in Tampa, where he began his professional career, and Baton Rouge, Louisiana, where he grew up. In December of 2007, his organization expanded to Tallahassee, Florida, assisting a single father and Florida State University employee (Taylor, 2007). Major League Baseball recognizes the power athletes have in their communities and encourages athletes to be active by awarding the Roberto Clemente award each year to recognize devotion to work in the community. The 2007 winner, Craig Biggio of the Houston Astros, was recognized for his work with The Sunshine Kids, a support group for children with cancer. Over the last 16 years, Biggio has raised over $2.5 million for the organization (Footer, 2007).

Sometimes this responsibility extends beyond the local community. American speedskater Joey Cheek provides a great example. After winning a gold medal at the 2006 Winter Olympics in Turin, Cheek donated his gold medal bonus to Right to Play, an international humanitarian organization. In addition, he used his influence as an athlete to encourage Olympic sponsors to do the same (Crouse, 2006).

BENEFITS OF BEING A GOOD CORPORATE CITIZEN

Just as socially responsible organizations deliver benefits to their stakeholders, they may also reap benefits, as organizations contributing to the *public good* often enjoy business success as customers reward organizations for their roles in the community (Besser, 1999). There is some evidence to suggest that socially responsible activities can boost an organization's image, generate increased business, and keep organizations out of trouble. In addition, customers are more likely to buy from organizations that are socially responsible and less likely to purchase products from companies whose practices are viewed as being less socially responsible (Creyer, 1997; Sen & Bhattacharya, 2001). Good corporate citizenship often helps sport organizations attract fans and corporate sponsors (Babiak & Wolfe, 2006).

Socially irresponsible organizations can suffer negative effects. A good example of how irresponsible activities can have negative effects on the organization comes from the Salt Lake City Olympics scandal. In 1999, while Olympic officials involved in the Salt Lake City bid process were being investigated on bribery charges, John Hancock Financial Services, a major Olympic sponsor, decided to significantly scale back advertising for the Sydney Olympics (Bell, 1999) and a major donor withdrew a $10 million donation (Blevins, 2003).

Summary

- Morality and ethics in the workplace should be key components of all industries, including the sport industry.
- Sport managers routinely face ethical situations and the decisions they make impact a variety of stakeholders such as athletes, coaches, staff, corporate sponsors, and fans.

- Sport managers will be better equipped to deal with the daily dose of dilemmas if they have a sound grasp of their personal values, a commitment to professional ethics, a basic understanding of ethical theories, and the ability to apply moral reasoning and ethical decision-making to resolve problems.

- It is important for sport managers to develop and enforce codes of ethics to ensure appropriate actions of constituents.

- Social responsibility should be strongly encouraged by our sport leaders at both the organizational and individual levels.

- Reflection upon the ethical choices currently being made in the world of sports coupled with the knowledge and appreciation of ethical principles and moral behavior can help guide future sport managers toward making the "right" decisions.

DISCUSSION ACTIVITIES

1. Do sport organizations have a responsibility to their communities? Is the level of responsibility different for professional teams? College teams? Youth teams?

2. Do athletes have a higher standard for behavior than non-athletes? Should more be expected of professional athletes? Should college athletes be expected to behave better than other college students?

3. Your minor-league baseball team has regularly sold out each game, and you expect to sell out again this season. Despite the sellouts, your organization is experiencing a budget crunch and you are under pressure to deliver as much revenue as possible. You feel you could sell all of your seats, but the local Drug Abuse Resistance Education (D.A.R.E.) program has asked for you to set aside 250 tickets for each game to be used as rewards for school children who agree not to use drugs. Do you sell the tickets to the public or do you donate them to the D.A.R.E. program?

4. Your men's basketball coach, who has coached for 15 successful years, has been arrested for drunk driving and has admitted to the crime. You have to formulate some sort of disciplinary action. How severe should the penalty be for this type of offense? Should the coach be treated like any other university employee in a similar situation?

5. You have a football player who has been accused of a crime. The local police claim he signed for a package containing steroids and other illegal drugs. The athlete claims he did not know what was in the package. Should the athlete be able to continue to play? Will you support the player or take disciplinary action? What type of disciplinary action would be appropriate?

6. You are operating a youth baseball league. Throughout the season, the parents have gotten more vocal in criticizing coaches, umpires, and league officials. It has gotten to the point that the kids are becoming distracted on the field. What policies can you put into place to avoid this type of behavior? What could happen if this behavior is not controlled?

7. The day before the championship game you find out your star player may be ineligible because of a minor paperwork error. It appears that the player lives

one block outside the district and should be playing for another team. The player has been on your team all season and you have received no complaints. The league office is not aware of the oversight, and it is possible that no one may ever notice. Should you report this to the league office? What is the right thing to do?

SUGGESTED READINGS

Badaracco, J. (2003). *Harvard Business Review on corporate ethics.* Cambridge, MA: Harvard Business School Press.

Bowie, N. E., & Duska, R. R. (1990). *Business ethics* (2nd ed.). Englewood Cliffs, NJ: Prentice Hall.

Boxill, J. (2002). *Sports ethics: An anthology.* Oxford, UK: Blackwell Publishers.

NCAA Division I Manual (2003–2004 ed.). (2003). Indianapolis, IN: National Collegiate Athletic Association.

Simon, R. (2003). *Fair play: The ethics of sport* (2nd ed.). Boulder, CO: Westview Press.

Seglin, J. (2003). *The right thing: Conscience, profit and personal responsibility.* Rollinsford, NH: Spiro Press.

The Arizona Sports Summit Accord (1999). *Pursuing victory with honor.* Retrieved July 2, 2004, from http://www.charactercounts.org/sports/accord.htm

Babiak, K., & Wolfe, R. (2006). More than just a game? Corporate social responsibility and Super Bowl XL. *Sport Marketing Quarterly, 15,* 214–222.

Barnhouse, W. (2004, February 13). Brand says ethics tops the NCAA's agenda. *Fort Worth Star-Telegram,* p. D1.

Bauchamp. T. L. (1988). Ethical theory and its application to business. In T. L. Beauchamp & N. E. Bowie (Eds.), *Ethical theory and business* (3rd ed., pp. 1–55). Englewood Cliffs, NJ: Prentice-Hall.

Bell, A. (1999, June 7). John Hancock fights to clean up Olympics. *National Underwriter, 103*(23), 3.

Besser, T. L. (1999). Community involvement and the perception of success among small business operators in small towns. *Journal of Small Business Management, 37,* 16–29.

Billington, R. (1988). *Living philosophy: An introduction to moral thought.* London: Routledge.

Blevins, J. (2003, January 23). Major sponsors stand by U.S. Olympics despite ethical scandal. *Knight Ridder Tribune Business News,* p. 1.

Branvold, S. (2001). Ethics. In B. L. Parkhouse (Ed.), *The management of sport: Its foundation and application* (3rd ed., pp. 162–176). New York: McGraw-Hill.

Broussard, C. (2003, September 26). NBA rookies get lessons in life skills. *The New York Times,* p. D 7.

Carroll, A. B. (1999). Corporate social responsibility: Evolution of a definitional construct. *Business and Society, 38,* 268–295.

Ciokajlo, M. (2002, October, 10). Chicago Cubs face ticket-fraud lawsuit. *Knight Ridder Tribune Business News,* p. 1.

Creyer, E. H. (1997). The influence of firm behavior on purchase intention: Do consumers really care about business ethics? *Journal of Consumer Marketing, 14,* 421–32.

Crosset, T. W., & Hums, M. A. (1998). Ethical principles applied to sport management. In L. P. Masteralexis, C. A. Barr, & M. A. Hums (Eds.), *Principles and practice of sport management* (pp. 117–136). Gaithersburg, MD: Aspen Publishers, Inc.

Crouse, K. (2006, February 14). Recognizing good fortune, Cheek shares gold medal. *New York Times,* p. D 1.

DeSensi, J. T., & Rosenberg, D. (2003). *Ethics and morality in sport management.* Morgantown, WV: Fitness Information Technology.

Footer, A. (2007) *Biggio receives Clemente award honor: Astros star exemplifies sportsmanship, community service.* MLB.com. Retrieved January 7, 2007, from http://mlb.mlb.com/news/article.jsp?ymd=20071027&content_id=2284369&vkey=news_mlb&fext=.jsp&c_id=mlb

Greenwell, T. C., Geist, A. L., Mahony, D. F.,

Jordan, J. S., & Pastore, D. L. (2001). Characteristics of NCAA conference codes of ethics. *International Journal of Sport Management, 2*, 108–124.

Hitt, W. D. (1990). *Ethics and Leadership: Putting theory into practice.* Columbus, OH: Battelle Press.

International Olympic Committee. (2004). *IOC Code of Ethics.* Lausanne Switzerland: Author

ISU adopts ethics code after Salt Lake scandal. (2003, August 12). *The Toronto Star,* p. E05.

Kluger, J. (2004, March 1). Entirely out of bounds. *Time, 163*(9), 59.

Kohlberg, L. (1987). *Child psychology and childhood education: A cognitive-developmental view.* New York: Longman.

Lere, J. C., & Guamnitz, B. R. (2004). The impact of codes of ethics on decision making: Some insights from information economics. *Journal of Business Ethics,* 48, 365–379.

Mahony, D. F., Geist, A. L., Jordan, J., Greenwell, T. C., & Pastore, D. (1999). Codes of ethics used by sport governing bodies: Problems in intercollegiate athletics. *Proceedings of the Congress of the European Association for Sport Management, 7,* 206–208.

McNamara, C. (1999). *Complete guide to ethics management: An ethics toolkit for managers.* Retrieved July 2, 2004, from http://www.mapnp.org/library/ethics/ethxgde.htm

Moran, M. (2003, October 16). Coaches, NCAA agree to chart new course. *USA Today,* p. 7C.

NCAA Division I Manual (2003–2004 ed.). (2003). Indianapolis, IN: National Collegiate Athletic Association.

Powers, J. (2007, September 15). Sports debate: When to cry foul: Edge-seeking becoming win-at-any-cost cheating. *The Boston Globe,* p. A1.

Rokeach, M. (1973). *The nature of human values.* New York: The Free Press.

Sen, S., & Bhattacharya, C. B. (2001). Does doing good always lead to doing better? Consumer reactions to corporate social responsibility. *Journal of Marketing Research, 38,* 225–243.

Shields, D. L. L., & Bredemeier, B. J. L. (1995). *Character development and physical activity.* Champaign, IL: Human Kinetics.

Solomon, R. C. (1992). *Above the bottom line: An introduction to business ethics.* Fort Worth, TX: Harcourt, Brace.

Smith, A. C. T., & Westerbeek, H. M. (2007, Spring). Sport as a vehicle for deploying corporate social responsibility. *Journal of Corporate Citizenship,* p. 43–54.

Snider, J., Hill, R. P., & Martin, D. (2003). Corporate social responsibility in the 21st century: A view from the world's most successful firms. *Journal of Business Ethics, 48,* 175–187.

Stead, W. E., Worrell, D. L., & Stead, J. G. (1990). An integrative model for understanding and managing ethical behavior in business organizations. *Journal of Business Ethics, 30,* 185–195.

Taylor, A. J. (2007, December 19). Warrick Dunn, Habitat join forces. *Tallahassee Democrat.*

Useem, J. (1998, May 19). Ball club of the new economy. *Inc., 20*(7), 31–32.

USA Gymnastics. (1996). *USA Gymnastics Code of Ethics.* Indianapolis, IN: Author.

Weinberg, R. S., & Gould, D. (2003). *Foundations of sport & exercise psychology.* Champaign, IL: Human Kinetics.

Weiss, M. R. (1987). Teaching sportsmanship and values. In V. Seefeldt (Ed.), *Handbook for youth sports coaches* (pp. 137–151). Reston, VA: AAHPERD.

Wood, G., & Rimmer, M. (2003). Codes of ethics: What are they really and what should they be? *International Journal of Value-Based Management, 16*(2), 181–195.

Veeck, B., & Linn, E. (1962). *Veeck as in wreck.* New York: Putnam.

Zinn, L. M. (1993). Do the right thing: Ethical decision making in professional and business practice. *Adult Larning, 5,* 7–8; 27.

Chapter Thirteen

GLOBAL SPORT INDUSTRY

ARTEMISIA APOSTOLOPOULOU · DIMITRA PAPADIMITRIOU

© 2003 Universal Press Syndicate   5-24

MOORE

www.ucomics.com

"Henry! It's the rest of the world. They want to know why you still haven't embraced the game of soccer."

LEARNING OBJECTIVES

After reading this chapter, the student should have gained an understanding of
- Globalization trends occurring in the sport industry;
- Challenges facing organizations considering international expansion;
- The Olympic Movement, its member associations and main functions;
- U.S. professional leagues' efforts to expand internationally;
- The structure of the European sport industry; and
- Opportunities for a career in international sport management and skills needed.

Introduction

During the 2003–2004 NBA season, American Express aired an advertisement tag-lined "Global Village." The ad featured Don Nelson, then coach of the Dallas Mavericks, shopping for international dictionaries and using his newly acquired vocabulary to communicate during practice with his international players: Tariq Abdul-Wahad from France, Dirk Nowitzki from Germany, Eduardo Najera from Mexico, even Steve Nash from Canada!

The message was simple: long gone were the days when U.S.-born players monopolized NBA rosters. During the 2003–2004 NBA season, 67 international players from 33 countries competed in the world's top basketball league ("International Players," 2004), a dramatic increase from the number of international players in the NBA 10 years ago. An examination of Major League Baseball and the National Hockey League rosters around the same time reveals similar diversification trends. According to a *Sports Illustrated* (*SI*) special report on globalization published in 2004, the percentage of U.S.-born players in MLB in the 2003 season was 72.7 (compared to 83.4 percent in 1993), while the number of North American players in the NHL dropped to 67.7 percent in 2003–2004 (from 81.3 percent in 1993–94) (Wertheim, 2004a).

The influx of international players into professional sport leagues is not the only indication that sport is increasingly becoming a global product. To further fuel international interest, the NBA is conducting basketball clinics in Africa, while MLB is holding season-openers in Japan and the NFL is taking regular season games across the Atlantic. Other indicators that point to this trend are the estimated 26.29 billion viewers (cumulative audience) that tuned in to one of the 376 channels in one of the 214 countries broadcasting the 2006 FIFA World Cup soccer matches, the record 205 countries participating in the Beijing 2008 Olympic Games, Nike's 3,000 retail stores in China, and IMG's 60-plus offices in 30 countries around the world. It is obvious that sport products and services are now being consumed by a greater number of nations than ever before. Welcome to the era of globalization in sport.

Globalization has been defined as "a phenomenon by which the experience of everyday life, as influenced by the diffusion of commodities and ideas, reflects a standardization of cultural expressions around the world. Propelled by the efficiency or appeal of wireless communications, electronic commerce, popular culture, and international travel, globalization has been seen as a trend toward homogeneity that will eventually make human experience everywhere essentially the same" ("Cultural globalization," 2008). The key concept is "the diffusion of commodities and ideas," which is illustrated by the sharing of information, products and services, labor, culture, and, of course, sport. In their book *Sport Business in the Global Marketplace*, Westerbeek and Smith (2003) identify seven driving forces of globalization: (1) economy, (2) technology, (3) social science, resources and natural environment, (4) demography, (5) governance, (6) conflict and war, and (7) religion and cultural identity. The authors point to the release of trade barriers and the increase of trade agreements between nations, the high-speed flow of information through new and improved communication vehicles (e.g., the Internet), and privatization as conditions that have facilitated the globalization of sport (Westerbeek & Smith, 2003).

Given these trends, it is imperative for sport managers to understand the *international environment* in which they operate. Sport professionals must be aware of the opportunities that are available on a global scale, as well as the challenges that arise from conducting business in this new, global market. For sport managers focused on selling their U.S.-based product globally, as well as those looking to capitalize on international imports, an understanding of the global sport industry is paramount.

The purpose of this chapter is to provide students preparing for a career in the sport industry insight into the global marketplace. The Olympic Games are considered to be the original international sport product and provide an excellent starting point for the examination of the international sport environment. Analysis of the Olympic Movement—more specifically, its member organizations and main revenue sources—will provide valuable insight into the international sport industry. We will also examine the impact of sport globalization in the U.S. and discuss the international expansion of the four major professional sport leagues: MLB, NBA, NFL, and NHL. The next section of this chapter addresses the European sport industry, particularly aspects of the football (soccer, for American readers) sector. The chapter concludes with a discussion of career opportunities for sport managers as well as skills necessary to become a successful international sport manager.

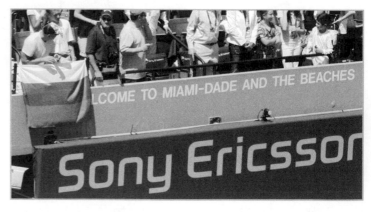

"SPORT IS PART OF EVERY MAN AND WOMAN'S HERITAGE AND ITS ABSENCE CAN NEVER BE COMPENSATED FOR."

—PIERRE DE COUBERTIN

So grab your passport (maybe your visa, too), dictionaries, and travel pack and get ready to embark on a tour of the global sport marketplace!

The Olympic Movement

Photo by Lucretious, courtesy of ©stock.xchng iv

There is little doubt that the modern *Olympic Games*, revived in 1896 by Pierre de Coubertin, represent one of the strongest examples of globalization in sport. Every four years the Games bring together a great number of nations to showcase a variety of athletic events and participants. Over the years, the world's most prestigious sporting event has grown to the point of incomparable international exposure, worldwide audience appeal, and multicultural activities that draw the attention of virtually every demographic. The *Olympic Movement* is a global phenomenon that transcends the boundaries of sport and culture and extends to education, politics, economy, and technology. This is clearly manifested through the IOC's global promotional campaigns: In 2004, the campaign "Celebrate Humanity" highlighted the Olympic values of hope, dreams and inspirations, friendship, and fair play, while in 2008 the IOC began campaigning with the message "The Best of Us" to promote excellence, friendship, and respect. The Olympic Movement includes the International Olympic Committee, National Olympic Committees, the Organizing Committees of the Olympic Games, International Federations, National Governing Bodies, and the athletes. These parties work closely to promote the fundamental principles of Olympism and to effectively operate business functions vital to the continuity of the Movement.

The *International Olympic Committee* (IOC) is "the supreme authority of the Olympic Movement" ("Mission," 2008). It is an international, non-governmental, nonprofit organization, and has its offices in Lausanne, Switzerland. The IOC's main responsibilities are to preserve and grow the Olympic Movement globally, to promote the use of sport as a vehicle of development, to select host cities for the Olympic Games, and to oversee the celebration of the Olympic Games every four year ("Mission," 2008). The IOC, which is governed by the *Olympic Charter*, exclusively owns the marketing rights to all Olympic properties, namely the Olympic symbol, flag, motto, emblem, anthem, flame, and torch. The IOC is represented in individual countries by *National Olympic Committees* (NOCs), which are responsible for promoting the Olympic Movement nationally, developing athletes, and sending delegations to the Games ("National Olympic Committees," 2008). Currently, there are 205 NOCs recognized by the IOC. The NOC for the U.S. is the *United States Olympic Committee* (USOC), located in Colorado Springs, Colorado. An *International Federations* (IF) is responsible for developing its sport(s) worldwide and for staging world championships. Some of the largest IFs include FIFA (football), FIBA (basketball), IAAF (athletics), and FIG (gymnastics). The IOC currently recognizes 35 IFs. On a national level, each sport is developed through respective *National Governing Bodies* (NGBs), such as USA Track and Field and USA Basketball.

The *Organizing Committee of the Olympic Games* (OCOG) is formed once a city is awarded the honor and responsibility of hosting the Olympic and Paralympic Games. The role of the OCOG is to handle all operational aspects of the Games and to ultimately put on the event. Some of the responsibilities of OCOGs include venue construction, accommodations, ticketing, national sponsorships, media authorizations, medical provisions, and security. Each OCOG is disbanded about two years following the completion of the Games.

In addition to the aforementioned organizations, the promotion of the Olympic ideals is supported by a number of *IOC commissions* (e.g., ethics, finance, juridical, marketing, medical, sport and environment, TV rights and new media, women and sport) and other organizations affiliated with the Olympic Movement, including the Court of Arbitration for Sport (CAS), the International Olympic Academy (AIO), the *International Paralympic Committee* (IPC), and the World Anti-Doping Agency (WADA) ("The Olympic Movement," 2008). Furthermore, recognizing the value of its marketing properties, the IOC has created the *IOC Television and Marketing Services SA* with the task of developing and executing marketing and branding strategies on behalf of the IOC ("IOC Television," 2008). This group operates out of two offices, one in Lausanne and the second in Atlanta, Georgia.

The most significant driving force for the financial stability of the Olympic Movement is the IOC *Olympic Marketing Programme*. From 2001 to 2004, the program exceeded US$4 billion in revenues. More than half of those moneys (53 percent or US$2.229 billion) came from broadcasting rights fees, 34 percent (or US$1.459 billion) from international and national sponsorship agreements, 11 percent (or US$441 million) from ticketing, and 2 percent (or US$86.5 million) from licensing and other revenues ("Revenue Sources," 2008). These significant resources support the entire family of the Olympic Movement as 92 percent of the revenues is distributed to the NOCs, IFs, and OCOGs and only 8 percent is used for the operation of the IOC ("Olympic Marketing Revenue Distribution," 2008).

As worldwide interest in the Olympic Games grows, so does the desire of multinational corporations and broadcasting agencies to share in the Olympic glory. The 2000 Olympic Games in Sydney were watched by more than 3.7 billion people from 220 countries, while that number increased to 3.9 billion viewers during the 2004 Athens Games. The Winter Olympic Games typically draw great audiences as well, evidenced by the 2.1 billion viewers from 160 countries who tuned in to watch the 2002 Salt Lake City Olympics ("Olympic Broadcasting History," 2008). Because of this increasing worldwide attention, the European Broadcasting Union (EBU) had to pay a total of US$ 837.4 million to obtain control over the IOC broadcast rights in Europe (excluding Italy) for the 2004 and 2008 Olympics ("Broadcast Rights," 2008). For the United States, NBC spent US$2.3 billion for the right to broadcast the 2004, 2006, and 2008 Olympic Games, and another US$2.001 billion for the 2010 and 2012 Games ("The Authoritative," 2003).

Olympic sponsorship agreements at the top level are handled through *The Olympic Partner (TOP) Programme*, which was created in 1985. (OCOGs also sell sponsorships, but at a lower level.) This TOP program, operated by the IOC, gives a handful of sponsors *exclusive* rights for four years to associate with the Summer and Winter Olympic Games and use all Olympic properties. Recognizing the tremendous effect that Olympic sponsorships can have on building a global brand, companies pay a lofty fee for the chance to be associated with the world's premiere sporting event. The total sponsorship revenue generated from the TOP partners has increased exponentially since the inception of the program: TOP I (1985–1988) delivered US$96 million, a mere fraction of TOP V's (2001–2004) US$663 million and the most recent TOP VI's (2005–2008) whopping US$866 million ("TOP Programme Evolution," 2008). Current TOP sponsors include Atos Origin, Coca-Cola, General Electric, Johnson & Johnson, Kodak, Lenovo, Manulife, McDonald's, Omega, Panasonic, Samsung, and VISA ("TOP Programme," 2008). As part of becoming Olympic sponsors, companies also invest heavily in leveraging this partnership. For example, VISA recently extended its global sponsorship agreement for four consecutive Olympic Games and has spent more than $100 million worldwide to support Olympic athletes.

The Olympic Games are idiosyncratic in that they are as much a global phenomenon with worldwide reach as they are a local project. This contradictory reality demands that the Organizing Committees involved in bidding or hosting the Olympic Games address strategic issues that extend to many sectors in the society, including politics, economy, technology, transportation, sporting infrastructure, communication and media, culture and national representation, tourism, and so on. Greece, a comparably small European country that hosted the 2004 Olympic Games, faced that challenge.

THE ATHENS 2004 OLYMPIC GAMES

For many cities and countries, worldwide exposure and financial gains are the two most important motivational factors for bidding to organize the Olympic Games. In Athens, the case was a bit different. The special attachment of Greece to the Olympic Movement—as it is the birthplace of the Games—remained the main driving force to "Welcome Home" the world. Many believed that the gigantic endeavor of hosting the Olympic Games seemed like perfect suicide for a small nation like Greece, at least in terms of finances and social policy. It was estimated that Greece spent approximately $4.238 billion from its public expenditure on the construction or upgrade of public transportation and medical facilities throughout the country. Furthermore, approximately $2.668 billion was additionally invested for the development of the required sports infrastructure (20 new and five upgraded sports venues) (Manou, 2003).

As the opening ceremony lavishly introduced the new Olympic venues and athletes to the world, and with the hopes that the most expensive and sophisticated security systems in the world would adequately protect the world's largest athletic celebration, Athens was there, proudly fulfilling its obligation toward the Olympic Movement and its own history. The world's best athletes competed in authentic settings (e.g., the original marathon course for the marathon race, ancient Olympia for the shot put event, and a route through the historical sites of Athens for cycling) and the winners were crowned with olive wreaths. What remains to be seen is how the rich history of Greece and the intangible assets of the 2004 Olympic Games will affect the future of the Olympic Movement.

CHALLENGES IN THE OLYMPIC MOVEMENT

The Olympic Movement faces numerous challenges, not the least of which is doping control issues and over-commercialization. *Drug testing* at the Olympic Games has become a sophisticated and quite successful process, especially since the establishment of the World Anti-Doping Agency (WADA). However, there will always be incidents of cheating that go undetected. The scandal that followed the 2007 revelation that track and field superstar and Olympian Marion Jones had used steroids in preparation for her participation in the 2000 Olympics is just one example of the challenges facing the International Olympic Committee and International Federations as they attempt to ensure "clean" and fair competitions. The IOC, in cooperation with its member nations, should maintain upgraded techniques and technologies, rigorous control, and strict measures in order to protect the integrity and spirit of the Games. The second issue, *over-commercialization*, is potentially as harmful for the IOC. Marketing studies have repeatedly documented the positive outcomes that multinational brands receive by associating with the Olympic ideals, but scarcely acknowledge the backlash that could result for the Olympic Movement. The Organizing Committee of the Athens Games claimed that they dealt with this challenge by notably confining the number of national sponsors affiliated with the Games to 36 (from 100 sponsors in the 2000 Olympics) and by taking out some of the needless show. A lot remains to be done, however, to balance sponsors' commercial interests with the Olympic image.

Another major issue that awaits future Organizing Committees of the Olympic Games is *gigantism*. The Olympic Games have progressively expanded through the years. The large number of participants (athletes, delegation members, media, and visitors) and the number of competitions creates immense pressure for host cities, especially in the areas of security and infrastructure. Furthermore, environmental concerns stemming from the magnitude of the event and the number of people involved cannot be ignored. The IOC might have to impose new regulations in order to address this issue and secure manageable competitions. As Viviane Reding, a member of the European Commission responsible for Education and Culture, stated, the challenge lies in organizing "less high-flown games, smaller games closer to their Olympic roots" ("Europa," 2004).

With the occasion of the 2008 Beijing Olympic Games, debate and controversy surfaced from allegations of the host country's *human rights violations* (in Tibet, in particular) and censorship, as well as their questionable ties with and actions (or *in*-actions) concerning the African nation of Sudan. Images of protests and violent incidents during the Olympic Torch Relay, as well as threats from several world leaders about boycotting the Games' opening ceremony became prevalent in international news circuits. The responsibility of the IOC to raise awareness about social, political, and environmental issues facing the world and the ability of the Olympic Games to become a platform for discussion and change is certainly an interesting topic of debate.

Although the Olympic Movement has not yet fulfilled one of its most historical aims, to end war, it has experienced dramatic growth and attracted huge economic and political support from the private and public sector. Safeguarding its future and further development might not be as easy as it has been in the past.

International Expansion of U.S. Sport

As the U.S. sport industry continues to mature, professional sport leagues are investigating growth possibilities through expansion into foreign markets and the development of new fans. International markets have become the source of not only talent, but also substantial revenue for the leagues through the signing of broadcasting deals, the sale of licensed merchandise, and the acquisition of foreign-based sponsors.

The recent technological and communication advances allow U.S.-based sport organizations to reach new consumers almost anywhere in the world. Even though their choices for global expansion might vary, one thing is constant: U.S. professional leagues consider international expansion the cornerstone for their future growth. Evidence to that is the creation of league International Divisions and the establishment of international offices to handle their business outside the borders.

The following sections provide some specific examples of initiatives that each of the four major leagues (MLB, NBA, NFL, and NHL) has taken to expand their reach in other countries. Sport management students interested in pursuing a career in the international sport setting must realize that U.S. leagues' efforts worldwide provide avenues for employment, as the leagues depend on qualified professionals with an understanding of the sport industry as well as the global market to design global strategies and successfully execute international programs.

MAJOR LEAGUE BASEBALL (MLB)

For baseball fans in the United States and in many countries around the world, October means one thing: the World Series. But are these games between the two best teams in Major League Baseball a true *World* Series? After all, the competition involves teams from North America only. Nevertheless, the games could be considered a *World* Series if one takes into account the number of international players on MLB team rosters. At the start of the 2007 season, 246 of the 849 MLB players, or about 29 percent, were born outside the United States, while 46.2 percent of minor league players also came from places other than the 50 states ("National Pastime," 2007). Another indication that North American baseball is becoming a global product is the widespread interest in and delivery of the game. In 2007 MLB games were broadcast in 229 countries and territories in 13 different languages, with the league's latest push involving China ("MLB International," 2007).

Major League Baseball has had an international presence for at least a century, mainly with exhibition games and tours, as well as spring training, preseason, and regular season games held outside the U.S. The league has held games in Japan, Mexico, Puerto Rico, even Cuba, while in March of 2008 the Dodgers and Padres played the league's first ever exhibition games in China ("MLB China Series"). Furthermore, an off-season All-Star Tour has visited Japan since 1986 (Graczyk, 2003), and with baseball stars such as Hideki Matsui, Ichiro Suzuki, and Hideo Nomo pursuing their baseball careers in the U.S. the popularity of MLB in Japan has increased immensely. The Red Sox and Athletics opened their 2008 season in Tokyo.

MLB established Major League Baseball International (MLBI) in 1989 and operates offices in Beijing, London, New York, Sydney, and Tokyo—a clear investment in growing the game of baseball and MLB's business globally. In addition to performances, the league sponsors grassroots, development, and promotional programs all around the world. Examples include the *Envoy Program*, which, since 1991, has sent baseball coaches to non-traditional baseball countries around the globe in order to teach the game to native players, coaches, and umpires; the *Elite Camps* (1999); and the *Baseball Festival* (1995), which tours the world and promotes the game of baseball in a fun atmosphere ("Development Initiatives," 2008).

Scheduling conflicts and differences in drug-testing policies are two of the main reasons MLB players have been kept from competing in the Olympic Games. However, the benefits of an international competition were not lost by baseball officials. In 2004, Bud Selig, the Commissioner of MLB, announced plans for a *Baseball World Cup Tournament*, a tournament that would be sanctioned by the International Baseball Federation and created jointly by baseball leagues and players' associations around the globe. The first *World Baseball Classic* (WBC) came to life in March of 2006 and included 16 teams: Australia, Canada, China, Chinese Taipei, Cuba, the Dominican Republic, Italy, Japan, Korea, Mexico, the Netherlands, Panama, Puerto Rico, South Africa, USA, and Venezuela. Games were hosted in seven different venues in Japan, Puerto Rico and the U.S. and delivered an impressive 737,112 sold tickets (Bloom, 2008a). At the end of the competition, Japan defeated Cuba 10-6 to become baseball's first true *world* champion. Plans are already underway for the second World Baseball Classic to be held in March 2009. In addition to the original three countries, games will be played in Toronto, Canada and Mexico City, Mexico.

The success of the inaugural tournament in terms of fan attendance and TV ratings serves as evidence that bringing high-caliber players from all over the world together in one global competition is an attractive property—and a significant tool for the worldwide expansion of the sport of baseball. As Commissioner Selig noted, "The 2009 World Baseball Classic will further demonstrate the remarkable global growth of our game" (Bloom, 2008b).

NATIONAL BASKETBALL ASSOCIATION (NBA)

Basketball is an Olympic sport that is played worldwide in structured leagues and prestigious tournaments (e.g., Euroleague Basketball). In the 1992 Summer Olympic Games held in Barcelona, Spain, millions of basketball fans around the world were mesmerized by the stars of the first ever "Dream Team." Seen by many as a landmark in the league's international expansion, the participation of professional players in the Olympics provided the NBA with a vehicle to showcase to the world the talent available in the basketball Mecca. Some things have changed since then. Sub-par performances and game results have "embarrassed" NBA superstars and have showcased the strength of other countries in the sport. However, one thing has remained constant: the NBA's focus on developing and exploiting new markets and its unparalleled strength in creating new, loyal fans. Currently the league operates over 10 international NBA offices worldwide (controlled by the International Division of the league) that handle local television and sponsorship deals and promote the NBA brand in the respective markets.

The NBA—the envy, according to some, of other U.S. leagues in terms of its success in international efforts—has been able to generate global interest by using exhibition and preseason games, regular season games, and grassroots programs to promote its brand. Since 1988 the league has held numerous exhibition, preseason and/or regular season games in Europe, the Middle East, Latin America, and Asia. In 2006 the NBA launched its *NBA Europe Live Tour*, with four teams holding training camps abroad and competing against each other and against European basketball clubs in multiple European cities and countries ("History of Games," 2008). The NBA is taking full advantage of the fact that the last few years its team rosters have boasted some 70 to 80 international players, including many superstars, who are seen as heroes in their native countries and whose careers in the U.S. are followed closely by their countrymen. Conveniently, the selection of teams and locations of the league's international competitions reflect an effort to match the international players on the teams' rosters with their native countries, bringing Tony Parker (San Antonio Spurs) back to Paris, Pau Gasol (while a player of the Memphis Grizzlies) back to Barcelona, and Yao Ming (Houston Rockets) back to Shanghai.

Basketball tournaments and clinics are another effective tool used by the league to develop fans around the globe. According to information provided on the global section of the league's website, during the 2007 off-season period the NBA ran an impressive 262 events in 162 cities on five continents involving over 200 of its current and retired players and coaches ("NBA to Host," 2007). Those initiatives included interactive fan events (e.g., NBA *Jam Van* in China), camps and clinics (e.g., NBA *Development Camp* in Korea), exhibition games (e.g., NBA *China Games*), tournaments (e.g., NBA *3-on-3* in Canada), and community outreach programs (*Basketball Without Borders* in Brazil).

So, where does the NBA stand today? Is the league's investment in global initiatives providing a return? The answer is *yes*. There are many indications that the league's international efforts are returning a profit: NBA games and shows are televised in 215 countries and territories around the globe in 41 languages, adding a notable portion to the league's broadcasting revenues ("NBA to Host," 2007). More than half of the visitors on the NBA's website (which is available in many different languages besides English) live outside the U.S. (Sandomir, 2007). And a significant percentage of the league's merchandise sales come from overseas. In fact, at the end of 2006 it was reported that the NBA's international business, which contributed 10 percent to the league's bottom-line, was the fastest growing operation of the league ("NBA to Open," 2006).

One market that is rapidly developing for the NBA is China. In June of 2002, audiences witnessed what may be considered by many the one most important development for the further global expansion of the NBA: the first-ever selection of an international player, Yao Ming of China, as the No.1 draft pick of the NBA. Yao's move to the United States and the Houston Rockets created a chain of positive outcomes both for his franchise and the league as a whole, including a lucrative naming rights deal for the Rockets' Toyota Center, thousands of Chinese Rockets' fans, and more national and regional television deals in the country that holds 1.3 billion of the world's population. It was reported that in April of 2007 2.8 million visitors to NBA.com came from China (Hefflinger, 2007). In an effort to strengthen its merchandise sales in the region, the NBA signed a 5-year deal with Reebok, making the manufacturer the exclusive league licensee in China (Lombardo, 2003b). Also, in 2006 the league opened its first international store in Beijing ("NBA to Open," 2006). China is opening up to the world, and there is no question that the NBA has front row seats. Having NBA stars on the USA team roster as it won the 2008 Olympic gold medal in men's basketball, and WNBA stars on the women's gold medal winning team further entrenched the league in all of Asia.

Many are looking to see what the NBA will do next. There has been an ongoing discussion regarding expansion of the NBA to countries outside North America by placing an NBA team or an NBA division in Europe. However, the league has refrained from acting on these discussions. The lack of adequate facility infrastructure in Europe, other financial considerations, and increased security concerns following the incidents of 9/11 have the league reviewing the feasibility of international expansion at this time (Lombardo, 2003a). Additionally, established European leagues and franchises could pose a significant challenge should the NBA decide to introduce a European division. Although an international division might not be in the league's near-future, be on the lookout for NBA teams holding more regular season games abroad, an NBA All-Star team touring overseas, and more NBA stores and restaurants opening up in European and Asian cities.

NATIONAL FOOTBALL LEAGUE (NFL)

Images of tailgating, Thanksgiving Day games, and Super Bowl Sunday are enough to get any American sports fan excited. However, these words have limited meaning outside U.S. borders. Being a specifically American sport—and not an Olympic sport, for that matter—with more than 95 percent of its players born in the

U.S. (Wertheim, 2004a), the NFL is presented with a greater challenge when considering international expansion. Any effort to become popular in other countries would have to include the education of audiences first.

Nevertheless, that has not stopped the league from spreading the word about the sport that captivates an entire nation from August to January every year. The NFL has held preseason, exhibition games in a number of countries (Canada, England, Germany, Japan, and Mexico, among others) since 1986, when the first *American Bowl* was played in London, England ("History," 2008). In 2005 the Arizona Cardinals met the San Francisco 49ers in Mexico City for what was the first-ever, regular season game to be played outside of the U.S. The 2007 season marked the first time that a regular season NFL game was played outside of North America, with the Miami Dolphins meeting the New York Giants in London's Wembley Stadium in front of a sellout crowd of 81,176. The next game to be played in London has already been scheduled for October 26, 2008, and will feature the San Diego Chargers and New Orleans Saints. In fact, the interest in that game has been so great that the first 40,000 tickets that became available sold in 90 minutes and the 15,000 tickets released subsequently sold in 30 minutes ("15,000 London," 2008).

For the 2005 season, NFL programming was received in 234 countries and territories worldwide in 31 languages ("International Programming," 2008), while Super Bowl XLI was seen by audiences in 232 countries and territories and covered in 33 different languages ("Super Bowl XLI," 2007). And even though the NFL has yet to stumble across the football equivalent of Yao Ming, the league is looking to develop fans in the world's most populated country not only through their broadcasting agreements, but also with community programs such as the *NFL Flag Football Clinics*, a newly developed NFL China website, and plans for a preseason NFL game ("China Bowl") in 2009.

However, the most aggressive international move to date made by the NFL came in 1991 when the league launched the *World League of American Football* (WLAF) —which marked the first time a U.S.-based professional sport league expanded to Europe. According to former NFL Commissioner Paul Tagliabue, that extension league provided a platform for the NFL to showcase the game of American Football to those outside the U.S. (Madkour & Kaplan, 2003). In addition, the international league was seen as grounds to develop talent among players, officials, and management. In its original structure, the WLAF consisted of 10 teams from North America and Europe and involved weekly intercontinental play from March through May. The extension league ceased operations after two seasons and was reintroduced in 1995 in European cities only. In 1998 the league changed its name to *NFL Europe* and in 2006 the league's name was modified to *NFL Europa*. In its latest form NFL Europa consisted of six teams, five in Germany and one in the Netherlands. However, in June 2007, under the leadership of new Commissioner Roger Goodell, the NFL decided to disband its European league that was reportedly losing $30 million per year in favor of a different international strategy, one focused on playing regular season games abroad (potentially adding a 17th game to the regular season NFL schedule) and utilizing new technology to develop and reach fans worldwide ("NFL Folds," 2007).

NATIONAL HOCKEY LEAGUE (NHL)

Ice hockey is played all over the world, with established and internationally recognized championships held in the Czech Republic, Finland, Russia, and Sweden, among other countries. Although it has been an Olympic sport since 1924, it wasn't until the mid-1990s that the NHL and the International Ice Hockey Federation (IIHF) agreed to allow NHL players to participate in the 1998 Nagano Winter Olympic Games in hope of increasing the sport's profile and worldwide interest (Lapointe, 1997). Hockey fans around the world will tune in again for the upcoming 2010 Vancouver Winter Olympic Games to enjoy performances by NHL stars—amidst discussions, however, that it might be the last time something like this occurs.

Of the four U.S. major professional sport leagues, the NHL has the highest percentage of players born outside North America, with about 30 percent of its players originating from countries other than the U.S. (Burnside, 2007). To reflect the increasing number of foreign-born players on team rosters, in 1998 the NHL changed its traditional All-Star Game format and introduced a North America *vs.* The World All-Stars competition—until 2003, that is, when the league went back to its classic East *vs.* West format. The international flavor of its rosters has also provided a unique opportunity for the NHL to promote its product in the native countries of its stars. In 2003, NHL programming was distributed to 217 countries, while the league's revenue from international television deals has reportedly tripled since 1998 (Wertheim, 2004a; Wertheim, 2004b).

As early as 1938, NHL teams played exhibition games in Europe. Building on ice hockey's global appeal, in 1989 the Calgary Flames and Washington Capitals held part of their training camps in (then) Czechoslovakia and Sweden, followed by preseason games in the (former) Soviet Union, while the league has also held exhibition and preseason games in Austria, England, Finland, and Germany, and a number of other European destinations ("NHL Overseas History," 2007). In 1997 the NHL opened its regular season in Tokyo, Japan ("NHL Overseas History," 2007). It was London's turn in 2007 to host the Los Angeles Kings and Anaheim Ducks as they competed in the first NHL regular season game to be held in Europe (Burnside, 2007).

In 2004, four European cities and three North American cities held the *World Cup of Hockey*, an international tournament including eight of the world's ice hockey powerhouses. This tournament, which is a joint effort of the NHL and NHLPA, is only the second of its kind (the first World Cup of Hockey was held in 1996) (Bernstein, 2004). Besides the Olympics and IIHF-sanctioned world championships, other international ice hockey competitions over the years have included the Summit Series (1972), the Challenge Cup (1979), Rendez-Vous (1987), and Canada Cup (1976, 1981, 1984, 1987, and 1991) ("World Cup," 2004).

The examples described in this section indicate that the potential for growth in foreign markets is immense. However, this growth does not come without risks. In his overview of the global sport industry, Schaaf (2004) pointed to five considerations that sport organizations need to keep in mind when looking to become global brands: (1) geography; (2) competition from existing events; (3) perception; (4) patience; and (5) talent. Schaaf suggested that international expansion could be hindered by geographical and time constraints, as well as the challenge of creating meaningful competitions for fans that are already loyal to existing events. He also stressed the importance of having business relationships that will give the perception of legitimacy to a new international initiative, patience from owners and/or other investors, and, finally, the cooperation from the actual players in securing a successful venture.

Challenges in the International Expansion of U.S. Sport

Even though international expansion is a promising avenue for future growth, there are some inherent challenges for U.S. sport organizations to consider when planning their international initiatives, not the smallest of which is *competition* from existing leagues and events in the markets where they are expanding. This becomes especially relevant when the leagues are considering the creation of international divisions. Along with this come *financial considerations*. Given its financial losses, it is questionable whether the WLAF/NFL Europe/NFL Europa would have been in business for as long as it was without the backing of the National Football League. The challenge lies in balancing the need for growth with the financial stability of the leagues' operations. Finally, another major concern for the global expansion of U.S. sport that should not be overlooked is the possible *resistance* from foreign nations. The tragedy of September 11, 2001 and the events that followed were a clear indication that sentiments about the "American way" can vary greatly throughout the world. As LaFeber (1999) pointed out, U.S.-driven efforts for global expansion might be viewed not as a form of globalization but rather as Americanization. Being sensitive to local cultures and taking into account national idiosyncrasies could make for a more successful international expansion.

The European Sport Industry

The turn of the century has brought a number of major sporting events to Europe, the most notable of those being the 2004 Summer Olympic Games in Athens, Greece; the 2006 Winter Olympic Games in Turin, Italy; the 2006 FIFA World Cup in Germany; and the 2008 UEFA European Football Championship in Austria and Switzerland. The Olympic Games are scheduled to return to the continent (London, England) in 2012. A recently published report by the *European Commission* (the *European Union*'s executive arm) attributed 3.7 percent of European Union GDP ($638.8 billion) for the year 2004 to sport ("White Paper," 2007). The same report noted that 15 million people were employed in sport-related positions.

The rapid growth evident throughout the continent has given the European sport industry a distinctive position within the international sport industry. It has also encouraged the European Union (EU) to include sport as a key element in its newly formulated Constitution discussed during 2004. Following a European year dedicated to the concept of "Education through Sport," the EU recognized the need to take an active role in European sport policy and related sporting issues. This role, yet ambiguous, concerns "promoting fairness and openness in sporting competitions and cooperation between bodies responsible for sports, and by protecting the physical and moral integrity of sportsmen and sportswomen, especially young sportsmen and sportswomen" ("European Union Recognises," 2004).

The organization of sport in Europe is based on a broad network of European sport governing bodies (e.g., UEFA, FIBA Europe) and umbrella sport organizations (e.g., European Olympic Committees [EOC], European University Sports Association [EUSA]) that aim to promote sports across the continent. These organizations are right holders of a huge number of major sporting events held regularly in European countries, including European championships in all recognized sports and various categories (e.g., Euroleague Basketball). In addition, National Governing Bodies of the various sports (e.g., Hellenic Basketball Federation) operate in each country and, along with the National Olympic Committees and state or non-governmental umbrella organizations, make up the sporting structure at a state level. Historically, however, it has been the sport clubs (e.g., Manchester United, Real Madrid) that have formed the backbone of the European sport system. Most often, these are voluntary associations, trying to satisfy the needs and interests of their members (Rubingh & Broeke, 1998).

The continuously expanding European Union (currently consisting of 27 member-countries) has provided a platform for the exchange of goods, players, and capital in relation to sport. For example, the 1995 *Bosman ruling* by the European Court of Justice, which established free agency for out-of-contract players, has been considered a landmark decision with significant impact on the structure, development, and economics of professional football (soccer) clubs throughout Europe (Dobson & Gerrard, 1999). The freedom of contract significantly enhanced the transfer opportunities of professional football players in Europe and created millionaires who have more control than ever over their sporting career (Szymanski & Kuypers, 1999).

As the European Union expands, issues of cultural integration and state equality are becoming more prevalent. Sport can serve as a stabilizer in this process. It can be used as the platform to pursue social objectives by encouraging European cultures to come close to each other in this joint European effort. This opportunity has not been lost by the European Commission, as will be discussed further below in this section.

FOOTBALL IN EUROPE

Over the last fifteen years there have been dramatic developments in the European football (soccer) industry. The 2003 Deloitte and Touche annual review estimated the total European football market to be around approximately $15.7 billion for 2001–2002, with *English Premiership* (the Division I Football League in England) accounting for 25 percent of this market. Furthermore, data indicate that gate attendance revenues have gone up, television revenues have increased significantly, and huge investments have been made in football's infrastructure over the last ten years (Deloitte & Touche, 2003; Dobson & Gerrard, 1999). This provides strong evidence that European football is growing in commercial terms and, consistent with the U.S. model, clubs are becoming profit-maximizing corporations (Drewes, 2003).

Professional football clubs in Europe vary significantly in terms of their legal structure and ownership. For example, the typical German club is a nonprofit entity with a large number of supporters sharing part of its ownership; whereas a few Italian clubs are often controlled by major companies (e.g., Juventus, AC Milan) (Hoehn & Szymanski, 1999). In Spain, the professional clubs are private companies, often with a single owner who works together with local and regional authorities to overcome financial problems. This is because most clubs, like Barcelona and Real Madrid, are associations with political power resulting from the large number of their members who are also fans (Garcia & Rodriguez, 2003). In France, clubs can vary from associations to corporations, while in Greece clubs are treated as commercial corporations.

In spite of the complexity in the legal structure of European football, many clubs have increasingly looked to the financial markets to supply investment capital. For example, Manchester United, a club that stands as a striking case of a business-like operation, represents one of the most attractive stock market investments, generating significant profits. Another good example of a club with global appeal is Real Madrid. By acquiring some of the world's greatest players (Beckham, Zidane, Raul, Figo, and Ronaldo) over the years, Real Madrid has achieved vast international exposure and created new fans around the globe, making former team president Florentino Perez proclaim that expected revenues from marketing alone in 2004 could reach approximately $217 million, which would be equal to the total team income from 2000.

Moreover, the UEFA European Football Championship, most commonly referred to as *Euro*, is another clear indicator of the growth of European football. This tournament is considered the third-largest sporting event in the world based on viewership, following FIFA's World Cup and the Summer Olympic Games ("A Whole New," 2008). The *Euro 2004* tournament, held in Portugal, scored record television audiences. It was estimated that 2.5 billion individuals, or about 80 million per match, watched the quadrennial soccer tournament, even though perennial favorites England, France, Germany, and Italy were knocked out before the semifinal round and Greece was crowned champion after defeating host Portugal. Furthermore, the event was also considered a unique opportunity to communicate with tens of millions of viewers, as eight main sponsors, including fast-food chain McDonald's and soft drink seller Coca-Cola, paid more than $15 million each to be associated with the Euro 2004 tournament. For Euro 2008, which was co-hosted by Austria and Switzerland, organizer UEFA opted to sell television rights on a market-to-market basis instead of working with the European Broadcasting Union. This approach brought an impressive increase of 32 percent in the television rights fees received by UEFA compared to those of the 2004 tournament ("A Whole New," 2008).

The European football model differs significantly from the American model in that it is based on a league hierarchy and the relegation rule, which allows changes in the clubs that are eligible to compete at various levels (Drewes, 2003). The right to play in the *UEFA Champions League* and the *UEFA Cup* is linked to the clubs' sporting performance in their national competitions, which again involve a relegation system. However, the most contemporary challenge for the European football industry is to come closer to the American model of professional leagues. In one such effort, 14 power football clubs from seven European countries (e.g., Ajax,

Manchester United, Milan, Real Madrid) came together in 2000 to form the *G-14*, an organization of clubs that served as a negotiating partner with FIFA and UEFA on behalf of the clubs and their players, and which also explored plans for the creation of a closed Super League. Although the G-14 was disbanded in 2008, it was replaced by the *European Club Association* (ECA), an organization representing the interests of over 100 European football clubs.

Challenges in the European Sport Industry

As the European Union expands in geographical and political terms, so do the challenges related to the continent's sport industry. As described earlier, the European sport industry has special characteristics in terms of how sport is structured, developed, and governed in different countries. This raises major concerns over *the role of the European Union*, and its ability to intervene and promote pan-European rules and regulations in issues such as club licensing, broadcasting rights, professional players' transfer and salaries, anti-doping, youth sportsmanship, and others.

In November of 2007 the Commission of European Communities published a "White Paper on Sport" that explored the social, economic, and organizational dimensions of sport and offered suggestions on how sport can be used to address challenges that are present in European society. According to the document, "The Commission acknowledges the essential role of sport in European society, in particular when it needs to bring itself closer to citizens and to tackle issues that matter directly to them" ("White Paper," 2007, p. 2). Some of the issues discussed in this white paper include public health, doping, integration, racism, violence, movement of players, protection of young athletes from exploitation, and corruption. The Commission has also highlighted the need for sport organizations "to maintain and develop a sustainable financing model" that will ensure their long-term support ("White Paper," 2007, p. 12).

Other challenges involving especially the most powerful professional football clubs in Europe include the *leadership* and *management* of these organizations, as well as their global growth. With the Middle East (Qatar, United Arab Emirates, Saudi Arabia, Bahrain) and Asia (e.g., China) entering the global sport industry through big investments in infrastructure and bids for major sporting events (e.g., Formula One Grand Prix in the Bahrain International Circuit, Olympic Games in Beijing, etc.), the *competition* becomes tighter for everybody (including the U.S.). The primary aim of the expansion plan of any professional club is to build not only a global but also a profitable brand. This creates additional challenges in terms of the management of European clubs, which need to develop their marketing operations even further in order to be competitive and take advantage of growth opportunities.

Career Opportunities in International Sport

The globalization trends evident in today's sport world—including the increasing expansion of U.S. sport organizations internationally—provide numerous career opportunities for sport management professionals. Job titles such as Director of International Sports Marketing, VP of Global Sponsorships, Senior VP of International Division, VP of International Television and Media, and Director of Global Market Development are common among those involved in international sport.

However, some of these career lines might not be obvious choices. This section outlines some areas that students interested in a career in international sport should examine.

1. **The Olympic Movement.** Many opportunities for a career in the international sport setting are related to the Olympic Movement and its organizations. In the U.S., this means becoming involved with the National Olympic Committee, the USOC, or any one of the national governing bodies (e.g., USA Basketball, USA Gymnastics, USA Track & Field, etc.). Another avenue is to pursue an internship or job with the International Olympic Committee (IOC) or the International Paralympic Committee (IPC), the International Federations (e.g., FIFA), or even any of the Olympic Games Organizing Committees nationally or internationally (e.g., ATHOC, BOGOC). A majority of NGBs place their job announcements on www.teamworkonline.com.

2. **U.S. Professional Leagues.** Each of the four major professional sport leagues is very active in global initiatives and even has international divisions to handle that part of its business. Whether it is in licensing, television, the Internet, events, or any one of their international offices, there are a number of opportunities through the leagues for someone interested in a career in international sport.

3. **U.S. Professional Teams.** With the increasing number of international players on the rosters of U.S. professional teams, franchises require people who can assist those international players (e.g., interpreters), or can help the organization capitalize on the opportunities that are presented. For example, the signing of Yao Ming in Houston has created a unique opportunity to reach out to the Asian population in the area and also to deal with Chinese organizations (e.g., sponsors, television stations) interested in forming business relationships with the franchise.

4. **Sport Management Agencies.** U.S.-based sport marketing and management agencies have long conducted business on a global scale. Companies such as IMG and Octagon each have international divisions as well as more than 50 offices worldwide. Becoming involved in one of those offices could be the avenue to an international career in sport.

5. **Athletic Apparel and Footwear Companies.** For those interested in entering the apparel and footwear side of the industry, there are opportunities for an international career. U.S.-based companies Nike and Reebok do business worldwide, from production and distribution to product promotion and sponsoring of international events. Furthermore, foreign-based companies like adidas and Puma have offices in the U.S and actively promote their products in North America. Working for one of those companies can provide the opportunity to be stationed overseas and pursue a career internationally. Take, for example, Puma. On its website (http://www.puma.com), the company advertises positions available not only in the United States but also in Belgium, Canada, France, Germany, Hong Kong, Mexico, the Netherlands, Russia, South Korea, and Switzerland.

6. **U.S. Companies with International Sponsorships.** In 2002, *Sports Business Journal* published a special report on international sport. In that issue, it was

reported that at the time there were 30 U.S. companies with overseas sports sponsorships and 65 overseas companies with U.S. sports sponsorships ("Overseas Companies," 2002; "U.S. Companies," 2002). Companies such as Coca-Cola, MasterCard, and Xerox have for years sponsored international sport organizations and events (e.g., Olympic Games). Consequently, they require personnel to handle those relationships. Although not always an obvious choice, this could be a great way to become involved in international aspects of the sport industry.

So, how does one prepare for such a career? What are those skills that will make you an attractive candidate for such a position? Here are some of the qualifications that employers will be looking for when hiring for a position in the international sector of the sport marketplace:

- **Educational background in international sport management.** Even if the program in which the student is enrolled does not offer an international sport management–type course, the student could take general business or international studies courses covering international business affairs.

- **Practical experience in international sport.** Especially if one is in the beginning of his or her career, the most appropriate way to obtain some experience in international sport might be through internships with an international sport organization or a U.S. organization doing business in other countries (Masteralexis & McDonald, 1997).

- **Foreign language skills.** The knowledge of a second (and even third) language enhances the appeal of a candidate when being considered for a position that involves dealing with people who speak another language. Although individuals would be advised to avoid doing business in a foreign language unless they were fluent, a basic knowledge of a foreign language could help form a warm relationship with international business partners (Gillentine, Goldfine, & Orejan, 2004; Gillentine & Orejan, 2003; Masteralexis & McDonald, 1997).

- **Knowledge and proficiency in new media.** As sport becomes more global, advances in technology, such as the Internet, web TV, and international cell phones, become more commonplace. Students preparing for careers in international sport should be knowledgeable about such devices and able to incorporate them into their business operations.

- **Cultural sensitivity and the ability to adapt to other cultures.** An international sport manager should be able to effectively communicate and work with partners from different parts of the world and also adapt to various working environments. Openness and sensitivity to other cultures are essential skills. The best way to obtain those skills, of course, would be to live in another country. But since that is not always possible, participating in a study abroad or exchange program could provide one with an understanding of cultural nuances and with a tolerance for differences in cultures. Other ways to obtain cultural training would be through university courses (e.g., history, geography, world politics) or through interaction with people from other cultures.

- **Willingness to travel and/or relocate to another country.** Flexibility is important when working in the sport industry. It becomes even more important when one is involved in the international sector, since spending a great deal of time overseas might be a large component of one's job description.

Summary

- Over the past decade we have witnessed significant movement and expansion in our industry; sport is becoming a more global business. This globalization is facilitated by technological advances (e.g., the Internet) as well as administrative, political, and social developments across the globe.

- The Olympic Movement—which consists of the International Olympic Committee (IOC), National Olympic Committees (NOCs), Organizing Committees of the Olympic Games (OCOGs), International Federations (IFs), and National Governing Bodies (NGBs) and is responsible for organizing the Summer and Winter Olympic Games—has experienced tremendous growth not only in participation and attendance figures, but also in broadcasting and sponsorship revenue.

- U.S. professional leagues (MLB, NBA, NFL, and NHL) are reaching consumers in new markets by holding games, tours, and clinics internationally. In addition, the increasing number of foreign players participating in U.S.-based leagues has created inroads for expansion in those players' native countries through lucrative broadcasting, sponsorship, and licensing agreements.

- The structure of European sport is based on European sport-governing bodies (e.g., UEFA) and umbrella organizations (e.g., EOC) that promote the growth of sport throughout the continent. European sport differs from the league-based organization of U.S. sport; sport clubs (e.g., Manchester United) operate within a league hierarchy and relegation rules.

- Opportunities for a career in international sport exist with the Olympic Movement associations (e.g., IOC, USOC), with U.S. professional leagues and teams, sport management agencies (e.g., IMG), athletic apparel and footwear companies, and with corporations involved in international sponsorships.

- For those considering a career in the global sport industry, an educational background in international business, practical experience internationally, foreign language skills, proficiency in new media, cultural sensitivity, an ability to adapt to other cultures, and a willingness to travel or relocate to another country are some of the skills needed to be successful.

DISCUSSION ACTIVITIES

1. Have you had any indications in your everyday involvement in sport and study of sport management of the globalization process occurring in the sport industry? If so, please identify five specific examples of this process.

2. Identify two national governing bodies (NGBs) that operate in the United States. What are the functions of those organizations? What is their relationship with their respective international federations and with the Olympic Movement?

3. This chapter provided examples of the international expansion of U.S. sport (particularly the four major leagues). What do you think are the positive consequences of their global expansion? What, if any, are the negative consequences?

4. What are the major differences between the structure of the U.S. and European professional leagues? Based on your understanding of the European sport industry, would an expansion U.S. league be successful in Europe? Please provide justification for your response.

5. What do you think is the best way for one to develop the suggested skills necessary for a career in the international sport industry? In addition to those characteristics discussed in this chapter, are there any other skills that could also be useful?

SUGGESTED READINGS

Fay, T. G. (2003). International sport. In J. B. Parks & J. Quarterman (Eds.), *Contemporary sport management*. Champaign, IL: Human Kinetics.

Gladden, J. M., & Lizandra, M. (1998). International sport. In L. P. Masteralexis, C. A. Barr, & M. A. Hums (Eds.), *Principles and practices of sport management*. Gaithersburg, MD: Aspen Publishers, Inc.

Hums, M. A., & MacLean, J. C. (2004). *Governance and policy in sport organizations*. Scottsdale, AZ: Holcomb Hathaway, Publishers, Inc.

LaFeber, W. (1999). *Michael Jordan and the new global capitalism*. New York: W. W. Norton & Company, Inc.

Maguire, J. (1999). *Global sport: Identities, societies, civilizations*. Cambridge, UK: Polity Press.

Riordan, J., & Krüger, A. (1999). *The international politics of sport in the 20th century*. New York: Routledge.

Rubingh, B., & Broeke, A. (1998). The European sports club system. In L. P. Masteralexis, C. A. Barr, & M. A. Hums (Eds.), *Principles and practices of sport management*. Gaithersburg, MD: Aspen Publishers, Inc.

Schaaf, P. (2004). *Sports, Inc.: 100 years of sports business*. Amherst, NY: Prometheus Books.

Senn, A. E. (1999). *Power, politics, and the Olympic Games*. Champaign, IL: Human Kinetics.

Thoma, J. E., & Chalip, L. (1996). *Sport governance in the global community*. Morgantown, WV: Fitness Information Technology.

Westerbeek, H., & Smith, A. (2003). *Sport business in the global marketplace*. New York, NY: Palgrave Macmillan.

References

15,000 London game tickets sell quickly. (2008, June 27). *15,000 London game tickets sell quickly*. Retrieved June 28, 2008, from http://www.nfl.com/news/story?id=09000d5d80909291&template=with-video&confirm=true

A whole new ball game: The corporate winners and losers in the quest for footballing glory. (2008, June). *CNBC European Business*. Retrieved July 6, 2008, from http://www.cnbceb.com/Articles/2008/June/43/a-whole-new-ball-game.aspx

Bernstein, A. (2004, January 26–February 1).

NHL, union team up to fill World Cup roster. *Street & Smith's SportsBusiness Journal, 6*(39), 4.

Bloom, B. M. (2008a, March 23). Inaugural Classic was . . . a classic. *The Official Site of Major League Baseball*. Retrieved June 27, 2008, from http://mlb.mlb.com/news/article.jsp?ymd=20080323&content_id=2453253&vkey=news_mlb&fext=.jsp&c_id=mlb

Bloom, B. M. (2008b, March 23). Venues set for World Baseball Classic. *The Official Site of Major League Baseball*. Retrieved June 27, 2008, from http://mlb.mlb.com/news/article

.jsp?ymd=20080323&content_id=2452760
&vkey=news_mlb&fext=.jsp&c_id=mlb

Broadcast rights fees history: Olympic Games: Europe. (2008). *Olympic Marketing Fact File—2008 Edition*. Retrieved July 1, 2008, from http://multimedia.olympic.org/pdf/en_report_344.pdf

Burnside, S. (2007). By traveling to London, Ducks, Kings taking one for the team. *ESPN—NHL*. Retrieved June 6, 2008, from http://sports.espn.go.com/nhl/preview 2007/columns/story?columnist=burnside_scott &id=3036914

Cultural globalization. (2008). *Encyclopædia Britannica*. Retrieved July 7, 2008, from http://www.britannica.com/EBchecked/topic /1357503/cultural-globalization#tab=active ~checked%2Citems~checked&title=cultural %20globalization%20—%20Britannica%20 Online%20Encyclopedia

Deloitte & Touche. (2003, July). *The annual review of football finance*. United Kingdom: Deloitte & Touche LLP.

Development initiatives. (2008). *The Official Site of Major League Baseball: International: Feature*. Retrieved June 27, 2008, from http ://mlb.mlb.com/mlb/international/index.jsp ?feature=development.

Dobson, S., & Gerrard, B. (1999). The determination of player transfer fees in English professional soccer. *Journal of Sport Management, 13*(4), 259–279.

Drewes, M. (2003). Competition and efficiency in professional sports leagues. *European Sport Management Quarterly, 3*(4), 240–252.

Europa: European Commission, Sport. (2004). *Press Releases*. Retrieved July 20, 2004, from http://europa.eu.int/comm/sport/action_sports/ aees/aees_overview_en.html

European Union recognises the importance of sport in its new constitution. (2004, June 21). *International Olympic Committee—News*. Retrieved July 6, 2004, from http://www .olympic.org/uk/news/media_centre/press_release_uk.asp?id=902

Garcia, J., & Rodriguez, P. (2003). From sports clubs to stock companies: The financial structure of football in Spain, 1992–2001. *European Sport Management Quarterly, 3*(4), 253–268.

Gillentine, A., Goldfine, B., & Orejan, J. (2004). *An examination of the need for international education and second language acquisition in the sport industry*. Paper presented at North American Society for Sport Management Conference, Atlanta, GA.

Gillentine, A., & Orejan, J. (2003). *An examination of second language requirements and international sport education at selected sport administration/management academic pro-*

grams. Paper presented at the North American Society of Sport Management Proceedings, Ithaca, NY.

Graczyk, W. (2003). *Major League Baseball opens Tokyo office Aug. 1*. Retrieved July 26, 2004, from http://www.weekender.co.jp/new/030 801/sports_news-030801.html

Hefflinger, M. (2007). *Report: 54% of NBA.com traffic in April came from overseas*. Retrieved June 30, 2008, from http://www.dmwme dia.com/news/2007/05/30/report-54-of-nba -com-traffic-in-april-came-from-overseas

History: 1981–1990. (2008). *NFL History by Decade*. Retrieved June 28, 2008, from http://www.nfl.com/history/chronology/1981 –1990#1986

History of games played by NBA teams in Europe: 2006. (2008). *NBA.com: Europe Live 2007*. Retrieved June 6, 2008, from http:// www.nba.com/europelive2007/history

Hoehn, T., & Szymanski, S. (1999). The Americanization of European football. *Economic Policy*, 203–204.

International players in the NBA. (2004, March 15). *NBA.com*. Retrieved July 26, 2004, from http://www.nba.com/players/interna tional_player_ directory.html

International programming. (2008). *International Programming*. Retrieved June 28, 2008, from http://www.nfl.com/global/pro gramming

IOC television and marketing services. (2008). *International Olympic Committee Organisation—Facts and Figures*. Retrieved July 1, 2008, from http://www.olympic.org/uk/or ganisation/facts/structure/index_uk.asp

LaFeber, W. (1999). *Michael Jordan and the new global capitalism*. New York, NY: W. W. Norton & Company, Inc.

Lapointe, J. (1997, September 16). HOCKEY: The N.H.L.'s Olympic gamble; Stars' participation in Nagano could raise sport's profile. Retrieved July 6, 2008, from http:// query.nytimes.com/gst/fullpage.html?res=99 01EFD91438F935A2575AC0A961958260

Lombardo, J. (2003a, October 27–November 2). Game plan calls for growth overseas. *Street & Smith's SportsBusiness Journal, 6*(27), 25.

Lombardo, J. (2003b, October 27–November 2). League scores big with merchandise sales. *Street & Smith's SportsBusiness Journal, 6*(27), 26.

Madkour, A., & Kaplan, D. (2003, September 1–7). Tagliabue keeps his focus on the future. *Street & Smith's SportsBusiness Journal, 6*(19), 1, 26–27.

Manou, N. (2003). Greece faces the challenge of growth. *Trade with Greece, the official magazine of the Athens Chamber of Commerce and Industry, 23*, 6–9.

Masteralexis, L. P., & McDonald, M. A. (1997). Enhancing sport management education with international dimensions including language and cultural training. *Journal of Sport Management, 11,* 97–110.

Mission of the International Olympic Committee. (2008). *International Olympic Committee-Organisation-Structures.* Retrieved July 6, 2008, from http://www.olympic.org/uk/organisation/ioc/organisation/index_uk.asp

MLB International and Shanghai Media Group bring World Series to China. (2007, October 22). Retrieved June 28, 2008, from http://mlb.mlb.com/content/printer_friendly/mlb/y2007/m10/d22/c2276156.jsp

National Olympic Committees: Missions of the NOCs. (2008). *International Olympic Committee-Organisation-Structures.* Retrieved July 6, 2008, from http://www.olympic.org/uk/organisation/noc/index_uk.asp

National pastime takes on international flavor. (2007, April 3). *ESPN—MLB.* Retrieved June 28, 2008, from http://sports.espn.go.com/mlb/news/story?id=2824295

NBA to host a record 262 global events in 162 cities on five continents this offseason. (2007). *NBA.com.* Retrieved June 30, 2008, from http://www.nba.com/global/nba_host_offseason_070827.html

NBA to open first overseas store in China. (2006). *Asia Times Online : China News.* Retrieved June 30, 2008, from http://www.atimes.com/atimes/China_Business/HL01Cb01.html

NFL folds Europe league, to focus on regular-season games abroad. (2007, June 29). *ESPN.com.* Retrieved June 6, 2008, from http://sports.espn.go.com/nfl/news/story?id=2920738

NHL overseas history. (2007). *Greatest Hockey Legends.com: NHL Overseas History.* Retrieved June 30, 2008, from http://www.greatesthockeylegends.com/2007/09/nhl-overseas-history.html

Olympic broadcasting history. (2008). *Olympic Marketing Fact File—2008 Edition.* Retrieved July 1, 2008, from http://multimedia.olympic.org/pdf/en_report_344.pdf

Olympic marketing revenue distribution. (2008). *Olympic Marketing Fact File—2008 Edition.* Retrieved July 1, 2008, from http:// multimedia.olympic.org/pdf/en_report_344.pdf

Overseas companies and their U.S. sports sponsorships. (2002, April 22–28). *Street & Smith's SportsBusiness Journal, 4*(53), 23–24.

Revenue sources 2001–2004. (2008). *International Olympic Committee Organisation— Facts and Figures.* Retrieved July 1, 2008, from http://www.olympic.org/uk/organisation/facts/introduction/index_uk.asp

Rubingh, B., & Broeke, A. (1998). The European sports club system. In L. P. Masteralexis, C. A. Barr, & M. A. Hums (Eds), *Principles and practices of sport management* (1st ed.). Gaithersburg, MD: Aspen Publishers, Inc.

Sandomir, R. (2007, June 30). *N.F.L. pulls the plug on its league in Europe.* Retrieved June 6, 2008, from http://www.nytimes.com/2007/06/30/sports/football/30nfl.html?_r=1&fta=y &oref=slogin

Schaaf, P. (2004). *Sports, Inc.: 100 years of sports business.* Amherst, NY: Prometheus Books.

Super Bowl XLI broadcast in 232 countries. (2007, August 7). Retrieved June 28, 2008, from http://www.nfl.com/news/story?id=09000d5d80022760&template=without-video&confirm=true

Szymanski, S., & Kuypers, T. (1999). *Winners and losers.* Harmondsworth: Viking.

The Authoritative Annual Research Guide & Fact Book. (2003, December 29). Broadcast rights to major sports properties. *SportsBusiness Journal, 6*(36), 82.

The Olympic movement. (2008). *International Olympic Committee Organisation.* Retrieved July 1, 2008, from http://www.olympic.org/uk/organisation/index_uk.asp

TOP programme. (2008). *International Olympic Committee—Organisation—Facts and Figures* Retrieved July 1, 2008, from http://www.olympic.org/uk/organisation/facts/programme/sponsors_uk.asp

TOP programme evolution. (2008). *Olympic Marketing Fact File—2008 Edition.* Retrieved July 1, 2008, from http://multimedia.olympic.org/pdf/en_report_344.pdf

U.S. companies and their overseas sports sponsorships. (2002, April 22–28). *Street & Smith's SportsBusiness Journal, 4*(53), 22.

Wertheim, L. J. (2004a, June 14). The whole world is watching. *Sports Illustrated,* 70–86.

Wertheim, L. J. (2004b, June 21). Hot prospects in cold places. *Sports Illustrated,* 62–66.

Westerbeek, H., & Smith, A. (2003). *Sport business in the global marketplace.* New York: Palgrave Macmillan.

White paper. (2007). *White Paper on Sport.* Brussels, Belgium: Commission of the European Communities.

World Cup of Hockey 2004 to feature eight national teams. (2004). *WCH2004.com Official site of World Cup of Hockey 2004.* Retrieved July 29, 2004, from http://wch2004.com/news/ release.html

Chapter Fourteen

SPORT MANAGEMENT INTERNSHIPS

JOHN J. MILLER

UNDER NEW MANAGEMENT!

HELP WANTED

"EVEN IF YOU'RE ON THE RIGHT TRACK, YOU'LL GET RUN OVER IF YOU JUST SIT THERE."

—WILL ROGERS

Introduction

Selecting a career path is among the most important proactive decisions a young person can make. Future sport management professionals can "stack" the odds in their favor or empower themselves by obtaining a specific internship in sport management. In fact, the internship experience has been identified as *the most critical element for the professional preparation* of future sport managers (Coco, 2000; Cuneen & Sidwell, 1993; Li, Cobb, & Sawyer, 1994; Mason, Higgins, & Wilkinson, 1981; Stier, 2002; Sutton, 1989). According to Coco (2000), whereas only 1 out of 36 students had completed an internship prior to graduation in 1980, 75 percent of graduates had fulfilled an internship experience in 2000. A prime reason for this increase may be due to students viewing internships as a way to *improve their likelihood of obtaining employment* (Cook, Parker, & Pettijohn, 2004).

Scott (1992) revealed that placement directors, graduates, and current students thought that internships were the single most effective strategy for gaining employment. Cannon and Arnold (1998) also reported that internships are often used by students as a way to improve their job searches. Additionally, Pianko (1996) reported that some organizations hired as many as 70 percent of their new full-time college individuals who had participated in their company's internship program. A 2001 survey of graduates conducted by the National Association of Colleges

LEARNING OBJECTIVES

After reading this chapter, the student will be able to
- Explain the concept of the sport management internship experience as well as its advantages;
- Identify the primary capabilities or abilities of a competent professional sport manager;
- Understand the importance of networking during the internship experience;
- Describe the importance of investigating potential organizations prior to beginning the internship;
- Identify potential legal concerns in the internship experience; and
- Explain the different types of evaluation processes and their importance to the sport management internship experience.

and Employers ("NACE") revealed that 57 percent of interns were offered full-time positions by the organization that had previously sponsored them (Altschuler, 2002). Six years later employers reported, in NACE's 2007 *Recruiting Benchmarks Survey*, that they offered full-time jobs to nearly two out of three of their interns. More than 70 percent of those offers were accepted and almost 50 percent of the interns came on board as full-time hires. Moreover, the results also indicated that nearly 31 percent of all new college graduate hires from the class of 2006 came from the organization's internship program ("Internships 'Pay' in Multiple Ways," 2007). The survey further reported that internship experiences enhance the likelihood of a student gaining employment, if the internship agency doesn't result in a job offer. For example, 62 percent of the responding employers revealed that new hires possessed internship experience ("Internships 'Pay' in Multiple Ways,' 2007).

Concerning wages, the new hires who had taken part in the organization's internship program earned as much as *$2,000 more* in terms of starting salary (Pianko, 1996). Gault, Redington, and Schlager (2000) supported this finding by indicating that students who successfully completed internships found employment faster at higher starting salaries and higher levels of job satisfaction than those who did not participate. Finally, a more recent survey revealed that among employers who paid their interns, the average hourly wage for an intern with a bachelor's degree was $15.99, or more than twice the minimum wage ("Internships 'Pay' in Multiple Ways," 2007).

While an internship can assist the future sport manager in obtaining a professional position at a higher salary, it is important to understand "how" to have a successful internship experience. Internships, when designed and implemented effectively, can help future sport managers learn to navigate the sport business world, as well as offer an opportunity to gain insights from mistakes that would likely be damaging under other conditions. Internship experiences are effective ways to "test the waters" before taking a permanent position and have been shown to be valuable devices in helping to recruit candidates and direct career paths, as well as enlarging the number of individuals who maintain their career paths (Leach 1998). This type of experience can give sport management interns an opportunity to re-evaluate and re-adjust their specific professional expectancies.

Some studies have suggested that organizations tend to hire students who have obtained experience within their organization through an internship program (Altschuler, 2002; Goetz, 1995; Pianko; 1996). A previous report indicated that the cost of hiring an intern as a permanent employee of the organization was approximately one-third the

Networking in Internships

It's not only what you know or who you know. It's what you know *and* who you know.

—Anonymous

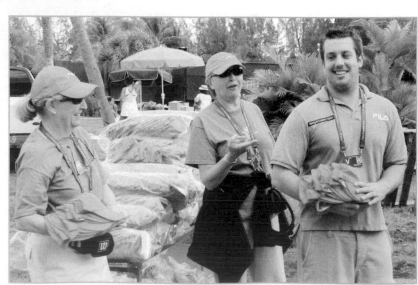

cost of recruiting and training a person with no previous familiarity of the workings of the organization (Croan, 1996). One of the reasons that students obtain positions may have been their *ability to network within the cooperating organization*. While the cooperating agency may not hire the intern, the potential for developing significant professional relationships exists. These relationships can then provide student interns with important networking opportunities that may positively impact their future.

| **Establishing Network Ties** | Some estimates indicate that approximately 50 percent of professional industry hiring in the United States is accomplished through *network-based referrals* (Tomaskovic-Devey & Stainback, 2007). Using social networks to recognize and hire an employee has been reported to be favored by a number of organizations because of its efficiency, low cost, and ability to provide information unavailable through formal sources (Granovetter & Tilly, 1988; Marsden, 1994; Resnick & McBrier, 2000). According to the *social network theory* (Granovetter, 1983), while network-based referrals can come from close friends or relatives (otherwise referred to as strong ties), the majority of such referrals come from professional acquaintances or "weak ties" in which there is relatively infrequent contact. Granovetter (1973) reported that *weak ties* possessed an important role in an individual's prospects for job attainment since there is a |

> structural tendency for those to whom one is only weakly tied to have better access to job information one does not already have. Acquaintances, as compared to close friends, are more prone to move in different circles than oneself. Those to whom one is closest are likely to have the greatest overlap in contact with those one already knows, so that the information to which they are privy is likely to be much the same as that which one already has. (pp. 52–53)

In other words, information about a new position may have a higher probability to be ascertained through weak ties rather than strong ones. Thus, it is important for the student intern to identify significant individuals who may be considered "weak ties."

It is essential to remember that the use of weak ties in finding jobs is best done when it connects the intern with someone who is in a position of authority within the occupational structure of the organization or who may have influence on similar authority outside of the organization. For example, a student who interned with the San Antonio Spurs may have worked indirectly under the Director of Marketing but directly under the Assistant Director of Marketing. During the internship experience the student also became familiar with the Director and Assistant Director of Event Management for the San Antonio organization.

In this scenario, it is the intent of the intern to remain with the San Antonio Spurs on a professional level in the area of marketing. While the intern may have done a good job, no marketing positions were open. However, a desired position is available in another NBA team. Because of the intern's positive relationship with "weak ties" such as the Director and Assistant Directors of Marketing and Event Management, the likelihood of obtaining the position with the other NBA team is greatly enhanced.

PERSONAL CONTACTS

Generally, job searches may be categorized into *informal or formal methods*. Formal methods of locating a position include employment agencies, placement offices, newspapers, and recruiters. Informal methods include finding a job through organizational networking (Drentea, 1998). Granovetter (1995) conducted an investigation to determine of how people locate jobs and reported that the majority of respondents used informal methods such as personal contacts of any kind. Within the context of this study *personal contacts* were defined as

> some individual known personally to the respondent, with whom he originally became acquainted in some context unrelated to a search for job information, from whom he has found out about his new job, or who recommended him to someone who then contacted him. (Granovetter, 1995, p. 11)

IDENTIFYING PERSONAL NETWORK TIES

To fully take advantage of networking within a sport organization, one needs to keep in mind the identity of potential personal contacts. As a guide, it is suggested that the student intern develop a list of individuals identifying weak ties as well as personal contacts as defined by Granovetter (1973, 1995) (see Table 14.1). As can be seen, the individuals identified in the table are those with which there may be infrequent interaction, even to the extent that a person uses friends in other sport organizations.

Table 14.1.					
People in Authority in Sport Organizations Where Internship Took Place	People in Authority in Other Sport Organizations	Acquaintances in the Sport Organization Where the Internship Took Place	Friends in Other Sport Organizations	Sport Management Professors or Internship Coordinator	Would This Person Give Me a Positive Recommendation?

"HOW EMPTY IS THEORY IN THE PRESENCE OF FACT."

—MARK TWAIN

Linking Theoretical to Practical

According to Stark and Lowther (1988) a competent professional should exhibit *conceptual, technical, and integrative capabilities*. Thus, competent professionals are often depicted as possessing the ability to link theoretical knowledge with suitable values and attitudes when making multifaceted judgments within vague parameters (Stark and Lowther, 1988). Skills that the intern should understand as being particularly important in a management-oriented setting are: (1) learning to learn; (2) reading and writing; (3) oral communication and listening; (4) creative and critical thinking and problem solving; (5) personal management; (6) group effectiveness; and (7) organizational effectiveness and leadership (Carnevale, Gainer, & Meltzer, 1990; McCormick, 1993).

Jones (1997) reported that employers thought college graduates often did not possess the ability to solve complex, ill-structured problems. According to Jones (1997) the employees frequently tried to develop a single "right" answer while infrequently suggesting alternatives, even when they were requested to develop more than one strategy. In fact, Useem (1995) questioned whether students will "be prepared to acquire knowledge later in a work environment that stresses personal initiative and collaborative work" if they "acquire knowledge by passively listening to authoritative figures at the lectern and experience no dialogue with them or with themselves" (p. 23).

The Business Higher Education Forum (1995) revealed that corporate leaders, nationwide, believed that graduates did not possess "leadership and communication skills; quantification skills; interpersonal relations; the ability to work in teams; the understanding to work with a diverse work force at home and abroad; and the capacity to adapt to rapid change" (p. 3). As such, it is not surprising that Van Horn (1995) found that over two-thirds of corporate employers felt that college graduates were incompetent. Thus, it appears that a significant amount of research points to potential interns, while not lacking conceptual or technical competencies, are sorely deficient in the integrative competency.

Examination of Sport Management Internship Policies

"SUPPOSING IS GOOD, BUT FINDING OUT IS BETTER."

—MARK TWAIN

While standards established through the Council on Sport Management Accreditation (COSMA; see Chapter 1) and the joint efforts of the National Association for Sport and Physical Education and the North American Society for Sport Management (NASPE/NASSM) (2008) endorse the internship experience, they provide little support of any specific, consistent standards and/or practices for internships within a sport management program. Therefore, a student must develop an understanding about the university's required standards for internship application. To accomplish this comprehension, the student should identify the *internship policies* required by the department. The following are some potential policy areas that the student intern should investigate:

1. Credit requirements: General requirements may include being a sport management major, successfully completing at least 50 percent of the total credit hours required at the institution, and possessing an overall grade point average of 3.0.

2. Grade point average: Many sport management departments may specify that students must hold a cumulative 3.0 GPA to qualify for internships. Possessing an overall GPA makes sense since an individual who has shown to be better educationally prepared may attain better internship opportunities (Beard 1997; Maynard, 1999).

3. Deadlines for application: Students who desire to apply for an internship may be required to submit an application (along with a résumé) by a deadline. The deadline should be during the term prior to the term that the internship is to

take place so that there is sufficient time to help the student find appropriate placement (Verner, 2004).

4. Identification of organizations: Sport management departments sometimes have a list of organizations in which a previous student(s) had a successful experience. The potential student intern may consider asking if any policies regarding internship sites exist. These policies may outline the responsibility of the organization to willingly provide students with appropriate supervision and with an opportunity to perform professional-quality work. These policies can also identify the characteristics of the person who is knowledgeable about the professional-quality work that the student is supposed to perform. For example, if a facility management supervisor fails to communicate or delegate job responsibilities to the intern, this will result in a "non-learning" experience for the intern.

5. Number of hours required to complete the internship: The student should inquire whether the internship must be completed in one semester or if it can be taken over continuous semesters. This is especially critical for students initiating an internship during the university's summer session.

6. Evaluation of internship: Henry, Razzouk, and Hoverland (1988) indicated that the internship should be graded as a pass/fail system for evaluating the performance of the intern. However, the evaluation process is totally at the discretion of the university. Additional concerns regarding evaluation and assessment of the internship experience will be addressed later in this chapter.

The potential intern may also investigate policies that address: (a) the anticipation that the intern will work the agreed-upon hours and present professional, excellent work; (b) professional attitude, dress, and appearance requirements of the student during the internship; (c) potential of unethical or illegal requests; (d) need for confidentiality; and/or (e) what to do if an organization where a student is interning goes out of business or relocates (Somerick, 2001).

Screening and Selecting the Sport Management Site

Once the potential intern has adequately addressed policies that impact the internship, consideration should be given to ensuring that time is not wasted, since an internship program should satisfy both the industry reality and student expectation. Hite and Bellizzi (1986) indicated that if the internship site is *not carefully investigated* the intern may have an *unsatisfactory experience* due to three key points: (a) unclear standards; (b) misinterpretation or misrepresentation by students regarding the expectancies of the position and; (c) misrepresentation by the firm concerning the required responsibilities. To prevent any of these from occurring, the student intern must identify, screen, and monitor potential sport management sites well in advance of the commencement of the internship. Suggested ways for students to gain this knowledge are to review literature related to their specific strengths and desires in sport management, visit the websites of the potential internship sites, attend professional conferences and conventions, and/or volunteer for activities within their field(s) of interest.

Students should also be very wary of any agency that uses them as clerical staff. A general rule of thumb for the potential intern to consider regarding whether the experience will be meaningful is: if the assignment may be carried out by the intern's on-site supervisor or by a person of equal status in the organization, the internship has potential to be a meaningful experience (Verner, 2004). By thoroughly investigating the organization regarding internships, students can assess their strengths and desires as they relate to the organization, thereby providing them with a positive experience. These assessments can provide students with an opportunity to apply their theoretical and technical competencies to further develop their skills.

An additional consideration when *screening* for an appropriate sport management internship site concerns the recognition and competency of the organization as it applies to the area of student interest. The sport management intern should not look at the experience as important simply to obtain any professional position but to also help in identifying his or her specific sport management career path. Sometimes students searching for an internship site apply to organizations that may have an availability that is close to, but not specifically within, the area in sport management they desire to work. For example, if students want to learn about facility management, it may not be beneficial for them to apply for an internship in sport marketing. While these areas are within the confines of sport management, the principles for each of these sub-areas are totally different, potentially depriving the students of an appropriate learning opportunity. Whereas the students may successfully pass the internship class in the immediate future, the actual impact may prevent them from being adequately prepared for the professional sport management position they desire.

The potential organization should also provide the intern opportunities to *observe* and *participate* in management-related issues. To make certain these items occur, the intern, in conjunction with the on-site supervisor and faculty member, should compose a written list of responsibilities expected of the student. At the start of the semester in which the internship will be conducted, it is generally a good idea for the students to meet with the on-site mentors to talk about how they will be evaluated. The intern and mentor then sign an internship evaluation agreement that outlines specific evaluation criteria. Although the evaluations may vary slightly because of differences in tasks across the organizational areas, normal criteria to be evaluated include quality of task performance, attendance and punctuality, attitude and enthusiasm, communication skills, creativity, honesty, and initiative.

Interns need to have a *clear picture of all the duties and responsibilities* that are expected of a sport manager. Questions that sport management interns may ask when screening organizations may include the following:

1. Will the organization allow them to be actively involved and receive ongoing feedback?

2. Will interns be put into positions that will allow them to apply theoretical knowledge to long-standing and new real-world, open-ended issues and problems?

3. Will interns be put into positions that will allow them to integrate discipline-based knowledge with their process skills, including problem solving, information literacy, critical thinking, analysis, communications, and teamwork?

4. Will interns be put into positions that will allow them to become increasingly more advanced in their abilities and skills?

5. Will interns be provided time for continuous evaluation and reflection?

Failure to ask these questions may result in students not only finding themselves in an unsuitable environment, but also one in which they are not able to integrate their classroom knowledge. This is especially true since the quality of task performance is generally regarded as having the most importance in the evaluation process in many internships experiences.

Research has indicated legal issues such as *paid internships, workers' compensation, sexual harassment, and general liability* issues should be investigated when screening a potential organization (Brown-Foster & Moorman, 2001; Miller, Anderson, & Ayres, 2002; Swift & Russell, 1999). The following will describe specific areas that the student should take into consideration when searching for an internship site.

Legal Concerns of Internship Experiences

PAID INTERNSHIPS

Many, if not most, student interns work for free. It is commonly estimated that at least 50 percent of all internships are unpaid (Barry, 2001; Gilbertson, 1997). According to Cook, Parker, and Pettijohn (2004) payment was not found to be a primary issue regarding a student's involvement with the internship program. Under the Fair Labor Standards Act (FLSA), *employers are not required to pay interns who qualify as trainees.*

However, if the internship is paid, the organization can limit the hours of the intern, thus preventing him or her from becoming eligible for benefits. This allows the organization to categorize the intern as a temporary employee (Sturges, 1993). Should this situation arise, the intern should still expect the organization to pay at least minimum wage or a wage comparable to those earned by others in the organization performing similar duties (Sturges, 1993).

WORKERS' COMPENSATION

An organization may not provide an intern with enough hours to be considered an employee, and therefore the intern is not eligible for certain benefits such as *workers' compensation*, in which the organization is held liable for medical benefits and wages if the intern is injured on the job (Kaplan, 1994). There are several reasons for this. First, many state workers' compensation laws do not distinguish between employees and trainees (Swift & Russell, 1999). Second, workers' compensation boards may determine that interns contribute enough to a company to qualify as employees and receive this benefit (*Evanson v. Univ. of Hawaii*, 1971). Third, some courts have held that even though a student is not paid for an internship, he or she gains important training and valuable experience that is equivalent to wages. For example, in *Hallal v. RDV Sports, Inc.* (1996) the plaintiff was enrolled in a sports internship class that was required within the university's curriculum. Although he was involved in the program only for academic reasons, the court held that he was still considered an employee. Therefore, it would be wise for the student intern and faculty advisor to investigate whether the potential organization possesses an effective risk-management program to cover interns under workers' compensation even though it is not required to do so.

The student intern as well as the faculty advisor must also note that the workers' compensation statute may hold that an internship employer in a university-sponsored internship program is considered to be an employer of a student intern, unless that internship is not paid. If the internship is an unpaid experience, the responsibility for coverage reverts back to the university (Henry, Razzouk, & Hoverland, 1988; *Kinder v. Industrial Claim Appeals Office*, 1998).

SEXUAL HARASSMENT

An area that the student intern should be particularly aware of is sexual harassment. While researching a specific organization, the intern should consider whether the organization provides any orientation to company policies concerning sexual harassment. This is an especially critical step since interns may be more vulnerable to sexual harassment than students or full-time employees (Bowen & Laurion, 1994). Therefore, sexual harassment may be a chief consideration when the institution is sending students to an organization as interns. However, the intern must understand that it is the responsibility of the organization to protect all employees from harassment; thus, interns should be encouraged to follow the same avenues of reporting incidents of harassment as the regular, full-time employees (Kaplan, 1994).

GENERAL LIABILITY

There is a potential that during the internship experience the student may be injured or may injure someone else. While workers' compensation can protect the intern as well as the sponsoring organization, the organization may be generally liable for the negligent act of a regular employee resulting in an injury to another. It is imperative for interns to understand whether they will be categorized as "regular" or "non-regular" employees.

Miller et al. (2002) reported that factors that may sway the intern's description as an employee include number of hours worked, wages earned, indirect benefits received, discretionary decision-making power, and genuine benefit to the ongoing operations of the organization. Thus, it is recommended that individuals entering an internship experience review the internship agreement with the on-site and faculty supervisors to gain a better understanding of their position or designation within the organization. The agreement must include provisions that assign legal responsibility for potential injuries that may take place during the internship (Miller et. al, 2002).

Evaluating the Student Intern	The National Society for Experiential Education identified *two key stratagems* for the student and faculty member to consider in creating strong, academically related

internships (Inkster & Ross, 1995). First, it is suggested that the student work closely with faculty member(s) and an on-site mentor to recognize and express acceptable educational objectives relating to what the student intends to learn and do in the internship. Duly (1982) proposed this step is critical so that students and supervisors understand how the skills and knowledge can be demonstrated as end products of the experience as well as the conditions that are likely to help promote these types of skills. Second, while many internships concentrate on the attainment of specific techniques and skills related to appropriate professional practices, the internship can also aid a student's intellectual development. Internships can help students learn how to reflect in action, develop new methods of reasoning, construct and test new categories of understanding, experiment with different action strategies, and try new ways of framing problems (Schön, 1987).

Despite the major differences between college and work environments, there are ways that student interns can involve themselves in the learning experience to more effectively prepare for the transition to the workplace. The primary objective of a student engaged in an academic internship should be to *integrate* classroom teaching with field-based application opportunities to develop management skills. Clear objectives regarding the proposed learning outcomes provide the basis for internship evaluations. Therefore, the assessments of student learning in internships should provide a precise and comprehensible description of learning, just as the methods and reporting strategies used should enhance learning (Guskey, 1994). A series of goals in communications, listening, writing, problem solving, critical thinking, and critical reading can be useful to help the intern identify priorities (Jones, 1997). Each objective may be based on a comprehensive review of the literature, which outlines a comprehensive framework for each major skill and then defines, in greater specificity, key dimensions associated with strong mastery. Thus, while true learning is multifaceted, appropriate evaluation should be also. With that in mind, interns should understand the importance of the following strategies that they may be required to complete.

WEEKLY JOURNALS

McCormick (1993) suggested that journal essays are one of the best ways available for the intern to develop *reflective learning*. Research has found that interns who have incorporated weekly journal reports as an integrative activity demonstrated the ability to transfer classroom knowledge to the "real world" (Eyler, 1994). The journal essays may be beneficially used for interns to think critically about the aptitudes required for a particular sport management position (Young & Baker, 2004). The interns then can reflect on their particular strengths and weaknesses for the position and indicate how they plan to improve the future quality of their work. The internship journal can also provide interns with the opportunity to identify specific situations that may be encountered in the organization and think critically about how they might handle the situation if they were in a decision-making position. Additionally, not only will these weekly reports allow interns time to reflect upon their internship experience, but they also help maintain regular contact between interns and instructors when class meetings are not possible. In some cases, the faculty supervisor cannot make regular visits. However, through reading the weekly essays, the faculty advisor can keep track of the students' progress and the quality of their experiences while recognizing potential problems.

ON-SITE SUPERVISOR EVALUATIONS

The on-site supervisor may be asked to provide a mid-term and a final grade for their interns based upon the interns' performance in the organization. At the start of the semester, interns meet with their faculty and on-site supervisor to discuss how the intern will be assessed. The intern, faculty, and on-site supervisor all sign an internship grade agreement that outlines detailed evaluation criteria. Items that are often included within the internship grade agreement are (a) the quality of task performance; (b) attendance and punctuality; (c) attitude and enthusiasm; (d) communication skills; (e) creativity, honesty, and initiative; and (f) professionalism. On predetermined mid-term and final due dates, the intern's on-site supervisor submits a grade as well as a detailed written evaluation of the intern to the faculty supervisor.

INTERNSHIP PROJECTS

Often the most significantly weighted item when grading an intern is the *quality* or professionalism of task performances. For example, after a careful mentoring and observation phase, the on-site supervisor may ask the intern to evaluate a marketing plan to increase the number of season ticket holders. This would involve integrating academic knowledge with information acquired by the intern through his or her organizational experiences. Other projects in which a sport management intern may be included are the renovation of a sport facility, designing media guides, developing fundraising plans, or creating policy manuals (Cuneen & Sidwell, 1994). Therefore, interns should be given or, even better, ask for projects that allow them to integrate their conceptual competencies with the technical to develop novel solutions to a problem.

MID-SEMESTER INTERNSHIP EVALUATION

During the middle of the respective semester the intern may be required to meet with the faculty supervisor to present verbal reports, indicate any problems they are having, help provide solutions to other interns who might be having problems, and obtain information on policies, performance appraisal strategies, and portfolio preparation. If the intern cannot meet directly with the faculty supervisor, other options such as phone conversations can be supplemented by faxes, e-mail, or regular mail. The intern should also meet with the on-site supervisor on a formal basis to receive an assessment at the middle and end of the semester. This assessment should address the strengths and weaknesses of the intern as well as offer suggestions concerning how the intern may improve on his or her responsibilities. The mid-semester evaluation conference is significant as it provides an opportunity for well-thought-out feedback, from the faculty as well as the on-site supervisor, regarding the intern's performance up to that time. Additionally, it gives the student and respective supervisors a chance to reevaluate goals for the remainder of the internship. At no time should the intern become defensive when given appropriately constructive feedback by either supervisor during the mid-semester evaluation.

FINAL EVALUATION REPORT PORTFOLIO

Most interns are required to complete *final portfolio reports* that indicate their overall sport management experience as well as critique their own performance. To best critique the internship experience, the interns are provided the opportunity to reflect on which learning outcomes they have fully achieved and how those outcomes were reached. Additionally, the intern reflects on areas of the internship that could be stronger or improved, what behaviors they engaged in most often, which courses best equipped them for their experiences, and whether these experiences had an effect on their career interests (Palomba & Banta, 1999).

Portfolios can also be used to measure interns' development and progress. Interns place in the portfolio a collection of materials that they have produced through the internship. Items such as evaluations written by colleagues or the supervisor as well as the intern's work—proposals, brochures, reports, workshop outlines, memos, or letters may be included.

Conclusion

Significant differences exist between the cultures of college and work (Holton, 1998). Usually, university students get regular feedback about their performance through grades and comments from faculty and peers. Feedback in the workplace is infrequent and less precise (Holton, 1998). Students usually participate in highly structured professional preparation programs that provide a great deal of direction. Employees usually work in highly unstructured environments, engage in tasks that have limited directions, experience less personal support than in college, and encounter frequent and unexpected changes.

How can a sport management student productively make the transition to becoming a competently skilled professional as previously identified? Internships provide opportunities for students to network with sport management professionals and learn about life in the "real world" without the commitment of a full-time position. Internships can present sport management students with an opportunity to evolve from learning career-related skills in the classroom to the application of these skills in a management-oriented environment. This can help the intern not only get a leg up on the competition but also obtain a position at a higher salary.

To better prepare themselves for the internship experience and, ultimately, the workplace, sport management student interns should consider the following recommendations. First, sport management interns should investigate and select sport-related organizations that will allow them to integrate their conceptual and technical competencies to further develop such skills as leadership, teamwork, problem solving, time management, communication, and analytical thinking. Second, potential student interns should focus on developing such personal traits as ethics, adaptability, self-management, global consciousness, and a passion for life-long learning. Finally, the potential student intern should take any opportunity to apply theoretical concepts of sport management and apply them to "real" learning experiences such as volunteer or summer work prior to the internship experience.

Summary

- The internship experience has been identified as the most critical element for the professional preparation of future sport managers as a way to improve their likelihood of obtaining employment.

- While it is important for the intern to gain experience in the sport management profession, it is also essential that the intern learn how and who to network with during the experience.

- Interns should be able to develop their integrative skills in addition to their technical and conceptual capabilities to become effective sport managers. Specific integrative competencies include: (1) learning to learn; (2) reading and writing; (3) oral communication and listening; (4) creative and critical thinking and problem solving; (5) personal management; (6) group effectiveness; and (7) organizational effectiveness and leadership.

- The student must understand the university's required standards before applying for an internship.

- The student intern must identify, screen, and monitor potential sport management sites well in advance of the commencement of the internship to ensure student expectations are met.

- The student should investigate such legal issues as paid internships, workers' compensation, sexual harassment, and general liability issues when screening a potential organization

- Since true learning is multifaceted, appropriate internship evaluation may include such strategies as weekly journals, internship projects, and evaluation report portfolios.

DISCUSSION ACTIVITIES

1. Develop a list of 5–10 potential internship sites based on the criteria addressed in this chapter.
2. List your expectations from completing an internship in the sport industry. List how you believe the organization benefits from hiring an intern.

References

Altschuler, G. C. (2002, April 14). A tryout for the real world: Interning is good for the résumé. Better yet, it may get you hired. *New York Times*, p. 4A.

Barry, G. (2001, February 11). Interns get head start at careers. *St. Petersburg Times*, p. 9B.

Beard, F. K. (1997, August). *Inside the advertising and public relations internship*. Paper presented to the Internships and Careers Interest Group of the Association for Education in Journalism and Mass Communication, Chicago, IL.

Bowen, M., & Laurion, S. (1994, August). *Incidence rates of sexual harassment in mass communications internship programs: An initial study comparing intern, student, and professional rates*. Available at WL ED374485

Brown-Foster, S., & Moorman, A. M. (2001). *Gross v. Family Services Agency, Inc.*: The internship relationship in creating negligence liability. *Journal of Legal Aspects of Sport, 11*(3), 245–267.

Business-Higher Education Forum. (1995). Higher education and work readiness: The view from the corporation. Washington, DC: Business-Higher Education Forum and the American Council on Education.

Cannon, A. J., & Arnold, M. J. (1998). Student

expectations of collegiate internship programs in business: A 10-year update. *Journal of Education for Business, 73*(4), 202–205.

Carnevale, A. P., Gainer, L. J., & Meltzer, A. S. (1990). *Workplace basics: The essential skills employers want.* San Francisco: Jossey-Bass.

Coco, M. (2000). A try before you buy arrangement. *Advanced Management Journal, 65*(2), 41–43.

Cook, S. J., Parker, R. S., & Pettijohn, C. (2004, January/February). The perceptions of interns: A longitudinal case study. *Journal of Education for Business, 79*(3), 179–85.

Croan, M. (1996, August 12). They aren't paid, but interns' experience will pay off. *Roanoke Times & World News*, p. C1.

Cuneen, J., & Sidwell, M. J. (1993). *Sport management field experiences.* Morgantown, WV: Fitness Information Technology.

Drentea, P. (1998). Consequences of women's formal and informal job search methods for employment in female-dominated jobs. *Gender and Society, 12*, 321–338.

Duly, J. S. (1982). Learning outcomes: The measurement and evaluation of experiential learning. PANEL Resource Paper, no. 6. Raleigh, NC: National Society for Internships and Experiential Education.

Evanson v. University of Hawaii. 483 P.2d 187, 190 (Haw. 1971).

Eyler, J. (1994). Comparing the impact of two internship experiences on student learning. *Journal of Cooperative Education, 29*, 41–52.

Gault, J., Redington, J., & Schlager, T. (2000). Undergraduate business internships and career success: Are they related? *Journal of Marketing Education, 22*(1), 45–53.

Gilbertson, D. (1997, October 19). Glamorous internships with a catch: There's no pay. *New York Times*, p. A16.

Goetz, T. (1995, January 17). To serve them all my days: Are internships education or exploitation? *Village Voice*, p. A6.

Granovetter, M. (1973). The strength of weak ties. *American Journal of Sociology, 78*, 1360–1380.

Granovetter, M. (1983). The strength of weak ties: A network theory revisited. *Sociological Theory, 1*, 201–233

Granovetter, M. (1995). *Getting a job: A study of contacts and careers.* Chicago, IL: The University of Chicago Press.

Granovetter, M., & Tilly, C. (1988). Inequality and labor process. In N. J. Smelser (Ed.), *Handbook of Sociology* (pp. 175–221). Newbury Park, CA: Sage.

Guskey, T. (1994). Making the grade: What benefits students? *Educational Leadership, 52*(2), 14–20.

Hallal v. RDV Sports, Inc. 682 So. 2d 1235 (Fla. Dist. Ct. App. 1996).

Henry, L. G., Razzouk, N. Y., & Hoverland, H. (1988). Accounting internships: A practical framework. *Journal of Education for Business, 64*(1), 28–31.

Hite, R., & Bellizzi, J. (1986). Student expectations regarding collegiate internship programs in marketing. *Journal of Marketing Education, 8*(3), 41–49.

Holton, E. F., III. (1998). Preparing students for life beyond the classroom. In J. N. Gardner & G. Van der Veer (Eds.), *The senior year experience: Facilitating integration, reflection, closure, and transition* (pp. 95–115). San Francisco: Jossey-Bass.

Inkster, R. P., & Ross, R. G. (1995). The internship as partnership: A handbook for campus-based coordinators and advisors. Raleigh, NC: The National Society for Experiential Education.

Internships "pay" in multiple ways. (2007). Retrieved December 27, 2007, from http://www.collegerecruiter.com/internships/archives/2007/09/internships_pay_in_multiple_wa .php

Jones, E. A. (1997). *Goals inventories: Writing, critical thinking, problem-solving, speech communications, listening, and critical reading.* University Park, PA: National Center on Postsecondary Teaching, Learning, and Assessment.

Kaplan, R. K. (1994). The legal side of internship programs. *CPC Journal, 19*(5), 47–49.

Kinder v. Industrial Claim Appeals Office. 976 P.2d 295 (Colo. Ct. App. 1998).

Leach, T. (1998, May). College internship: An aid to recruitment. *Law and Order*, 57–59.

Li, M., Cobb, P., & Sawyer, L. (1994). Sport management graduate programs: Characteristics of effectiveness. *Journal of Physical Education, Recreation, and Dance, 65*(5), 57–61.

Marsden, P. V. (1994). The hiring process: Recruitment methods. *American Behavioral Scientist, 37*, 79–91.

Maynard, M. L. (1999, Winter). Challenging the 3.0 GPA eligibility standard for public relations internships. *Public Relations Review, 25*(4), 495–507

Mason, J. G., Higgins, C., & Wilkinson, O. (1981). Sports administration 15 years later. *Athletic Purchasing and Facilities, 5*, 44–45.

McCormick, D. W. (1993). Critical thinking, experiential learning and internships. *Journal of Management Education, 17*, 260–262.

Miller, L. K., Anderson, P. M., & Ayres, T. D. (2002). The internship agreement: Recommendations and realities. *Journal of Legal Aspects of Sport, 12*(1), 37–60.

National Association for Sport and Physical Education/North American Society for Sport Management. (2000). *Sport management program: Standards and review protocol*. Reston, VA: National Association for Sport and Physical Education.

Palomba, C. A., & Banta, T. W. (1999). *Assessment essentials: Planning, implementing, and improving assessment in higher education*. San Francisco: Jossey-Bass.

Pianko, D. (1996). Power internships. *Management Review, 85*(12), 31–33.

Reskin, B. F., & McBrier, D. B. (2000, April). Why not ascription? Organizations' employment of male and female managers. *American Sociological Review, 65*(2), 210–233.

Schön, D. A. (1987). *Educating the reflective practitioner: Toward a new design for teaching and learning in the professions*. San Francisco: Jossey-Bass.

Scott, M. E. (1992). Internships add value to college recruitments. *Personnel Journal, 71*(4), 59–62.

Somerick, N. M. (2001, Spring). Strategies for managing an intern's performance. *Public Relations Quarterly, 46*(1), 23–25.

Stark, J. S., & Lowther, M. A. (1988). *Strengthening the ties that bind: Integrating liberal and professional study*. Report of the Professional Preparation Network. Ann Arbor: University of Michigan.

Stier, W. F. (2002). Sport management internships: From theory to practice. *Strategies, 15*(4), 7–9.

Sturges, J. S. (1993, October). When is an employee truly an employee? *HR Magazine, 38*(10), 56–58.

Sutton, W. A. (1989). The role of internships in sport management curricula: A model for development. *Journal of Physical Education, Recreation, and Dance, 60*(7), 20–24.

Swift, C. O., & Russell, K. (1999). Business school internships: Legal concerns. *Journal of Education for Business, 75*(1), 23–26.

Tomaskovic-Devey, D., & Stainback, K. (2007). Private sector workplaces since the Civil Rights Act discrimination and desegregation: Equal opportunity progress in U.S. *American Academy of Political & Social Science, 609*(1), 49–84.

Useem, M. (1995). Corporate restructuring and liberal learning. *Liberal Education, 81*(1), 18–23.

Van Horn, C. E. (1995). *Enhancing the connection between higher education and the workplace: A survey of employers*. Denver: State Higher Education Executive Officers and the Education Commission of the States.

Verner, M. E. (2004). Internship search, selection, and solidification strategies. *Journal of Physical Education, Recreation, and Dance, 75*(1), 25–27.

Young, D. S., & Baker, R. E. (2004). Linking classroom theory to professional practice: Internship as a practical learning experience worthy of academic credit. *Journal of Physical Education, Recreation, and Dance, 75*(1), 22–24.

Chapter Fifteen

YOUR FUTURE IN THE SPORT INDUSTRY

BENJAMIN D. GOSS • COLBY B. JUBENVILLE • CRAIG CROW

© 2007 Universal Press Syndicate

10-4   www.gocomics.com

"It's a text message from Jeff at home plate. It says, 'Heads up!' ... I think he's kidding, but there's no smiley face."

LEARNING OBJECTIVES

By the end of this chapter, students should be able to:
- Identify areas for future employment in the sport industry
- Identify growth areas in the sport industry
- Appreciate the breadth and scope of the sport industry
- Understand entrepreneurial opportunities in sport
- Develop a personal philosophy about the sport industry

Introduction

By this stage of your study of sport management, many questions with which you entered have no doubt been answered. However (and hopefully), many more have probably been raised. Some questions may be concrete in nature, such as, "How do facility managers balance security demands with enhanced fan experiences?" or they may be abstract in nature, such as, "How do I pull all of this information together as a professional?" or "Where do I go from here?" While your instructor and/or contacts in your newly emerging professional network can help you answer some of the more concrete questions, the aim of this chapter is to help answer some of the more abstract ones by pulling together some of the basic principles of this text and giving you a solid professional launch into one of the most exhilarating yet convoluted industries in the entire marketplace.

The Power of the Sport Product

Previous chapters have clearly illustrated the unique nature of the sport product and sport industry on a topic-by-topic basis. Let's pull them together collectively in one example to illustrate how they appear in a professional context.

ECONOMIC PROFITABILITY

Located in Trafford, Greater Manchester, England, Manchester United Football Club (ManU) of the English Premiere League is one of the world's most popular and visible sport properties. In early 2008, the soccer franchise announced record revenues (approximately $490 million) and profits approximately ($119.2 million) for 2007 (Sport Business International,

2008). According to ManU Chief Executive David Hill, Manchester United credits its success to developing three specific interrelated areas that have built its brand. First, the Red Devils have worked tirelessly for decades to produce a tradition of quality play on the soccer pitch, including filling its roster with the likes of mega-star David Beckham and Brazilian fireball Ronaldo. Second, Manchester United's on-field success has translated into an ability to sell out every game at their Old Trafford stadium, even after a substantial expansion, thereby generating large amounts of event-related revenue. Third, the relevance and quality of the Red Devils' live events have generated tremendous media rights and sponsorship revenues. Accordingly, Hill said, these rising revenues have enabled ManU to support the team's quest for further on-field achievements, thereby perpetuating the Red Devils' cycle of success (Sport Business International, 2008). Though ManU enjoys perhaps a more advantageous global business platform than the average sport property, the formula for the success of the Red Devils' financial success speaks to the obvious power of sport as a selling platform.

Beyond the potential for monetary profitability, however, lies another dimension of value for sport. Previous chapters have detailed what a powerful human institution sport is and can become. From a social perspective, hardly any other human construct can rival sport's universal pervasiveness or appeal. Perhaps only the institutions of religion, education, government, and music can even come close, and in some cases, they clearly take a back seat. At some point, the business and social facets of sport entwine inextricably to create the unique field of sport management. Accordingly, sport becomes a unique selling platform that exists with infinite managerial facets or aspects to it (and that's *great* news for you as an up-and-coming sport manager!).

To illustrate, consider another example from European soccer. Rangers Football Club and Celtic Football Club of Glasgow, Scotland, were founded in 1873 and 1888, respectively. However, the crux of their rivalry can be traced back to the Protestant Reformation of the early 1500s, as Celtic was founded to empower the immigrant Irish Catholic population of Glasgow. Consequently, Rangers became an adopted rallying point for Protestants and Unionists who supported a unified United Kingdom that included Ireland, providing a symbolic feuding ground for a cultural conflict dating back to the Reformation of the 1500s (Foer, 2005).

Accordingly, the rivalry proves sport's power as a cultural transmitter. A fan choosing to cheer for one side or another goes beyond adopting a favorite player, liking one side's colors better, or enjoying greater media access to one over the other. Instead, choosing sides in the Old Firm rivalry is an expression of social orientation for fans (Catholicism and Irish independence for Celtic, Protestantism and Unionism for Rangers), just as is the selection of which newspapers they read and which shops they patronize. However, from a business perspective, their bitterly divisive, socially based sporting rivalry has served to make both clubs exponentially richer than any other SPL teams, enabling the two franchises to compete in signing some of the most expensive player talent in the world, giving them their distinction as "the Old Firm" (Foer, 2005).

Social Responsibility

Beyond the complicated marriage of money and humanity lies another dimension of value for sport. Specifically, this dimension involves the ability to initiate, engage, and/or accomplish social change. Sport as a social institution contributes considerably to the health and cohesion of society as a whole and can build on this role with activities that address social issues connected to it (UEFA, 2007). However, this concept of social responsibility involves more than simple charitable acts. Instead, a better model involves a program such as the one approved by the Union of European Football Associations (UEFA) Executive Committee in 2007, which provides for a number of core partnerships with both trusted partners and other organizations that will help UEFA spread essential messages and provide vital support to it (UEFA, 2007). Suddenly that sign on the scoreboard takes on a new dimension, doesn't it?

Stakeholder Management

Coupling sport's charge of social responsibility with the high stakes of the industry clearly illustrates that, when more hangs in the balance to be won or lost than games and money, managing in such an environment can become quite precarious. In a results-driven industry like sport, managers are always under pressure because, by its very nature, sport is a high-risk business with many stakeholders at every level. As such, the concepts of stakeholder management and the open systems approach become a vitally important part of management in sport, no matter the type of sport property. Understanding these principles will allow you to effectively and efficiently strategize as a sport manager, no matter where your employment in sport takes you, whether it's managing players, coaches, and/or competitive structures; managing fans and their experiences; or managing brands, sponsorships, or content. Each of these areas of professional endeavor in sport requires an understanding of stakeholder management to meet the demands of fickle constituents and an understanding of the open systems approach to understand how your organization works internally and interacts with its environment externally.

"How do I start to collectively apply these concepts?" you may rightfully wonder. To help give you a push in the right direction, let's look at some big-picture trends that will affect the short- and long-term operations of sport systems:

They include:

- Developing an appreciation for research;
- Identifying new areas of future growth & entrepreneurship;
- Developing your own professional philosophy;
- Finding your niche; and
- Tackling the first steps in a new career.

DEVELOPING AN APPRECIATION FOR RESEARCH

As in any other industry, modern sport professionals and organizations must employ information as their most powerful competitive asset. As the sport management industry grows in both size and scope, its body of knowledge continues to evolve, as does the need for accessible, credible data to advance, promote, and preserve the sport industry. Therefore, developing an understanding of and appreciation for research has become a critical professional component for students and practitioners alike. Not only must sport managers have access to solid, timely, and relevant information to make business decisions, but they must be able to make judgment calls about that information before using it, specifically regarding how knowledge is developed, produced, consumed, and utilized (Thomas, 1996).

Epistemology

Why is epistemology (i.e., knowledge about knowledge) so important? Quite simply, we live in the Information Overload Age (a Google search of the term "New York Yankees" produced approximately 18,400,000 hits as of this writing). Though information is plentiful and we are hopelessly addicted to it, that does not mean that it is always reliable, accessible, or relevant (Rubel, 2008). As we determined in the previous section, sport managers make decisions daily that shape and define the character and meaning of sport, its leaders, and its future. To that end, if sport is to fulfill its role as a prominent social institution and social product, its managers must begin to fully and completely acknowledge and embrace research as the foundation upon which to build sound business models, formulate ethical imperatives, and generate long-term goals that are good for society (Lumpkin, Stoll, & Beller, 1999).

In many cases, research is often cast as such a high-level endeavor filled with intensive statistical manipulation it becomes misunderstood, feared, or ignored (if not all of these!). Unfortunately, a negative attitude toward research will not be just an inconvenient gap in an individual's sport management repertoire, but it will become a major void in a sport organization's ability to function as a stakeholder-serving business or institution. Many practicing sport management professionals complain (and rightfully so) that most academic-based research presents itself as impossibly cluttered theory that is not very applicable to them or their organizational environments. Accordingly, a fresh, practical perspective on the power and potential of research is clearly needed (Davis, 1994).

Phenomenology

One way to refresh the professional perspective of research is to use it to successfully examine specific issues and problems in the sport management industry, commonly known as the case study approach. Research that is both grounded in academic theory and driven by the needs of practitioners can be shifted toward a more precise study of distinct phenomena, ideas, and events (Goss & Jubenville, 2007a). Scientifically known as *phenomenology*, such a perspective on research in both short-term and long-term decision making and problem solving is anything but new.

This phenomenological approach to research in the sport industry is important because it will allow for the development of a new prototype of sport manager and leader. We call this new prototype the *scholarly sport practitioner* (Goss & Jubenville, 2007b).

The Scholarly Sport Practitioner

The scholarly sport practitioner (SSP) is the needed next-generation evolution in the sport industry's work force. This new kind of employee understands how to unite sport organizations through management practices and utilizes the power of knowledge to build a culture of continuous learning for successful organizational and stakeholder management. This critical thinker and learner will embrace research and understand how to apply the information it yields as part of day-to-day and strategic approaches to management (Goss & Jubenville, 2007b). This ability to interpret, analyze, and synthesize information will help the SSP in his or her career.

NEW AREAS OF GROWTH AND ENTREPRENEURSHIP

If recent past and present are accurate indicators, sport will not lack for future areas of growth and entrepreneurship. Over recent decades, sport has demonstrated a remarkable knack to both develop its current core business competencies and exhibit a resilient entrepreneurial spirit. This section provides a quick overview of the current areas that will present both challenges and opportunities for future sport managers.

Growth

Numerous well-established areas of the sport market have witnessed burgeoning development over the past decade, and for many of them, no end to their growth patterns appears to be in sight.

Facilities Development

Growth and expansion of sport facilities have been major drivers of the sport industry boom, including wondrous new dimensions of architecture and engineering, a constant retrofitting of established facilities, their acknowledged places as centerpieces of economic development, and the sales of naming rights.

Facility Design

From retractable roofs in 1989, to "Magic Carpet" retractable turfs in 1995, to entirely retractable fields in 2006, facility design technology has played a major role in the construction and management of sport facilities and should continue to influence the entire sport industry in very exciting ways (Rogers Centre, n.d.; St. Louis Rams, n.d.; University of Phoenix Stadium, n.d). Such major innovations have raised stakes and expectations across the field of sport management, but obviously, the evolutions continue. Because of its critical importance in creating a wide variety of revenue streams, facility design will remain a vital aspect of innovation into the foreseeable future of sport management.

Naming Rights

Sales of facility naming rights have become one of the most important revenue streams available to many sport properties. However, new issues and models associated with this practice are evolving and will require innovative thinking from future sport managers.

While naming rights sales have gained widespread acceptance in professional sport, the practice still is an issue of contention for some university administrators. However, a quick glance at the college stadiums and arenas opening in recent and coming years appears to reveal less resistance to corporate naming of college facilities, particularly among NCAA Division I athletic programs looking to increase their competitiveness with well-established programs.

Interscholastic Athletics Facilities

The naming rights trend is also an emerging issue in high school athletics, as school districts find increasing challenges in funding athletic programs because of rising costs and decreasing government support. The ethical debate centers on the easily influenced student populations that would be exposed to such sponsorships. School districts across the United States have weighed the positives and negatives associated with selling corporate naming rights to school-owned sport facilities. A growing number of school districts are deciding that the positives of selling naming rights, mainly increased funding, outweigh the negatives. This trend is likely to continue despite the apparent ethical concerns and will likely represent a lucrative emerging market.

Sectional Naming Rights

Another emerging trend in facility naming rights is the practice of selling rights for specific sections of facilities. The new Yankee Stadium, scheduled to open in 2009, will manifest such an approach. Rather than lose any tradition associated with the Yankee Stadium name, the New York Yankees decided to sell naming rights to specific sections of the stadium (entrances, concourses), which could fetch up to $75 million annually (Birger & Arango, 2007). This practice is not confined to just professional sport. Missouri State University's new JQH Arena was named to honor benefactor John Q. Hammons, who donated $30 million toward the project. However, to maximize naming revenue from the facility, Missouri State sold corporate naming rights to each of the arena's four concourses (8 projects, 2008).

Niche Events/Programming Development

Sport properties such as World Wrestling Entertainment (WWE), Ultimate Fighting Championship (UFC), and International Fight League (IFL) will likely continue to carve their own slice of the sport industry pie in the coming years. While the core product of the UFC and IFL is combat-style mixed-martial arts (MMA), the WWE is an integrated media and entertainment company whose business relies primarily on scripted professional wrestling matches. Despite the drastic difference between the core product of the MMA organizations and the WWE, similarities exist between the business models used by each company. Each attempts to reach the young 18- to 35-year-old male demographic through live events, basic cable and pay-per-view television broadcasts, online and wireless media, ancillary product development, and even sex appeal.

Smaller sport properties will continue to find their niche in the sport industry in coming years. Sports like poker, pool, and bowling, as well as rodeo and bass fishing, will continue to be of interest to a loyal minority. The continuing desire for sport programming will permit each of the aforementioned sports to gain television exposure, albeit mostly on cable and sometimes during not-so-primetime hours. The challenge for the future for each of these sports will be to see if one or more can develop a business model that will catapult the sport beyond its current status as a niche sport.

The competition for sport consumer viewership will only intensify in the future as niche networks increasingly dot cable and satellite channel lineups. Channels such as Versus (formerly the Outdoor Life Network), Outdoor Channel, Speed Channel, and CBS College Sports Network (formerly CSTV) offer programming that differs somewhat from the broad, general, premiere programming found on more established modern cable networks such as ESPN. Emerging sport networks, especially sport-specific ones, must focus on niche markets in order to survive such a competitive sport and entertainment marketplace. Such focus can be quite risky from a business perspective, given the tendency of large firms to ignore niche markets, despite their lucrative potential (Mullin, Hardy, & Sutton, 2000). Without marquee sport programming with broad appeal (NFL, NBA, MLB, etc.) sport networks must offer programming that will attract a highly devoted niche audience that will likely result in repeat viewership.

Niche segments, based on various demographic and psychographic characteristics, will become increasingly important for well-targeted marketing campaigns. For example, the U.S. Census Bureau estimates that by 2030, the Latino population in the United States will be approximately 73 million and comprise 20 percent of the U.S. population (U.S. Census Bureau, n.d.). Such a dramatic shift in the composition of the U.S. population is guaranteed to have an impact on the sport industry. To their credit, sport properties both large and small have recognized this trend and developed initiatives to attract Hispanic consumers. The Northwest Arkansas Naturals, the AA affiliate of MLB's Kansas City Royals, immediately took an aggressive approach to reach the burgeoning Latino population in its market in its first season after relocating from Wichita, Kansas. The Naturals purchased ads in Spanish media, held a Cinco de Mayo celebration, offered a Spanish section on its website, and broadcast some games in Spanish (Minton, 2008). The NFL has also taken steps to reach the Hispanic market, including the establishment of Hispanic Heritage Month, production of a Spanish-language television ad campaign, offering select game broadcasts in Spanish, presenting Super Bowl specials on Telemundo, and launching NFLatino.com (National Football League, 2007).

Technology Development

While discussing sport media consumption patterns with the *SportsBusiness Journal* in 2005, ESPN and ABC Sports head George W. Bodenheimer commented that, "It's a three-screen world now. TV is your first screen. The computer is your second screen. And your digital device is going to be your third screen" (King, 2005).

Bodenheimer's statement is critical to analyzing the future of sport media. Because of increased viewing alternatives, competition will be intense in the future for the attention of consumers. Thus, networks and sport properties will be faced with the challenge of deciding which content best matches each screen, as illustrated by the National Football League (NFL).

In addition to its television broadcast agreements with broadcast networks (CBS, Fox, NBC) and cable outlets (ESPN networks), the league created the NFL Network to offer year-round league programming with in-depth analysis and insider information of league events, such as training camp, games, and the NFL Draft. On the computer, the league reaches consumers through NFL.com's plethora of exclusive news, analysis, scores, videos, statistics, player profiles, and photos that are available at the click of a mouse. The NFL has also been active in developing third-screen content. Through a partnership with Sprint, the league offers NFL Mobile, which provides a live streaming of the NFL Network, video highlights, and access to statistics and news to Sprint mobile customers (NFL Mobile, n.d.).

Control of Content

Professional sport franchises and athletic departments have looked to the Internet for over a decade as a source of revenue. Internet broadcasts of games are now common. Tickets and merchandise can easily be purchased online. Official athletic department sites provide additional sponsorship inventory to sell. However, many sport properties are going beyond more traditional Internet revenue sources to offer fans even more insider access to their programs. One such area is the annual National Letter of Intent (NLI) signing day. Capitalizing off of the buzz created by message board posts on sites such as Rivals.com and Scout.com, many intercollegiate athletic departments are offering their fans up-to-the-minute information on the signing of recruits on a pay-per-view basis.

One unique characteristic of the sport business is that, unlike typical markets, a large percentage of its consumers consider themselves experts on the products they consume. One need not look any further than the growth of sports talk radio for evidence, and the Internet continually lends further credence to the fans-as-experts theory. Internet blogs have always served as a way for fans to converse or vent about their favorite teams (as well as teams they don't like).

Further evidence of the growth of consumer engagement through fan input can be found on ESPN.com. In addition to providing news and expert opinion, the front page of ESPN.com now includes a Featured Comment section with input from readers on current topics. As more individuals consume blog content and use it as a primary source of information, source and credibility distinctions for sport-related content and distribution have become less clear in recent years and will likely continue to be blurred further in the future. Such convolution highlights the primary issue with which sport properties must wrestle in future assessments of their multimedia rights and content development: how much control of branded content is optimal to cede to third parties? This will be a major area of future policy development, particularly for those in the public relations/sports information fields within the sport industry.

Areas of Entrepreneuship

According to Robbins and Coulter (2007), *entrepreneurship* can be defined as the process whereby an individual or group of individuals uses organized efforts to create value and growth by fulfilling wants and needs through innovation and uniqueness. Accordingly, entrepreneurship involves the pursuit of opportunities through innovation in products, services, or business methods and is accompanied by desire for continual organizational growth. Sport's entrepreneurial spirit is alive and well, but it must remain that way to sustain the growth needed to propel the industry forward. Two major current areas that will no doubt evolve themselves and also lead to further entrepreneurial efforts include the action sports and fantasy sports industry segments.

Action Sports

Action sports have come a long way since their primitive demonstrations on early episodes of *ABC's Wide World of Sports*. In fact, action sports have become key growth segments of the sport industry. With skateboarding legend Tony Hawk following Michael Jordan's example and conflating his roles as athlete and businessman to become a culturally iconic brand unto himself, action sports have attained new heights in public consciousness.

Competitively, the action sports segment has adopted the touring tournament model used by golf and tennis in previous decades, thereby offering many attractive sponsorship opportunities for various brands to target the desirable teen/young adult demographics. For example, the AST Dew Tour offers sponsors tremendous fit by blending action sports with an outdoor festival to create a sponsor's dream for reaching its target markets through signage and product demonstrations. Among the Dew Tour's partner brands are Panasonic, Right Guard, Vans, Toyota, and Sony PlayStation.

A dramatically increasing need for programming content on television, online, and mobile outlets will also likely spur the growth of action sports. Conveniently, each action sports property is closely aligned with (and in some cases owned by) a media corporation. For example, ESPN created the X Games, while NBC Universal owns the AST Dew Tour. News Corporation (FOX Network's parent company) went a step further in 2003, adding Fuel TV, the only cable/satellite action sports niche channel in the U.S., to its lineup of Fox cable networks. Fuel TV currently reaches 24 million homes in the U.S. (Fuel TV, 2008). Regarding new media, the unpredictability and sense of danger found in action sports footage easily translates into short video clips that can be distributed on the Internet, most notably through

YouTube. Also, ESPN developed EXPN.com as part of ESPN.com specifically to highlight action sports and offer a wide swath of content, including news articles, podcasts, video, and photos.

Increased event sponsorship and television affiliations have resulted or will soon result in a number of age-old sport management issues finding their way to the doorstep of the action sports segment. Substantial prize monies available to action sports athletes have impacted the earnings potential of action sports athletes and have already resulted in the formation of collective bargaining units, the power and scope of which will no doubt evolve in the near future. Subsequently, new governance models for action sports are also likely to emerge. Current action sports structures largely operate as one cohesive unit, but future governance models may branch out to be more sport-specific, thus impacting current properties such as the X Games and AST Dew Tour. Another primary consideration not to be overlooked is whether or not increased organizational structure among action sports and their athletes will result in some or all action sports losing their most important attribute: the cultural edginess that has given them a competitive advantage in a crowded sport marketplace.

Fantasy Sports

Fantasy sports competition now exists for nearly every major sport, as well as variations of competition for several sports (Birch, 2004). While estimations concerning the exact size and scope of the fantasy sports industry vary (pegged at $2 billion in 2005), its status as a maturing industry with escalating numbers of participants and increasing marketplace fertility remains unchallenged (Janoff, 2005; Fisher, 2007a). More than 25 magazines devoted to fantasy football were published in 2005, with sales for more successful titles ranged from 150,000 to 400,000 (Fisher, 2006).

Less well known are the underlying dynamics of the unique market of fantasy players and the major transformations occurring within the fantasy sports business (Russo & Walker, 2006). The explosion of popularity in fantasy sports participation and the dearth of research about it create a need for investigation in this relatively new form of sport spectatorship (Davis & Duncan, 2006), not to mention new challenges for marketers, media companies, and others within the sport industry who wish to capitalize on the fantasy sports audience (Russo & Walker, 2006).

Roy and Goss (2007) proposed a three-pronged model of fantasy sports consumption that involves the interactivity of psychological influences (escape, control, achievement), social influences (community, socialization), and marketer-controlled influences (product, price, promotion). The model, based on literature from psychology, sociology, sport management/marketing, general management/ marketing, and consumer behavior, resulted in three major points of importance to managers charged with growing fantasy sports businesses. First, reasons for fantasy sports participation can vary widely, meaning that a one-size-fits-all marketing strategy for fantasy sports products is impossible. Second, the role of marketer-controlled influences can escalate players' commitment to fantasy game play and purchase of related products and services beyond their initial attraction to fantasy sports games. Third, while recent growth in fantasy sports participation has been substantial, opportunities for continued growth exist, including attracting demographic groups with lower participation and through product development, specifically the creation of fantasy games by team sports properties (Roy & Goss, 2007).

DEVELOPING YOUR OWN PROFESSIONAL PHILOSOPHY

By now, you clearly know that the sport product is a breed apart, as is management of that product. You shouldn't be surprised to learn that the careers of sport managers are a different breed, too.

Some of these differences are fairly superficial.

For instance, you probably have learned by now that entry-level positions in sport management are difficult to obtain without a well-established professional network. Internships are critical not only for résumé building, but for establishing a network of contacts that will propel you into that entry-level job. Before securing a quality internship, however, a sport management pre-professional will likely need to engage in numerous unpaid volunteer work hours with various sport properties. Since sport management is a profession largely void of pre-professional certifications, licensures, and/or board examinations, these important career-building steps may or may not be structured by your college curriculum and will need to become an extracurricular pursuit for you.

Other facts of life that you've no doubt learned as a pre-professional sport manager include the need to remain mobile, the lack of effectiveness of blindly sent résumés, and the dangers of initially over-focusing upon a career in one certain sport or one certain level of a sport. Your instructors have also no doubt told you that the glitz, glamour, and high salaries are exclusively reserved for the players and upper-level managers, and that much of your work will involve long hours, low pay, and little praise by organizations that are besieged with a pool of job applicants so eager that they will gladly take on those conditions just for the chance to work in the sport field, and in some cases, leave established, lucrative careers in mainstream industries to do it (Chelladurai, 2001).

Other differences are much more subtle, and since most sport properties can have their pick of sport management talent, what will set you apart from the competition, give you a competitive edge in the job sweepstakes, and give you the ability to find an organization that values you, your skill sets, and your long-term growth potential within the sport industry?

Think about that statement from this perspective.

Anyone with enough money can purchase a car, but few people really know how one works beyond keys, pedals, and buttons. A mechanic, however, knows how a car works and is trained to take specific actions to make it work properly. Beyond the mechanic, though, lies the engineer, who truly understands the intricacies and inter-working of the car and its various parts and systems. The engineer sees the systematic relationships, can analyze them for individual effectiveness and improvement, and can create the synthesis needed for optimal system performance. Successful future elite sport managers must work to emulate the engineer and achieve true understanding by assimilating all aspects of their formal and informal education.

Admittedly, this process is difficult to initiate, but it starts with the realization that while a college degree is important, its true purpose is only to certify that you are currently in possession of a certain body of knowledge; it is a commodity that makes no guarantee that the knowledge you possess will do you any good just a few short years after graduation. Learning to think, however, is not a commodity, and that's the source from which true understanding springs and is the mold from which future leaders in the sport management field will be cast.

To prepare yourself for such a journey, we recommend that you examine the list of questions in the Discussion Activities section at the conclusion of this chapter. At first glance, if you find them deep and philosophical, that's because they are, but we believe they will give you a solid pre-professional foundation. You may not be able to instantly answer all of them, but that's okay. As question 7 implies, we encourage you to work on doing something each day to contribute to answering them successfully. After all, education is not just a product; it is also a process, and as much can be learned from your movement through the process as any actual learning outcome thereafter (maybe more).

THE RIGHT FIT

It is very important then, when searching this industry for the right "fit" between what the industry needs and what qualified applicants offer, to gather pertinent information. It is time to apply all the concepts you have learned in this class, and this textbook, and begin to develop a résumé that best reflects your strengths in this industry.

RÉSUMÉ DEVELOPMENT

As experience grows and the résumé begins to build, students are confronted with two serious professional dilemmas. First, almost every person in the Office of Career Services will promote and insist on developing a one-page résumé. In addition, they demand that, at the bottom of one's résumé, the phrase "References Available Upon Request" be inserted, again to maximize the potential to keep the résumé to one page. Once you begin to accumulate the experience required for that first job (internships, practica, volunteerism), there will be too much stuff to put on one page. A two-page résumé is perfectly acceptable, especially if the experiences won't fit onto one page in a readable format.

Second, if a potential employer wishes to check one's references and they are not listed on the résumé, it becomes a challenging ordeal for the employer. Why put him or her throughthat hardship? Just list your professional references (not your pastor or your family friend) at the end of your résumé. Who knows—the interviewer may be friends with one of your references, and now you move to the top of the list. In summary, it is very important to make the job of selecting the successful candidate as easy as possible. Anything that creates a barrier to entry may

The sport industry has some big shoes that need to be filled. Are you ready to fill them?

Photo by Marcus Cheng

Table 15.1.

List of Common Reasons that Résumés Don't Pass the Critique

- No objective statement or statement is vague or unclear
- Use of personal pronouns such as I, me, and my
- Education and/or experience not listed in reverse chronological order
- Accomplishment statements don't provide enough information (use action words)
- Bullets NOT used in experience section (bullets aid in readability and the flow of the résumé)
- Use of periods at the end of bullet statements
- Use of dates under "Honors" and/or "Activities" section (too much congestion)
- Lack of organization
- Format and/or style is not consistent
- Length is not appropriate for education and experience
- Spelling and grammatical errors
- Improper use of acronyms and abbreviations

Source: University of Miami Toppel Center

be the difference in one candidates' success versus another's failure (see Appendix 15.1 for a sample résumé).

TAKING YOUR TEMPERATURE

For you to be successful, know the following:

- What you want to do
- What you don't want to do
- What you're good at
- What you're not so good at

Then and only then can you rationally begin the process of understanding what "fit" would be right for you. It is important to "know thyself" in this regard.

Taking stock of your attributes—what you can offer as a set of skills and abilities to a sport organization—is the crucial part of this "fit" arrangement. This personal assessment and evaluation process is as important as anything else in getting one's "foot in the door" and ensuring the rest of you is invited inside. It is one thing to "talk the talk," but sometimes quite another to "walk the walk." You must demonstrate to a potential employer that you have the "right stuff" to secure the opportunity you seek.

Individuals can be "invited" into the sport industry only if they can contribute something *of substance* and be able to demonstrate that their contribution is *substantially different* from everyone else's. What are you prepared to do better than anyone else? What can you positively and unquestionably prove you are able to do better than anyone else?

THE COMPANY YOU KEEP

Fortunately, for most internship/job seekers today, they are not alone in their search process. Most sport management program coordinators and advisors have established a network of industry experts to assist them in their search. All programs have an established network of graduates who are currently in the sport industry. Use this program's legacy of alumni and the networks developed by program faculty to get an edge in the search.

First impressions are important, so be sure to dress for success—regardless of how informal the setting. Pay very close attention to those you meet—you want to take from this experience some insight into how they act, how they speak, how they carry themselves, how they dress, and how they project confidence, enthusiasm, and professionalism. For example, a student who attended the Stadium Managers Association annual meeting in Key West in 2007 was awarded an internship with an NFL team because of the manner in which she presented herself during the association's golf outing. The point is you must begin to model or imitate their persona. Individuals are more likely to hire those like themselves. Professionals in this industry are no different than those in other industries—they are interested in conformity and "team" players, not renegades and non-conformists. In the sport industry, you are clearly defined by the company you keep. It is important to surround yourself with successful people or those who share your desire to be successful.

Summary

The scope of this chapter has been fairly broad and has covered quite a variety of topics, making it a bit difficult to neatly summarize. However, we did try to create a common theme centered on things that the next generation of sport managers needs to know to become effective industry leaders. With that in mind, we believe this chapter should conclude with a few words about the differences between managers and leaders.

As detailed by Robbins and Coulter (2007), managers can influence people only to the extent of the formal authority of their position. On the other hand, leaders are people who can influence others toward the achievement of goals. Therefore, though managers are not necessarily leaders, imagining someone being a good manager without being a good leader would be next to impossible.

The topic of leadership produces thousands of books, videos, and seminars each year, and even if we tried, we couldn't summarize them all in the scope of this chapter. However, we did find an article entitled "Preparing Leaders for Change-Oriented Schools" by Thurston, Clift, and Schacht (1993) in which we saw a framework for leadership that fits closely with the topics that were covered in this chapter about developing a professional philosophy in sport management. Here are the main principles that it advocates:

> To truly build successful organizations, employees must become empowered to innovate by confidently making decisions in the face of turbulent business conditions. Successful decision making depends directly upon how much those employees trust the leadership of their managers and the ideology of the organization. Innovative leaders, therefore, spawn innovative employees by setting the bars of expectations in four ways.

> First, innovative leaders foster engaging relationships with their employees to inspire the acceptance and accomplishment of goals that are transformational and transcend self-interest. Second, innovative leaders foster transformation by creating collaborative, inclusive decision-making processes. Third, innovative leaders are continuous learners, define the organization's needs according to its specific context, and tailor responses accordingly. Fourth, innovative leaders assess the effects of changes by examining a variety of outcomes with a variety of measures.

We applaud you for accepting the incredible challenge to be a successful sport manager and wish you every success on your journey!

DISCUSSION ACTIVITIES

The following are some introspective pre-professional questions:

1. Who am I, and why am I here?
2. Is my focus on preparation for continuous learning and not just a college degree?
3. What are the elements of a life well lived?
4. Do I want to become an expendable commodity or a valuable resource?
5. What skill sets do I possess that an organization would be willing to pay for?
6. What are my values, and in what organizations do I see them reflected?
7. What am I doing today to help me answer these questions?

References

8 projects to watch in 2008. (2008, January 21). *SportsBusiness Journal*, p. 17.

Birch, D. (2004, August 25). Fantasyland. *Modesto Bee*, p. F1.

Birger, J., & Arrango, T. (2007, August 10). The Yankees stadium windfall. Retrieved September 18, 2007, from http://www.cnnmoney.com

Brown, L. R. (2008, February 1). Mayor Slay 'losing patience' with Cordish on Ballpark Village. *St. Louis Business Journal*. Retrieved February 18, 2008, from http://www.bizjournals.com/stlouis/stories/2008/02/04/story4.html

Chelladurai, P. (2001). *Managing organizations for sport and physical activity: A systems perspective*. Scottsdale, AZ: Holcomb Hathaway, Publishers.

Davis, K. A. (1994). *Sport management: Successful private sector business strategies*. Madison, WI: Brown & Benchmark Publishers.

Davis, N. W., & Duncan, M. C. (2006). Sports knowledge is power: reinforcing masculine privilege through fantasy sport league participation. *Journal of Sport & Social Issues, 30*(3), 244–264.

Dick's Sporting Goods Park. (n.d.). Stadium info. Retrieved February 10, 2008, from http://www.dickssportinggoodspark.com/Stadium/Facts.aspx

Fisher, E. (2006c, July 31). Fantasy football gets early jump on season. *SportsBusiness Journal*, p. 7.

Fisher, E. (2007a, April 30). Women fuel NASCAR's fantasy growth. *SportsBusiness Journal*, p. 1.

Fisher, E. (2007b, October 1). Indians execs rethink The Jake for a new era. *SportsBusiness Journal*, p. 7.

Foer, F. (2005). *How soccer explains the world: An unlikely theory of globalization*. New York: HarperCollins.

Fuel TV. (n.d.). About Fuel TV. Retrieved January 21, 2008, from http://www.fuel.tv/help/about

Goss, B. D., & Jubenville, C. B. (2007a). *Phenomenology*. Retrieved February 12, 2008, from: http://www.jsasonline.org/vision.htm

Goss, B. D., & Jubenville, C. B. (2007b). *Scholarly sport practitioner*. Retrieved February 12, 2008, from: http://www.jsasonline.org/level2/scholar.htm

Goss, B. D., & Jubenville, C. B. (2007c). *Social responsibility*. Retrieved February 12, 2008, from: http://www.jsasonline.org/level2/social.htm

Home Depot Center. (n.d.). About us. Retrieved February 18, 2008, from http://www.homedepotcenter.com/aboutus_thehdc.php

Janoff, B. (2005, April 11). Marketers of the next generation. *Brandweek, 46*(15), 38.

King, B. (2005, March 14). Reaching today's fans. *SportsBusiness Journal*, pp. 17–21.

Lumpkin, A., Stoll, S. K., & Beller, J. M. (1999). *Sport ethics: Applications for fair play*. Boston: Edward E. Bartell.

Minton, M. (2008, February 18). Team pitches to new fan base. *Arkansas Democrat Gazette*. Retrieved February 19, 2008, from http://www.nwanews.com/adg/News/217205/

Mullin, B. J. (2007). *Sport marketing*. Champaign, IL: Human Kinetics.

Mullin, B. J., Hardy, S., & Sutton, W. A. (2000). *Sport marketing*. Champaign, IL: Human Kinetics.

National Football League. (2007, September 19). NFL celebrates Hispanic Heritage Month. Retrieved February 19, 2008, from http://www.nfl.com/news/story;jsessionid=8035032292E0A61200B844D83D3651E0?id=09000d5d80282851&template=without-video&confirm=true

NFL Mobile. (n.d.). NFL Mobile Features. Retrieved February 18, 2008, from http://www.nfl.com/mobile

Patriot Place. (n.d.). About Patriot Place. Retrieved February 18, 2008, from http://www.patriot-place.com/contents.aspx?About

Robbins, S. P., & Coulter, M. (2007). *Management* (9th ed.). Upper Saddle River, NJ: Pearson Prentice Hall.

Rogers Centre. (n.d.). Fun facts and figures. Retrieved February 18, 2008, from http://www.rogerscentre.com/about/facts/index.html

Roy, D. P., & Goss, B. D. (2007). A conceptual framework of influences on fantasy sports consumption. *Marketing Management Journal, 17*(2), 96–108.

Rubel, S. (2008, February 18). Too much info-technology can lead to brain overload. *Advertising Age*. Retrieved February 18, 2008, from http://adage.com/article?article_id=125099

Russo, C., & Walker. C. (2006, May 8). Fantasy sports growth hinges on marketing, offline efforts. *SportsBusiness Journal*, p. 21.

Sport Business International. (2008, January 11). *United success underpins record financial results*. Retrieved January 14, 2008, from http://www.sportbusiness.com/news/163232/united-success-underpins-record-financial-rsults.html

St. Louis Rams. (n.d.). Dome facts. Retrieved February 11, 2008, from http://www.stlouisrams.com/edwardjonesdome/facts/

Thomas, J. R. (1996). *Research methods in physical activity*. Champaign, IL: Human Kinetics.

Thurston, P., Clift, R., & Schacht, M. (1993). Preparing leaders for change-oriented schools. *Phi Delta Kappan, 75*(3), 259–265.

UEFA. (2007, October 12). UEFA's social responsibility. Retrieved October 25, 2007, from http://www.uefa.com/news/newsid=601933

University of Phoenix Stadium. (n.d.). Stadium facts. Retrieved February 18, 2008, from http://www.universityofphoenixstadium.com/index.php?page=stadium_facts&section=statistics

U.S. Census Bureau. (n.d.). *Hispanics in the United States*. Retrieved February 19, 2008, from http://www.census.gov/population/www/socdemo/hispanic/files/Internet_Hispanic_in_US_2006.pdf

Wheatley, M. J. (1993). *Leadership and the new science: Learning about organization from an orderly universe*. San Francisco: Berrett-Koehler Publishers, Inc.

Zolli, A. (2007, March). Business 3.0. Retrieved February 13, 2008, from http://www.fastcompany.com/magazine/113/open_fast50-essay.html

SEBASTIAN D. IBIS

sdibis@miami.edu

Permanent Address	Local Address
1234 Anyplace Lane	1987 Collins Ave.
Memphis, TN 39402	Miami, FL 33126

OBJECTIVE

To obtain a full-time position that affords a broad range of experiences in the field of sport finance.

EDUCATION

University of Miami, Coral Gables, FL
Bachelor of Science Sport Administration, May 2009
Major in Sport Administration, Minor in Business Administration, GPA 3.5

EXPERIENCE

Mucho Sport Properties, Miami, FL
Database and Marketing Team Lead, 9/08 to Present
Research information about stocks and mutual funds for current and prospective clients
Assist in the maintenance of a client base of over $100 million
Design database to allow for client retention through the use of various ACT tools

Bobbleheads R Us, New York, NY
Financial Analyst Intern, 5/08 to 8/08
Presented results on a project to reconcile $500,000 discrepancy between perpetual inventory levels and general ledger
Developed weekly director labor reports in order to better align production efforts with business plan budgets
Assisted in yearly inventory audit by designing an Access database

Beach Front Health and Fitness Center, Miami Beach, FL 33142
Practicum Intern, 5/06 to 9/07
Provided service training for a 43-member staff meeting including ice breaker, handouts and PowerPoint presentations
Updated 2400 member list into active monthly statistics using Microsoft Excel
Calculated fiscal year Health and Fitness Center ratios that increased 9 percent
Researched and collected data for PowerPoint presentation for the CEO to present at the ACSM conference

Department of Residence Halls, University of Miami, Coral Gables, FL
Resident Assistant, 8/05–5/06
Responsible for the safety and well-being of 50 resident students
Ensured resolution of all floor conflicts and disciplinary situations
Planned educational programs to foster positive environment for learning and living

HONORS/ACTIVITIES

Sport Professionals Organization of Research & Training (S.P.O.R.T.)
Alpha Kappa Psi (President and Treasurer)
Golden Key National Honor Society
School of Business Peer Counselor
Toppel Career Center Student Advisory Board

SKILLS

Microsoft Word, Excel, Access, PowerPoint, FrontPage, Bloomberg
Fluent in Spanish

SEBASTIAN D. IBIS
sdibis@miami.edu

Permanent Address	Local Address
1234 Anyplace Lane	1987 Collins Ave.
Memphis, TN 39402	Miami, FL 33126

References
John Q. Citizen
President, Mucho Sports Properties
111 Calle Ocho
Miami, FL 33146
(O)305-212-8965
(F)305-212-4562
jqcitzen@mucho.net

I.M. Wobblen
Finance Director, BobbleheadsRus
1357 Bobble Dr.
New York, NY 22156
(O)212-564-9137
(F)212-564-9515
imwobblin@bobbleheads.com

R. U. Fitt
Manager, Beach Front Health and Fitness Center
5792 Ocean Dr.
Miami Beach, FL 33142
(O)305-595-9874
(F)305-595-9632
rufitt@beachfront.net

Glossary

80/20 principle: a marketing principle suggesting that a focus be made on moving consumers up the consumer escalator while keeping the existing heavy user segment content, as heavy users are known to be responsible for up to 80% of all purchases, though they may represent as few as 20% of all consumers.

action sports: athletic endeavors considered to have a higher level of inherent danger than others, involving speed, height, extreme physical exertion, highly specialized gear, or spectacular stunts; also called adventure sports or extreme sports.

ad valorem taxes: a tax, duty, or fee that varies based on the value of the products, services, or property on which it is levied.

administrative rules and regulations: directives enforced by administrative agencies that generally carry the force of law as if they were passed by Congress or the state legislature, and violators of the rules and regulations are subject to the penalties provided in them.

The Age Discrimination in Employment Act (ADEA) of 1967: U.S. law initially passed to protect workers age 40 and older from age discrimination. The ADEA was amended by the Older Workers Benefit Protection Act of 1990 (OWBPA) to include a focus on age discrimination and loss of workplace benefits.

agencies: businesses or services authorized to act for others.

AIDA: advertising concept that stands for awareness, interest, desire, and action, which is designed to move consumers along in the progression toward actual product purchase.

alternative dispute resolution (ADR): resolving a dispute through any means other than litigation or negotiation.

ambush marketing: a direct competing brand in the same product category staging a presence to create confusion in the mind of the consumer regarding who is the official sponsor.

The Americans with Disabilities Act (ADA) of 1990: U.S. law that protects individuals with disabilities from being discriminated against in the workplace.

appeal: the transfer of a case from a lower to a higher court for a new hearing.

arbitration: the submission of a dispute to a neutral third party (arbitrator) who listens to all parties, considers the legal position of each, then renders a decision to resolve the dispute.

arbitrator: neutral third party who acts much like a judge and listens to all parties in an arbitration, considers the legal position of each, then renders a decision to resolve the dispute.

Arizona Sports Summit Accord: edict issued in May of 1999 by a gathering of nearly 50 influential sport leaders that encourages greater emphasis on the ethical and character-building aspects of athletic competition. The goal of formulating this document was to establish a framework of principles and values that would be adopted and practiced widely by those involved with sport organizations.

assumed risk: the inherent danger within an activity.

Athlete Agent statutes: laws that seek to protect prospective professional athletes and regulate athlete agents.

balance sheet: a snapshot of a business's financial condition at a specific moment in time, usually at the close of an accounting period, which comprises assets, liabilities, and owners' or stockholders' equity.

barriers to effective communication: variables that impede productive interaction and correspondence, the three most notable being linguistic, psychological, and environmental.

Baseball World Cup Tournament: plan announced in 2004 by Bud Selig, the Commissioner of MLB, which called for a 16-team tournament to be held during spring training in warm-weather cities across the U.S.

behavioral approach: in conceptualizing leadership, this approach emphasized what leaders and managers actually did on the job, as opposed to their personal characteristics; theorists focused not only on what leaders would do, but also on how often and at what intensity they would do certain things to distinguish themselves as leaders.

benefits: the distinct advantages gained from an investment.

Bill of Rights: the first ten amendments to the U.S. Constitution, added in 1791 to protect the essential rights and liberties of all citizens.

blog: short for "weblog," a type of website that presents regular entries of an individual's commentary and descriptions of events, usually in reverse chronological order, and that gives readers the opportunity to comment.

booking: the act of engaging and contracting an event or attraction.

Bosman ruling: 1995 ruling by the European Court of Justice, which established free agency for out-of-contract players; it has been considered a landmark decision with significant impact on the structure, development, and economics of professional football (soccer) clubs throughout Europe.

brand equity: all of the distinguishing qualities of a commercial brand that results in personal commitment to and demand for the brand.

brand insistence: behavior in which the consumer wants or is willing to buy or purchase a specific product only.

brand loyalty: a more intense form of brand insistence in which the consumer develops a passion about or loyalty to a specific product.

brand preference: the extent to which a customer prefers to use a certain product or service.

brand recognition: the extent to which a brand is recognized for its advertised attributes or communications.

breach of warranty: a breach by a seller of the terms of a warranty.

business (personal) financial management: directing and controlling the use of cash flow and monetary operations and funds.

buy in: the incentive for companies or potential sponsors to invest in a program, event, team, etc.

case law: law based on judicial decision and precedent rather than on statutes.

case study method: a curriculum that presents students with the opportunity to read previous cases in order to learn how courts make legal decisions by applying relevant law to the facts of the case.

cash budget: a forecast of estimated cash receipts and disbursements for a specified period of time.

cash flow: money entering and exiting an organization; cash inflows and outflows in your personal life and in various business enterprises.

casuals: types of visitors who were not drawn in by the event being studied.

Certificates of Participation (COPs): public financing instruments that involve the governmental entity creating a corporation to buy/build a public assembly facility, such as an arena or convention and visitors' center; financing is obtained by buying a share of the lease revenues of an agreement made by a municipal or governmental entity, rather than the bond being secured by those revenues.

charitable immunity: immunity from civil liability, especially for negligent torts that is granted to a charitable or nonprofit organization.

charitable organizations: institutions or organizations established to help the needy or for humanitarian or philanthropic purposes beneficial to the public.

circuits: the area or district under the jurisdiction of a judge in which periodic court sessions are held.

civil law: the body of laws dealing with the rights of private citizens; includes everything that is not criminal law.

civil rights: the rights belonging to an individual by virtue of citizenship, especially the fundamental freedoms and privileges guaranteed by the 13th and 14th Amendments to the U.S. Constitution and by subsequent acts of Congress, including civil liberties, due process, equal protection of the laws, and freedom from discrimination.

Clayton Antitrust Act: law passed by the U.S. Congress in 1914 as an amendment to clarify and supplement the Sherman Antitrust Act of 1890, which prohibited exclusive sales contracts, local price cutting to freeze out competitors, rebates, interlocking directorates in corporations capitalized at P1 million or more in the same field of business, and intercorporate stock holdings.

clutter: the result of too many sponsors being associated with a sport entity in which no single brand image stands out as the sponsor.

code of ethics: a system of principles governing morality and acceptable conduct.

collective bargaining agreement (CBA): a negotiation contract outlining the collective bargaining terms drawn up by the owners and union representatives, who are acting on the behalf of workers and employees.

Commission on Sport Management Accreditation (COSMA): an independent accrediting body that promotes and recognizes excellence in sport management education through specialized accreditation.

commitment: in sport, the frequency, duration, and intensity of involvement, or the willingness to expend money, time, and energy in a pattern of sport involvement.

common law: the system of laws originated and developed in England and based on court decisions, on the doctrines implicit in those decisions, and on customs and usages rather than on codified written laws.

competitive balance: when conditions exist within competition that cause parity, or equality, in amount, status, or value.

competitive imbalance: when conditions exist within competition that cause a disparity in amount, status, or value.

compliance: observance of official requirements.

compound interest: interest that is calculated not only on the initial principal but also the accumulated interest of prior periods.

conceptual skills: in sport management terms, these skills involve the ability to conceptualize how all the different parts of the organization fit together so that established goals and objectives can be achieved.

conduct: the way a person acts, especially from the standpoint of morality and ethics.

consideration: the payment of money by one party to the other, who in turn provides something of value.

consumer escalator: a marketing model in which the goal is to move consumers from non-aware/non-consumers onto a consumption "escalator" and ultimately up each level from light to medium to heavy users.

contemporary theories: leadership theories, developed in the past two decades, that presented a broader perspective of the leader-follower relationship as they examined the changes in the followers that came as a result of leader influence, and characterized the leader as charismatic, inspirational, visionary, and/or transformational.

content: the subject matter or essential meaning of something.

contingency approaches: see definition for *situational approaches.*

contract: an agreement, or exchange of promises, that creates legally enforceable duties and obligations for all parties to the contract.

conventional: the second of Kohlberg's three stages of moral reasoning, which is based on a person's conformance to society's rules and is the level of most adolescents and adults in societies.

Copyright Act of 1976: law that extended the length of protection for individual authors to the author's entire life plus fifty years and did the same for works for hire with seventy-five years.

core: the basic or most important part.

corporate social responsibility: obligation of a corporate business to fulfill a role within the surrounding community, assuming economic, legal, ethical, and philanthropic responsibilities.

corporation: a company formed by an agreement between the state and the persons forming the company, with the state requiring legal documentation of the agreement.

counteroffer: an offer made in return by one who rejects an unsatisfactory offer.

Courts of Appeals: a court to which appeals are made on points of law resulting from the judgment of a lower court.

credibility: the quality of being believable or trustworthy.

crime: an act committed or omitted in violation of a law forbidding or commanding it and for which punishment is imposed upon conviction.

criminal law: law that deals with unlawful acts committed against the public as a whole, in which a defendant is accused of violating a statute defining a criminal act, thereby committing a crime.

crowd management: organizational tool used to assist venue directors and/or event coordinators in providing a safe and enjoyable environment for patrons.

culture: the socially transmitted behavior patterns, arts, beliefs, institutions, and all other products of human work and thought.

damages: money ordered to be paid as compensation for injury or loss.

decision making: choosing a course of action based on the evaluation of necessary information.

Declaration of Independence: the declaration of the Congress of the Thirteen United States of America, on the 4th of July, 1776, by which they formally declared that these colonies were free and independent States, not subject to the government of Great Britain.

defection: to abandon a position or association; in sport sponsorships, to cause a company or sponsor not to renew.

demographics: the characteristics of human populations and population segments that are used to identify consumer markets, and those that describe their state of being, such as income level, education level, zip code, marital status, age, race, religious affiliation, occupation type, number of children in the home, and gender.

deontology: ethical theory concerned with duties and rights, based on the idea of absolute rules of moral behavior.

Department of Education: the United States federal department, created in 1979, that administers all federal programs dealing with education, including federal aid to educational institutions and students.

depreciation: the allocation of the cost of an asset over a period of time for accounting and tax purposes.

direct spending: dollars spent explicitly for a specific program or purpose.

director of finance: assistant to the head of the management team who is responsible for fiscal accountability, budgeting, cost control, contract negotiations, and financing.

director of marketing: assistant to the head of the management team who is responsible for market planning, advertising, and sales (i.e., sponsorships, merchandise, and tickets).

director of operations: the primary assistant to the head of the management team who has a wide variety of departmental responsibilities, including event coordination; engineering; security, safety, and medical services; and maintenance and housekeeping.

discretionary expense: a recurring or non-recurring expense for goods and services that are either non-essential or more expensive than necessary; examples include entertainment expenses, wellness programs, and speakers; also referred to as step cost.

discrimination: treatment or consideration based on class or category rather than individual merit; partiality or prejudice.

disseminator: an informational role filled by the sport manager in which he or she screens information and passes it along to employees who otherwise would probably not have access to it.

disturbance handler: a decisional role filled by a sport manager in which the individual is responsible for reacting to changes affecting the organization that are unexpected and beyond his or her immediate control.

diversity: a range or variety; having difference among the assembled or included parts of a group.

diversity of citizenship: a condition in which the parties to an action are of diverse state or national citizenship.

division of labor: a directive that shows the separation of departments by function or specialization.

drug testing: testing administered to detect the presence of drugs, especially from a blood or urine sample and especially for illegal substances.

economic benefit: a measure of the economic gain in the local economy.

economic impact: the total economic gain or loss after accounting for an event's costs.

economic responsibilities: implicit requirement of organizations to produce goods and services and sell them at a profit, because that is how a capitalist society operates.

eduselling: a process by which sport professionals approach new users of the products or services more as "teachers" than as salespeople.

emotional content: the emotions or feelings inherent in a communication that often offers information other than that of the intended message.

English Premiership: the Division I Football (Soccer) League in England.

entrepreneur: a decisional role filled by a sport manager in which he or she looks for ways to improve his or her work group, adapt to internal and external changes, and direct the organization toward opportunities that initiate growth.

entrepreneurship: the process whereby an individual or group of individuals uses organized efforts to create value and grow by fulfilling wants and needs through innovation and uniqueness.

environment: the totality of circumstances or conditions surrounding an individual or group of individuals.

epistemology: the branch of philosophy that studies the origin and nature of human knowledge, its presuppositions, and its validity.

Equal Access Act: act that prohibits any school receiving federal funds from denying equal access to, or discriminating against, any student desiring to conduct a meeting on school premises, when the meeting deals with religious, political, or philosophical subjects.

equilibrium price: the point at which the supply curve and the demand curve overlap, where the amount of product demanded equals the amount of product supplied.

equitable treatment: handling or dealing with equally.

Establishment Clause: a clause in the U.S. Constitution forbidding Congress from establishing a state religion.

ethical challenge: moral conflict; an ethical situation that requires a choice between options that are or seem equally unfavorable or mutually exclusive; also called an ethical dilemma.

ethical dilemma: see **ethical challenge**.

ethical responsibilities: requirement of organizations to operate by established norms defining suitable behavior.

ethics: a set of principles or values that are used to determine right and wrong.

Euro 2004: 2004 European soccer tournament that saw record TV audiences, topping those from the 2000 tournament by more than 15 percent; it was estimated that 2.5 billion individuals, or about 80 million per match, watched.

European Union: an economic and political union established in 1993 after the ratification of the Maastricht Treaty by members of the European Community, which forms its core. In establishing the European Union, the treaty expanded the political scope of the European Community, especially in the area of foreign and security policy, and provided for the creation of a central European bank and the adoption of a common currency by the end of the 20th century.

evaluation: the process of examining a system to determine whether or not certain criteria were met.

exclusivity: having the exclusive right or privilege.

expense: any cost of doing business resulting from revenue-generating activities.

expense budget: a calculation of projected future expenses analyzed in relationship to cash available, which is used to make planning and management decisions.

explicit expenditures: the cost of explicitly making one choice over another.

fad: a fashion that is taken up with great enthusiasm for a brief period of time; a craze.

fantasy sports: sports competitions with imaginary teams that the participants own, manage, and coach, with the games based on statistics generated by actual professional sports players and teams.

federal court system: court system established by the federal government and having jurisdiction over questions of federal law.

federal question: a question that falls under the jurisdiction of a federal court because it requires a resolution of the construction or application of federal law.

The Federal Trademark Act of 1946: statute that authorizes owners of trademarks to register them with the U.S. government, and provides protection against others who seek to use the trademark without permission; also known as the Lanham Act.

federal trial courts: courts that operate essentially the same as state trial courts, providing a trial of the case before a judge and jury; also called U.S. District Courts, followed by a geographical description of the location of the court (e.g., United States District Court

for the Western District of Pennsylvania), of which there are 94 throughout the U.S., with at least one located in every state.

figurehead: the first of three interpersonal roles a sport manager must fulfill, which involves fulfilling certain ceremonial functions as the result of being in charge of a certain department or the organization as a whole.

final portfolio reports: formal assessments written at the conclusion of an internship by interns in order to assess their overall experience as well as critique their performance.

financial considerations: concerns about cost or funding.

fit: in sport marketing, the compatibility of the sport property's image with the desired image of the brand, as well as how well needs are matched between the target market of the sport entity and the target market of the brand.

fixed cost: a cost that does not vary depending on production or sales levels, such as rent, property, insurance, or interest expense; also referred to as non-variable cost.

foundations: institutions founded and supported by an endowment.

future value: the value at some point in the future of a present amount of money.

G-14: a proposal, also referred to as Super League, offered by the European football (soccer) industry to come closer to the American model, which would include football giants like Ajax Amsterdam, Manchester United, AC Milan, and Real Madrid.

gender discrimination: discrimination based on sex.

general liability: liability for bodily injury, death, or damage to property owned by others to which an employer may be subject either directly or by reason of liability arising out of an act, error, or omission of its employee, agent, or officer in the course and scope of employment.

general obligation bonds: bonds typically used to finance traditional capital projects such as highways, roads, and sewers that will be paid back through the taxing power of the issuing authority. General obligation bonds are issued against the general full faith and credit of state and local governments.

generally accepted accounting principles (GAAP): a combination of authoritative standards, set by policy boards made up of the American Institute of Certified Public Accountants (AICPA) and Financial Accounting Standards Board (FASB), in addition to the Security

Exchange Commission (SEC), an agency of the federal government, that establish the accepted ways of doing accounting.

gigantism: excessive growth of a body or any of its parts.

globalization: the process by which the experience of everyday life, marked by the diffusion of commodities and ideas, is becoming standardized around the world.

goals: in regard to a mission statement, the achievable statements provided by management, ideally developed through consultation with all stakeholders in the venue, usually based on the mission statement and used to justify the fiscal resources requested in a budget document.

grassroots programs: programs that focus on people or society at a local level rather than at the center of major political activity.

gross negligence: acting in such a reckless manner that the court will consider that the defendant exhibited a conscious indifference toward the safety of the plaintiff, even though the defendant did not intend to injure the plaintiff.

hazing: to persecute or harass with meaningless, difficult, or humiliating tasks.

human skills: in sport management terms, these skills involve aspects of leading, communicating, motivating, and, in general, dealing with all aspects of employee relations on a daily basis.

idealized influence: the position of role model that the transformational leader assumes in the eyes of his or her followers.

image: a distinctive but intangible quality that surrounds a product that is to make it appealing to the consumer.

image enhancement: the positive effects done to the image of a company or sponsor as part of being associated with a certain event, team, or fundraiser.

implicit expenditures: the intangible benefits lost by making one choice over another.

income statement: a business financial statement that lists revenues, expenses, and net income throughout a given period.

indirect spending: dollars spent as a secondary result of direct spending.

individualized consideration: the role of coach or mentor that the transformational leader assumes in the eyes of followers in an organization.

induced spending: dollars spent by wage earners as a result of increased money flow caused by direct and indirect spending.

induction: the act or process of inducing or bringing about.

infringement: encroachment of a right or privilege.

inspirational motivation: the idea that transformational leaders will inspire and motivate those around them, encouraging others to find challenge and personal meaning in their work, and will thereby foster enthusiasm throughout the organization.

instrumental values: in ethical theory, the means that one will use to achieve the ends.

intellectual stimulation: the component of transformational leadership theory that resides in the leader's ability to challenge followers to be more creative and innovative, and to be supportive of follower efforts even when in error.

intentional torts: civil wrongs that occur when the party acting wrongfully, called the tortfeasor, intends to cause the harm by committing the act that causes the injury.

intermediate appeals court: a court whose jurisdiction is to review decisions of lower courts or agencies.

International Association of Assembly Managers (IAAM): a group comprised of leaders who represent a diverse industry—entertainment, sports, conventions, trade, hospitality, and tourism—and manage, or provide products and services to, public assembly facilities like arenas, amphitheaters, auditoriums, convention centers/exhibit halls, performing arts venues, stadiums, and university complexes.

international environment: cultural or social conditions extending across or transcending national boundaries.

international federations (IFs): federations that are responsible for developing their sport(s) worldwide and for staging world championships.

International Olympic Committee (IOC): an international, non-governmental, nonprofit organization whose main responsibility is to organize the Olympic Games, but that also owns the rights to the Olympic properties, including the Olympic symbol, flag, motto, emblem, anthem, flame, and torch.

internship policies: the rules, guidelines, and specifications given by the department that is offering the internship.

interviews: a formal meeting in person in which questioning is used to gather data and opinions.

involvement: to occupy or engage the interest of; when referring to sport consumers, can be behavioral (the actual doing of a sport activity), cognitive (seeking out information and knowledge about a sport), and affective (the feelings and emotions a sport consumer has for a particular activity or team).

IOC commissions: groups whose duty is the promotion of Olympic ideals (e.g., marketing, medical, ethics, nominations, press, TV and Internet rights, Olympic solidarity).

job description: a summary of all the roles and responsibilities of a particular job.

judgment: a determination of a court of law; a judicial decision.

justice: the upholding of what is just, especially fair treatment and due reward in accordance with honor, standards, or law.

kinesics: the appearance and physical mannerisms of a speaker.

Lanham Act: statute that authorizes owners of trademarks to register them with the U.S. government, and provides protection against others who seek to use the trademark without permission; also known as the Federal Trademark Act of 1946.

law: a body of enforceable rules, established by the lawmaking authorities of a society, governing the relationships among individuals, and between individuals and their government.

law of demand: the law that states that when the price of an item declines, the demand for that item increases.

leader: the second interpersonal role a sport manager must fulfill, which involves directing subordinates toward the achievement of assigned tasks and may require the manager to hire, train, supervise, motivate, and evaluate employees in the workplace.

legal capacity: a person's capability and power under law to engage in a particular undertaking or transaction or to maintain a particular status or relationship with another.

legal responsibilities: requirements for organizations to reach goals within legal constraints.

legality: adherence to or observance of the law.

legislature: an officially elected or otherwise selected body of people vested with the responsibility and power to make laws for a political unit, such as a state or nation.

levels of branding: the levels used to assess consumer enthusiasm or intensity toward a specific brand, starting with brand recognition and brand preference, on through to brand insistence and brand loyalty.

leveraging: developing an integrated plan that specifies the role promotional tools will play and the extent to which each will be used.

liaison: the third interpersonal role a sport manager must fulfill, which involves developing and cultivating relationships with individuals and groups in other departments or from different organizations.

lifestyle marketing: type of marketing technique in which the company attempts to cut through all the other selling messages by appealing to consumers who have or desire the lifestyle depicted in the sport sponsorship relationship.

limited duty: the limited responsibility of management to protect those involved in an event who are at risk for injury, such as the obligation of baseball franchises to protect their fans from foul balls.

limited liability company (LLC): a business entity formed upon filing articles of organization with the proper state authorities and paying all fees; LLCs provide the limited liability to their members and are taxed like a partnership, preventing double taxation.

linguistics: the study of the nature, structure, and variation of language, including phonetics, phonology, morphology, syntax, semantics, sociolinguistics, and pragmatics.

litigation: the process of filing a lawsuit so that a court can resolve the disagreement.

marginal cost: how much more an individual has to spend to get more of what he or she wants, without worrying about what already has been spent.

marketing objectives: the reasons or goals behind a particular promotion or marketing campaign that clearly identify the desired results.

mediation: the submission of a dispute to a disinterested third person who intervenes between the parties in an attempt to settle their dispute without going to court.

mediator: the third party in a mediation who communicates with all parties to the dispute, presents proposals from each party to the other, and facilitates resolution of the dispute, if possible.

message credibility: believability or trustworthiness associated specifically with the source and content of a message.

minors: in legal terms, persons under the age of 18.

mission statement: guidelines that outline the parameters for operating a venue and provide the basis for the development of goals and objectives for the venue.

monitor: an informational role filled by the sport manager in which he or she must search the internal and external environment for information that could affect the organization.

monopoly: a company or group having exclusive control over a commercial activity.

moral behavior: the execution of an act deemed right or wrong.

moral development: a process of growth in which a person's capacity to reason morally is developed through cognitive maturation and experiences.

moral reasoning: the decision process in which an individual determines whether a course of action is right or wrong.

morals: the fundamental baseline values that dictate appropriate behavior within a culture or society.

municipal bonds, or **munis:** bonds in the capital market issued by state and local governments to finance their capital spending programs for building arenas, stadiums, parking lots, and infrastructure upgrades, including roads, water/sewer, utility right of way, and other utility needs. The bonds are issued by municipalities, subdivisions of states; they are tax exempt because the interest investors receive is exempt from federal taxation.

myopia: in sport marketing, the result of sport personnel focusing solely on the sport product and not considering the needs and wants of consumers.

myth: a popular belief or story that has become associated with a person, institution, or occurrence, especially one considered to illustrate a cultural ideal, which may often seem like fact but is not always the case.

National Governing Bodies (NGBs): respective organizations that develop sport on a national level; e.g., USA Track and Field.

National Olympic Committees (NOCs): individual countries representing the IOC that are responsible for promoting the Olympic Movement nationally, developing athletes, and sending delegations to the Games.

natural rights: rights that are not derived from any government, but are God-given and inherent to all people.

negligence: the failure to exercise ordinary care, or the degree of care that the law requires, by acting differently than a person of ordinary care would have acted under the same or similar circumstances.

negotiation: a process involving formal or informal discussions in order to reach an agreement.

negotiator: a decisional role filled by the sport manager in which he or she is responsible for conferring with employees and work groups located within the organization, as well as those that are on the outside.

NFL Europe: extension league created after the World League of American Football (WLAF) disbanded after two seasons, which was reintroduced in 1995 in European cities only; currently consists of six teams in the Netherlands, Germany, and Scotland.

niche events: events specially suited to a person's interests, abilities, or nature; appealing to a distinct segment of a market.

noise: the collective dissonance caused by radio, television, the Internet, billboards, print advertisements, etc. that helps desensitize the consumer to all messages.

non-price promotions: publicity other than price promotions that are designed to make the activity or event more attractive and enjoyable to consumers, such as giveaways, fireworks, autograph-signing sessions, and concerts.

non-variable cost: a cost that does not vary depending on production or sales levels, such as rent, property, insurance, or interest expense; also referred to as fixed cost.

objectives: the activities to be implemented to reach the overall goal, sometimes called action strategies.

observational studies: a data-gathering procedure used primarily in the psychology and sociology fields in which information is obtained by observing and recording subjects' behavior without their knowledge.

offer and acceptance: a process that involves the involved parties making a series of proposals to the other until the negotiations culminate with an agreement.

Office of Civil Rights (OCR): the division of the Department of Education has been charged with enforcing Title IX, which is the law that prohibits sex discrimination in education agencies that receive federal funding.

Older Workers Benefit Protection Act of 1990 (OWBPA): amendment to the Americans with Disabilities Act of 1990 meant to include a focus on age discrimination and loss of workplace benefits. The OWBPA also provided for older worker protection in the area of protocol establishment that must be followed when employers are asked to waive their rights when filing settlement claims regarding age discrimination.

Olympic Games: a group of modern international athletic contests, revived in 1896 by Pierre de Coubertin, held as separate winter and summer competitions every four years in a different city.

Olympic Marketing Programme: the driving force for the financial stability of the Olympic Movement, which produces revenues through broadcasting rights, sponsorship, ticketing, licensing, and other means.

The Olympic Movement: the term used to refer to the incomparable growth of international exposure, worldwide audience appeal, and multicultural activities that draw the attention of virtually every demographic of the Olympic Games.

The Olympic Program (TOP): introduced for the first time in the 1984 Los Angeles Olympic Games, this program, operated by the IOC, handles Olympic sponsorship agreements and gives sponsors exclusive rights to associate with the Olympic Games and use all Olympic properties.

operating expense: expense arising in the normal course of running a business, such as an office electricity bill.

opportunity cost: what one gives up in turn for obtaining what one wants.

Organizing Committee of the Olympic Games (OCOG): formed after a city has been awarded the honor and responsibility of hosting the Olympic and Paralympic Games, its role is to handle all operational aspects of the Games and to ultimately put on the events.

over-commercialization: the overwhelming presence of commercial business, marketing, etc. that may be so saturated as to deter consumers.

paid internships: a paid appointment in which the individual undergoes supervised practical training for future employment.

participant-oriented organizations: organizations often managed by individuals with very specialized skill sets, such as municipal parks, YMCAs, recreation departments, collegiate recreation settings, and special events.

partnership: a company owned by two or more individuals who have entered into an agreement.

perception: recognition and interpretation of sensory stimuli based chiefly on memory.

personal credibility: believability or trustworthiness associated specifically with a person or organization's character or past actions.

phenomenology: the study of distinct phenomena, ideas, and events; a description, history, or explanation of phenomena.

philanthropic responsibilities: requirement for organizations to give back to their communities.

planning: formulating a scheme or program for the accomplishment or attainment of a specific goal.

podcast: a digital media file distributed over the Internet using syndication feeds for playback on portable media players and computers.

postconventional: the third of Kohlberg's three stages of moral reasoning, in which the individual's values are formed independently of social norms.

pouring rights: the exclusive ability to sell soft drinks, bottled water, and beer in a facility.

precedent: a judicial decision that may be used as a standard in subsequent similar cases.

preconventional: the first of Kohlberg's three stages of moral reasoning, which is characterized by a separation between conventions and the individual.

The Pregnancy Discrimination Act: an amendment to Title VII of the Civil Rights Act of 1964, which provides protection for pregnancy-based discrimination including pregnancy, childbirth, and pregnancy-related medical conditions.

present value: the value of what a cash flow to be received in the future is worth in today's dollars.

price promotions: type of publicity in which the actual cost of consuming an event is manipulated or lowered to encourage people to attend.

primary skills: in sport management terms, these are the skills necessary to direct employees toward the achievement of established goals and objectives, without which a sport manager would be ineffective.

private law: law that governs the relationship among private citizens.

private seat licenses (PSLs): an amenity offered at certain venues in which the purchaser obtains exclusive use of his or her own private seat(s).

pro forma statements: statements based on hypothetical figures used as a means of assessing how assets might be managed under differing future scenarios.

procedural law: the method of enforcing rights and obligations given to citizens by substantive law.

product adoption process: an extension of the AIDA concept that awareness builds interest and knowledge of a brand's associated benefits, which in effect, creates an image in the mind of the consumer.

products liability: liability imposed on a manufacturer or seller for a defective and unreasonably dangerous product.

product purchase intentions: a key sales objective that is most often measured to assess consumers' tendencies and perceptions when buying certain products.

proxemics: the study of how individuals communicate through their use of space.

psychographics: the use of demographics to study and measure attitudes, values, lifestyles, and opinions, as for marketing purposes; often refer to consumers' state-of-mind, exploring the likes and dislikes of consumers and using the similarities to create the segments.

psychological: of, relating to, or arising from the mind or emotions.

public assembly facilities: assembly halls, conference centers, stadiums, arenas, etc. that are available to fulfill the needs of public meetings, conventions, and conferences, as well as host a number of different events such as athletic contests, concerts, conventions and trade shows.

public good: the well-being of the general public.

public law: law that governs the relationship between citizens and their government.

public relations: a program designed to influence the opinions of people within a target market through responsible and acceptable performance, based on mutually satisfactory two-way communication.

racism: discrimination or prejudice based on race.

reasonably prudent person standard: standard applied by the court that will determine if the defendant acted as a reasonably prudent person would have acted under the same or similar circumstances.

recall: the ability of a spectator to remember and correctly identify a sponsor's brand without input or prompting.

recognition: the ability of a spectator to correctly identify the brand of a sponsor from a list.

Recreational Use statutes: legislation that provides liability protection to owners and operators of recreational facilities by placing responsibility for injury on the participant who voluntarily assumed the risk; the statutes cover activities such as equestrian activities, snow skiing, roller skating, whitewater rafting, snowmobiling, amusement rides, and, in a few cases, provides protection for "any sport or recreational opportunity."

reflective learning: an educational philosophy meant to engage one's knowledge about the world and others critically and analytically, including self-assessment of teaching goals, responsibilities, and effectiveness.

regional multiplier: the value multiplied by direct spending to estimate total spending, or economic benefit, which is used to measure how many times money changes hands in the community before it leaves or leaks out of the region.

relational: of or arising from kinship; indicating or constituting relation.

renewal: the act of restoring or resuming a contract.

request for proposal (RFP): an invitation for providers of a product or service to bid on the right to supply that product or service to the individual or entity that issued the RFP.

resource allocator: a decisional role filled by a sport manager in which he or she distributes organizational resources to different employees or work groups.

return on investment: the income that an investment provides in a year.

revenue bonds: bond issued by a municipality to finance a specific public works project and supported by the revenues of that project.

revenue budget: a calculation of projected future revenue used to make planning and management decisions.

risk management: the process to reduce or limit risk exposure in a venue.

risk management plan: a document defining how reducing or limiting risk exposure will be implemented in the context of a particular project.

Robert's Rules of Order: procedures that assure legislative fairness, maximum participation, and an orderly process by participants, while protecting individuals from domination by certain vocal sub-groups.

S-Corporation: a C Corporation—also known as a standard business corporation—that files IRS form 2553 to elect a special tax status with the IRS.

Scalar Principle: principle referring to the chain of command that denotes a clear line of authority from the top to the bottom of the organization.

scheduling: the reservation process and coordination of all events to the venue's available time.

scholarly sport practitioner (SSP): the next-generation evolution in the sport industry's work force, which understands how to unite sports organizations through management practices and utilizes the power of knowledge to build a culture of continuous learning for successful organizational and stakeholder management.

screening: to examine (a job applicant, for example) systematically in order to determine suitability.

segmentation: the process of dividing large, unlike groups of consumers into smaller, more defined groups of people who share similar characteristics.

semantics: the meaning or interpretation of a word and/or sentence.

semi-variable cost: a cost that has a fixed cost component and a variable expense component.

sexism: discrimination based on gender.

sexual harassment: employment discrimination consisting of unwelcome verbal or physical conduct directed at an employee because of his or her sex.

Sherman Antitrust Act: an 1890 federal antitrust law intended to control or prohibit monopolies by forbidding certain practices that restrain competition.

simple interest: the interest calculated on a principal sum, not compounded on earned interest.

situational approach: in the study of leadership (also referred to as "contingency theories"), this approach resulted in an understanding that the traits and behaviors identified previously would be successful only to the degree to which any particular situation allowed; intervening, or moderating, factors were considered in this approach.

social institution: any place where there is a set of rules for behavior; examples include churches, colleges, and places of business.

sociodemographic: of or relating to characteristics of a particular group or demographic, such as certain age groups, people of the same income levels, gender, etc.

sociolinguistics: the impact that differing social and/or cultural groups have on the meaning and interpretation of language.

sociological analysis: thorough examination of a social institution or societal segment as a self-contained entity or in relation to society as a whole.

sole proprietorship: a company owned by one person

sovereign immunity: an exemption that precludes bringing a suit against the sovereign state without the state's consent; often known by the maxim "the king can do no wrong."

Span of Management: principle that refers to the number of employees reporting to a specific manager.

spokesperson: an informational role filled by the sport manager in which he or she communicates information to groups that are outside the organization.

sponsorship: the provision of resources (e.g., money, people, equipment) by an organization (the sponsor) directly to an individual, authority or body (the sponsee), to enable the latter to pursue some activity in return for benefits contemplated in terms of the spon-

sor's promotion strategy, and which can be expressed in terms of corporate, marketing, or media objectives.

sponsorship activation: the idea that for every dollar spent on a sponsorship fee, an equivalent dollar is typically spent in the promotion of the sponsorship.

sport sociologist: one who studies human social behavior in sport, including the analysis of sport as an industry, the political and cultural implications of sport, sport and globalization, the relationship between gender, class and economics, deviance in sport, and the social organization of sport.

sport sociology: the method of analyzing sport from a cultural perspective that concerns itself mainly with how humans relate to each other in the sport context, how values affect these relationships, and how humans organize sport activities.

sportsmanship: conduct and attitude considered as befitting participants in sports, especially fair play, courtesy, striving spirit, and grace in losing.

standard: a requirement of moral conduct.

state action: an action in which the federal or state government is responsible for the specific conduct about which the plaintiff complains.

state court system: court systems that generally hear matters that occur within the boundaries of the state, and involve disputes that involve state law.

statement of cash flow: a financial statement that show the sources and uses of cash for a business over a certain period of time.

statutes: particular laws passed by the U.S. Congress or a state legislature that declare, command, or prohibit some conduct, or require citizens to act in a certain manner.

step cost: a recurring or non-recurring expense for goods and services that are either non-essential or more expensive than necessary; examples include entertainment expenses, wellness programs, and speakers; also referred to as discretionary expense.

strict liability: liability that is imposed without a finding of fault .

substantive law: the law that defines, describes, or creates legal rights and obligations.

Super League: a proposal, also referred to as G-14, offered by the European football (soccer) industry to come closer to the American model, which would include football giants like Ajax Amsterdam, Manchester United, AC Milan, and Real Madrid.

supply: the quantity of a product that an owner is willing to offer or make available at a given price.

Supreme Court: the highest federal court in the United States, consisting of nine justices and having jurisdiction over all other courts in the nation.

surveys: paper forms used to gather a sample of data or opinions considered to be representative of a whole group, sometimes referred to as questionnaires.

symbiotic: a relationship of mutual benefit or dependence.

target market: the group of people at which all marketing efforts are aimed.

technical skills: in sport management terms, these skills involve a knowledge of operations, activities, and processes necessary to accomplish organizational goals and objectives.

teleology: a doctrine explaining phenomena by their ends or purposes; a focus on the consequences of an action.

terminal values: in ethical theory, the ends toward which one is striving.

time-switchers: people who plan to attend an event, but cancel or change time in order to attend to something else.

timetable: a chart used to provide the schedule of tasks and when they need to be completed; can be seen as a countdown to an event.

time value of money: the idea that a dollar now is worth more than dollar in the future, even after adjusting for inflation, because a dollar now can earn interest or other appreciation until the time the dollar in the future would be received.

Title VII: law passed in 1964 that protects employees and prospective employees from discrimination by making it unlawful for an employer to discriminate against a person in employment activities (i.e., hiring, firing, compensation, promotion, classification) based on race, color, religion, sex, or national origin; formally referred to as Title VII of the Civil Rights Act of 1964.

Title IX: law passed in 1972 as part of the Educational Amendments Act that prohibits sex discrimination in education agencies that receive federal funding; formally referred to Title IX of the Education Amendments of 1972.

TOP sponsors: companies that have been granted a four-year contract deal with The Olympic Partner Programme that includes both the Summer and Winter Games; they are granted the right to Olympic affiliation in every participating country with worldwide exclusivity in their product category.

tort: a civil wrong—other than a breach of contract—for which an injured party can recover damages.

tort claims acts: statutes in which the state has agreed to accept liability for certain tort claims.

tortfeasor: a person who commits a tort.

trademark: word, phrase, logo, or other graphic symbol used by a manufacturer to distinguish its product from those of others.

trait theories: some of the earliest systematic attempts to conceptualize leadership, these approaches focused on the characteristics, or attributes, that distinguished leaders from non-leaders; traits under investigation included physical characteristics (e.g., height, appearance), personality traits (e.g., arrogance, self-esteem), and general ability traits (e.g., intelligence, insight, energy).

trial court: the court before which issues of fact and law are tried and first determined as distinguished from an appellate court.

UEFA Champions League: the Union of European Football Associations' football (soccer) league that is open to each national association's domestic champions, as well as clubs who finish just behind them in the domestic championship table.

UEFA Cup: championship title of the UEFA Champions League.

Uniform Athlete Agents Act: act that provides for the uniform registration, certification, and background check of sports agents seeking to represent student athletes who are or may be eligible to participate in intercollegiate sports; also imposes specified contract terms on these agreements to the benefit of student athletes, and provides education institutions with a right to notice along with a civil cause of action for damages resulting from a breach of specified duties.

Unity of Command: principle that states that an employee should only have one boss to which he or she reports.

U.S. Congress: the national legislative body of the United States, consisting of the Senate and the House of Representatives.

U.S. Constitution: the fundamental law of the United States, framed in 1787, ratified in 1789, and variously amended since then, which prescribes the nature, functions, and limits of the government.

U.S. District Courts: courts that operate essentially the same as state trial courts, providing a trial of the case before a judge and jury; also called federal trial courts. There are 94 throughout the U.S., with at least one located in every state.

utilitarianism: an ethical theory whereby morality is assessed by whether or not the action creates the greatest good for the greatest number of people.

value: worth in usefulness or importance to the possessor.

variable expenses: unavoidable periodic cost that does not have a constant value, such as electric, gas, and water bills.

verdict: the finding of a jury in a trial.

vertical integration: the degree to which a firm owns its upstream suppliers and its downstream buyers.

Volunteer Protection Act: act that provides protection to volunteers, employees, and the volunteer organization itself, so long as the organization has insurance in the amount required by the statute to cover losses sustained by injured participants.

waived: given up; relinquished.

warranty: a promise or guarantee that products will comply with a certain standard.

welfare: health, happiness, and good fortune; well-being.

word of mouth: advertising through personal recommendations among consumers.

workers' compensation: compensation for death or injury suffered by a worker in the course of his or her employment.

World Cup of Hockey: an international ice hockey tournament, introduced in 2004 in four European cities and three North American cities, which included eight of the world's ice hockey powerhouses.

World League of American Football (WLAF): extension league introduced in 1991 that provided a platform for the NFL to showcase the game of American Football to those outside the U.S., especially in Europe.

Writ of Certiorari: a common law writ issued by a superior court to one of inferior jurisdiction demanding the record of a particular case.

Index

80/20 principle, 156, 299

A
Abbott and Costello, 31
Abdul-Wahad, Tariq, 243
action sports, 289–290, 299
ad valorem taxes, 120, 299
administration, 8–9
Administrative Rules and Regulations, 193–194, 299
Age Discrimination in Employment Act (ADEA), 20–21, 23, 299
agent, 204
agents, athlete, 201, 299, 310
AIDA (Awareness, Interest, Desire, and Action), 147, 155, 299, 307
alternative dispute resolution (ADR), 189, 299
Amateur Athletic Union (AAU), 214
ambush marketing, 151–152, 299
Americans with Disabilities Act (ADA), 23, 200, 299
Angelou, Maya, 20
appeal, 195–196, 299
arbitration, 189, 299
arbitrator, 299
Aristotle, 189
Arizona Sports Summit Accord, 227–228, 299
Armstrong, Lance, 10, 153, 156
Arnold, Mark J., 265
articulation, 33
assumed risk, 190, 201, 299
Athlete Agent statutes, 201, 299
Attribution Theory, 61
Avolio, Bruce J., 62

B
balance sheet. *See* financial statements
Barnum, P. T., 162
Baseball World Cup Tournament, 250, 299
Bass, Bernard M., 61, 62
Bearman v. University of Notre Dame, 177
behavioral approach. *See* leadership
Bellizzi, J., 270
benefits, 146
Biggio, Craig, 238
Billington, Ray, 226
Bonds, Barry, 19, 187, 225
booking, 173, 300
Bosman ruling, 256, 300
brand
    equity, 147, 300
    insistence, 155, 300
    loyalty, 155, 300
    preference, 155, 300
    recognition, 155, 300
Brand, Myles, 322
breach of warranty, 203, 300
Bridges, Francis J., 46, 213
Brown v. Board of Education, 194
Bryant, Kobe, 16, 19
Bryman, Alan, 60
business financial management, 93
"buy in," 150–152, 300

C
Cannon, Andrew J., 265
career opportunities
    in international sport, 258–268
Carroll, Archie B., 235
case study method, 191, 300
cash budgets, 105–106, 300
cash flow, 80, 92–94, 115–117, 300
cash flow statement. *See* financial statements
casuals, 82, 300
Certificates of Participation (COPs), 119, 120, 300
Chalip, Laurence H., 53
charisma, 60–61, 62, 64
Charitable Immunity, 201, 300
charitable organization, 201, 300
Cheek, Joey, 238
Chelladurai, Packianathan, 51, 63
circuits, 196, 300
Civil Rights Act of 1964, 200
Clayton Antitrust Act, 200, 300
Clemens, Roger, 193, 237
club seating, 98–100
clutter, 151, 300
Coco, Malcolm, 266
Collective Bargaining Agreement (CBA), 192, 300
Commission on Sport Management Accreditation (COSMA), 7, 300
commitment, 124–125, 300
communication (interpersonal and small group)
    barriers to, 31–32, 299
    emotional content, 30–31, 302
    flow of, 32–33
        downward, 32–33
        lateral, 33
        upward, 33
    keys to, 30–31
    listening, 34
    message content, 30, 301

non-verbal, 33, 34–35
tempo, 33
verbal, 33–34
volume, 34
communication (mass media)
Internet, 37–38
"The Medium Is the Message," 35
print media, 35–36
radio, 36
sport media, 35
sports information, 38–39
television, 36–37
communication (styles), 64–66
six main ways people communicate, 65–66
competitive balance and imbalance. *See* economics
compliance, 234, 301
compound interest, 108–109, 301
conceptual skills, 51, 301
concessions, 102–103
conduct, 234, 301
Conger, Jay A., 61
Congress, 192–193, 310
consideration, 198, 301
Constitution. *See* U.S. Constitution
constraints, 45
consumer escalator, 156, 301
contemporary theories. *See* leadership
content, control of, 288–289
content (emotional). *See* communication
content (message). *See* communication
contingency approach. *See* leadership
contract, 197, 301
Cook, S. J., 272
core product, 127
corporate social responsibility, 235–237, 301
corporation, 95–96, 301
Cosell, Howard, 124
Coubertin, Pierre de, 244, 245
counteroffer, 198, 301
Courts of Appeals, 195–197, 301
credibility, 30, 301
message, 30, 305
personal, 30, 307
crime, 192, 301
Crompton, John, 82, 84, 87
Crosset, Todd, 232
crowd management, 178, 301
culture, 17, 301
"curse of the Bambino," 125

D
damages, 201–202, 301
Davis, Timothy, 190–191
decision making, 51, 56–57, 106, 232, 301
defection, 147, 149, 301
demographics, 133, 301
deontology, 227, 301
Department of Education, 200, 302
depreciation, 113, 302
DeSensi, Joy T., 227
direct spending, 79–80, 302

directing, 44
director
of finance, 172, 302
of marketing, 172, 302
of operations, 172, 302
discretionary expense, 107, 302
discrimination, 20–21, 302
age, 23
disability, 23
race/color, 21
religious, 22–23
sex (gender), 21–22, 303
Disney Corporation, 214
disseminator, 55, 302
disturbance handler, 56, 302
diversity, 20, 302
and sport, 20–23
of citizenship, 196, 302
division of labor, 210, 302
Drucker, Peter, 43
drug testing, 248, 302
Duly, J. S., 274
Dunn, Warrick, 238

E
economic profitability, 281–283
economics
benefit, 79, 80, 87, 302
competitive advantage, 76–78
competitive balance, 75–76
definition of, 71
impact, 79–88
impact in sport, uses of, 81
impact study abuses, 82–83
intangible benefits, 83–84
is a social science, 88–89
opportunity and marginal costs, 72–73, 305, 307
responsibilities, 235, 302
steps to completing impact study, 81
supply and demand, 73–75
English Premiership, 256, 302
entrepreneur, 56, 302
entrepreneurship, 302
entrepreneurship, areas of
action sports, 289–290
fantasy sports, 290–291
environment, 31–32, 302
epistemology, 284, 302
equilibrium price, 74, 302
equitable treatment, 234, 302
ESPN, 36, 288–289
Establishment Clause, 199, 302
ethics
and morals, 226
code of, 233–234, 300
decision making, 232
definition of, 226, 303
dilemmas (challenges), 231–232, 302
moral development and reasoning, 229–231
personal and professional, 228–229
responsibilities, 236, 302

social responsibility, 235–238, 283
theories, 226–227
values, 227
values clarification exercise, 228
values in sport, 227–228
Euro 2004, 257, 303
European Union, 255, 256, 258, 303
evaluation, 148, 303
evaluations, intern, 275–276
exclusivity, 147, 303
expense budgets, 104, 107, 303
explicit expenditures, 72, 303

F

facilities development, 285
facility design, 285
fad, 303
fantasy sports, 290–291, 303
federal court system, 196–197, 303
federal question, 196, 303
federal trail courts, 196, 303
feedback, 33
figurehead, 55, 303
final portfolio reports, 276, 303
finance
    accounting as a partner, 93–94
    budgets and analysis, 105–107
    essentials, 108–110
    importance in sport, 93
    organizational structure, 95–96
    revenue sources, 96–102
financial considerations, 255, 303
financial statements, 103–105
    balance sheet, 103, 299
    cash flow statement, 103–104
    income statement, 103–104, 304
    pro forma statements, 104–105, 307
fit, 150, 292, 303
fixed cost, 107, 303
flow of communication. *See* communication
foundations, 303
France, Bill, 125
Freedom of Information Act (FOIA), 94
French, John, 64
future value, 109, 303

G

G-14, 258, 303
Garvey, Ed, 204
Gasol, Pau, 251
Gault, Jack, 266
Geist, Alan L., 233
general liability, 272, 273, 303
General Obligation (GO) bonds, 120, 303
generally accepted accounting principles (GAAP), 103, 303
Giamatti, Bart, 188
gigantism, 248, 304
global sport industry
    career opportunities in international sport, 258–261
    challenges in the European sport industry, 258
    challenges in the international expansion of U.S. sport, 255

international expansion of U.S. sport, 249–255
    the Athens 2004 Olympic games, 247–248
    the European sport industry, 255–256
    the Olympic movement, 259
globalization, 244, 304
goals, 172, 304
Goldwyn, Samuel, 197
Gore, Al, 34
grassroots programs, 251, 304
Gravity Games, 149–150
Greenwell, T. Christopher, 233
gross negligence, 202, 304
growth in sport, areas of
    control of content, 288–289
    facilities development, 285
    facility design, 285
    naming rights, 286
    niche events, 286–287
    technology development, 288
Gruden, John, 34

H

Hallal v. RDV Sports, Inc., 272
Hamm, Mia, 237
Hardy, Stephen, 124, 154
Hawk, Tony, 289
hazing, 202, 304
Henry, L. G., 270
Hill, David, 282
Hite, R., 270
"home rule," 218
House, Robert J., 59, 61
Huizenga, Wayne, 236
human skills, 51, 304
Hums, Mary A., 52, 53, 208, 232

I

idealized influence, 62, 304
image, 304
    enhancement, 150, 304
implicit expenditures, 72, 304
income statement. *See* financial statements
Indiana Sports Corporation (ISC), 79
indirect spending, 80, 304
individualized consideration, 62, 304
induced spending, 80, 304
induction, 59, 304
inspirational motivation, 62, 304
intellectual stimulation, 62, 304
intermediate appeals court, 195, 304
International Association of Assembly Managers (IAAM), 170, 304
international environment, 244, 304
International Events Group (IEG), 98
International Federations (IFs), 245, 304
International Olympic Committee (IOC), 220, 245, 304
    IOC commissions, 246, 305
International Paralympic Committee (IPC), 246, 259
internships
    evaluating the student intern, 273–274
    examination of policies, 269–270

internships (cont.)
    legal concerns, 272–273
    linking theoretical to practical, 268–269
    networking, 266–268
    paid, 277, 307
    policies, 269, 304
    screening and selecting the site, 270–272
interviews, 24, 304
involvement, 124–125, 304

J

James, LeBron, 237
Jerry Maguire, 204
job descriptions, 181, 305
Jones, Adam (Pacman), 19
Jones, E. A., 269
Jones, Marion, 19, 225, 248
Jordan, Jeremy, 233
Joy, David, 83
Joyce Julius and Associates, 157
judgment, 195, 305

K

Kant, Immanuel, 225
Kanungo, Rabindra N., 61
Katwala, Sunder, 209
KDKA radio, 36
Kimball, David C., 211
kinesics, 34, 305
Knight, Phil, 58
Kohlberg, Lawrence, 229, 230

L

LaFeber, Walter, 255
Landis, Floyd, 19
Lanham Act. *See* Federal Trademark Act of 1946
Lapham, Lewis H., 91
LaRussa, Tony, 237
law
    administrative and statutory, 199–201
    case, 194, 300
    civil, 192
    classifications of, 192–193
    common, 194–301
    constitutional, 198–199
    contract, 197–198
    criminal, 192, 301
    definition of, 189, 305
    of demand, 73, 305
    practice areas, 194
    private, 192, 307
    procedural, 192, 307
    public, 192, 308
    sources in the United States, 193–194
    substantive, 192, 309
    the study of, 191
    tort, 201–202
    what it is, 189–190
Law of Demand, 73, 305
Le Gougne, Marie-Reine, 233
leader, 55, 305
leadership, 58–59

behavioral approach, 59, 299
contemporary theories, 60, 301
contingency approach, 59
evolution of leadership theory, 59–60
five primary sources of power, 64
multidimensional model of, 62
situational approach, 59, 309
transactional, 62
transformational, 61–63
legal
    capacity, 197, 305
    responsibilities, 236, 305
legality, 198, 305
legislature, 193, 305
Leslie, Lisa, 237
levels of branding, 155, 305
leveraging, 156, 305
liaison, 55, 305
licensing, 101–102
lifestyle marketing, 153, 305
limited duty, 190, 305
Limited Liability Company (LLC), 96, 305
Lincoln, Abraham, 173
linguistics, 31, 305
    components of, 31
litigation, 190, 305
Lowther, Malcolm A., 268
Lussier, Robert N., 211
luxury suites, 98–100

M

MacLean, Joanne C., 208
Mahony, Daniel F., 233
Major League Baseball (MLB), 249–251
Malthus, Thomas, 88
management
    functions of, 44–50
    roles, 54–57
        decisional, 56
        informational, 55
        interpersonal, 55
    skills, 51–54
    versus leadership, 57–63
marginal cost. *See* economics
marketing objectives, 146, 305
Martin, Bill, 220
Mason, James, 5
Matsui, Hideki, 250
McCallister, Linda, 65
McCormick, D. W., 274
McGwire, Mark, 73
McLuhan, Marshall, 35
McNamara, Carter, 232
media revenue, 100–101
mediation, 189, 305
mediator, 189, 305
merchandising, 101–102
Miller, L. K., 273
Ming, Yao, 251, 252, 253, 259
minors, 197, 305
Mintzberg, Henry, 54, 55, 56

mission statement, 213, 305
Monday Night Football, 100
monitor, 55, 306
monitoring, 49–50
    concurrent, 50
    feedback, 50
    preliminary, 50
monopoly, 200, 306
Moorman, Anita M., 52
morals
    behavior, 229, 306
    definition of, 226, 306
    development of, 229, 306
    reasoning, 229, 306
    stages of development, 229–231
        conventional, 230, 301
        postconventional, 230–231, 307
        preconventional, 229–230, 307
    See also ethics
Moreno, Arturo, 125
Morgan, William, 213
motivation, 48–49
motivation, employee, 152–153
Mullin, Bernard J., 9, 124, 154
municipal bonds (munis), 119, 306
myopia, 150, 306
myths
    in American sport, 16–17
    most frequently cited, 2–4

N

Naismith, James, 213
Najera, Eduardo, 243
naming rights, 286
    sectional, 286
Nash, Steve, 243
NASSM/NASPE, 7
National Association of Sports Commissions (NASC), 84–85
National Basketball Association (NBA), 251–252
National Collegiate Athletic Association (NCAA), 38, 92, 95,
    101, 207, 213, 218–220
National Federation of State High School Associations (NFHS),
    208, 213, 214–217
National Football League (NFL), 75–79, 221–222, 252–253
    NFL Europe, 253, 306
National Governing Bodies (NGBs), 246, 306
National Hockey League (NHL), 254–255
National Olympic Committees (NOCs), 245, 306
negligence, 202, 306
negotiation, 189, 306
negotiator, 56–57, 306
Nelson, Don, 243
newspapers, 35
niche events, 286–287, 306
Nike, 157, 259
noise, 151, 306
Noll, Roger G., 84
Nomo, Hideo, 250
non-price promotions, 130–132, 306
non-variable cost, 107, 306
Nowitzki, Dirk, 243

O

objectives, 44, 172, 306
    marketing, 146, 305
    sales, 154
observational studies, 24, 306
offer and acceptance, 197–198, 306
Office of Civil Rights (OCR), 200, 306
Older Workers Benefit Protection Act (OWBPA), 23, 306
Olympics
    games, 245, 306
    marketing programme, 246, 307
    movement, 245–249, 307
    The Olympic Partner (TOP) program, 246–247, 307
O'Malley, Walter, 5
O'Neal, Shaquille, 92–93, 163
operating expense, 106, 307
opportunity cost. See economics
organizing, 46
Organizing Committee of the Olympic Games (OCOG), 246, 307
over-commercialization, 248, 307
Ozanian, Michael, 1

P

Parker, R. S., 272
Parker, Tony, 251
parking, 102–103, 175
Parks, Janet B., 9
participant-oriented organizations, 162, 307
partnership, 95, 307
Pastore, Donna L., 233
Payne, Billy, 83
perception, 32, 207
Perez, Florentino, 257
personal financial management, 92, 300
Pettijohn, C., 272
Pfeffer, Jeffrey, 64
phenomenology, 284–285, 307
philanthropic responsibilities, 237, 307
Phillip Morris, 153
Pianko, Daniel, 265
planning, 30, 44–46, 307
Pope, Nigel, 145
pouring rights, 175, 307
precedent, 194, 307
Pregnancy Discrimination Act, 22, 307
present value, 109, 307
price promotions, 130, 307
primary skills, 51, 307
private seat licenses (PSLs), 173, 307
pro forma statements. See financial statements
problem-solving methodology, 52
product adoption process, 155, 307
product purchase intentions, 154, 307
products liability, 203, 307
proxemics, 34, 307
psychic income, 83–84
psychographics, 134, 308
psychological barriers, 32
public assembly facilities, 119, 162, 308
public good, 238, 308
public relations, 174, 308

Q

qualitative measures, 49
quantitative measures, 49
Quarterman, Jerome, 9

R

racism, 20, 308
radio, 36
Railey, Jim H., 52
Ramirez, Manny, 237
Raven, Bertram H., 64
"reasonably prudent person" standard, 202, 308
recall, 157, 308
recognition, 32, 308
recreational use statutes, 201, 308
Reding, Viviane, 248
Redington, John, 266
Reebok, 252, 259
reflective learning, 273, 308
regional multiplier, 80, 308
relational (leadership), 58, 308
renewal, 148, 308
request for proposal (RFP), 170, 308
resource allocators, 56, 308
resume, 292–293
return on investment (ROI), 146, 308
revenue bonds, 119, 308
revenue budgets, 106–107, 308
risk management, 175–176, 202–203, 308
    plan, 178, 202, 308
Robbins, S. P., 289
Robert's Rules of Order, 209, 308
Rodriguez, Alex, 72–73
Rogers, Will, 265
Rokeach, Milton, 227–228
Rolnick, Art, 83, 88
Roosevelt, Theodore, 218
Roquemore, Libby L., 46, 213
Rosenberg, Danny, 227
Rosentraub, Mark S., 82

S

S-Corporation, 96, 308
Sampson, David, 2
"sanity code," 218
Santa Fe Independent School District v. Doe, 192, 199
Scalar Principle, 210, 308
Schaaf, Phil, 254–255
scheduling, 173, 308
Scherr, Jim, 220
Schlager, Tammy, 266
scholarly sport practitioner, 284–285, 308
Schultz, Howard, 125
Scott, Mary E., 266
screening, 270–272, 308
segmentation, 133, 308
Selig, Bud, 76, 250
semantics, 31, 309
semi-variable cost, 107, 309
sexism, 20, 309
sexual harrassment, 22, 273, 309

Sherman Antitrust Act, 200, 309
simple interest, 108, 309
Simpson, O. J., 19
situational approach. *See* leadership
SLEEPE model, 53
SMARTS, 6
Smith, Aaron, 235, 244
Smith, Red, 161
Smith, R. K., 187
SMPRC, 6
Sobek, Joe, 213
social institution, 15, 309
social responsibility, 283
sociolinguistics, 31, 309
sociological analysis, 15, 309
sole proprietorship, 95, 309
Solomon, Jerry, 181
sovereign immunity, 201, 309
span of management, 210–211, 309
spokesperson, 55, 309
sponsorship, 97–98, 145–147, 309
    activation, 156, 309
Sport Business in the Global Marketplace (Westerbeek & Smith), 244
sport facility and event management
    event management—the process, 179–180
    facility/venue management, 162–170
    location, facilities, and equipment, 182–183
    public and media relations, 173–174
    types of venues, 170–171
    venue operations, 173–178
    venue organization, 171–173
sport governance
    importance of, 208
        professional sport organizations, 221–222
        the "how," 210–213
        the "what," 208
        the "when," 213–221
        the "where," 221–223
        the "who," 209–210
        the "why," 208–209
sport industry, challenges in European, 258
sport industry, unique aspects of
    career paths, 10
    customer base (fans), 10–11
    finance, 10
    marketing, 9
    social influence of sport, 10
    sport venues, 11
sport law. *See* law
sport management
    problems with the name, 8–9
    why it matters, 15–24
Sport Management Arts and Sciences Society (SMARTS), 6
Sport Management Program Review Council (SMPRC), 6
sport marketing
    definition of, 124–126
    role of research, 133–134
    the four Ps, 126–133
sport sociologists, 15, 309
    what areas they investigate, 18–19

sport sociology, 18, 309
sports information outputs, 39
sports journalism, 39
sportsmanship, 234, 309
stakeholder management, 283
standard, 202, 309
Stark, Joan S., 268
state action, 198–199, 309
state court system, 195–196, 309
statutes, 199, 309
step cost, 107, 309
Stern, David, 124
Stotlar, David, 153, 182
strict liability, 202, 309
Super League. *See* G-14
supply and demand. *See* economics
Supreme Court, 192–194, 310
"Supreme Law of the Land," 193
surveys, 23, 310
Sutton, William A., 124, 135
Suzuki, Ichiro, 250
symbiotic, 146, 310

T
Tagliabue, Paul, 253
target market, 151–152, 310
technical skills, 51, 310
technology development, 288
teleology, 226, 310
The Agent Game (Garvey), 204
"The Apprentice," 43
The Nature of Human Values (Rokeach), 228
ticket revenue, 97
time-switchers, 82, 310
timetable, 181, 310
time value of money, 108–109, 310
Title VII, 200
    definition of, 21, 310
    myths about it, 17
Title IX, 199–200
    definition of, 21, 310
    myths about it, 17
Tollefson, Jeff, 83
TOP sponsors, 147, 247, 310
tort, 201–202, 310
    claims acts, 201, 310
    intentional, 202, 304
tortfeasor, 202, 310
trait theories, 59, 310
trial court, 195, 310
Tribune Company, 92
Tschauner, Peggy R., 52
Twain, Mark, 268, 269
Tyson, Mike, 19

U
Ueberroth, Peter, 220–221
UEFA
    Championship League, 255, 257
    Cup, 257
Uniform Athlete Agents Act, 201, 310

United States Olympic Committee (USOC), 214, 220–221, 245
unity of command, 210, 310
U.S. Constitution, 193, 198–199, 310
U.S. District Courts, 196, 311
Useem, M., 269
utilitarianism, 226, 311

V
values
    instrumental, 227–228, 304
    terminal, 227–228, 310
    See also ethics
Van Fleet, David D., 60
Van Horn, C. E., 267
variable expenses, 107, 311
variable pricing, 97, 129
Veeck, Bill, 237
verdict, 195, 311
vertical integration, 92, 311
Vick, Michael, 19
Volunteer Protection Act, 201, 311

W
waived, 301, 311
Walker, M. L., 182
warranty, 203, 311
Wayne, John, 126
Weber, Max, 60–61
Weiss, Maureen R., 230
welfare, 234, 311
Westerbeek, Hans, 235, 244
Wie, Michelle, 153
Williams, George, 213
Wolf, Eli A., 52–53
Wong, Glenn M., 215
Wooden, John, 17
Woods, Tiger, 237
word of mouth, 156, 311
Workers' Compensation, 272–273, 311
World Cup of Hockey, 254, 311
World League of American Football (WLAF), 253, 311
Wright, Frank Lloyd, 182
Writ of Certiorari, 196, 311

X
X Games, 149, 150

Y
Young Men's Christian Association (YMCA), 213–214
Yukl, Gary A., 60, 63, 64

Z
Zimbalist, Andrew, 84
Zinn, Lorraine M., 232

About the Editors

Andy Gillentine served as the associate dean and director of the sport administration programs at the University of Miami (2002–2008) and at Mississippi State University (1995–2002). In 2009, he received the *Sport Management Outstanding Achievement Award* from the National Association of Sport and Physical Education. Additionally, he served as athletic director and coach for more than 15 years and is nationally recognized for his expertise in sport management curriculum and program development. In 2008, he was appointed as a Commissioner of the Council of Sport Management Accreditation (COSMA). Prior to this appointment, Gillentine served as chair of a joint task force of NASPE/NASSM charged with formalizing the curricular standards required for accreditation. In 2007, he was appointed to serve as a board member of the Miami Dade Sports Commission, which is charged with developing and expanding the presence of the sport industry in Miami Dade County and South Florida. Previously he served on the Sport Management Program Review Council Executive Board and as chair of the National Sport Management Council.

Dr. Gillentine's research interests are sport marketing, professional development, and management issues in sport. He has conducted research projects for numerous sport organizations that have resulted in more than 50 publications and more than 100 national and international presentations. In 2007 he was appointed as a research fellow of the Research Consortium of the AAHPERD, the largest professional organization of sport and physical educators in the United States.

R. Brian Crow is an associate professor in the Department of Sport Management at Slippery Rock University, where he teaches courses related to sport marketing, sport finance, selling in sport, and current issues in sport. Dr. Crow also serves SRU as the NCAA faculty athletics representative. Prior to his appointment at SRU, he taught at Hampton University for four years and at the University of Southern Mississippi for three years. He earned his Ed.D. in higher education administration and master of business administration degrees from West Virginia University, and his bachelor of science degree from West Liberty State College. Professionally, Dr. Crow has served as editor-in-chief of *Sport Marketing Quarterly* and has held various positions within the North American Society for Sport Management, including president. He has co-authored another text, *Profiles of Sport Industry Professionals*, with friends and colleagues Matt Robinson, Mary Hums, and Dennis Phillips.

In 2004, Dr. Crow founded GameDay Consulting, LLC, a full-service consulting firm providing customer-service training to various sport organizations and entities. Current and past clients include the Pittsburgh Steelers (Heinz Field), Baltimore Ravens (M & T Bank Stadium), Buffalo Bills (Ralph Wilson Stadium), Houston Texans (Reliant Stadium) and several NCAA Division I institutions, including WVU, Bowling Green, and Pitt.

Dr. Crow is the proud father of Samuel (13) and Hannah (9).

About the Authors

Artemisia Apostolopoulou is an associate professor of sport management in the Robert Morris University School of Business. She teaches courses in sport marketing and promotion. Her research interests include branding and brand extension strategies, sport sponsorship, and the fusion of sport and entertainment. She has presented work in numerous national and international conferences, and her publications have appeared in *Sport Marketing Quarterly*, the *International Journal of Sports Marketing & Sponsorship*, the *Journal of Product & Brand Management*, and the *Journal of Promotion Management*. Dr. Apostolopoulou is originally from Greece.

Paul J. Batista is an associate professor at Texas A & M University. He earned his bachelor's degree at Trinity University and his J.D. at Baylor Law School. Professor Batista is admitted to practice before the U.S. Supreme Court, licensed in all Texas courts, has previously served as county judge of Burleson County, Texas, and is a former player agent. He has taught sport law at Texas A&M since 1991 and has received numerous teaching excellence awards. He is a member of the Sport and Recreation Law Association and serves on the editorial board of the *Journal of Legal Aspects of Sport*. His primary research interest is sports related liability issues in school settings, with particular emphasis on First Amendment religion and free speech matters.

Matt Bernthal received his Ph.D. in marketing from The University of South Carolina, where he is associate professor in the Sport and Entertainment Management Department. Bernthal teaches numerous courses related to sport and entertainment marketing and serves as graduate director for USC's master's of sport and entertainment management program. His research has appeared in the *Journal of Consumer Research*, *Sport Marketing Quarterly*, *Journal of Nonprofit and Public Sector Marketing*, *School Psychology International*, *Journal of Sport Behavior*, and other journals. He also consults with numerous firms in the sport and entertainment industry.

Cheri Bradish is an assistant professor of sport management at Brock University, responsible for the sport marketing and sponsorship course offerings. While at Brock, she has served as the chair of the Department of Sport Management and currently is a member of the University Board of Senate. Bradish earned both her Ph.D. and M.Sc. in sport management from Florida State University. She has presented and published at more than 30 related international forums. She has also held positions in the Communications Department with the NBA's Vancouver Grizzlies and with the Sport Marketing Department at Nike Canada.

Matthew Brown has been at the University of South Carolina since 2005 where he teaches and researches in the areas of sport business and finance. His research has led to publications in journals including the *Journal of Sport Management*, *Sport Marketing Quarterly*, *Entertainment and Sport Law Journal*, the *International Journal of Sport Finance*, and *Sport Management Review*. In addition, Dr. Brown has made more than 40 national and international research presentations. Dr. Brown currently serves as the faculty advisor for the Sport and Entertainment Management Club and the newly formed club tennis team. He also serves as a liaison between the department and the Columbia Blowfish, a wood bat baseball team in the Coastal Plain League.

John Clark is an associate professor of sport management, and the director of the MBA program at the Robert Morris University School of Business. He has conducted and published research in the areas of sport marketing such as sport sponsorship, customer loyalty, sport sales, and cause-related sport marketing programs.

Craig Crow is the former assistant director of compliance at West Virginia University. He previously served as an instructor in the sport management at East Stroudsburg University. Crow earned an M.S. in sport management from West Virginia University and a B.S. in business administration from West Liberty State College. He is currently completing his doctorate at West Virginia University.

Bernie Goldfine is a professor at Kennesaw State University. He has taught a variety of undergraduate and graduate courses throughout his 17 years in higher education, including venue and event management. Additionally, Dr. Goldfine oversaw the operations and management of a wide variety of facilities and events in his 13 years as a high school athletic director. He has completed numerous presentations and articles for publication at the state, national, and international levels, as well as contributed to textbooks on facility and event management. Dr. Goldfine has also served as a consultant on a number of athletic facility design projects. Dr. Goldfine received his bachelor of arts from the University of California, Santa Barbara, and his master of arts and Ph.D. from the University of Southern California.

Benjamin D. Goss earned his bachelor's and master's degrees at Louisiana Tech University and his doctorate at The University of Southern Mississippi. Currently he serves as an assistant professor in the entertainment management program within the Department of Management and the College of Business Administration at Missouri State University in Springfield, Missouri. Goss has also taught courses in Missouri State's joint business degree program with Liaoning Normal University in Dalian, China. In 2007, Goss co-founded the *Journal of Sport Administration & Supervision* and currently serves as its editor.

T. Christopher Greenwell is an associate professor at the University of Louisville. He holds a Ph.D. in sport management from The Ohio State University, an M.S. in sport management from Georgia Southern University, and a B.B.A. from McKendree College. He teaches in the areas of sport marketing, sport publicity, and event management. He has had recent articles published in the *Sport Marketing Quarterly, The International Journal of Sport Management*, and *Contemporary Athletics*.

Josh Harris is the business development manager for IMG Tickets, a division of IMG, the world's premier and most diversified sports, entertainment, and media company. Harris received his master's degree in sport administration from the University of Miami in 2006 and his bachelor's of business administration from Mississippi State University in 2004. He has previously held sales positions with the University of New Hampshire Athletic Department and the University of Miami Athletic Department. Harris currently resides in Coconut Grove, FL.

Catriona Higgs is a professor in the Sport Management Department at Slippery Rock University. She is a sport sociologist who specializes in gender and diversity issues. She teaches in the areas of diversity, sport sociology and research methods. She has presented nationally and internationally numerous times, and her research has appeared in a number of journals, including the *Journal of Sport Sociology, Nine: A Journal of Baseball and Social Policy Sociology*, the *Journal of Sport and Social Issues*, the *Women in Sport and Physical Activity Journal*, and the *Journal of Homosexuality*. Dr. Higgs completed her master's degree at the University of Stirling (Scotland, UK) and her Ph.D. at Texas Woman's University.

Jeremy S. Jordan is an assistant professor in the sport administration program at Temple University. His research focuses on organizational behavior and human resource management issues within sport organizations, specifically, examination of the influence of organizational justice on employee attitudes and behaviors demonstrated in the workplace. He teaches courses in management, organizational behavior, and legal issues in sport. Published manuscripts have appeared in the *International Journal of Sport Management, International Sports Journal, Physical Educator*, and the *Journal of Applied Research in Coaching and Athletics*.

Colby B. Jubenville earned his bachelor's degree at Millsaps College and his master's and doctorate degrees at The University of Southern Mississippi. He currently serves as an associate professor, coordinator of the graduate sport management program, coordinator of the doctoral program in the Department of Health and Human Performance, and the director of the Center for Sport Policy and Research at Middle Tennessee State

University in Murfreesboro, Tennessee. Previously, he served as the sport management program coordinator at Belhaven College and Eastern Kentucky University. At Belhaven, he also served as an assistant coach on Belhaven's inaugural football team. In 2007, Jubenville cofounded the *Journal of Sport Administration & Supervision*; he now serves as its publisher.

Aubrey Kent is an associate professor in the sport management program at Temple University. His primary areas of interest are leadership and organizational behavior within sport organizations. He teaches courses in management and the current issues facing the sport industry. His published work includes articles in the *Journal of Sport Management*, *The European Journal of Sport Management*, *Sport Marketing Quarterly*, *The Journal of Park and Recreation Administration*, the *International Sports Journal*, and the *Journal of Applied Sport Psychology*.

Nancy L. Lough is an associate professor at the University of Nevada Las Vegas, where she is the director of the sport administration graduate program. Dr. Lough has worked in sport extensively, with experience as a collegiate coach, athletic administrator, and consultant. Her research has focused primarily on marketing of women's sport and on leadership development for women in sport. She is currently the associate editor for *Sport Marketing Quarterly*, the editor of the *Journal of Contemporary Athletics*, and the director of the Center for Sport Education at UNLV.

Betsy McKinley is an associate professor at Slippery Rock University, where she serves as chairperson of the Physical Education Department. She is a pedagogist, specializing in differentiated planning and teaching for physical education. She presents internationally and nationally on topics including program and learner assessment, socially responsible pedagogy, and constructivist teaching in the physical education environment. She is past president of Pennsylvania AHPERD, and serves as a standards-based curriculum consultant for K-12 physical education. Dr. McKinley completed her master's degree at Slippery Rock University and her Ph.D. in physical education curriculum an instruction at Temple University.

John Miller is an associate professor at Texas Tech University. He coached at the intercollegiate level for 16

years and is recognized for his expertise in several sport management–related issues including student internships. He has been instrumental in the development and implementation of the graduate internship experience at Texas Tech as well as teaching legal aspects of sport, sport facility design and management, sport leadership, and sport marketing. His areas of research include legal aspects of sport and recreation, sport facility design and management, and sport management education. He can be contacted at john.miller@ttu.edu.

Dimitra Papadimitriou teaches in the Department of Business Management at the University of Patras, Greece. Her research interests include organizational performance of national sport governing bodies and local sports clubs, as well as nonprofit board effectiveness. In addition, she is involved in multi-disciplinary research in the areas of volunteer management, brand management, and Olympic sponsorship. She has published in *Sport Management Review*, *European Journal of Sport Management*, *Sport Marketing Quarterly*, the *International Journal of Sports Marketing & Sponsorship*, and *Managing Leisure*, and she has presented her work in numerous national and international conferences.

Dennis Phillips is the assistant director for undergraduate studies at the University of Southern Mississippi. He has strong research interests in sport law, sport governance, sport economics and finance, and sport management. Dr. Phillips has a great deal of interest in college athletics and has served as the faculty athletics representative at Southern Miss for the past six years. He has played and coached basketball and has been a sport administrator in more than 22 countries worldwide. He is currently teaching a sport global studies class in the United Kingdom during the summers.

Tom H. Regan is an associate professor in the Department of Sport and Entertainment Management at the University of South Carolina. Research emphasis focuses on the economic impact of sport and entertainment events on regional economies and the financing and feasibility of live entertainment events. He has completed numerous studies on professional, collegiate, and touring sports. Publications have highlighted his work on the Denver Broncos Football Club, the University of South Carolina athletic department, NASCAR, golf in South Carolina, USTA and WTA professional tennis, and other studies involving live entertainment. He was invited to the Brookings Institute to discuss the impact of professional sport facilities on regional economies. He has consulted with many professional organizations concerning financing venues and determining the economic benefit of facilities, events, and teams. Dr. Regan's education experience includes bachelor and master of accounting degrees from the University of Wyoming and a doctorate degree in sports administration at the University of Northern Colorado.

Lynn L. Ridinger is an associate professor of sport management at Old Dominion University in Norfolk, Virginia. Her research focuses on issues related to sport consumer behavior and involvement with women's sports. Her published work includes articles in *Sport Marketing Quarterly*, *Sport Management Review*, *International Journal of Sport Management*, *Journal of Sport Behavior*, and *Leisure Sciences*. She teaches courses in sport marketing, event planning, sport ethics, sport psychology, and research methods. Dr. Ridinger holds a Ph.D. from The Ohio State University, an M.A. from Kent State University, and a B.S. from Central Michigan University. Prior to earning her doctorate, she worked as a high school athletic director and coach.

Tom Sawyer is currently a professor and graduate coordinator for the sport management program at Indiana State University. His research interests fall into four general areas: facility design and development, school law and risk management, sport finance, and sport governance and policy development. He was the 2008 NASPE Outstanding Sport Management Professional as well as the 2008 Indiana AHPERD Sport Management Professional of the Year.

Matthew B. Walker is an assistant professor in the College of Tourism, Recreation, and Sport Management at the University of Florida. His primary research interest lies generally in the area of organizational theory, but more specifically in the areas of corporate social responsibility (CSR) and philanthropic practices of organizations within the sport industry. Dr. Walker has presented his research at numerous academic conferences and his published manuscripts have appeared in the *Journal of Sport Management*, *Management Decision*, *Journal of Business Ethics*, *International Journal of Sport Management*, *International Journal of Sport Finance*, and *Business Research Yearbook*.

David Matthew Zuefle works as a consultant, writer, and columnist. He earned his Ph.D. from Texas A&M University in recreation resource development, with an emphasis in environmental ethics. He is the associate editor and book review editor for the journal *Schole*, and he has two book manuscripts in preparation. He lives in Oxford, Mississippi, and divides his time between there and Charlottesville, Virginia.